Modern American Prose

A Reader for Writers

Modern American Prose

A Reader for Writers

John Clifford
University of North Carolina, Wilmington

Robert DiYanni
Pace University, Pleasantville

Random House
New York

First Edition

9876543

Copyright © 1983 by Random House, Inc.

All rights reserved under International and Pan-American Copyright Conventions. No part of this book may be reproduced in any form or by any means, electronic or mechanical, including photocopying, without permission in writing from the publisher. All inquiries should be addressed to Random House, Inc., 201 East 50th Street, New York, N.Y. 10022. Published in the United States by Random House, Inc., and simultaneously in Canada by Random House of Canada Limited, Toronto.

Library of Congress Cataloging in Publication Data

Main entry under title:

Modern American prose.

    1. College readers.   2. English language—Rhetoric. 3. American prose literature—20th century.   I. Clifford, John.   II. DiYanni, Robert.
PE1417.M57   1982   808′.0427   82–14988
ISBN 0–394–32896–5

Manufactured in the United States of America

Cover design by Gina Davis.

Acknowledgments

"On Going Home" (pp. 164–168) from *Slouching Towards Bethlehem* by Joan Didion. Copyright © 1961, 1967, 1968 by Joan Didion. Reprinted by permission of Farrar, Straus and Giroux, Inc.

"The Iks" and "The Lives of a Cell" from *The Lives of a Cell: Notes of a Biology Watcher* by Lewis Thomas, copyright © 1974 by Lewis Thomas. These essays were originally pub lished in the *New England Journal of Medicine*, copyright 1971, 1973 by the Massachusetts Medical Society. Reprinted by permission of Viking Penguin, Inc.

"The Tucson Zoo," "To Err Is Human," "On Natural Death" from *The Medusa and the Snail: More Notes of a Biology Watcher* by Lewis Thomas, copyright © 1976, 1977, 1979 by Lewis Thomas. Some of these essays were originally published in the *New England Journal of Medicine*. Reprinted by permission of Viking Penguin, Inc.

"On Being a Journalist" from *Close to Home* by Ellen Goodman. Copyright © 1979 by The Washington Post Company. Reprinted by permission of Simon & Schuster, a Division of Gulf & Western Corporation.

"The Company Man" (pp. 18–19) from *Close to Home* by Ellen Goodman. Copyright © 1979 by The Washington Post Company. Reprinted by permission of Simon & Schuster, a Division of Gulf & Western Corporation.

Lobrano Guth. Copyright © 1976 by E. B. White. Reprinted by permission of Harper & Row, Publishers, Inc.

"Goodbye to Forty-eighth Street" (pp. 3–6) from *Essays of E. B. White* by E. B. White. Copyright © 1957 by E. B. White. Reprinted by permission of Harper & Row, Publishers, Inc. This essay originally appeared in *The New Yorker*.

"The Ring of Time" (pp. 142–145, ending with the words "the combustion of stars") from *Essays of E. B. White* by E. B. White. Copyright © 1956 by E. B. White. This essay originally appeared in *The New Yorker*.

"Once More to the Lake" (pp. 197–202) from *Essays of E. B. White* by E. B. White. Copyright © 1941 by E. B. White. Reprinted by permission of Harper & Row, Publishers, Inc.

"Men at Forty" from *Night Light* by Donald Justice. Copyright © 1966 by Donald Justice. Reprinted by permission of Wesleyan University Press. This poem first appeared in *Poetry*.

"Seeing" (pp. 15–19 spliced with pp. 30–32) from *Pilgrim at Tinker Creek* by Annie Dillard. Copyright © 1974 by Annie Dillard. Reprinted by permission of Harper & Row, Publishers, Inc.

"Jest and Earnest" (pp. 5–9) from *Pilgrim at Tinker Creek* by Annie Dillard. Copyright © 1974 by Annie Dillard. Reprinted by permission of Harper & Row, Publishers, Inc.

"Design" from *The Poetry of Robert Frost* edited by Edward C. Lathem. Copyright 1936 by Robert Frost. Copyright © 1964 by Lesley Frost Ballantine. Copyright © 1969 by Holt, Rinehart and Winston. Reprinted by permission of Holt, Rinehart and Winston, Publishers.

"Musée des Beaux Arts" from *W. H. Auden: The Collected Poems* by W. H. Auden. Copyright © 1940 and renewed 1968 by W. H. Auden. Reprinted by permission of Random House, Inc. and of Faber and Faber Ltd.

"Fecundity" (pp. 159–162 spliced with 165–170) from *Pilgrim at Tinker Creek* by Annie Dillard. Copyright © 1974 by Annie

"Nocturne in Silver" (p. 159) from *The Star Thrower* by Loren Eiseley. Copyright © 1978 by the Estate of Loren C. Eiseley. Reprinted by permission of Times Books, a division of Quadrangle/The New York Times Book Co., Inc.

"The Running Man," Loren Eiseley, in *All the Strange Hours. The Excavation of a Life.* Copyright © 1975 by Loren Eiseley (New York: Charles Scribner's Sons, 1975). Reprinted with the permission of Charles Scribner's Sons.

"Carnal Indifference" (pp. 3-6) from *The Fight* by Norman Mailer. Copyright © 1975 by Norman Mailer. Reprinted by permission of Little, Brown and Company.

"Into Orbit" (pp. 215-219) from *Of a Fire on the Moon* by Norman Mailer. Copyright © 1969, 1970 by Norman Mailer. Reprinted by permission of Little, Brown and Company.

"The Siege of Chicago" from *Miami and the Siege of Chicago* by Norman Mailer. Copyright © 1969 by Norman Mailer. Reprinted by permission of the author and the author's agents, Scott Meredith Literary Agency, Inc., 845 Third Avenue, New York, New York 10022.

"Why Are We in Vietnam?" (pp. 202-209) from *The Armies of the Night* by Norman Mailer. Copyright © 1968 by Norman Mailer. Reprinted by arrangement with The New American Library, Inc., New York, New York.

"A Confrontation by the River" (pp. 146-149) from *The Armies of the Night* by Norman Mailer. Copyright © 1968 by Norman Mailer. Reprinted by arrangement with The New American Library, Inc., New York, New York.

"Autobiographical Notes" (pp. 3-9) from *Notes of a Native Son* by James Baldwin. Copyright © 1955 by James Baldwin. Reprinted by permission of Beacon Press.

"The Discovery of What It Means to Be an American" (pp. 3-12) from *Nobody Knows My Name* by James Baldwin. Copyright © 1954, 1956, 1958, 1959, 1960, 1961 by James Baldwin. Permission granted by The Dial Press.

"Fifth Avenue, Uptown: A Letter from Harlem" (pp. 56–71) from *Nobody Knows My Name* by James Baldwin. Copyright © 1954, 1956, 1958, 1959, 1960, 1961 by James Baldwin. Permission granted by The Dial Press.

"Notes of a Native Son" (pp. 85–114) from *Notes of a Native Son* by James Baldwin. Copyright © 1955 by James Baldwin. Reprinted by permission of Beacon Press.

For Joan, Christine, and Pamela;

for Mary, Karen, and Michael.

Preface

Modern American Prose: A Reader for Writers is based upon our conviction that reading and writing are reciprocal acts that should be integrated rather than separated. Because reading and writing stimulate and reinforce one another, we believe that the best way to go about either is to ally it with the other. Associated with this belief in the reciprocity of reading and writing is another: that in addition to their own writing, students can profit most as readers and writers from reading essays that are accessible, engaging, thought-provoking, and, above all, well crafted. In saying this we do not mean to deny that students learn to write primarily by writing, but rather to suggest that in learning to read and respond critically to their own writing and to the writing of others—both amateurs and professionals alike—students mature as writers themselves.

The essayists whose works we anthologize are among the best of contemporary American writers. Taken together they have produced a diversified and substantial body of outstanding nonfictional prose. Ranging widely in subject, style, structure, and tone, their prose includes autobiographical and polemical essays, observations and speculations, reminiscences and sketches, meditations and expostulations, celebrations and attacks. Overall, our selections from their works offer a balance of the flamboyant and innovative with the restrained and classically lucid.

Our aim in choosing selections for *Modern American Prose* was simply to collect between the covers of one book some of the most distinctive nonfiction of the last forty years, written by American writers who have something to say and know how to say it powerfully. It has been our experience that nonfictional prose in general, and the essay in particular, has been underrated as literature. Traditionally accorded secondary status behind the major genres of fiction, poetry, and drama, the essay has consistently been relegated to a literary limbo. But this has recently begun to change. Nonfictional prose has benefited from the revitalization of studies in rhetoric and composition as well as from the upsurge of scholarly work in linguistics and style. Also contributing to the belated recognition of the literary stature of nonfictional prose has been the rise of the new journalism. New journalistic experiments with the novel-as-history and with the nonfiction novel along with a general elevation in the significance of brute fact and sharply observed details of social and personal history have all contributed to the acceptability of the essay as a flexible instrument for recording reality and expressing the self.

By restricting ourselves to twelve writers, we have been able to include at least four essays by each. We have done this because we believe students can come closer to an understanding of an author's ideas, style, and tone by encountering more than one example of his or her work. Within the selections from a particular writer we have tried to offer variety of subject, purpose, tone, and length of essay. And we have included, for the most part, either complete essays, complete chapters, or self-contained sections of books. In addition, we have tried to show each writer working in the four rhetorical modes: narration, description, exposition, and argumentation. Sometimes these modes are kept fairly pure. Far more often, however, they are mixed in complex and interesting ways, as in Joan Didion's essay "On Going Home," which is reprinted along with an extended commentary in the Introduction.

To help students simultaneously become more critical readers and more confident writers, we have provided a thorough discussion of how to read and respond to essays (the Introduction). In addition, following each essay selection is an extensive set of questions designed to guide students through a careful reading—or re-reading—of the pieces, and to assist them in analyzing their style, structure, and meaning. The group of questions headed "Ideas" is meant to serve as a set of probes, a series of ways into the author's main point or central idea. The questions on "Organization," "Sentences," and "Words" invite students to look closely at the writer's craft. Our "Suggestions for Writing" invite students to learn to write by writing, with the essayists as exemplars and fellow writers. Some of these writing suggestions ask for short, informal opinions, often as reactions to an author's ideas. Other assignments ask for more considered assessments of style, form, and meaning. Still others ask students to imitate effective patterns of language and form, in phrase, sentence, paragraph, essay. For a few essays we have avoided categories for our questions because we wanted to focus less on style than on content in those essays which share a common feature: they are all about writing.

Beyond these aids to reading and writing we have written, for each writer, an introduction that subordinates biographical and bibliographical information to focus on how and why each writes. In these introductions we have explored different facets of the writer's world: his or her writing habits, reasons for writing, methods of composition, conceptions of intention, purpose, and design. And in each introduction we have commented briefly on the essays in that section.

Throughout *Modern American Prose* our intent has been to help students read, understand, and imitate good writing in the belief that, by providing students with guided practice in reading and writing, we will help them increase both their competence and their confidence. Through repeated acts of attention to their own writing and to the writing of others, we hope students will gain a renewed sense of the original meaning of "essay": a foray into thought, an attempt to discover an idea, work out its implications, and share it with others. And we hope further that our students will come to see the essay as a way of both enriching their experience and discovering effective ways to communicate it.

John Clifford
Robert DiYanni

Editors' Acknowledgments

For assistance of varying kinds at different stages of our work we would like to thank our friends and colleagues who inspired, criticized, and sustained by listening carefully and giving good advice. Appreciation and thanks to Cynthia Bathurst-Rogers, Lil Brannon, Janis Forman, Kathleen Kelly, Dennis Jarrett, Robert Lyons, Bill Naufftus, Steve Schmidt, Karen Thomas, Myron Tuman, and Dick Veit. Special appreciation to Richard Garretson and Christine Pellicano, who believed in the book early on and gave support in abundance. Thanks also to our reviewers Victoria Casana, Northeastern University; Fred Crews, University of California, Berkeley; Richard Hootman, University of Iowa; Paula Johnson, New York University; Dick Larson, Lehman College; and Don McQuade, Queens College.

We have been fortunate in working with a knowledgeable and exacting professional staff at Random House. We would like to thank especially Fred Burns, David Follmer, Steve Pensinger, and June Smith.

Finally, we would like to thank our wives, Joan and Mary, who helped us in less academic but no less enduring ways.

Contents

Rhetorical Table
of Contents

Description

Narration

Exposition

Persuasion

Modern American Prose

A Reader for Writers

ONE

Introduction

I: READING ESSAYS

When they read essays, most students assume that the meaning is there, in the text. But that is only partially true. A writer certainly does have a theme in mind as he or she composes an essay, but equally important is what a competent reader brings to the work. The author's intention is only one of the three important ingredients in literary nonfiction. In a complete reading, the writer, the reader, and the text must all play their parts.

Critical reading, therefore, is a creative process, requiring active minds. The black marks on the white page have potential meaning, but they remain inert until readers bring the words to life in the reading process. That's not an exaggeration or a metaphor. Critical reading is not simply decoding from printed symbol to sound to meaning. It is, rather, an interaction or a transaction. What a particular reader gets from the page is a blend of that reader's experiences, ideas, and attitudes and the experiences, ideas, and attitudes the writer put in the text. Readers do not simply discover what is already there, like solving a puzzle. Instead, engaged readers use their familiarity with the conventions of writing as tools to make meaning. As readers, our previous knowledge of vocabulary, syntax, and organization join with a writer's intention at the crossroads of meaning. Although the road has already been paved by the writer, only an active reader can give the journey significance.

An active response to a written text has long been considered an important dimension of the reading of literary texts, especially fictional ones. And although most college students think of essays as merely the packages that information comes in, we want to suggest that nonfiction

1

texts, especially essays, require a similar kind of attentiveness and an equal degree of critical response. Even when the author's primary purpose is to convey information, as it is in many essays, the reader's contribution is also crucial. Reading involves two minds—the mind of the writer and the mind of the reader. And even though the writer isn't there to respond to your questions and criticisms or to your expressions of approval and disapproval, a real conversation can occur, as long as you respond honestly and fully.

Although some writing—the scientific prose in your biology text, for example—does try to minimize creative contributions, it still demands your participation. Whereas literature asks that you be an active reader, technical prose tries to keep you passively receptive to its purely informational or directional goal. Some scientific writers strive to be objective and detached through techniques such as omitting the use of "I," letting the subject of the sentence receive the action (via verbs in the passive voice), avoiding highly connotative words, and appealing primarily to logic. In technical writing, snappy, personal anecdotes, wide swings of feeling, and literary language are inappropriate.

Even so, if your background is inadequate on a particular subject, you will not make much sense of sophisticated scientific prose, regardless of how clearly and objectively it is written. Try reading a bridge or chess column without any practical experiences of those games: you will know the words, but because you do not bring enough background with you, you will not be able to read for meaning. If you can't bring the relevant knowledge to the reading, the content will be opaque. Of course, this need for background information is not limited just to reading. We all know people who think quality rock bands like The Rolling Stones, Pink Floyd, and Fleetwood Mac all sound alike—noisy; while others think Bach, Mozart, and Beethoven all sound alike—classical. They can't "read" or hear the differences because they don't have the necessary knowledge and experience of the kind of music in question. The result is a blurring of distinctions, an oversimplifying and stereotyping of complex, individual forms of expression. Discrimination comes with experience. You rarely find what you don't even know exists: you see more when you know what to look for.

Although some of the essays in this collection deal with technical matters, they cannot be considered scientific writing. This may sound odd, but it isn't. The content of the essays is not the deciding factor. More telling is the way the ideas are presented. In distinguishing literary from scientific prose, an author's style, attitude, purpose, and organizational pattern are all more important than the essay's content, its facts. Lewis Thomas, for example, writes about DNA, symbiants, rhizobial bacteria, and death, with emotion and grace, in the most natural language. Perhaps Thomas's audience is crucial. He is not writing to fellow scientists, reporting on his latest research; he is writing to a much wider lay audience (of which you are a part). At times he tries to explain his deepest feelings about life and death, cells and computers; at times he tries to change your mind about the nature of man, hoping to share with you his awe at the complexity and wonder of our world. And he does all this with imagination and style. His aim is not exclusively to tell you particular factual information; he wants instead to engage your intellect and imagination; he wants you to bring your own experiences to his essay so that reader and writer are both present, ready for an active conversation, an intellectual transaction. This invitation to the reader helps make his essays literature.

In fact, many of the essays in this book *are* literature, and should be read as such. Although students generally know that poems, drama, and fiction are literature, they often assume that nonfiction is not. They figure that since literature involves the imaginative and the fanciful, nonfiction, especially essays, do not qualify as serious literature. This attitude, we believe, denies status to undeniably great works of imagination and literary art—works like Boswell's *Life of Samuel Johnson*, Gibbon's *Decline and Fall of the Roman Empire*, essays such as Swift's "A Modest Proposal" and Lamb's "A Dissertation on Roast Pig." Because these works don't fall under the canonized literary categories of poetry, drama, or fiction, they are accorded an inferior place as literary or belletristic works, but not literature.

Without pursuing the complex issue of just how "literature" ought to be defined, we want to suggest that works of nonfiction such as the essays included in this collection should be accorded the same status, granted the same respect, and read with the same care as a poem by Robert Frost or a story by Ernest Hemingway. Like a Frost poem or a Hemingway story, many of the essays in this volume will reward repeated readings. They invite and gratify a considered and deliberate reading primarily because the authors gave more attention to diction, voice, image, form, and theme than they gave to information.

The distinction between fiction and nonfiction raises one other problem: the problem of what is real, of what a fact is. Norman Mailer's book *The Executioner's Song* and some of his earlier work, including *Miami and the Siege of Chicago* and *The Armies of the Night,* are based on fact, on historical events, on real people. But they are also novelistic in technique. His books oscillate uneasily between fact and fiction, history and novel, objective reality and subjective response. As a result, there is considerable confusion about how to read them and what to label them.

The traditional division between factual and fictional discourse creates more problems than it solves. The notion that nonfiction mirrors reality while literature creates its own reality is oversimplified. Joan Didion has a relevant comment in her essay "On Keeping a Notebook": "Not only have I always had trouble distinguishing what happened and what merely might have happened, but I remain unconvinced that the distinction, for my purposes, matters." The essays in this anthology use language in such a way that they help readers give birth to a new creation. They are nonfiction, but they are also literature.

And literature, as we have said, demands more than your attention: it demands your active participation as well. Without you, these essays are merely texts; with your imaginative participation they become something more: literary experiences. And to do your part you don't have to be a highly skilled reader, knowledgeable about esoteric writing techniques and about a wide range of topics. Yet, there is no denying that these essays were written to be read by good readers. We expect that you are one of these good readers, or that in working through the essays, you will become one.

II: READING TECHNIQUES

To emphasize our point that literature requires active readers, we said that scientific writing tries to discourage imagination, to make the words point to specific objects in the world. That is true, in a way. It would be better, however, to think of prose as a continuum with imaginative literature on one end and pure scientific discourse on the other. The essays in this book would lie somewhere in between. Strangely enough, much will depend on your attitude and on the special reading you give each essay. One thing to observe as you read essays is how much the language differs from conventional practice. Poetry, for example, consciously calls attention to its language. Technical language, on the other hand, tries for anonymity, with attention focused only on the message. When you are trying to read instructions for defusing a bomb, for example, you want the language to be as clear as a pane of glass. Essays generally fall between the density and resonance of poetry and the clarity and directness of a set of directions, often containing something of each.

Because this is so, we suggest you read each essay twice: once for content and once for form; once for what the piece says and once for how it says it, keeping in mind, however, that these are ultimately inseparable.

There are, nonetheless, different ways to read. You can, if you want, read the most lyrical of poems for information; or you can read a physics text for its syntax and structure. Here, we are asking for a synthesis, for a balanced reading, attending first to ideas, then to structure and syntax. To get a full reading, you will be called on to use your imagination and your analytical ability, or in the current formulation, to integrate the right and left sides of your brain, to blend intuition with logic.

Reading literature is not a one-shot event; it is a process that involves repetition and reflection. Meaning emerges out of the fog only after you read, reflect, reread, and reflect again. As with writing, few people get it right the first time, or even the second. If, as Thoreau noted, books should be read with the same care and deliberation with which they were written, then your investment of time in repeated readings of these essays will be essential for real understanding. This kind of investment of time and effort will also be a necessary first step toward literary competence and confidence. To gain that competence and to acquire that confidence, we suggest the following reading sequence:

1. Read the essay through in one sitting. When you finish, jot down some notes indicating what the piece was about, if only in a literal sense. Be sure to notice your personal reactions, your subjective responses, to the events and the ideas of the essay. These seemingly random associations are part of the unique baggage each of us brings to reading. In reading an essay about death, for example, we can't ignore our preconceptions about suicide, nor can we forget our biases against disco when reading an article about popular music. Meaning exists, Kenneth Burke suggests, in the "margin of overlap between the

writer's experience and the reader's." Don't try to deny that you are a person whose experiences and ideas are relevant. Since the writer of the essay certainly didn't, neither should you.

The easiest way to bring these valuable associations to the surface is to write quickly for a few minutes, sketching your immediate feelings and thoughts in any order that occurs to you. Concentrate on getting down an honest, detailed response: if you were bored or confused, say so. But try to locate the source of the boredom or confusion. Finally, write one or two sentences about your impression of the author's point in this piece, that is, the theme or generalization that might cover or bind together most of the information the essay presents. Remember: depending on your experiences and attitudes, or even on your present mood, you will probably have different notions about what this general statement might be, especially after one reading.

2. Do your second reading, remembering that it will probably be different from the first: no two readings can be the same, especially since you will be integrating the memory of the first reading experience with this more informed second reading. This is the excitement and surprise of reading literary exposition: each encounter is unique, each reading unfolds new insights and new possibilities. As you read, try to fill in the gaps, to creatively participate in the literary experience. After this reading, jot down your reaction. Has the writer's focus now become clearer to you? What minor points are developed?

This is also the time to begin seeing how the parts of the essay work together. A crucial question in this regard is the relation between the theme (or the purpose) and the material the author presents to support it. What is the relationship between the general and the specific, the abstract and the concrete? Another important consideration is whether the writer presents the main point in the introduction and then supports it in the body, or whether he or she builds up to the point, arranging facts, anecdotes, events, and arguments in such a way that the point is made forcefully in the conclusion. Ask yourself also about the major parts, and whether there are natural "blocks of discourse," that is, paragraphs that go together, that develop the same idea. Although it may sound strange to you, the purpose of taking an essay apart like this is to better understand how it was put together. An active reader first analyzes, then synthesizes.

3. At the end of your second reading, take note of the voice, the personality, you hear. It may be forceful and direct; it may be effacing

and oblique. Sometimes you'll hear the same writer being alternately sarcastic and tender. Each time we write we need to decide anew what mask—or persona—will work best. Of course, the writer's ideas are important in determining tone, but equally crucial is how they are stated. Read groups of sentences out loud, slowly. Try to see how close the writing is to the rhythms of speech. Some writers, like Didion and Thomas, will seem clear and natural; others, like Baldwin and Eiseley, will seem elaborate, formal, and complex. Try to explain to yourself why this is so.

4. You are now ready for the third and best reading of all, the one that should clarify your impressions of the author's purpose, persona, and arguments. You will also be more aware of why you are responding to certain ideas and images. If you focus primarily on one thing, and another reader focuses on something else, it doesn't mean one of you is wrong. Perhaps you are both responding openly to the rich possibilities of literature. If in discussing your responses and in analyzing the craft of expository writing you find yourself differing from others in the class, you should look to the text to see if you can support your reading. If you think the text validates your minority view, it might be because your experiences, your attitudes, or your expectations differ from those of your classmates. Fine. Literary critics have been arguing for hundreds of years over Hamlet's madness and Macbeth's motives. As a dissenter, you are in the best of company. What is important is that you learn to engage intelligently in the process of analytical reading.

We will try to illustrate some ideas by looking at the following essay by Joan Didion. One editor of this book, John Clifford, then presents his reading of the essay in order to illustrate one person's individual response. See how his comments compare with yours.

On Going Home

I am home for my daughter's first birthday. By "home" I do not mean the house in Los Angeles where my husband and I and the baby live, but the place where my family is, in the Central Valley of California. It is a vital although troublesome distinction. My husband likes my family but is uneasy in their house, because once there I fall into their ways, which are difficult, oblique, deliberately inarticulate, not my husband's ways. We live in dusty houses ("D-U-S-T," he once wrote with his finger on surfaces all over the house, but no one noticed it) filled with mementos quite without value to him (what could the Canton dessert plates mean to him? how could he have known about the assay scales, why should he care if he did know?), and we appear to talk exclusively about people we know who have been committed to mental hospitals, about people we know who have been booked on drunk-driving charges, and about property, particularly about property, land, price per acre and C-2 zoning and assessments and freeway access. My brother does not understand my husband's inability to perceive the advantage in the rather common real-estate transaction known as "sale-leaseback," and my husband in turn does not understand why so many of the people he hears about in my father's house have recently been committed to mental hospitals or booked on drunk-driving charges. Nor does he understand that when we talk about sale-leasebacks and right-of-way condemnations we are talking in code about the things we like best, the yellow fields and the cottonwoods and the rivers rising and falling and the mountain roads closing when the heavy snow comes in. We miss each other's points, have another drink and regard the fire. My brother refers to my husband, in his presence, as "Joan's husband." Marriage is the classic betrayal.

Or perhaps it is not any more. Sometimes I think that those of us who are now in our thirties were born into the last generation to carry the burden of "home," to find in family life the source of all tension and drama. I had by all objective accounts a "normal" and a "happy" family situation, and yet I was almost thirty years old before I could talk to my family on the telephone without crying after I had hung up. We did not fight. Nothing was wrong. And yet some nameless anxiety colored the emotional charges between me and the place that I came from. The question of whether or not you could go home again was a very real part of the sentimental and largely literary baggage with which we left home in the fifties; I suspect that it is irrelevant to the children born of the fragmentation after World War II. A few weeks ago in a San Francisco bar I saw a pretty young girl on crystal take off her clothes and dance for the cash prize in an "amateur-topless" contest.

There was no particular sense of moment about this, none of the effect of romantic degradation, of "dark journey," for which my generation strived so assiduously. What sense could that girl possibly make of, say, *Long Day's Journey into Night?* Who is beside the point?

That I am trapped in this particular irrelevancy is never more apparent to me than when I am home. Paralyzed by the neurotic lassitude engendered by meeting one's past at every turn, around every corner, inside every cupboard, I go aimlessly from room to room. I decide to meet it head-on and clean out a drawer, and I spread the contents on the bed. A bathing suit I wore the summer I was seventeen. A letter of rejection from The Nation, an aerial photograph of the site for a shopping center my father did not build in 1954. Three teacups hand-painted with cabbage roses and signed "E.M.," my grandmother's initials. There is no final solution for letters of rejection from The Nation and teacups hand-painted in 1900. Nor is there any answer to snapshots of one's grandfather as a young man on skis, surveying around Donner Pass in the year 1910. I smooth out the snapshot and look into his face, and do and do not see my own. I close the drawer, and have another cup of coffee with my mother. We get along very well, veterans of a guerrilla war we never understood.

Days pass. I see no one. I come to dread my husband's evening call, not only because he is full of news of what by now seems to me our remote life in Los Angeles, people he has seen, letters which require attention, but because he asks what I have been doing, suggests uneasily that I get out, drive to San Francisco or Berkeley. Instead I drive across the river to a family graveyard. It has been vandalized since my last visit and the monuments are broken, overturned in the dry grass. Because I once saw a rattlesnake in the grass I stay in the car and listen to a country-and-Western station. Later I drive with my father to a ranch he has in the foothills. The man who runs his cattle on it asks us to the roundup, a week from Sunday, and although I know that I will be in Los Angeles I say, in the oblique way my family talks, that I will come. Once home I mention the broken monuments in the graveyard. My mother shrugs.

I go to visit my great-aunts. A few of them think now that I am my cousin, or their daughter who died young. We recall an anecdote about a relative last seen in 1948, and they ask if I still like living in New York City. I have lived in Los Angeles for three years, but I say that I do. The baby is offered a horehound drop, and I am slipped a dollar bill "to buy a treat." Questions trail off, answers are abandoned, the baby plays with the dust motes in a shaft of afternoon sun.

It is time for the baby's birthday party: a white cake, strawberry-marshmallow ice cream, a bottle of champagne saved from another party. In the evening, after she has gone to sleep, I kneel beside the crib and touch her face, where it is pressed against the slats, with mine. She is an open and trusting child, unprepared for and unaccustomed to the ambushes of family life, and perhaps it is just as well that I can offer her little of that life. I would like to give her more. I would like to promise her that she will grow up with a sense of her cousins and of rivers and of her great-grandmother's teacups, would like to pledge her a picnic on a river with fried chicken and her hair uncombed, would like to give her *home* for her birthday, but we live differently now and I can promise her nothing like that. I give her a xylophone and a sundress from Madeira, and promise to tell her a funny story.

III: A PERSONAL RESPONSE

Since I grew up in a large family in a working-class neighborhood in Brooklyn, New York, and am now writing this response in Beverly Hills, you might expect my initial reading to reflect this juxtaposition. I should say, however, that this is my first reading of the essay in five or six years. I remember reading it earlier, but I cannot remember my response, except a sense that Didion was writing broadly about the difficulty of returning to an older America.

The following are my unedited notes written in response to "On Going Home," and in accord with the sequence described earlier, they are not meant as a formal essay, merely the kind of notes you might write as you read. In a sense, they are writer-based, prepared not for readers but to help me understand my response to Didion's essay. I would have to do lots of rearranging and cutting to make these notes into a reader-based essay. Because I am trying to illustrate a technique I have tried to be detailed. Perhaps you will not want to do as much. And because I have different goals and a different reading background from you, you should not compare yours to mine, except to see how each of us follows the suggested steps.

1. The essay seems to be about the difference between Didion's sense of home now—as a grown woman—and her sense of it when she was a child. Is she talking about home as a place or as a point in time? Somehow I think she means both. I am wondering why she stayed for so long; her visits are probably infrequent. Her husband was uncomfortable in her house. I can understand that. Families seem to develop their own idiosyncratic ways of doing things, of relating to each other. I can understand his uneasiness: he couldn't bear all that real estate talk; neither could I.

I'm not sure what she means by marriage as the "classic betrayal." Perhaps she thinks her family felt rejected when she left home. But she takes that idea away in the second paragraph: "Perhaps it is not any more." I can see that time will be important here. This is probably an essay that comes to a resolution at the end. Didion is giving me a record of her thinking; she is showing me how she arrived at her conclusion about the possibility of going home. Going home surely has a wider meaning than just physically returning. She says hers is the last generation to carry the burden of home. "Burden" is a strong word.

She claims she was normal but then talks about crying and about a nameless anxiety. Then she says it is different for those born of the "fragmentation after World War II." I guess that is the key to her concept of home. She seems to be focusing on the differences between the extended and the nuclear family. That's interesting for me, since I grew up in the forties and fifties during the break-up of the traditional family structure. My grandparents lived around the corner from me, and their nine children and their families all lived within ten city blocks. Their house was the center around which our lives revolved. Gradually, however, my aunts and uncles drifted off, first to the edges of the city and then to the growing suburbs of Long Island and New Jersey. And now, some thirty years later, we are scattered throughout the East, with a few grandchildren testing the exotic climes of Los Angeles and San Diego.

My grandmother's house was also a moral and cultural center. At holiday parties we had to ask her permission to play American music instead of traditional Irish ballads and dance music. So I can understand the poignancy of Didion's feeling that she was "beside the point," of feeling irrelevant. She had to struggle, as I did, to break away from the established moral and cultural traditions of an extended family. The topless girl, of course, never had those rules to begin with. And as I read this essay, I am thinking that my daughters, thousands of miles from my childhood neighborhood and decades from the conformity and pressure of a religious upbringing, will also never experience Didion's "dark journey." Their sense of morality will be mostly their own construction; they will have themselves to answer to, not to scores of relatives and to a tradition many centuries old.

As Didion walks through her former home, I also sense her mixed feelings of nostalgia and distance. I read the last sentence of the third paragraph several times: I'm not sure why she says "guerrilla war"; isn't that a contradiction of normal and happy? Perhaps not. But her not understanding makes sense. I don't think I ever understood the reasons for the disagreement, the points missed, the tension.

I am surprised that she dreads her husband's evening call. I would have thought she would be anticipating it, as an escape. Maybe her old ways are taking over again. When she visits her old aunts, I could not help but remember my last visit to my grandmother, then ninety-five: she thought I was several people, never me. And questions trailed off, answers were abandoned. Her description here seems very real.

In her conclusion she paints a vivid picture, one I've experienced many times: staring at my sleeping children, wondering about their future, their "possibilities," my hopes and dreams for them, and my fears about the world they will have to cope with. Will it be easier or harder? Didion's thoughts are clear: she wants for her daughter the myth of the happy extended family, a sense of roots and shared values, a connection to a rich cultural heritage, a sense of community, of belonging somewhere with people who accept and support your efforts. But realistically, she promises what she can: a xylophone, a sundress, and a story. I like that. She seems to be coming to grips with her break with the home she can never go back to. Instead of depression or anger, she thinks positively. She seems to be saying: "OK, things are not what they were or what they could be, but given the way I live now, this is the best I can do."

I am still wondering if she thinks her "home" in the Central Valley of California is worth going back to—back in the sense of becoming a part of an extended family, adopting its values, its idiosyncratic customs—or if she wants to go back in time to a simpler America, one with common purposes and dreams. Looking back to the first paragraph,

I notice her description of her family's ways: "difficult, oblique, deliberately inarticulate." Then I remember the "nameless anxiety" of the
second paragraph and the "guerrilla war" and "my mother shrugs."
Finally, I looked at the third sentence in the last paragraph, especially
the phrase "unprepared for and unaccustomed to the ambushes of family
life, and perhaps it is just as well that I can offer her little of that life."
All this certainly sounds negative, as if her daughter is better off without
that home in the Central Valley. I am wondering why she didn't put
a "Yet" before the next sentence: "I would like to give her more." More
of what? Of the comforts and benefits of community? Surely Didion
realizes that the positive feelings of belonging cannot be separated from
the disadvantages of conformity.

    2. After my second reading the focus does seem clearer. I think
she is talking about accepting the present without attempting to recapture
the past, a past that had a good many problems anyhow. I think she
realizes that America has changed, that the old center—the extended
family rooted for generations in the same place—is no more. New ways
are replacing the old. But even if things fall apart, even if we cannot
go home again, I do not sense pessimism or despair here. I sense rather
a need to confront reality, to see what's possible. She is a realist; she
does not offer false hope for a world that isn't (and perhaps wasn't).

    Didion is not afraid to admit that her moral concerns are, in the
modern world, irrelevant. She is not afraid to admit that she has ambiguous, contradictory feelings about her home: she longs for and flees
from the "picnic on a river with fried chicken." After all, if the "young
girl on crystal" taking off her clothes is the result of the atomization of
modern life, then perhaps an alternative is to be hoped for. Somehow
winning an amateur topless contest strung out on acid in front of tipsy
strangers doesn't seem like much of a victory for freedom.

    As I turn my attention to the organization, I notice that there are
only six paragraphs. Didion begins concretely, with lots of specific
details (dust, plates, real estate talk, people committed to mental hospitals) to suggest what she means by the first three sentences. This place
is different from her home in Los Angeles. She is surely making this
point, but indirectly. She lets her details do the work—or rather she
invites you to make the connections, to work out the implications. She
respects the reader's ability to do just that. I respond to that challenge
positively; I know it will pay off.

The second paragraph picks up the last sentence of the first. Here, however, she is both more explicit and more abstract. She is, in a sense, thinking out loud about the links between her generation (those born in the 1930s) and their childhood homes. Her opening sentence clearly states the idea she wants to explore: she left a clearly defined home, and the young girl in the bar never had one. I assume she wants us to imagine that she's making a point about different generations, not just one or two people. She seems to be setting herself up as typical, as representative. This universality is, in fact, one of the touches of art that makes this essay literature. So she makes her point again by ending with a concrete and provocative image. Her concluding question is at this point rhetorical, since today she would have little of the old morality to rebel against. Again she weaves this last sentence into the pattern of the next paragraph. And again she supports this abstract topic sentence by poignantly detailing specific items from her past, a past that makes little sense to the present generation.

The next paragraph, however, is loosely tied to the previous one. The first three paragraphs form a block; the last three, another. She picks up the abandoned narrative again. She tells us about the dread and then gives us the details of her drive to the graveyard. Is this incident meant to suggest the present generation's lack of respect for death, for the past and its traditional values? I think so.

The fifth paragraph focuses on a specific visit to the edges of her family. The details here are rich and telling. It is clear that this is only a ritual visit: no real contact is made. Didion seems comfortable with specific details; she seems to shy away from the announced theme, the explicit point. That is one of the things I like about her work: I'm included; I'm asked to see the relation between the abandoned answers and her inability to go "home."

And finally her snapshot of the party. We have come back now to the essay's opening sentence. The details here are sharply drawn: crisp and appropriate. The final statement, the wrap-up, is, typically, given in concrete form. She cannot bear to say "this is what I meant." No, that would break the cooperative bond with the reader. She wants more; she wants creative involvement, a partner in her art. Perhaps I am going beyond what she calls for, but I think Didion is saying that we can give our children culture, style, grace and love, or whatever else the presents suggest to our imagination. These can create a new definition of home.

IV: CONCLUSION

The traditional essays usually written in college bear little resemblance to "On Going Home," at least when the editors of this anthology were in college in the sixties. We were usually asked, instead, to begin with an explicit thesis statement (or to lead up to it, placing it dramatically as the last sentence of the first paragraph). We were then asked to support that generalization with three paragraphs all beginning with clear topic sentences and providing detailed evidence for our thematic assertion. It is clear that Didion chose not to follow that mode; yet, we suspect that she wrote many of these traditional deductive essays at Berkeley in the fifties. Her choice, however, was not arbitrary; she selected a structure that would best fit her meaning. If a traditional five-paragraph theme were appropriate, she would not hesitate to use it.

Organization is not neutral. It suggests a writer's attitude toward his or her readers and material. If Didion had begun, as is typical in academic articles, with a strong thematic statement, such as "After World War II, the American family was transformed from a closely knit community to a mobile nuclear unit," she would then have developed and supported this thesis with evidence from sociology. She would have been the authority telling us something she knows. Didion, however, chose to begin with a specific incident from her own experience, which she hedges on throughout. She is suggesting that her abstract thinking is firmly rooted in her own experiences. She does not begin with a strong thesis because she doesn't feel that secure about it. She is exploring and wondering. She is also presenting us with a tentative persona, one who is willing to look at the topic with us. Only after she has illustrated her experiences of going home does she make her point about "we live differently now." And even then it is couched in concrete details, not in the usual abstractions that often refer only vaguely to a world the reader knows.

Didion's honest voice is reinforced by her unadorned style. There is little flowery or pompous diction here. Look at the opening sentences of each paragraph: simple, clear, declarative sentences. Notice how she varies the rhythm and length of her sentences in the first paragraph, ending with a crisp and powerful expression of her thought. Her vivid, stark prose suggests that she is trying not to delude herself or us with uncalled-for optimism or self-defeating pessimism. She is just trying to see clearly, to understand. Cluttered sentences would fog that understanding. That seems a realistic alternative to the sometimes artificial authority of the deductive essay.

There is, of course, no doubt that the generalization-support pattern is useful and necessary. You will find some fine examples of that form in this anthology. But Didion's essay demonstrates that a writer can also be forceful, focused, and informative by developing a structure that parallels her intention. Writers usually try to let their content and purpose determine their organization, not the other way around.

This discussion of Didion's essay, and the questions in the text, are intended to turn your attention to two things: the essay as a finished product and crafted work, and the essay as an action and a process. By attending actively to the essays collected here, we hope you will learn to see in the writing of others, and to initiate and maintain in your own writing, a respect for vitality, variety, honesty, and surprise. Moreover, we hope you will gain a renewed sense of the original meaning of the word "essay": a foray into thought and an attempt to discover an idea, work out its implications, and share it with others. We hope, finally, that you will come to see the essay, and nonfiction in general, as a way of both enriching your experience and discovering effective ways to communicate it.

TWO

Lewis Thomas
(1913–   )

Lewis Thomas uses science to tell us something important about the human predicament. Missing, however, is Eiseley's cosmic melancholy. Instead, Thomas celebrates life, seeing "possibilities where others see only doom."

In "To Err Is Human," he turns our typically negative reaction to error completely around, finding in mistakes progress and growth. He sees hope everywhere. In "On Natural Death," instead of wincing at the spectacle of a dying field mouse in "the jaws of an amiable household cat," he uses the incident to speculate that, instead of being an abomination, nature is wise and kind. Since there are scientific reasons for thinking that fear releases peptide hormones that have the "pharmacologic properties of opium," it is plausible to think that the mouse does not feel pain. He goes on to cite a passage from Montaigne that suggests that nature will teach us all how to die, "take you no care for it."

This is typical Lewis Thomas: after something in nature is encountered, he lets it reverberate in his mind until he comes to a tentative hypothesis. He then tests it and invariably arrives at an encouraging vision of both man and nature. It is a traditional and logical thought process and one that is made more plausible because of its simplicity.

Although he doesn't share Eiseley's mood, Thomas has a similar purpose in writing about scientific matters: "to communicate truths too mysterious for old-fashioned common sense." Ironically, even though Eiseley and Thomas have both contributed significantly to scientific understanding, they both stress how much we *don't* know about the workings of nature.

This is not to say that there is not a great deal of scientific information in Thomas's essays. His two collections of essays, *The Lives of a Cell: Notes of a Biology Watcher* (1974) and *The Medusa and the Snail: More Notes of a Biology Watcher* (1979), explore a wide range of complex scientific topics, from pheromones and embryology to cloning and germs. He is also not afraid to deal with such diverse subjects as linguistics, music, computers, and literature. In exploring these complex issues, he is never dogmatic, even when he is clearly the expert. He always invites the reader to join in, to share with him the joy of "being dumbfounded."

Indeed, it is refreshing to be told we are better than we think. In "The Iks," for example, he strongly disagrees with a famous anthropologist's depressing idea that a repellent mountain tribe from Uganda is an appropriate symbol for mankind. Thomas argues that it is society that corrupts man, not the opposite. At heart, he believes, we are all good. In his characteristically plain and exact style, Thomas rejects the view that man is inherently evil with "He's all right."

In "The Lives of a Cell," he develops another of his central concerns—our connection to nature. Symbiosis, in fact, is one of his favorite notions. He seems quite upset by our nineteenth-century view that man is superior to and independent from nature. In his graceful, gently persuasive prose, he argues instead that "man is embedded in nature." We can, he believes, no longer see ourselves as separate and detached entities. In fact, it is an illusion to see ourselves as autonomous. In this regard he echoes Annie Dillard's almost mystic urge toward the total unity of all life.

Even though Chekhov, William Carlos Williams, and other creative writers have been medical doctors, it still seems unusual for a famous pathologist to write about scientific matters with such grace, clarity, and eloquence. For the president of a world-famous cancer center to have the reputation of being one of America's best essayists is a tribute to Thomas's diversity as a scientist and humanist.

The Iks

1   The small tribe of Iks, formerly nomadic hunters and gatherers in the mountain valleys of northern Uganda, have become celebrities, literary symbols for the ultimate fate of disheartened, heartless mankind at large. Two disastrously conclusive things happened to them: the government decided to have a national park, so they were compelled by law to give up hunting in the valleys and become farmers on poor hillside soil, and then they were visited for two years by an anthropologist who detested them and wrote a book about them.

2   The message of the book is that the Iks have transformed themselves into an irreversibly disagreeable collection of unattached, brutish creatures, totally selfish and loveless, in response to the dismantling of their traditional culture. Moreover, this is what the rest of us are like in our inner selves, and we will all turn into Iks when the structure of our society comes all unhinged.

3   The argument rests, of course, on certain assumptions about the core of human beings, and is necessarily speculative. You have to agree in advance that man is fundamentally a bad lot, out for himself alone, displaying such graces as affection and compassion only as learned habits. If you take this view, the story of the Iks can be used to confirm it. These people seem to be living together, clustered in small, dense villages, but they are really solitary, unrelated individuals with no evident use for each other. They talk, but only to make ill-tempered demands and cold refusals. They share nothing. They never sing. They turn the children out to forage as soon as they can walk, and desert the elders to starve whenever they can, and the foraging children snatch food from the mouths of the helpless elders. It is a mean society.

4   They breed without love or even casual regard. They defecate on each other's doorsteps. They watch their neighbors for signs of misfortune, and only then do they laugh. In the book they do a lot of laughing, having so much bad luck. Several times they even laughed at the anthropologist, who found this especially repellent (one senses, between the lines, that the scholar is not himself the world's luckiest man). Worse, they took him into the family, snatched his food, defecated on his doorstep, and hooted dislike at him. They gave him two bad years.

5   It is a depressing book. If, as he suggests, there is only Ikness at the center of each of us, our sole hope for hanging on to the name of humanity will be in endlessly mending the structure of our society, and it is changing so quickly and completely that we may never find the threads in time. Meanwhile, left to ourselves alone, solitary, we will become the same joyless, zestless, untouching lone animals.

6   But this may be too narrow a view. For one thing, the Iks are extraordinary. They are absolutely astonishing, in fact. The anthropologist has never seen people like them anywhere, nor have I. You'd think, if they were simply examples of the common essence of mankind, they'd seem more recognizable. Instead, they are bizarre, anomalous. I have known my share of peculiar, difficult, nervous, grabby people, but I've never encountered any genuinely, consistently detestable human beings in all my life. The Iks sound more like abnormalities, maladies.

7   I cannot accept it. I do not believe that the Iks are representative of isolated, revealed man, unobscured by social habits. I believe their behavior is something extra, something laid on. This unremitting, compulsive repellence is a kind of complicated ritual. They must have learned to act this way; they copied it, somehow.

8   I have a theory, then. The Iks have gone crazy.

9   The solitary Ik, isolated in the ruins of an exploded culture, has built a new defense for himself. If you live in an unworkable society you can make up one of your own, and this is what the Iks have done. Each Ik has become a group, a one-man tribe on its own, a constituency.

10   Now everything falls into place. This is why they do seem, after all, vaguely familiar to all of us. We've seen them before. This is precisely the way groups of one size or another, ranging from committees to nations, behave. It is, of course, this aspect of humanity that has lagged behind the rest of evolution, and this is why the Ik seems so primitive. In his absolute selfishness, his incapacity to give anything away, no matter what, he is a successful committee. When he stands at the door of his hut, shouting insults at his neighbors in a loud harangue, he is city addressing another city.

11   Cities have all the Ik characteristics. They defecate on doorsteps, in rivers and lakes, their own or anyone else's. They leave rubbish. They detest all neighboring cities, give nothing away. They even build institutions for deserting elders out of sight.

12   Nations are the most Iklike of all. No wonder the Iks seem familiar. For total greed, rapacity, heartlessness, and irresponsibility there is nothing to match a nation. Nations, by law, are solitary, self-centered, withdrawn into themselves. There is no such thing as affection between nations, and certainly no nation ever loved another. They bawl insults from their doorsteps, defecate into whole oceans, snatch all the food, survive by detestation, take joy in the bad luck of others, celebrate the death of others, live for the death of others.

13   That's it, and I shall stop worrying about the book. It does not signify that man is a sparse, inhuman thing at his center. He's all right. It only says what we've always known and never had enough time to worry about, that we haven't yet learned how to stay human when assembled in masses. The Ik, in his despair, is acting out this failure, and perhaps we should pay closer attention. Nations have themselves become too frightening to think about, but we might learn some things by watching these people.

QUESTIONS

Ideas

1. How does Thomas react to the Iks? To the book about them? The anthropologist, in his book, does indeed suggest "that man is a sparse, inhuman thing at his center." Does Thomas think so? Do you think so? What is Thomas's position in paragraph 3? Does he think man is basically good at heart? Does his view seem reasonable? Fair? Flexible? Why or why not?

2. Thomas lets us follow his train of thought as he comes to terms with the nature of the Iks and finally with the nature of man. After he sketches the necessary background, he asserts, in paragraph 5, that this "is a depressing book." Try to outline, in brief sentences, his reasoning from this point on. How does he counter the anthropologist's thesis?

3. What is the effect of "That's it," in the last paragraph? Has he convinced you that "he's all right"? Who is this "he"?

Organization

4. Go back through this essay, reading only the first and last sentences in each paragraph. What does this tell you about Thomas's view of the paragraph's

opening sentence? Notice paragraphs 11 and 12. After the opening sentence, what do the rest of the sentences try to do?

5. What do you make of the one-sentence paragraph 8? Is this effective?

6. How is the last sentence of paragraph 3 related to and connected with the five sentences before it?

7. Where does the essay seem to change direction? To shift in ideas?

8. Do you think the organization represents Thomas's actual thinking process? Would the essay have been more effective if he had begun with a thesis and then set out to defend it? What organization would you have chosen?

9. As part of his organization and thematic plan Thomas compares the Iks first to cities, then to nations. How does he do this? What aspects of each does he compare?

Sentences

10. Is the repetition of "they" effective in paragraph 4?

11. When Thomas wants to be emphatic he usually writes short, assertive sentences. Can you point to some that seem especially effective? (Read paragraphs 3 and 4 aloud.)

12. There don't seem to be many compound sentences here. There's one in paragraph 10; can you find others? What is the effect of making sentences simple?

13. Take a close look at Thomas's use of commas in the first sentence. Why does he use the first two? Could he have used a colon instead of the third comma? Can you explain the function of these commas?

Words

14. What words and specific details does Thomas repeat in the essay? To what effect?

15. What words, in paragraphs 5 and 6, carry negative connotations? Which describe or define "Ikness"?

Suggestion for Writing

Write an essay that supports either the anthropologist's or Thomas's position on the Iks. Try to use personal experience to support your stand.

The Lives of a Cell

1   **W**e are told that the trouble with Modern Man is that he has been trying to detach himself from nature. He sits in the topmost tiers of polymer, glass, and steel, dangling his pulsing legs, surveying at a distance the writhing life of the planet. In this scenario, Man comes on as a stupendous lethal force, and the earth is pictured as something delicate, like rising bubbles at the surface of a country pond, or flights of fragile birds.

2   But it is illusion to think that there is anything fragile about the life of the earth; surely this is the toughest membrane imaginable in the universe, opaque to probability, impermeable to death. We are the delicate part, transient and vulnerable as cilia. Nor is it a new thing for man to invent an existence that he imagines to be above the rest of life; this has been his most consistent intellectual exertion down the millennia. As illusion, it has never worked out to his satisfaction in the past, any more than it does today. Man is embedded in nature.

3   The biologic science of recent years has been making this a more urgent fact of life. The new, hard problem will be to cope with the dawning, intensifying realization of just how interlocked we are. The old, clung-to notions most of us have held about our special lordship are being deeply undermined.

4   *Item.* A good case can be made for our nonexistence as entities. We are not made up, as we had always supposed, of successively enriched packets of our own parts. We are shared, rented, occupied. At the interior of our cells, driving them, providing the oxidative energy that sends us out for the improvement of each shining day, are the mitochondria, and in a strict sense they are not ours. They turn out to be little separate creatures, the colonial posterity of migrant prokaryocytes, probably primitive bacteria that swam into ancestral precursors of our eukaryotic cells and stayed there. Ever since, they have maintained themselves and their ways, replicating in their own fashion, privately, with their own DNA and RNA quite different from ours. They are as much symbionts as the rhizobial bacteria in the roots of beans. Without them, we would not move a muscle, drum a finger, think a thought.

5   Mitochondria are stable and responsible lodgers, and I choose to trust them. But what of the other little animals, similarly established in my cells, sorting and balancing me, clustering me together? My centrioles, basal bodies, and probably a good many other more obscure tiny beings at work inside my cells, each with its own special genome, are as foreign, and as essential, as aphids in anthills. My cells are no longer the pure line entities I was raised with; they are ecosystems more complex than Jamaica Bay.

6   I like to think that they work in my interest, that each breath they draw for me, but perhaps it is they who walk through the local park in the early morning, sensing my senses, listening to my music, thinking my thoughts.

7   I am consoled, somewhat, by the thought that the green plants are in the same fix. They could not be plants, or green, without their chloroplasts, which run the photosynthetic enterprise and generate oxygen for the rest of us. As it turns out, chloroplasts are also separate creatures with their own genomes, speaking their own language.

8   We carry stores of DNA in our nuclei that may have come in, at one time or another, from the fusion of ancestral cells and the linking of ancestral organisms in symbiosis. Our genomes are catalogues of instructions from all kinds of sources in nature, filed for all kinds of contingencies. As for me, I am grateful for differentiation and speciation, but I cannot feel as separate an entity as I did a few years ago, before I was told these things, nor, I should think, can anyone else.

9   *Item.* The uniformity of the earth's life, more astonishing than its diversity, is accountable by the high probability that we derived, originally, from some single cell, fertilized in a bolt of lightning as the earth cooled. It is from the progeny of this parent cell that we take our looks; we still share genes around, and the resemblance of the enzymes of grasses to those of whales is a family resemblance.

10   The viruses, instead of being single-minded agents of disease and death, now begin to look more like mobile genes. Evolution is still an infinitely long and tedious biologic game, with only the winners staying at the table, but the rules are beginning to look more flexible. We live in a dancing matrix of viruses; they dart, rather like bees, from organism to organism, from plant to insect to mammal to me and back again, and into the sea, tugging along pieces of this genome, strings of genes from that, transplanting grafts of DNA, passing around heredity as though at a great party. They may be a mechanism for keeping new,

mutant kinds of DNA in the widest circulation among us. If this is true, the odd virus disease, on which we must focus so much of our attention in medicine, may be looked on as an accident, something dropped.

11   *Item.* I have been trying to think of the earth as a kind of organism, but it is no go. I cannot think of it this way. It is too big, too complex, with too many working parts lacking visible connections. The other night, driving through a hilly, wooded part of southern New England, I wondered about this. If not like an organism, what is it like, what is it *most* like? Then, satisfactorily for that moment, it came to me: it is *most* like a single cell.

QUESTIONS

Ideas

1. From your experience, do you think Thomas's image in the first paragraph is correct? Have we been trying to detach ourselves from nature?

2. Does his "correction" of this scenario seem more or less optimistic? Does it worry you that he claims "we are the delicate part"?

3. In the last paragraph, what difference does it make whether we accept Thomas's analogy that the earth is an organism or a single cell?

Organization

4. Thomas chooses to put a traditional topic sentence (the assertion of an opinion) at the end of the second paragraph. What does he try to do in the succeeding paragraphs? Is this exposition (explanation), or is he trying to persuade you of something? Look especially at the last sentence in paragraph 8.

5. Thomas appears to be trying to alter our misconceptions about our "special lordship." In this regard, do you think he arranges his essay effectively?

6. Where does his introduction end? Where does his conclusion begin?

7. How does Thomas support his opening sentence in paragraph 4?

8. How does Thomas get us from paragraph 1 to 2 and on to 3? Underline all the connections; include the syntactic and semantic ways the paragraphs are linked.

Sentences

9. Look at the ways Thomas begins his sentences in the first two paragraphs. How many follow the normal subject, verb, object (S–V–O) pattern?

10. Look at the first sentence of the second paragraph. The two three-word phrases at the end are free modifiers, meaning they can be moved to other positions in the sentence. Where else might they go?

11. Count the words in each sentence in the second paragraph. Is there a reason for this pattern?

12. In paragraph 9, why did Thomas decide to use a semicolon in the last sentence? Are there other options?

Words

13. Unlike much of "scientific writing," Thomas opens this piece on a technical subject with an attention-getting image. Does this "popular technique" make his argument seem less serious?

14. Do you find Thomas mixing levels of diction, for example, using scientific jargon and informational speech? Where does he do it and for what effect? Does it work?

15. What kind of voice (or persona) do you hear in this essay? Try reading the last two paragraphs out loud. Is this a voice of authority? Is he trying to be down to earth? What voice might you take in handling this subject? Does it depend on your purpose? What do you think Thomas's purpose is?

Suggestions for Writing

A. Throughout the essay, Thomas frequently uses triplets—three words in parallel form, three phrases in parallel structure, three sentences in parallel motion. Paragraph 3 contains two examples, paragraph 5, one. Rewrite these sentences, destroying the parallelism or adding connecting words (like "and") to join the three elements. What is lost in these revisions?

B. Even more frequently than triplets, Thomas uses doublets of words and phrases, of sentences and paragraphs. What kinds of "pairs" can you find in the essay? How effective are they? Consider especially the balances and parallels of paragraphs 6, 7, and 11. Write a short paragraph describing a familiar scene using doublets.

C. Think of a scientific or technical subject that concerns you, say, pollution and protecting (or not protecting) the environment, or cloning, or chemical additives in our food. Try to write about it using the Thomas structure of beginning with a misconception our society shares and then demonstrating why the illusion is false. In writing your piece keep in mind how Thomas combines anecdote, comparison and contrast, exposition, persuasion, and description.

The Tucson Zoo

---

1   Science gets most of its information by the process of reductionism, exploring the details, then the details of the details, until all the smallest bits of the structure, or the smallest parts of the mechanism, are laid out for counting and scrutiny. Only when this is done can the investigation be extended to encompass the whole organism or the entire system. So we say.

2   Sometimes it seems that we take a loss, working this way. Much of today's public anxiety about science is the apprehension that we may forever be overlooking the whole by an endless, obsessive preoccupation with the parts. I had a brief, personal experience of this misgiving one afternoon in Tucson, where I had time on my hands and visited the zoo, just outside the city. The designers there have cut a deep pathway between two small artificial ponds, walled by clear glass, so when you stand in the center of the path you can look into the depths of each pool, and at the same time you can regard the surface. In one pool, on the right side of the path, is a family of otters; on the other side, a family of beavers. Within just a few feet from your face, on either side, beavers and otters are at play, underwater and on the surface, swimming toward your face and then away, more filled with life than any creatures I have ever seen before, in all my days. Except for the glass, you could reach across and touch them.

3   I was transfixed. As I now recall it, there was only one sensation in my head: pure elation mixed with amazement at such perfection. Swept off my feet, I floated from one side to the other, swiveling my brain, staring astounded at the beavers, then at the otters. I could hear shouts across my corpus callosum, from one hemisphere to the other. I remember thinking, with what was left in charge of my consciousness,

that I wanted no part of the science of beavers and otters; I wanted never to know how they performed their marvels; I wished for no news about the physiology of their breathing, the coordination of their muscles, their vision, their endocrine systems, their digestive tracts. I hoped never to have to think of them as collections of cells. All I asked for was the full hairy complexity, then in front of my eyes, of whole, intact beavers and otters in motion.

4   It lasted, I regret to say, for only a few minutes, and then I was back in the late twentieth century, reductionist as ever, wondering about the details by force of habit, but not, this time, the details of otters and beavers. Instead, me. Something worth remembering had happened in my mind, I was certain of that; I would have put it somewhere in the brain stem; maybe this was my limbic system at work. I became a behavioral scientist, an experimental psychologist, an ethologist, and in the instant I lost all the wonder and the sense of being overwhelmed. I was flattened.

5   But I came away from the zoo with something, a piece of news about myself: I am coded, somehow, for otters and beavers. I exhibit instinctive behavior in their presence, when they are displayed close at hand behind glass, simultaneously below water and at the surface. I have receptors for this display. Beavers and otters possess a "releaser" for me, in the terminology of ethology, and the releasing was my experience. What was released? Behavior. What behavior? Standing, swiveling flabbergasted, feeling exultation and a rush of friendship. I could not, as the result of the transaction, tell you anything more about beavers and otters than you already know. I learned nothing new about them. Only about me, and I suspect also about you, maybe about human beings at large: we are endowed with genes which code out our reaction to beavers and otters, maybe our reaction to each other as well. We are stamped with stereotyped, unalterable patterns of response, ready to be released. And the behavior released in us, by such confrontations, is, essentially, a surprised affection. It is compulsory behavior and we can avoid it only by straining with the full power of our conscious minds, making up conscious excuses all the way. Left to ourselves, mechanistic and autonomic, we hanker for friends.

6   Everyone says, stay away from ants. They have no lessons for us; they are crazy little instruments, inhuman, incapable of controlling themselves, lacking manners, lacking souls. When they are massed together, all touching, exchanging bits of information held in their jaws

like memoranda, they become a single animal. Look out for that. It is a debasement, a loss of individuality, a violation of human nature, an unnatural act.

7   Sometimes people argue this point of view seriously and with deep thought. Be individuals, solitary and selfish, is the message. Altruism, a jargon word for what used to be called love, is worse than weakness, it is sin, a violation of nature. Be separate. Do not be a social animal. But this is a hard argument to make convincingly when you have to depend on language to make it. You have to print up leaflets or publish books and get them bought and sent around, you have to turn up on television and catch the attention of millions of other human beings all at once, and then you have to say to all of them, all at once, all collected and paying attention: be solitary; do not depend on each other. You can't do this and keep a straight face.

8   Maybe altruism is our most primitive attribute, out of reach, beyond our control. Or perhaps it is immediately at hand, waiting to be released, disguised now, in our kind of civilization, as affection or friendship or attachment. I don't see why it should be unreasonable for all human beings to have strands of DNA coiled up in chromosomes, coding out instincts for usefulness and helpfulness. Usefulness may turn out to be the hardest test of fitness for survival, more important than aggression, more effective, in the long run, than grabbiness. If this is the sort of information biological science holds for the future, applying to us as well as to ants, then I am all for science.

9   One thing I'd like to know most of all: when those ants have made the Hill, and are all there, touching and exchanging, and the whole mass begins to behave like a single huge creature, and *thinks*, what on earth is that thought? And while you're at it, I'd like to know a second thing: when it happens, does any single ant know about it? Does his hair stand on end?

QUESTIONS

Ideas

1. Think of this essay as a counterpart to "The Iks." Do they have a common theme? What does Thomas hope is bound up in our DNA? What does this have to do with the Iks' problem? Look especially at the first two sentences in paragraph 8.

2. Like many writers, including Eiseley and Dillard, Thomas uses his response to an experience as a jumping-off place to further thinking. Try to outline the chain of reasoning that the beavers and otters of the Tucson Zoo set off in Thomas's mind.

3. What do you think Thomas means by "full hairy complexity" in paragraph 3? Why does he "want no part of the science of beavers and otters"?

4. What did Thomas learn about himself from his zoo experience? What does he mean by saying he is "coded for beavers"? (Consider paragraph 5 carefully.)

5. Do you agree that our conscious minds fight against the loss of individuality? What is Thomas's rejoinder to those who urge us "not to be a social animal"?

6. Even though Thomas is using the questions in the last paragraph for effect how might you answer them?

Organization

7. What is the function of the first paragraph? What do you think Thomas intended in the last sentence by, "So we say"?

8. Does Thomas come back to that opening paragraph to summarize or strengthen? Does he do so explicitly, implicitly, or not at all?

9. Why does Thomas begin paragraph 5 with "But"? Is this an effective device?

10. Read the first sentence of paragraphs 2 and 7. How does Thomas connect them to the previous paragraphs?

11. In paragraph 6, what is the relation between the first and the remaining sentences? How are the sentences in this paragraph connected to each other?

12. If you split the essay into two parts, where would you break it and why?

Sentences

13. Thomas is trying to make his prose seem effortless, but we know that prose that is easy to read is hard to write. Thomas's prose did not spontaneously flow from his typewriter. He worked at it, long and hard. All writers do. For example, read paragraph 3 out loud several times. Can you describe some of the techniques Thomas uses here to achieve fluency? Some hints: Do all the sentences begin the same way? How does he vary the S–V–O pattern? How many words are in each sentence?

14. How is the fifth sentence constructed? Why the specific detail (endocrine systems, etc.) and the repetition? Does this paragraph have a beginning, a middle, and an end? How would you partition it?

15. Thomas occasionally uses short sentences, sometimes only two or three words long. Look through paragraphs 1–4, noting those. What is the effect of each?

Words

16. Thomas uses some scientific words in this essay. Do they confuse you? Did you get lost while reading them?
17. Why does Thomas use personal pronouns? See paragraphs 2 (you), 3 and 4 (I), and 5 (we).

Suggestion for Writing

Write a letter to Lewis Thomas agreeing or disagreeing with paragraphs 6, 7, or 8—or with the whole essay

---

To Err Is Human

---

1   Everyone must have had at least one personal experience with a computer error by this time. Bank balances are suddenly reported to have jumped from $379 into the millions, appeals for charitable contributions are mailed over and over to people with crazy-sounding names at your address, department stores send the wrong bills, utility companies write that they're turning everything off, that sort of thing. If you manage to get in touch with someone and complain, you then get instantaneously typed, guilty letters from the same computer, saying, "Our computer was in error, and an adjustment is being made in your account."

2   These are supposed to be the sheerest, blindest accidents. Mistakes are not believed to be part of the normal behavior of a good machine. If things go wrong, it must be a personal, human error, the result of fingering, tampering, a button getting stuck, someone hitting the wrong key. The computer, at its normal best, is infallible.

3   I wonder whether this can be true. After all, the whole point of computers is that they represent an extension of the human brain, vastly

improved upon but nonetheless human, superhuman maybe. A good computer can think clearly and quickly enough to beat you at chess, and some of them have even been programmed to write obscure verse. They can do anything we can do, and more besides.

4   It is not yet known whether a computer has its own consciousness, and it would be hard to find out about this. When you walk into one of those great halls now built for the huge machines, and stand listening, it is easy to imagine that the faint, distant noises are the sound of thinking, and the turning of the spools gives them the look of wild creatures rolling their eyes in the effort to concentrate, choking with information. But real thinking, and dreaming, are other matters.

5   On the other hand, the evidences of something like an *unconscious*, equivalent to ours, are all around, in every mail. As extensions of the human brain, they have been constructed with the same property of error, spontaneous, uncontrolled, and rich in possibilities.

6   Mistakes are at the very base of human thought, embedded there, feeding the structure like root nodules. If we were not provided with the knack of being wrong, we could never get anything useful done. We think our way along by choosing between right and wrong alternatives, and the wrong choices have to be made as frequently as the right ones. We get along in life this way. We are built to make mistakes, coded for error.

7   We learn, as we say, by "trial and error." Why do we always say that? Why not "trial and rightness" or "trial and triumph"? The old phrase puts it that way because that is, in real life, the way it is done.

8   A good laboratory, like a good bank or a corporation or government, has to run like a computer. Almost everything is done flawlessly, by the book, and all the numbers add up to the predicted sums. The days go by. And then, if it is a lucky day, and a lucky laboratory, somebody makes a mistake: the wrong buffer, something in one of the blanks, a decimal misplaced in reading counts, the warm room off by a degree and a half, a mouse out of his box, or just a misreading of the day's protocol. Whatever, when the results come in, something is obviously screwed up, and then the action can begin.

9   The misreading is not the important error; it opens the way. The next step is the crucial one. If the investigator can bring himself to say, "But even so, look at that!" then the new finding, whatever it is, is ready for snatching. What is needed, for progress to be made, is the move based on the error.

10   Whenever new kinds of thinking are about to be accomplished, or new varieties of music, there has to be an argument beforehand. With two sides debating in the same mind, haranguing, there is an amiable understanding that one is right and the other wrong. Sooner or later the thing is settled, but there can be no action at all if there are not the two sides, and the argument. The hope is in the faculty of wrongness, the tendency toward error. The capacity to leap across mountains of information to land lightly on the wrong side represents the highest of human endowments.

11   It may be that this is a uniquely human gift, perhaps even stipulated in our genetic instructions. Other creatures do not seem to have DNA sequences for making mistakes as a routine part of daily living, certainly not for programmed error as a guide for action.

12   We are at our human finest, dancing with our minds, when there are more choices than two. Sometimes there are ten, even twenty different ways to go, all but one bound to be wrong, and the richness of selection in such situations can lift us onto totally new ground. This process is called exploration and is based on human fallibility. If we had only a single center in our brains, capable of responding only when a correct decision was to be made, instead of the jumble of different, credulous, easily conned clusters of neurones that provide for being flung off into blind alleys, up trees, down dead ends, out into blue sky, along wrong turnings, around bends, we could only stay the way we are today, stuck fast.

13   The lower animals do not have this splendid freedom. They are limited, most of them, to absolute infallibility. Cats, for all their good side, never make mistakes. I have never seen a maladroit, clumsy, or blundering cat. Dogs are sometimes fallible, occasionally able to make charming minor mistakes, but they get this way by trying to mimic their masters. Fish are flawless in everything they do. Individual cells in a tissue are mindless machines, perfect in their performance, as absolutely inhuman as bees.

14   We should have this in mind as we become dependent on more complex computers for the arrangement of our affairs. Give the computers their heads, I say; let them go their way. If we can learn to do this, turning our heads to one side and wincing while the work proceeds, the possibilities for the future of mankind, and computerkind, are limitless. Your average good computer can make calculations in an instant which would take a lifetime of slide rules for any of us. Think of what

we could gain from the near infinity of precise, machine-made miscomputation which is now so easily within our grasp. We could begin the solving of some of our hardest problems. How, for instance, should we go about organizing ourselves for social living on a planetary scale, now that we have become, as a plain fact of life, a single community? We can assume, as a working hypothesis, that all the right ways of doing this are unworkable. What we need, then, for moving ahead, is a set of wrong alternatives much longer and more interesting than the short list of mistaken courses that any of us can think up right now. We need, in fact, an infinite list, and when it is printed out we need the computer to turn on itself and select, at random, the next way to go. If it is a big enough mistake, we could find ourselves on a new level, stunned, out in the clear, ready to move again.

QUESTIONS

Ideas

1. How is the title of this piece relevant? What does it have to do with Thomas's theme? Where is that theme expressed? Underline at least three sentences you think are related to the thesis.

2. Do you agree that our ability to make mistakes is a "splendid freedom"? Does our society agree? Does your university, your instructor?

3. Again, Thomas takes an apparently negative topic and makes it seem optimistic. Do you see hope in our "faculty of wrongness, the tendency toward error"?

4. In paragraph 8 Thomas discusses "error." And he makes what at first might seem the rather strange remark ". . . if it's a lucky day, and a lucky laboratory, somebody makes a mistake: . . . when the results come in, something is obviously screwed up, and then the action can begin." Can you explain this paradoxical idea? (Look ahead to paragraph 9 for help.)

5. Why does Thomas celebrate choice and alternative, especially multiple alternatives most of which will be "wrong"? Explain his idea that exploration is based on human fallibility (paragraph 12).

6. Suppose Thomas is "wrong" about what he says in this essay. Does that invalidate his view entirely? Does it make what he says here useless? Why or why not?

7. To err means, of course, to be mistaken. But the original meaning of the word carries the idea of wandering (L. *errare*, to wander). How do Thomas's ideas about error reflect this aspect of the word's meaning?

8. Does what Thomas says about error have any bearing on learning? On writing?

Organization

9. What is the purpose of Thomas's opening two paragraphs? How do they compare to the introductions in "The Iks" and "The Lives of a Cell"?

10. In the overall scheme of these fourteen paragraphs, what is the function of paragraph 6?

11. Where does Thomas support his notion that we are "coded for error"?

12. The last paragraph is rather long for Thomas. What holds it together? Is there an implicit or explicit topic sentence?

13. How many paragraphs have a "this" in the first sentence? Why do you think he does this?

14. Experienced writers try to move between the abstract and the concrete, often supporting general statements with specific details. How does Thomas do this in paragraphs 8, 12, and 13?

Sentences

15. Thomas sometimes adds words, phrases, and clauses to sentences, clarifying an idea, making a general point more specific. See the last sentence, for example. Locate several similar examples.

Words

16. How would you distinguish among error, mistake, and accident?

17. What does "maladroit" mean? "Haranguing"? "Protocol"?

Suggestion for Writing

Now that Thomas has alerted the reader to the paradox of error, can you see mistakes you made in the past or are continuing to make as enabling you to be "in the clear, ready to move again"? Write an essay involving personal experience to support this optimistic view of error.

On Natural Death

1   There are so many new books about dying that there are now special shelves set aside for them in bookshops, along with the health-diet and home-repair paperbacks and the sex manuals. Some of them are so packed with detailed information and step-by-step instructions for performing the function that you'd think this was a new sort of skill which all of us are now required to learn. The strongest impression the casual reader gets, leafing through, is that proper dying has become an extraordinary, even an exotic experience, something only the specially trained get to do.

2   Also, you could be led to believe that we are the only creatures capable of the awareness of death, that when all the rest of nature is being cycled through dying, one generation after another, it is a different kind of process, done automatically and trivially, more "natural," as we say.

3   An elm in our backyard caught the blight this summer and dropped stone dead, leafless, almost overnight. One weekend it was a normal-looking elm, maybe a little bare in spots but nothing alarming, and the next weekend it was gone, passed over, departed, taken. Taken is right, for the tree surgeon came by yesterday with his crew of young helpers and their cherry picker, and took it down branch by branch and carted it off in the back of a red truck, everyone singing.

4   The dying of a field mouse, at the jaws of an amiable household cat, is a spectacle I have beheld many times. It used to make me wince. Early in life I gave up throwing sticks at the cat to make him drop the mouse, because the dropped mouse regularly went ahead and died anyway, but I always shouted unaffections at the cat to let him know the sort of animal he had become. Nature, I thought, was an abomination.

5   Recently I've done some thinking about that mouse, and I wonder if his dying is necessarily all that different from the passing of our elm. The main difference, if there is one, would be in the matter of pain. I do not believe that an elm tree has pain receptors, and even so, the blight seems to me a relatively painless way to go even if there were nerve endings in a tree, which there are not. But the mouse dangling

tail-down from the teeth of a gray cat is something else again, with pain beyond bearing, you'd think, all over his small body.

6   There are now some plausible reasons for thinking it is not like that at all, and you can make up an entirely different story about the mouse and his dying if you like. At the instant of being trapped and penetrated by teeth, peptide hormones are released by cells in the hypothalamus and the pituitary gland; instantly these substances, called endorphins, are attached to the surfaces of other cells responsible for pain perception; the hormones have the pharmacologic properties of opium; there is no pain. Thus it is that the mouse seems always to dangle so languidly from the jaws, lies there so quietly when dropped, dies of his injuries without a struggle. If a mouse could shrug, he'd shrug.

7   I do not know if this is true or not, nor do I know how to prove it if it is true. Maybe if you could get in there quickly enough and administer naloxone, a specific morphine antagonist, you could turn off the endorphins and observe the restoration of pain, but this is not something I would care to do or see. I think I will leave it there, as a good guess about the dying of a cat-chewed mouse, perhaps about dying in general.

8   Montaigne had a hunch about dying, based on his own close call in a riding accident. He was so badly injured as to be believed dead by his companions, and was carried home with lamentations, "all bloody, stained all over with the blood I had thrown up." He remembers the entire episode, despite having been "dead, for two full hours," with wonderment:

> It seemed to me that my life was hanging only by the tip of my lips. I closed my eyes in order, it seemed to me, to help push it out, and took pleasure in growing languid and letting myself go. It was an idea that was only floating on the surface of my soul, as delicate and feeble as all the rest, but in truth not only free from distress but mingled with that sweet feeling that people have who have let themselves slide into sleep. I believe that this is the same state in which people find themselves whom we see fainting in the agony of death, and I maintain that we pity them without cause. . . . In order to get used to the idea of death, I find there is nothing like coming close to it.

Later, in another essay, Montaigne returns to it:

> If you know not how to die, never trouble yourself; Nature will in a

moment fully and sufficiently instruct you; she will exactly do that business for you; take you no care for it.

9 The worst accident I've ever seen was on Okinawa, in the early days of the invasion, when a jeep ran into a troop carrier and was crushed nearly flat. Inside were two young MPs, trapped in bent steel, both mortally hurt, with only their heads and shoulders visible. We had a conversation while people with the right tools were prying them free. Sorry about the accident, they said. No, they said, they felt fine. Is everyone else okay, one of them said. Well, the other one said, no hurry now. And then they died.

10 Pain is useful for avoidance, for getting away when there's time to get away, but when it is end game, and no way back, pain is likely to be turned off, and the mechanisms for this are wonderfully precise and quick. If I had to design an ecosystem in which creatures had to live off each other and in which dying was an indispensable part of living, I could not think of a better way to manage.

QUESTIONS

Ideas

1. Thomas takes a rather controversial stand on the current interest in "death therapy." What is the tone of the first paragraph, especially the last sentence?

2. Where does Thomas present his point? Why? Has he earned the right to state his position at this point?

3. What do you make of the first sentence in paragraph 7? Do you think he has a right to make the statement he does in the last sentence in this paragraph, especially the last phrase?

4. Why does Thomas quote Montaigne? Is the quote necessary? Useful? Why or why not?

5. Is Thomas being too optimistic? Do you think nature "will exactly do that business for you"?

Organization

6. Notice how these ten paragraphs are put together. After the introductory first and second paragraphs, what is the purpose of the elm and mouse

paragraphs? Where do you think he shifts from specifics to a generalized notion of death? What is the function of paragraph 9? How about 10?

7. Exactly how does Thomas launch this essay? What does he do in the opening paragraph? Compare the opening of "The Iks" and of "To Err Is Human." How are these essays introduced?

8. What is the relation between the first and the last sentence in this essay?

Sentences

9. In paragraph 5, could Thomas have broken the first sentence into two separate sentences? How about the third one? Could any part of the last sentence stand by itself?

10. A clause is part of a sentence that contains a subject and a predicate. Some clauses can stand by themselves (independent); others cannot (dependent). In the ninth paragraph, is there an independent clause in the first sentence? Where are the depending clauses in the second sentence? Rewrite this first sentence as many ways as you can.

11. Read aloud the second quotation from Montaigne. Now read the next paragraph by Thomas. How would you describe the difference? Try to be specific.

Words

12. Where does Thomas use technical, scientific language? Is it necessary? Effective? Confusing?

13. What synonyms for "death" does Thomas use? What does each connote? (See especially paragraph 3.)

14. What does "natural" mean?

Suggestions for Writing

A. Do you think we should be instructed in how to die?

B. Do you think death is hidden away in our society? Freewrite for 15 minutes on either of these ideas, then find a focused opinion and develop that in a paragraph.

THREE

Ellen Goodman
(1941–   )

Ellen Goodman, a columnist for *The Boston Globe*, has described her job as "telling people what I think." This she has been doing for many years with honesty, intelligence, and verve. Collected in two books—*Close to Home* and *At Large*—Goodman's essays range over many subjects, both public and private: family life, television, friendship, the relations between men and women (and between adults and children), anxiety, violence, the role of women, and trends, fads, and established traditions.

Her writing about these and other issues is clear, direct, and personal. Because her essays are confined to a 750-word column, she writes to the point. Because she addresses a general audience—her work is nationally syndicated—she writes clearly and simply, without pomposity or ostentation. Prizing the personal, the concrete, and the familiar, Goodman fills her essays with anecdotes, vignettes, and characters; she tells stories with real people in them. This is her way of bringing important public issues down to earth or, as she puts it, "close to home."

In "The Company Man" Goodman describes Phil, a man who "worked himself to death" at fifty-one. In a few quick strokes she sketches Phil: a man who worked six days a week, had no interests beyond his job, and "ate egg salad sandwiches at his desk." Throughout "The Company Man" Goodman works by implication rather than outright statement. She presents facts about Phil's life and work along with comments from the wife and children he rarely saw and hardly knew. She allows her readers to draw their own conclusions, with the result that her argument, inviting the reader's participation, is the more powerfully advanced by remaining implicit.

Her views in two other essays are more explicitly aired. In "It's Failure, Not Success" Goodman argues against the ideas in Michael Korda's book *Success!* Countering Korda's advice to look out for Number One, to be greedy and selfish, she asserts that "it's not OK to be greedy, Machiavellian, dishonest. It's not always OK to be rich." Questioning the assumptions on which *Success!* rests, Goodman gets to the heart of the issue—an ethical one—and from her counter-perspective claims that Korda's book is less about success than about failure.

In a similar way she questions another bit of conventional wisdom in "Time Is for Savoring." Challenging the notion that faster is better, that time can be "saved," Goodman asks that we think more about how we use the time we have than about new ways to gain more of it. She asks us, in short, to examine our assumptions about time, to change the questions we ask about it.

Besides possessing a talent for description and a flair for argument and debate, Goodman is a shrewd and sensitive social analyst. In "The Tapestry of Friendships" she sharply contrasts the bonding styles of men and women, setting her ideas in the context of how friends are portrayed in a few recent films. Although the tone of the piece is authoritative, even judgmental, the thought is more speculative than polemical. The confident yet reasonable tone of this and many of her essays enhances their persuasiveness.

But whatever her subject and however pointedly expressed her views, Goodman is consistently witty, intelligent, and provocative. She entertains as she enlightens. Perhaps best of all, her essays reveal her as she wants to be revealed: as "a person, not a pontificator," as a writer who enjoys her work, one who communicates with intelligence and civility.

On Being a Journalist

1   When my daughter Katie was seven years old, I overheard her telling a friend, "My mommy is a columnist." "What's that?" asked the other little girl, reasonably enough. Katie thought about it awhile and finally said, "Well, my mother gets paid for telling people what she thinks."

2   All in all, that's not such a bad job description. The pieces collected in this book represent several years of "telling people what I think." They also represent two of the main qualifications for this business: nerve and endurance.

3   To write a column you need the egocentric confidence that your view of the world is important enough to be read. Then you need the pacing of a long-distance runner to write day after day, week after week, year after year. One journalist who dropped out of this endurance contest with a sigh of relief said that writing a column was like being married to a nymphomaniac: every time you think you're through, you have to start all over again. This was an unenlightened, but fairly accurate, analogy.

4   To meet my "quota," I need two opinions a week, although I assure you that some weeks I overflow with ideas, percolate opinions, while other weeks I can't decide what I think about the weather. Moreover, I have to fit these thoughts into a carefully reserved piece of newspaper property. I am allotted approximately the same number of words whether I am writing about life, love or the world-shattering problem of a zucchini that is sterile.

5   Despite these constraints, I tend to go through life like a vacuum cleaner, inhaling all the interesting tidbits in my path, using almost everything I observe, read or report. For me at least, this makes life more interesting and more integrated. I don't "go" to work or "return" to home life. The lines between the personal and professional sides of my life are far less rigidly drawn in this job than in virtually any other.

6   I suppose that is because I do write close to home.

7   I never wanted to be a package tour sort of columnist who covered thirteen countries in twenty-seven days. Nor do I want to write at arm's length about the Major Issues of Our Times. I think it's more important

for all of us to be able to make links between our personal lives and public issues.

8   The most vital concerns can't be divided into internal and external affairs. What is more private a concern than the public policy decisions made about the family? What is more public a concern than the impact of divorce, or the new isolation, or the two-worker family? The ups and downs of presidential polls are no more crucial to our society than the way we raise our children.

9   As a writer, I've wanted to be seen as a person, not a pontificator. Why should people believe what I have to say if they know nothing about me? I don't want to present myself as a disembodied voice of authority but as a thirty-eight-year-old woman, mother, vegetable gardener, failed jogger and expert on only one subject: the ambivalence of life.

10   I see myself in these pieces, and in fact, as a fellow struggler. In that sense too I write close to home.

11   What else can I say about the collection? The pieces show that I am more comfortable observing—people, change, events—than judging. I am more concerned with the struggles between conflicting values than the struggles between conflicting political parties. I don't think there is anything undignified about being silly when all about me are grave.

12   And maybe these columns also show how much I like my work.

QUESTIONS

1. How does Goodman define herself? Does she give you a good idea of what she does and why she does it?

2. What personal characteristics and attributes does a columnist need to do the job well? Does Goodman seem to possess these?

3. What does Goodman see as proper subjects for a columnist? What does she mean by saying she writes "close to home"?

4. Throughout this essay Goodman establishes a sense of her priorities by setting up a series of contrasts. Single out one or two of these and explain what point she makes in presenting the contrast. (See especially paragraphs 5–11.)

5. Goodman frequently uses comparisons to clarify her ideas. Explain the idea behind each of the following comparisons:

Writing a column is like being married to a nymphomaniac: every time you think you're through, you have to start all over again.

I tend to go through life like a vacuum cleaner, inhaling all the interesting tidbits in my path. . . .

6. One of the notable features of Goodman's style—in this piece as well as in her others—is a high degree of concreteness, of specificity. She talks about *things*, things you can get your hands on, things from everyday life. Make a list of all the specific things, the details that Goodman includes in this essay.

7. In paragraph 4 Goodman mentions one of the constraints of writing a column: limitations of space. How well does she succeed in saying what she has to, in making her point? What kind of audience is she writing for?

Suggestions for Writing

A. Write an essay in which you identify or define yourself. Try to imitate Goodman's down-to-earth tone and concreteness, even to the point of using comparisons from everyday life.

B. After you read what E. B. White or Edward Hoagland suggests about writing essays, assess Goodman's writing according to their standards and goals.

The Company Man

1   **H**e worked himself to death, finally and precisely, at 3:00 A.M. Sunday morning.

2   The obituary didn't say that, of course. It said that he died of a coronary thrombosis—I think that was it—but everyone among his friends and acquaintances knew it instantly. He was a perfect Type A, a workaholic, a classic, they said to each other and shook their heads—and thought for five or ten minutes about the way they lived.

3   This man who worked himself to death finally and precisely at 3:00 A.M. Sunday morning—on his day off—was fifty-one years old and

a vice-president. He was, however, one of six vice-presidents, and one of three who might conceivably—if the president died or retired soon enough—have moved to the top spot. Phil knew that.

4   He worked six days a week, five of them until eight or nine at night, during a time when his own company had begun the four-day week for everyone but the executives. He worked like the Important People. He had no outside "extracurricular interests," unless, of course, you think about a monthly golf game that way. To Phil, it was work. He always ate egg salad sandwiches at his desk. He was, of course, overweight, by 20 or 25 pounds. He thought it was okay, though, because he didn't smoke.

5   On Saturdays, Phil wore a sports jacket to the office instead of a suit, because it was the weekend.

6   He had a lot of people working for him, maybe sixty, and most of them liked him most of the time. Three of them will be seriously considered for his job. The obituary didn't mention that.

7   But it did list his "survivors" quite accurately. He is survived by his wife, Helen, forty-eight years old, a good woman of no particular marketable skills, who worked in an office before marrying and mothering. She had, according to her daughter, given up trying to compete with his work years ago, when the children were small. A company friend said, "I know how much you will miss him." And she answered, "I already have."

8   "Missing him all these years," she must have given up part of herself which had cared too much for the man. She would be "well taken care of."

9   His "dearly beloved" eldest of the "dearly beloved" children is a hard-working executive in a manufacturing firm down South. In the day and a half before the funeral, he went around the neighborhood researching his father, asking the neighbors what he was like. They were embarrassed.

10   His second child is a girl, who is twenty-four and newly married. She lives near her mother and they are close, but whenever she was alone with her father, in a car driving somewhere, they had nothing to say to each other.

11   The youngest is twenty, a boy, a high-school graduate who has spent the last couple of years, like a lot of his friends, doing enough odd jobs to stay in grass and food. He was the one who tried to grab

at his father, and tried to mean enough to him to keep the man at home. He was his father's favorite. Over the last two years, Phil stayed up nights worrying about the boy.

12   The boy once said, "My father and I only board here."

13   At the funeral, the sixty-year-old company president told the forty-eight-year-old widow that the fifty-one-year-old deceased had meant much to the company and would be missed and would be hard to replace. The widow didn't look him in the eye. She was afraid he would read her bitterness and, after all, she would need him to straighten out the finances—the stock options and all that.

14   Phil was overweight and nervous and worked too hard. If he wasn't at the office, he was worried about it. Phil was a Type A, a heart-attack natural. You could have picked him out in a minute from a lineup.

15   So when he finally worked himself to death, at precisely 3:00 A.M. Sunday morning, no one was really surprised.

16   By 5:00 P.M. the afternoon of the funeral, the company president had begun, discreetly of course, with care and taste, to make inquiries about his replacement. One of three men. He asked around: "Who's been working the hardest?"

QUESTIONS

Ideas

1. Goodman uses Phil as an example, a type of something. Of what is he a representative, and what is her attitude toward him and toward what he represents? What point does she make about the more general situation of which he is only a part?

2. What is implied by the boss's question at the end of the essay? Would this point have been more effective if made explicitly rather than by implication?

3. Why, in an essay about a company man, does Goodman include discussion of his family? What does this discussion contribute to her point?

Organization

4. Consider the structure of this essay. How could it be diagrammed? What figure could represent its structure—circle, square, triangle? Look at par-

agraph 1 in relation to paragraph 15, and at paragraphs 2 and 3 in relation
to paragraph 16.

5. Paragraphs 1, 3, and 15 repeat a particular point—the time of Phil's death.
Does Goodman employ other forms of repetition? For what purpose?

Sentences

6. In paragraphs 2 and 3 Goodman includes sentences that make use of the
double dash. Explain the function and tone of the information included
between the dashes in each sentence. Could the "sandwiched-in" information be left out of any of these sentences? Why or why not?

7. Goodman ends a number of her paragraphs with short, emphatic sentences—paragraphs 3, 4, 6, 7, 8, 9, 14, and 15. In fact, one paragraph—
14—consists of four consecutive short sentences. What tone is established
with these short, almost staccato sentences?

8. Another thing to notice about Goodman's sentences in this essay is their
uniformity of pattern, in this case, subject-verb-object. Almost all begin
with a noun or pronoun; many begin with "Phil," "He," or "His." Is this
uniformity of structure monotonous? What is the effect of such heavy use
of repeated sentence forms?

Words

9. Why does Goodman repeatedly use generic terms like "the widow," "the
company man," "the company president"? What is the tone of these?

10. Why are so many words and phrases in quotation marks? What tone is
established through their use?

Suggestions for Writing

A. Write an essay explaining what it means to be a company man or a company
woman. You might want to consider the pleasures and pressures, the
liabilities and assets, the opportunities and obligations such a position
accords.

B. Write an essay in which you use something that happened as an occasion
to explore an idea that the event illustrates. You might consider treating
the description of what happened ironically, as Goodman does in "The
Company Man."

C. Imagine that you are the president of the company for which Phil worked.
Write a letter to Phil's wife. Decide what you want the purpose and tone
of the letter to be.

D. Imagine that you are Phil's wife. Write a letter to the company president. You might want to write the letter before Phil dies. Or you could do it after. In either case, decide what the purpose and tone of your letter should be.

It's Failure, Not Success

1   **I** knew a man who went into therapy about three years ago because, as he put it, he couldn't live with himself any longer. I didn't blame him. The guy was a bigot, a tyrant and a creep.

2   In any case, I ran into him again after he'd finished therapy. He was still a bigot, a tyrant and a creep, *but* . . . he had learned to live with himself.

3   Now, I suppose this was an accomplishment of sorts. I mean, nobody else could live with him. But it seems to me that there are an awful lot of people running around and writing around these days encouraging us to feel good about what we should feel terrible about, and to accept in ourselves what we should change.

4   The only thing they seem to disapprove of is disapproval. The only judgment they make is against being judgmental, and they assure us that we have nothing to feel guilty about except guilt itself. It seems to me that they are all intent on proving that I'm OK and You're OK, when in fact, I may be perfectly dreadful and you may be unforgivably dreary, and it may be—gasp!—*wrong*.

5   What brings on my sudden attack of judgmentitis is success, or rather, *Success!*—the latest in a series of exclamation-point books all concerned with How to Make it.

6   In this one, Michael Korda is writing a recipe book for success. Like the other authors, he leapfrogs right over the "Shoulds" and into the "Hows." He eliminates value judgments and edits out moral questions as if he were Fanny Farmer and the subject was the making of a blueberry pie.

7   It's not that I have any reason to doubt Mr. Korda's advice on the way to achieve success. It may very well be that successful men wear

handkerchiefs stuffed neatly in their breast pockets, and that successful single women should carry suitcases to the office on Fridays whether or not they are going away for the weekend.

8   He may be realistic when he says that "successful people generally have very low expectations of others." And he may be only slightly cynical when he writes: "One of the best ways to ensure success is to develop expensive tastes or marry someone who has them."

9   And he may be helpful with his handy hints on how to sit next to someone you are about to overpower.

10   But he simply finesses the issues of right and wrong—silly words, embarrassing words that have been excised like warts from the shiny surface of the new how-to books. To Korda, guilt is not a prod, but an enemy that he slays on page four. Right off the bat, he tells the would-be successful reader that:

- It's OK to be greedy.
- It's OK to look out for Number One.
- It's OK to be Machiavellian (if you can get away with it).
- It's OK to recognize that honesty is not always the best policy (provided you don't go around saying so).
- And it's always OK to be rich.

11   Well, in fact, it's not OK. It's not OK to be greedy, Machiavellian, dishonest. It's not always OK to be rich. There is a qualitative difference between succeeding by making napalm or by making penicillin. There is a difference between climbing the ladder of success, and macheteing a path to the top.

12   Only someone with the moral perspective of a mushroom could assure us that this was all OK. It seems to me that most Americans harbor ambivalence toward success, not for neurotic reasons, but out of a realistic perception of what it demands.

13   Success is expensive in terms of time and energy and altered behavior—the sort of behavior he describes in the grossest of terms: "If you can undermine your boss and replace him, fine, do so, but never express anything but respect and loyalty for him while you're doing it."

14   This author—whose *Power!* topped the best-seller list last year—is intent on helping rid us of that ambivalence which is a signal from

our conscience. He is like the other "Win!" "Me First!" writers, who try to make us comfortable when we should be uncomfortable.

15   They are all Doctor Feelgoods, offering us placebo prescriptions instead of strong medicine. They give us a way to live with ourselves, perhaps, but not a way to live with each other. They teach us a whole lot more about "Failure!" than about success.

QUESTIONS

Ideas

1. How well does the title fit the essay? Where does Goodman echo the title and with what point?
2. Both near the beginning of the essay (paragraph 5) and at the end (paragraphs 14 and 15), Goodman goes beyond discussion of Korda's *Success!* Why does she do this, and what does she say about other books of this type? What is her main objection to Korda's book in particular?

Organization

3. Divide the essay into two major parts. Provide a subtitle for each and explain how they are related. Then divide the essay into three or four parts, and again provide subtitles and show how the parts are related.
4. One thing that quickly strikes the reader of this essay is the shortness of its paragraphs. Reorganize and rearrange the paragraphs, combining as many as you think can be logically connected. What differences do you detect between this new version and Goodman's present arrangement? Which do you prefer and why?

Sentences

5. Throughout the essay Goodman uses parallel sentences. She does this most noticeably in paragraphs 10, 11, and 15. Explain what is gained by use of the parallel structure.

> There is a qualitative difference between succeeding
> by making napalm
> or by making penicillin.

> There is a   difference between
> climbing the ladder of success
> or machete-ing a path to the top.

6. Examine the first four paragraphs, noting especially how Goodman varies the length of her sentences. Consider where and how she uses short sentences.

Words

7. What words and phrases are responsible for the personal, even familiar tone of the essay?
8. What point does Goodman make by comparing Korda with Fanny Farmer? How does the comparison convey her attitude toward Korda and his book?
9. Explain the function and effect of the comparisons used in paragraph 10:

> But he simply finesses the issues of right and wrong—silly words, embarrassing words that have been excised like warts from the shiny surface of the new how-to books.

> To Korda, guilt is not a prod, but an enemy that he slays on page four. . . .

Suggestions for Writing

A. Write an essay about a book you've read—perhaps a practical, how-to book or a self-help book such as Korda's. In your essay, summarize the author's views, then explain why you agree or disagree with them.
B. Write a how-to essay. Assume the role of a confident and comfortable and experienced person who knows and believes in the advice being given. If you like, you can write a humorous essay rather than a "straight" or serious one. Possible titles: "How to Annoy Your Friends"; "How to Con Your Teachers"; "How to Feel Good (or Bad) about Yourself." Try to make the essay an offering of general advice about the subject rather than a set of directions.
C. Write an essay defining and illustrating what you mean by Failure—or Success.

Time Is for Savoring

1   A few months ago, when a preening French official descended from his Concorde into Washington, he bragged to Tip O'Neill that he saved four, count 'em, four hours traveling supersonically.

2　　At that point the Speaker turned and asked him, benignly, what he had done with the four hours he'd saved. The official, as the story goes, was taken aback, right aback into silence. This exchange stuck in my mind, and not because I'm snooping into the Frenchman's activities. I'm not that sort of reporter.

3　　But it occurred to me that O'Neill's response was a nice healthy challenge to the time-saving obsession of our lives. I guess the Concorde is as good a place to begin as any.

4　　It has taken the accumulated wisdom of centuries to build this plane, and what have we got? For one thing, a noisier airplane which uses more fuel to carry fewer people in less comfort from one continent to the other at greater expense. We call this peculiar achievement "progress" for only one reason: It does all this absurd stuff in a shorter amount of time than a conventional plane.

5　　Saving time, it seems, has a primacy that's too rarely examined. From the Concorde to the microwave oven to the Speed Reading class, we value saving time more than the way we spend it and more than the values we may sacrifice to it. At times we behave like the efficiency expert in *Pajama Game* whose rationalization for his life was simple: "For a time-study man to waste time / is a crime."

6　　We tell ourselves that we are all busy people. Our lives are geared to the school bells and alarm clocks and factory whistles outside of our control. But on the whole, the time-saving devices—both mechanical and personal—that are supposed to help us save time, don't. They merely allow us to do more in the same number of minutes, leaving us with full schedules and the need to find more ways to save time.

7　　With the aid of the plane, the official and the businessman can turn a two-day trip into a one-day trip. But they are usually faced with two one-day trips. The people who learn to Speed Read don't spend less time reading; they just read more in the same time.

8　　The machines that make it possible for us to do things that we could never do before—like cook a roast in a half hour—also make it more likely that we will do things we never would have done before. Like cook that roast.

9　　These things don't save time, any more than the assembly line saves the worker time.

10　　There is actually no way to bank our minutes away. The best we can do, with the most sophisticated machinery products, is to redistribute those minutes. And, like the French official, we don't always do a good job of that. We have even become so addicted to saving time that we forget to differentiate between the things we like to do (dining with our families, for example) and the things we hate to do (cleaning the oven). We efficiently shorten them all.

11   At the end of a busy day, families often get dinner "down to a science": the science of convenience foods, mixes, and fifteen-minute "gourmet" recipes. In some houses, dinner goes from the refrigerator to the dishwasher in less than an hour. Then, having saved all these minutes, rather than spending them with each other, we drop them like quarters in a television slot machine.

12   Either we spend more and more energy processing ourselves through our days, doing more and more in the same amount of time, or we throw away our "free time" like Daddy Warbucks.

13   It's not that I want to go back to ox carts, let alone wooden washtubs, but it seems to me that we ought to make some personal judgments about the machines that are pushed on us in the name of the clock. We have to ask: Is it really going to save time? *My* time? Is it going to cut down unpleasant time, or pleasant time? And, as the Speaker would say, what am I going to do with the time I save?

14   Ultimately, time is all you have and the idea isn't to save it but to savor it. Like the man on the record, James Taylor, says, "The secret o' life is enjoying the passage of time."

QUESTIONS

Ideas

1. In this essay Goodman examines a common assumption about time and speed. What is this assumption, and what is her view of it?
2. What is Goodman's purpose? To entertain? To persuade? To provoke? Something else? Are you convinced by what she says? Why or why not?

Organization

3. Goodman begins the essay with an anecdote briefly recounting an event she heard about. From there she moves to the more general idea of "saving time." Could those opening paragraphs be dispensed with? What adjustments to the essay would be necessary if it were to begin with what is now paragraph 4 or paragraph 5? Which beginning do you prefer and why?

4. The conclusion of the essay consists of two paragraphs—13 and 14. How does each of these paragraphs bring the essay to an "end"? What point does Goodman make in this double-barrelled conclusion?

5. Paragraphs 9 and 12 are only a sentence each. Why? Explain what would be gained and what lost if paragraph 9 were attached to paragraph 8 and paragraph 12 to paragraph 11.

Sentences

6. Goodman uses the colon three times in this essay—in paragraphs 4, 5, and 11. For each sentence containing a colon, explain the relationship between the left-hand part and the right-hand part.

7. The following sentences begin with prepositional phrases, with introductory phrases. For each, decide whether the phrase can be moved to another position in the sentence or can be eliminated entirely. What effect would such changes have on the sentences and on the paragraphs in which they appear? Paragraph 5, sentences 2 and 3; paragraph 7, sentence 1; paragraph 11, sentences 1 and 2.

Words

8. What do the following excerpts suggest about the intensity of Goodman's feeling about the subject of her essay? What is their tone? "We call this peculiar achievement 'progress' " (4); "We have even become so addicted to saving time . . ." (10).

9. Twice in this essay Goodman uses allusions, one a reference to Daddy Warbucks, the other a quotation from James Taylor. Do these references aid or impede your understanding? Can they be dispensed with?

Suggestions for Writing

A. Rewrite Goodman's sentences containing colons to eliminate the colons. How do the revised versions compare with Goodman's originals?

B. Write an essay describing different ways to make efficient use of your time. Or write an essay explaining how and why you waste time, and how you might begin to savor it more.

C. Write a letter to Goodman either challenging her ideas or explaining why you accept them.

D. Write an essay in which you argue for a reconsideration of something taken for granted—as Goodman does here by questioning the idea that time can be "saved" by doing things more quickly.

The Tapestry of Friendships

1   It was, in many ways, a slight movie. Nothing actually happened. There was no big-budget chase scene, no bloody shoot-out. The story ended without any cosmic conclusions.

2   Yet she found Claudia Weill's film *Girlfriends* gentle and affecting. Slowly, it panned across the tapestry of friendship—showing its fragility, its resiliency, its role as the connecting tissue between the lives of two young women.

3   When it was over, she thought about the movies she'd seen this year—*Julia*, *The Turning Point* and now *Girlfriends*. It seemed that the peculiar eye, the social lens of the cinema, had drastically shifted its focus. Suddenly the Male Buddy movies had been replaced by the Female Friendship flicks.

4   This wasn't just another binge of trendiness, but a kind of *cinéma vérité*. For once the movies were reflecting a shift, not just from men to women but from one definition of friendship to another.

5   Across millions of miles of celluloid, the ideal of friendship had always been male—a world of sidekicks and "pardners," of Butch Cassidys and Sundance Kids. There had been something almost atavistic about these visions of attachments—as if producers culled their plots from some pop anthropology book on male bonding. Movies portrayed the idea that only men, those direct descendants of hunters and Hemingways, inherited a primal capacity for friendship. In contrast, they portrayed women picking on each other, the way they once picked berries.

6   Well, that duality must have been mortally wounded in some shootout at the You're OK, I'm OK Corral. Now, on the screen, they were at least aware of the subtle distinction between men and women as buddies and friends.

7   About 150 years ago, Coleridge had written, "A woman's friendship borders more closely on love than man's. Men affect each other in the reflection of noble or friendly acts, whilst women ask fewer proofs and more signs and expressions of attachment."

8   Well, she thought, on the whole, men had buddies, while women had friends. Buddies bonded, but friends loved. Buddies faced adversity

together, but friends faced each other. There was something palpably different in the way they spent their time. Buddies seemed to "do" things together; friends simply "were" together.

9   Buddies came linked, like accessories, to one activity or another. People have golf buddies and business buddies, college buddies and club buddies. Men often keep their buddies in these categories, while women keep a special category for friends.

10   A man once told her that men weren't real buddies until they'd been "through the wars" together—corporate or athletic or military. They had to soldier together, he said. Women, on the other hand, didn't count themselves as friends until they'd shared three loathsome confidences.

11   Buddies hang tough together; friends hang onto each other.

12   It probably had something to do with pride. You don't show off to a friend; you show need. Buddies try to keep the worst from each other; friends confess it.

13   A friend of hers once telephoned her lover, just to find out if he were home. She hung up without a hello when he picked up the phone. Later, wretched with embarrassment, the friend moaned, "Can you believe me? A thirty-five-year-old lawyer, making a chicken call?" Together they laughed and made it better.

14   Buddies seek approval. But friends seek acceptance.

15   She knew so many men who had been trained in restraint, afraid of each other's judgment or awkward with each other's affection. She wasn't sure which. Like buddies in the movies, they would die for each other, but never hug each other.

16   She'd reread *Babbit* recently, that extraordinary catalogue of male grievances. The only relationship that gave meaning to the claustrophobic life of George Babbitt had been with Paul Riesling. But not once in the tragedy of their lives had one been able to say to the other: You make a difference.

17   Even now men shocked her at times with their description of friendship. Does this one have a best friend? "Why, of course, we see each other every February." Does that one call his most intimate pal long distance? "Why, certainly, whenever there's a real reason." Do those two old chums ever have dinner together? "You mean alone? Without our wives?"

18   Yet, things were changing. The ideal of intimacy wasn't this

parallel playmate, this teammate, this trenchmate. Not even in Hollywood. In the double standard of friendship, for once the female version was becoming accepted as the general ideal.

19   After all, a buddy is a fine life-companion. But one's friends, as Santayana once wrote, "are that part of the race with which one can be human."

QUESTIONS

Ideas

1. What does Goodman see as the main difference between male and female friendships? Do you agree that men "bond" and "buddy" whereas women "love" and "befriend" one another? Why or why not?

2. How do the movies that Goodman mentions tie in with her main point? Are these movie references necessary?

Organization

3. The essay falls roughly into three parts: paragraphs 1–6; paragraphs 7–17; paragraphs 18–19. What would have been gained and lost if Goodman had omitted paragraphs 1–6?

4. Two paragraphs (11 and 14) are very short, even for journalism. Should these short paragraphs have been attached to the paragraphs before or after them? Why or why not? Could they be omitted?

Sentences

5. A notable feature of Goodman's style in this essay is her use of antithetical sentences such as the following:

> Buddies bonded, but friends loved. (8)
>
> Buddies try to keep the worst from each other; friends confess it. (12)
>
> Buddies seek approval. But friends seek acceptance. (14)

The basic thrust and the general idea of the three sentences are the same; the sentence structure is slightly different in the three instances. Find other sentences that make contrastive, antithetical points about buddies and friends—in still other, slightly different ways.

6. In the sentences that follow, Goodman uses the dash to set off part of her idea. For each, explain how the sentence would be different if a comma replaced the dash. And explain also whether the sentence could (or should)

end where the dash occurs. (That is, imagine a period where the dash is with the words after the period omitted.)

Slowly, it panned across the tapestry of friendship—showing its fragility, its resiliency, its role as the connecting tissue between the lives of two young women. (2)

When it was over, she thought about the movies she'd seen this year—*Julia, The Turning Point* and now *Girlfriends*. (3)

Across millions of miles of celluloid, the ideal of friendship had always been male—a world of sidekicks and "pardners," of Butch Cassidys and Sundance Kids. (5)

A man once told her that men weren't real buddies until they'd been "through the wars" together—corporate or athletic or military. (10)

7. In paragraph 17 Goodman asks a series of questions and then provides answers in quotation marks. What is the tone and the point of these questions (and of this paragraph)?

8. Goodman twice introduces quotations into the essay—Coleridge in paragraph 7 and Santayana at the end. What is the point of each quotation, and how well does each tie in with Goodman's main idea?

Words

9. In writing of herself in this essay, Goodman uses the third person: she refers to herself as "she," rather than as the more conventional and expected "I." What is the effect of this third-person self-reference? Try reading two or three paragraphs, mentally changing the "she" to "I." How does the tone change?

10. In the first five paragraphs Goodman uses the language of film, perhaps more so than she actually needs to. What is her purpose in using film language?

11. Explain the tone and word play of each of the following sentences:

Buddies faced adversity together, but friends faced each other. (8)

Buddies hang tough together; friends hang onto each other. (11)

You don't show off to a friend; you show need. (12)

Suggestions for Writing

A. Write imitations of the sentences discussed in questions 5, 6, and 7.
B. Write your own essay on the meaning and value of friendship.
C. Attend a film—or several films—and write an essay examining the kinds of friendships portrayed.

FOUR

Edward Hoagland

(1932–   )

Edward Hoagland is a city man with a love for the country. He splits his time between the wilds of New York and the wilderness of New England. He has written about both, producing different kinds of attractions in essays such as "City Rat," "Red Wolves and Black Bears," "City Walking," "Hailing the Illusory Mountain Lion," and "Home Is Two Places." Originally published in a wide variety of periodicals, including *The New York Times Book Review, The Village Voice, Harper's, Esquire, Life, Sports Illustrated,* and *The Saturday Review,* Hoagland's essays have been collected in four books: *The Courage of Turtles* (1971), *Walking the Dead Diamond River* (1973), *Red Wolves and Black Bears* (1976), and *The Edward Hoagland Reader* (1979). Hoagland has also written three novels and two travel books, *African Calliope* and *Notes from the Century Before.*

Hoagland has been characterized as a "nature writer," a term he objects to as too limiting, as not recognizing the range and variety of his work. Although he has written frequently and well about animals, he has written equally well about many other things: circuses, boxing, marriage, fame, power and success, tugboats and taxidermy, rodeos and writing, politics, people, and the golden rule. At the center of Hoagland's essays, whatever their subjects, is a concern for performance, for how people strive for perfection. In two essays that don't appear in this collection, "Tiger Bright" and "A Low Water Man," Hoagland describes and celebrates two men who are very good at what they do. In "Tiger Bright" it is the skill of Gunther Gebel-Williams in

61

handling lions and tigers for show that captivates Hoagland; in "A Low Water Man" it is the unusual performance of Henri LaMothe, who high-dives into a small pool containing only a few inches of water.

In addition to skill, to the success of devoted performance, Hoagland writes about people's pain, about what they endure. Perhaps his most successful performance on this subject is "The Threshold and the Jolt of Pain," an essay that explores many kinds of pain, both physical and mental: the pain of childbirth, the anguish of divorce, the torture of having knuckle ground against knuckle, the agony of death. Hoagland brings himself into this essay, as he does frequently in his work, by writing about his frustration and distress as a stutterer. He writes about his impediment with sensitivity and humor, providing us with an acute understanding of what it's like to suffer from this handicap.

The characteristic tone of a Hoagland essay is upbeat, optimistic. Even when he writes about pain, he celebrates the dignity of his subjects—whether men or animals—affirming their courage, their determination, their endurance. His optimism works its way into "A Run of Bad Luck," an essay whose title promises dire happenings. And even though Hoagland delivers on the direnesses, he approaches his unhappy experiences with equanimity, even with a touch of humor. That we endure pain, that we survive bad luck, that we yearn and strive for perfection—these are the centers of interest in Hoagland's essays. These, along with his respect for animals—whether in the wild, in the circus, or in the home—are what excite his imagination and spur his feeling, in essay after essay.

Hoagland was a devoted writer by the time he was twenty. He has been working hard at his craft ever since. And he likes it as well, once commenting that "writing for me is a very happy activity—I actually enjoy the time of writing more than publication day." But Hoagland doesn't deny the pleasure of being read: "Writers want to be read," he once noted. All of them, we might add, Hoagland included. Or else why write?

What has been most read of Hoagland's output are his essays, which, as he has written, "hang somewhere on a line between two sturdy poles: this is what I think, and this is what I am." As a prescription for what any writer can accomplish in an essay and as a description of what Hoagland has given us in his own essays, this is very good indeed. In presenting his thoughts and his very self, honestly and authentically, Hoagland speaks to us, as he puts it, "mind to mind." His essays, perhaps his best advertisements for himself, show us the possibilities of wedding mind with feeling, and both thought and feeling with form. His writing, finally, demonstrates the accuracy of his observation that "the fascination of the mind is the fascination of the essay."

What I Think, What I Am

---

1   **O**ur loneliness makes us avid column readers these days. The personalities in the *New York Post, Chicago Daily News, San Francisco Chronicle* constitute our neighbors now, some of them local characters but also the opinionated national stars. And movie reviewers thrive on our need for somebody emotional who is willing to pay attention to us and return week after week, year after year, through all the to-and-fro of other friends to flatter us by pouring out his (her) heart. They are essayists as Elizabeth Hardwick is, James Baldwin was. We sometimes hear that essays are an old-fashioned form, that so-and-so is the "last essayist," but the facts of the marketplace argue quite otherwise. Essays of almost any kind are so much easier for a writer to sell now than short stories, so many more see print, it's odd that though two fine anthologies remain which publish the year's best stories, no comparable collection exists for essays. Such changes in the reading public's taste aren't always to the good, needless to say. The art of telling stories predated even cave-painting surely; and if we ever find ourselves living in caves again, it (with painting) will be the only art left, after movies, novels, essays, photography, biography and all the rest have gone down the drain—the art to build from.

2   One has the sense with the short story form that while everything may have been done, nothing has been overdone, it has a permanence. Essays, if a comparison is to be made, although they go back 400 years

to Montaigne, seem a newfangled mercurial, sometimes hokey sort of affair which has lent itself to many of the excesses of the age, from spurious autobiography to spurious hallucination, as well as the shabby careerism of traditional journalism. It's a greased pig. Essays are associated with the way young writers fashion a name—on plain, crowded newsprint in hybrid vehicles like *The Village Voice, Rolling Stone, The Soho Weekly News* (also *Fiction* magazine), instead of the thick paper stock and thin readership of *Partisan Review.*

3   Essays, however, hang somewhere on a line between two sturdy poles: this is what I think, and this is what I am. Autobiographies which aren't novels are generally extended essays, indeed. A personal essay is like the human voice talking, its order the mind's natural flow, instead of a systematized outline of ideas. Though more wayward or informal than an article or treatise, somewhere it contains a point which is its real center, even if the point couldn't be expressed in fewer words than the essayist has employed. Essays don't usually "boil down" to a summary, as articles do, but on the other hand they have fewer "levels" than first-rate fiction—a flatter surface—because we aren't supposed to argue about their meaning. In the old distinction between teaching versus story-telling—however cleverly the author muddies it up—an essay is intended to convey the same point to each of us.

4   This emphasis upon mind speaking to mind is what makes essays less universal in their appeal than stories. They are addressed to an educated, perhaps a middle-class reader, with certain presuppositions shared, a frame of reference, even a commitment to civility—not the grand and golden empathy inherent in every man which the story-teller has a chance to tap. At the same time, of course, the artful "I" of an essay can be as chameleon as any narrator in fiction; and essays do tell a story just as often as a short story stakes a claim to a particular viewpoint.

5   Mark Twain's piece called "Corn-pone Opinions," for example, which is about public opinion, begins with a vignette as vivid as any in "Huckleberry Finn." When he was a boy of 15, Twain says, he used to hang out a back window and listen to the sermons preached by a neighbor's slave standing on top of a woodpile. The fellow "imitated the pulpit style of the several clergymen of the village, and did it well and with fine passion and energy. To me he was a wonder. I believed he was the greatest orator in the United States and would some day be

heard from. But it did not happen; in the distribution of rewards he was overlooked.

6   "He interrupted his preaching now and then to saw a stick of wood, but the sawing was a pretense—he did it with his mouth, exactly imitating the sound the bucksaw makes in shrieking its way through the wood. But it served its purpose, it kept his master from coming out to see how the work was getting along."

7   The extraordinary flexibility of essays is what has enabled them to ride out rough weather and hybridize into forms to suit the times. And just as one of the first things a fiction writer learns is that he needn't actually be writing fiction to write a short story—he can tell his own history or anyone else's as exactly as he remembers it and it will still be "fiction" if it remains primarily a story—an essayist soon discovers that he doesn't have to tell the whole truth and nothing but the truth; he can shape or shave his memories as long as the purpose is served of elucidating a truthful point. A personal essay frequently is not autobiographical at all, but what it does keep in common with autobiography is that, through its tone and tumbling progression, it conveys the quality of the author's mind. Nothing gets in the way. Because essays are directly concerned with the mind and its idiosyncrasy, the very freedom the mind possesses is bestowed on this branch of literature that does honor to it, and the fascination of the mind is the fascination of the essay.

QUESTIONS

1. Throughout this essay, Hoagland makes distinctions. He distinguishes between essay and story, between essay and article, between essay and autobiography. What does the essay have in common with each of these forms, and how, according to Hoagland, does it differ from each of them?

2. Is it true that, as Hoagland says, "an essay is intended to convey the same point to each of us"? Do you think that, as he suggests, an "emphasis upon mind speaking to mind is what makes essays less universal in their appeal than stories"?

3. What does Hoagland mean when he says that essays "hang somewhere on a line between two sturdy poles: this is what I think, and this is what I am"?

4. What does it mean for an essayist to be truthful? What is Hoagland's point concerning the essayist's freedom to select, distort, or partially tell the truth?

5. In paragraphs 5 and 6, Hoagland uses an example from Mark Twain. What does this example contribute to the essay? How does it refer to the point about the essay that Hoagland is making? Why does Hoagland quote so much of it in Twain's own words? (Would it have been better as a summary?)

6. What, finally, is Hoagland saying about the essay?

Suggestions for Writing

A. Taking your cue from Hoagland, write an essay explaining the relationship between what you think and what you are.

B. Modifying slightly Hoagland's title, write an essay developing the implications of one of the following titles: Why I Think; What I Think; What I Was, What I Am; What I Believe; Why I Believe X.

C. After reading E. B. White's "The Essayist," write a few paragraphs comparing what White says about the essayist with what Hoagland says.

D. After reading the other Hoagland essays in this book, write an essay explaining how Hoagland comes across as a writer and as a man. Try to do some literary detective work, looking for clues as to what kind of individual Hoagland is. Consider his subjects, his style, his selection of details, his tone.

A Run of Bad Luck

1 Bad ions in the air, bad stars, or bad luck: call it what you will—a run of bad luck, in fact. I was driving down the Thruway in Vermont to consult a doctor in New York, and hit a deer. Didn't see the deer till the impact, sharing its surprise. Deer, unlike domestic animals, are afraid of cars and leap as you pass, either into you or away. It lay in the deep grass, heaving like a creature stranded on the beach.

2 Sure enough, as befitted the omen, in New York City the doctor's news was bad. Then within a day or two, Pier 50, a huge ramshackle structure across the street from where I live, caught fire and burned hectically for seven hours, although surrounded by fireboats, as only

an abandoned pier can. The neighborhood was layered in smoke for a couple of days—for me, acrid testimony to what the doctor had said. There were also a few of the usual New York hang-up phone calls, and then, as if to push me into a sump of depression, somebody—a vandal aroused by the fire, or someone who thought I had parked in his parking space—poured sugar into the gas tank of my car, not enough to destroy the engine but enough so that I returned to Vermont in relief.

3   In the meantime, my mother, in another city, had gone into the hospital for surgery, and one evening that week my daughter and I were out walking along a wooded road (I was carrying her on my shoulders), when a car passing another car bore down on us at high speed, its roar not easy to distinguish from that of the slower one; I barely heard it in time. This, in the context of the other incidents, particularly shook me because it seemed to bear a hint of malevolence; I felt very small. Then, within days, my next-door neighbor there, an old man as close as a relative to us, died of a stroke. Another good friend and country mentor went into the hospital after a heart attack. News came from New York as well that a friend in the city had killed herself. I marshaled a motley assortment of tranquilizers and sleeping pills left over from the past— divorce, career crisis, other bad occasions. I had that feeling of luck running out, that I must be *very careful*, although, on the contrary, I was becoming deadened, not alert. At such a time, the opposite of invulnerable, one must take care to move in a gingerly fashion and not get so rattled that an accident happens. I had considered myself a sort of a Sunday's child much of my life, but suddenly intimations of death and calamity were all about.

4   I remembered talking to a woman who had survived a snowslide by swimming along on the surface while whooshing downhill for a hundred yards—as people caught in an undertow or even in quicksand save themselves by flattening out and floating if they can. Just so, I should ride the current until it turned. The best advice I have heard on bearing pain is to fix one's mind upon the idea that the pain is in one place—the other side of the room—and that you are in another; then, where you are, play cards or whatever. Cooking, fooling with my daughter, I realized more distinctly than at any time in years that although in fact my life was not at stake right now, I believed in some form of reincarnation or immortality—this a conviction, not a wish. I pray in airplanes during takeoff, but it is with a sense of praying *pro forma*, as if the location of my belief weren't really there, but were more

generalized, in a bigger God. There are ideas central to society which we seldom question in order that society will hold together—as, for instance, the notion basic to medical care that everybody has a contribution to make, or "a right to life." But there are other conceptions, such as the idea of God, which we disparage and scarcely consider, until later, smiling sheepishly in our mind's eye as if we had disputed the fact that the moon moves in the sky, we admit to having been wrong, and to having known all along that we were wrong.

5   Once, highborn ladies would flee to a convent if some unnerving sequence of events overtook them, not necessarily taking orders, but resting, collecting their wits. And when they strolled in the cloister around a bubbling fountain, the walkway itself possessed a soothing, perpetual quality, with each right-angle turn leading straight to another. Walking for many hours, they looked at the lindenwood saints, the robust faces—at the Virgin's implacable verve, or else at a dolor portrayed with an equally saving exaggeration. Coincidentally, I went to New York's own Cloisters, and because the reality of each bad event had been dulled by the others, it was for me one of those queer times when people recognize how much they can adjust to—how quickly, for example, they could settle into the routine of life in a prison camp.

6   Of course I had my daughter to entertain, and in the country I walked in the woods, watching the aspens quake (said by legend to occur because Christ's cross was of aspen). I have an old army siren, hand-cranked, that I climbed with up on the mountain at twilight, to persuade a family of coyotes nearby to answer. I was relieved that the random incidents seemed to have ended. I thought of two friends in the city who had recently suffered crises—heart attacks at forty. One fellow, as the pain surged through him, found himself muttering stubbornly, "No groveling, Death!" When he was out of danger he wrote seventy-some letters to friends from his hospital bed, each with a numbered series of thoughts directed to the recipient. The other man is that rare case where one can put one's finger exactly on the characteristics of which one is so fond. He married the same woman twice. Although it didn't work out either time, she was well worth marrying twice, and to my way of thinking this showed that he was at once a man of fervent, rash, abiding love, and yet a man of flexibility, ready to admit an error and to act to correct it.

7   Both my mother and country mentor were now on the mend, and my own doctor reported good news. Prospects began looking up.

What I'd gained from the period, besides a flood of relief, was the memory of how certain I'd been that the intricacy and brilliance of life cannot simply fold up with one's death—that, as in the metaphor of a fountain, or the great paradigm of rain and the ocean, it sinks down but comes up, blooms up and sinks down again.

QUESTIONS

Ideas

1. Is the title accurate as a clue to the content of the essay? What does the word "run" mean here?
2. How many examples of bad luck does Hoagland include? Are they all pretty much the same, or are they different in kind or degree? Are they all necessary? What is their cumulative effect on Hoagland? On you?
3. What advice does Hoagland give (and heed) in paragraph 4? What analogy is used to convey this advice, and how valuable are both the analogy and the advice?

Organization

4. Where does the bad news stop? Where and how does Hoagland turn the essay around to recount his change of fortune? Why does he include the near accident with his daughter?
5. How are the first two paragraphs related? How does the second paragraph develop the first? And how does the third paragraph follow from the first two?
6. Diagram, graph, or draw a picture of the structure of this essay. Explain your diagram to another student.

Sentences

7. The first sentence of "A Run of Bad Luck" is abrupt and direct. It has a no-nonsense tone: "Bad ions in the air, bad stars, or bad luck: call it what you will—a run of bad luck, in fact." Besides the repetition of "bad" (four times) what else contributes to the tone of the sentence?
8. The final sentence of the essay is quite different from the first. Explain how the two sentences differ in length, form, rhythm, and tone.
9. In the first two sentences of paragraph 3, Hoagland uses the semicolon to set off (or to connect) a long statement and a short one. For each sentence,

isolate the short section, the part following the semicolon. If you were to cut these short sections from each of the long sentences, putting a period where the semicolon is, what would be lost? How would the meaning change?

Words

10. In the first and last paragraphs of the essay, Hoagland uses comparisons. Explain how each comparison works and what it adds to the point of the essay.

   It [a deer] lay in the deep grass, heaving like a creature stranded on the beach. (1)

   What I'd gained from the period, besides a flood of relief, was the memory of how certain I'd been that the intricacy and brilliance of life cannot simply fold up with one's death—that, as in the metaphor of a fountain, or the great paradigm of rain and the ocean, it sinks down but comes up, blooms up and sinks down again. (7)

11. Hoagland italicizes certain words and places quotation marks around others. In each case explain why.

   very careful (3)
   pro forma (4)
   "a right to life" (4)
   "No groveling, Death!" (6)

12. Hoagland's vocabulary in this essay and in his others is a mix of the familiar and the less than usual. Check the context and the meaning of the following words: "sump," "acrid" (2); "malevolence" (3); "dolor" (5).

Suggestions for Writing

A. Write imitations of the first and last sentences of the essay.
B. Write an essay describing a period of good or bad luck in your life. Explain how and why the good or bad luck affected you as it did. And, of course, include specific examples of the kind of luck you experienced.
C. Write an essay exploring the meaning(s) of one or more of the following words: "luck," "chance," "fortune," "circumstance," "fate," "destiny."
D. Write an essay describing a bad time in your life—a day, a week, a month, even longer. Explain the effect of having lived through that time. Reflect on the meaning and importance of the experience.

E. Write an essay following the general form of Hoagland's "A Run of Bad Luck." Begin by briefly recounting experiences, by accumulating examples. At some point, turn from describing examples to thinking about them and explaining them.

F. Defend or attack the following statement: "There is no such thing as 'luck.' People who say they have 'bad luck' are simply looking for excuses for their failures."

On the Question of Dogs

---

1   The idea has gotten abroad in New York that nobody in a metropolis should keep a dog. There is a lot of shitting on dogs going on. "Children before dogs," and so on, as if most of the dog-owners didn't have children as well and as if children didn't love and profit from dogs. My daughter weighs half as much as our dog, stands shorter than he does, and in the absence of woods and a farmyard to wander around, learns a good deal about where her roots in the world are from him, learns about her own wellsprings of love and the initiative of love, because of course he's a different proposition from us and her affections as they encounter his are different—discovers that there are bigger things than herself in the world besides us.

2   He's a large country dog (both images that set the sort of person who objects to dogs to gnawing his elbows and toes), and during the winters he doesn't spend in the city is curled up asleep in his polar-bear coat in deep Vermont snow like a husky. He was middle-aged before he first smelled a stone building or went for a drive in a car. (He smelled a river that we were riding by and jumped right out of the window like a puppy to go for a swim, not realizing that we were traveling fast.) The city is a smorgasbord of new smells, but the cranks say it's mean of us to deprive him of that winter spent vegetating in the snow. What they fear most in a dog—these amateur sanitary engineers who would chop themselves off at the knees if it would free them entirely from their origins on the land—is that he actually may be an honest-to-goodness *animal*, and not some kind of substitute human being and therefore

fair game for them, comprehensible to them. They hate the fact that milk comes from the udders of cows and that grapefruit juice is mostly water which has been down percolating in the soil.

3   Admittedly, we live near the lower Manhattan waterfront, with its *Gold Star Mother* ferryboat, where the addicts line up for a methadone fix, its House of Detention, and many truck parks, gritty dead lots, and the West Side Highway and a derelict railroad spur running above. Find the right spot and what is a little uric acid there? But if our site is less citified than some, as a group we make up for that by the size of our dogs: hundred-pounders on occasion, Airedales, shepherds, Great Danes, Great Pyrenees, Afghans, Saint Bernards, Salukis, big wolfish chows, Malemutes, Newfoundlands, collies like mine. We are up with the sun, cold but alive to the morning because of the company we keep, smelling the sharp west wind, and much happier-looking than those other outlaws of the city who keep cars and are looking for some place to park. We are out kite-flying, if you want to know, our eyes fixed away on a reality as big and old as the sky. We have tugging on the end of our string the friendly spirit of *Canis*, fifteen thousand years removed from the Near Eastern wolf, fifteen million years removed from the fox, thirty million years distant from the ancestral bear-raccoon, forty million or fifty million years removed from ancestral weasels and cats, and from our own line by sixty million to seventy million years, perhaps. The dog family is thought to have originated in North America, dispersed, then come back. And here it is, with poundingly cheerful feet, kiting across the street, sniffing out traces of life. If after all this time the world of life is grinding to an end, it won't be by the agency of dogs. Nor will they give up the ghost without a final leap of the feet and grin of their pointy teeth. Even set down in this ultimate slag heap on the waterfront, if they can't find any life, then, nose to the ground, wagging their tails, they seek out the wastes of life.

4   The pennyworth psychology of the day would have it that keeping pets is a way of avoiding the mainstream concerns—of putting one's tenderness in a jewelbox, so to speak—a premise that, like any other, can be illustrated if you pick your cases carefully enough, because there are certainly some fanciers who confine their affections to a fish tank. My own impression is that a commoner, deeper motive than escapism

is the wish to broaden one's base, to find the fish in oneself. Another fascination, especially with small wild creatures hemmed into a terrarium or cage, is seeing how they cope, and helping them cope. Every man is an experimenter and every experimenter is a small boy, but in this day and age the observer's promptings are not generally cruel; it seems quite crucial to us to know how they *do* function and cope.

5   No matter how sensibly their needs have been anticipated, however, I wind up pitying wild animals and want them released. But where released? They are pushed face to face with us wherever they survive. Even in the effort to help them survive there are absurd misplays. Recently an entrepreneur somehow gathered together two hundred specimens of a South American sidenecked turtle which is on the list of endangered species and flew them to California, where he hoped to capitalize on their rarity. Instead they were identified and seized by federal officials. So the federal men confiscated the shipment of turtles to teach him a lesson. What did they do then—fly them back? No, killed them.

6   There's an excellent pet store on 14th Street called Fang and Claw, Aldo Passera, proprietor, where I go to look over the field. Burmese and Ceylonese pythons cost $150 or so, button quail are $25 apiece, sungazar lizards $30. Hornbills and stump-tailed macaques are for sale. The prettiest beast Passera has is an emerald tree boa for $125, and the biggest a regal python of seventeen feet, at $44 a foot. If I went in for wildlife, what I'd buy for my house to represent what has gone before and paralleled us and diverged from us and just stood still would be a common iguana, I think. An iguana as green as a tree, with a stillness about it, but undaunted, tall, gallant in posture, with a mouthful of teeth and a face like that of a god's palace guard, carved by the millennia as if by the workings of water and wind on a grim cliff, only more so. More sculpted than sculpture, an iguana's face is really a great double take, reacting maybe to what was going on in the room forty-five minutes ago and maybe to what was happening during the Triassic Age. It's a face like a trumpet blast, practically a caricature of fortitude, and so it's a face to come home to, a face to get a grip on, I should think. If I wanted a wild animal, it would be that.

7   But I go for the intelligence and good will and good spirits of my dog instead. He is my fish, my macaque, my iguana, and more.

QUESTIONS

Ideas

1. Scattered throughout this essay are a series of reasons why Hoagland owns and keeps a dog. What are these reasons? Does he convince you that it's not so bad to keep dogs—even large dogs—as pets in the city?
2. What is Hoagland's purpose in this essay, and who is his implied audience? How do you know?
3. What is Hoagland's attitude toward dogs? Toward other animals? Toward nature? And what does Hoagland mean by his last sentence: "My dog is my fish, my macaque, my iguana, and more"?
4. Why does Hoagland include a discussion of children, especially of his daughter?

Organization

5. How is the essay arranged? Go through it one paragraph at a time and explain how each paragraph follows from the one before and leads into the one after it.
6. Is the first paragraph an effective opening for the essay? Would Hoagland have done better to have used his second sentence as the lead sentence of the essay? How would the tone of the paragraph be affected by such a change?
7. If paragraph 7 were included as part of paragraph 6, how would the tone and emphasis change? Could paragraph 5 be omitted entirely? What would be the effect of omitting paragraph 5?

Sentences

8. Paragraphs 1–4 contain one long sentence each. Examine one or two of these long sentences, taking the sentence(s) apart section by section. Try to locate the basic idea—the central fact or act of the sentence—and discover just how Hoagland expanded it.
9. Paragraph 6 contains a fragment: "An iguana as green as. . . ." If you rewrote it as a complete grammatical sentence, would that improve upon or detract from the effect the sentence has as it now reads? Why?
10. Hoagland includes two questions—and answers—in paragraph 5. What is the purpose of these? Should the questions be converted to declarative statements? Why or why not?

Words

11. What is Hoagland's tone toward those who criticize him, those who challenge his right to own a pet? How and where does he respond to those who question his motives? What words and phrases in the first two paragraphs are especially important as carriers of tone?
12. How appropriate and how effective are the comparisons Hoagland uses in paragraph 3? What point does he make by means of these comparisons?
13. Reread the description of the iguana in paragraph 6. What impression of the animal do you have? How does Hoagland create this impression?

Suggestions for Writing

A. Write imitations of one or two of the long sentences from the first four paragraphs.
B. Write an essay explaining why you think more people should have pets—or why they should not have them. If you prefer, limit your discussion to keeping pets in the city, or perhaps to keeping one kind of pet in the city.
C. Write a defense of (or an attack on) a particular animal—any animal, including man. Explain specifically why the animal appeals to you, why you want to celebrate it—or why it repulses you, why you want to condemn it.

The Threshold and the Jolt of Pain

---

1   Like most boys in their teens, I wondered once in a while how I would take torture. Badly, I thought. Later I thought not so badly, as I saw myself under the pressures of danger or emergency, once when a lion cub grabbed my hand in its mouth and I wrestled its lips for half a minute with my free hand. Another summer when I fought forest fires in a crew of Indians in the West, we stood up under intense heat and thirst, watching the flames crackle toward us irresistibly while we

waited to see whether the fire lines that we had cut were going to hold. I've climbed over the lip of a high waterfall; I've scratched inside a hippopotamus's capacious jaws; I faced a pistol one day in Wyoming with some degree of fortitude. However, I knew that all this élan would vanish if my sex organs were approached. The initiation to join the Boy Scouts in our town was to have one's balls squeezed, so I never joined. Even to have my knuckle joints ground together in a handshake contest reduces me to quick surrender—something about bone on bone. I steered clear of the BB-gun fights in my neighborhood, and I could be caught in a chase and tied up easily by someone slower who yelled as if he were gaining ground, so I made friends with most of the toughies as a defensive measure.

2   As a boy I was much given to keeping pets and showering care on them, but I had a sadistic streak as well. In boarding school my roommate got asthma attacks when he was jumped on, and I always backed away laughing when his tormentors poured into the room. There was another nice boy whom I seldom picked on myself, and with sincere horror I watched a game grip the Florentine fancy of our corridor. Divided in teams, we would push him back and forth as a human football from goal to goal. The crush at the center, where he was placed, was tremendous, and though no one remembered, I'd invented the game.

3   My first love affair was with a Philadelphian, a girl of twenty-seven. That is, she was the first girl I slept with. She was a love in the sense that she loved me; I was close and grateful to her but didn't love her—I'd loved one girl earlier whom I hadn't slept with. She lived in one of those winsome houses that they have down there, with a tiled backyard and three floors, one room to each floor. We wandered along the waterfront and spent Saturdays at the street market, which is the largest and visually the richest street market in the United States. I was not an ogre to her, but I did by stages develop the habit of beating her briefly with my belt or hairbrush before we made love, a practice which I have foregone ever since. It may be indicative of the preoccupations of the 1950s that I worried less about this than about any tendencies I may have had toward being homosexual; but the experience gives me a contempt for pornography of that arch gruesome genre, quite in vogue nowadays as psychological "exploration," where whipping occurs but the flesh recovers its sheen overnight and the whippee doesn't perhaps

hang her(him)self, propelling the whipper into the nervous breakdown which he is heading for.

4   Seeing eventual disaster ahead, I didn't go deeply into this vein of sensation, just as I was shrewd enough as a boy not to be picked on often or to suffer more than a few accidents. Once I ran my hand through an apple crusher, and once I imitated a child's stutter at summer camp, thereby—or so I imagined (remembering what was supposed to happen to you if you crossed your eyes)—picking up the malady at the age of six. Almost my only pangs, then, were this stutter, which still remains in my mouth. It may strike other people as more than a spasm, but to me it's a spasm of pain of a kind which I haven't time for, or time to regard as anything else. It's like someone who has a lesion or twist in his small intestine, which hurts him abruptly and of which he is hardly aware otherwise. The well-grooved wince I make in shaking the words out seems to keep my face pliant and reasonably young.

5   Somerset Maugham described his bitter discovery when he was a boy that prayer was no help: he woke up next morning still clamped to his adamant stutter. I was more of a pantheist; I kept trusting to the efficacy of sleep itself, or to the lilting lift that caused birds to fly. Also I went to a bunch of speech therapists. At the Ethical Culture School in New York, for example, a woman taught me to stick my right hand in my pocket and, with that hidden hand, to write down over and over the first letter of the word I was stuttering on. This was intended to distract me from stuttering, and it did for a week or two. The trouble was that watching me play pocket pool that way was more unsettling to other people than the ailment it was meant to cure. At a camp in northern Michigan I was trained by a team from the university to speak so slowly that in effect I wasn't speaking at all; I talked with the gradualism of a flower growing—so absurdly tardy a process that my mind unhinged itself from what was going on. In Cambridge, Massachusetts, a young fellow from the University of Iowa—and oh, how *he* stuttered—took the most direct approach. He got me to deliberately imitate myself, which was hard on me since I was already terribly tired of stuttering, and to stare, as well, at the people whom I was talking to in order to find out what their reactions were. I found out, for one thing, that some of my friends and about a fifth of the strangers I met smiled when the difficulty occurred, though they generally turned their heads to the side or wiped their mouths with one hand to hide the smile. Thereafter, life

seemed simpler if I avoided looking at anybody, whoever he was, when I was stuttering badly, and I wasn't so edgily on the alert to see if I'd spit inadvertently.

6   Not that I lacked understanding for the smilers, though, because for many years I too had had the strange impulse, hardly controllable, to smile if somebody bumped his head on a low door lintel or received sad news. The phenomenologists say this is a form of defense. It goes with childhood especially, and I stopped indulging in it one night in Boston when I was in a police patrol wagon. A friend and I had been out for a walk, he was hit by a car, and as he woke from unconsciousness during the ride to the hospital and asked what had happened, I found myself grinning down at him while I answered. A few weeks later I was walking past an apartment building just as a rescue squad carried out a would-be suicide. He was alive, on a stretcher. When our eyes touched he smiled impenetrably, but I didn't smile back.

7   As a stutterer, I learned not to write notes. You put yourself at someone's mercy more when you write him a note than if you just stand there like a rhinoceros and snort. I could write a *Stutterer's Guide to Europe*, too: the titters in old Vienna, the knowing English remembering their King, the raw scorching baitings I met with in Greece, surrounded sometimes like a muzzled bear. The fourth means of effecting a cure I heard about was based on the fact that stutterers are able to sing without stuttering; hence, the victim should swing one of his arms like a big pendulum and talk in time to this—which again was obviously a worse fate than the impediment. Though I didn't try it, I was sent to a lady voice teacher who laid my hand on her conspicuous chest so that I could "feel her breathe." For just that moment the lessons worked wonderfully; if I wasn't speechless I spoke in a rush.

8   Stammering (a less obtrusive word I used to prefer) apparently is not unattractive to women. It's a masculine encumbrance; five times as many men as women suffer from it. I was seldom alone while I was in Europe, and once or twice girls told me by way of a pick-me-up that they'd loved someone "for" his stutter. When I went into my seizures at parties, if a woman didn't step back she stepped forward, whereas the men did neither. The female instinct does not apply nearly so favorably to other afflictions. In our glib age the stutterer has even been considered a kind of contemporary hero, a presumed honest man who is unable to gab with the media people. Beyond the particular appeal of this

image, it does seem to suit a writer. Publishers are fastidious types and some whom I've met have sidled away in distress from my flabbering face as soon as they could, but they probably remembered my name if they caught it. The purity image or Billy Budd stuff didn't intrigue them, just the hint of compulsion and complexity. Though I don't greatly go for either picture, in social terms I've thought of my stutter as a sort of miasma behind the Ivy League-looking exterior. People at parties take me for William Buckley until I begin, so I keep my mouth shut and smile prepossessingly just as long as I can.

9   Being in these vocal handcuffs made me a desperate, devoted writer at twenty. I worked like a dog, choosing each word. I wrote two full-length novels in iambic meter and a firehose style. Three hundred review copies of the second of these were sent out, but I received, I think, only three reviews. This was new pain, a man's career pain, with its attendant stomach trouble and neck and back cramps. A couple of years after that I got divorced from my first wife, and bawled like a half-butchered bull for an hour, rolled up on the floor of my apartment, while the two homosexuals next door listened in silence close to the wall, wondering what they ought to do. It was a purge, but the pain of that experience I remember best was an earlier scene. I'd announced to my wife, whom I loved and still love, my belief that we needed to separate. The next time we talked she crossed the room to my chair, knelt down beside me and asked what was going to become of each of us. That is the most painful splinter in my life, the most painful piece of the past. With variations the ache was prolonged through many fugitive suppers. In fact we still meet, holding hands and laughing at each other's jokes until we feel tears.

10   Who knows which qualities are godly? Pain probably makes us a bit godly, though, as tender love does. It makes us rue and summarize; it makes us bend and yield up ourselves. Pain is a watchdog medically, telling us when to consult a doctor, and then it's the true-blue dog at the bedside who rivals the relatives for fidelity. Last summer my father died of cancer. We had made peace, pretty much, a few years before. Although he had opposed my desire to be a writer, he ended up trying to write a book too, and he turned over to me at the last an old family history which he'd been hiding, partly because it mentioned a lot of muteness among my ancestors and partly in order to prevent my ex-ploiting the stories. My voice and my liberal opinions grew a little more

clarion in the household during the months he was dying. From a selfish standpoint, I suppose I was almost ready for him to die, but I was very earnestly sorry for every stage of rough handling involved in the process and for his own overriding regret that his life was cut off. Having lost our frank fear of death along with our faith in an afterlife, we have all adopted our fear of pain as a feeble alternative. Our regret, too, is magnified. When he was in discomfort I stuttered a great deal, but when he was not, when he was simply reminiscing or watching TV, I stuttered scarcely a bit. Then, as he was actually dying, during our last interview, he turned on the bed and asked me something. My answer was blocked in my mouth and his face went rigid with more pain than mine. He was startled because in the exigencies of dying he had forgotten that my infirmity was still there unhealed. He straightened, shutting his eyes, not wanting to end his life seeing it. Nevertheless, he'd often told me that it was my problems he loved me for rather than for my successes and sleekness. He loved my sister for being waiflike and my mother for being on occasion afraid she was mentally ill.

11   We were quite hardy while the months passed. Mother and he lay side by side on the bed clasping hands. Because of the pills, until nearly the end he was not suffering pain of the magnitude he had dreaded. The last couple of days there was a tossing, pitching, horrific pain, but the body more than the mind was responding—the body attempting to swallow its tongue. What I remember, therefore, of death's salutation to my father was that it came as a tickler, making his withered body twitch, touching him here and touching him there, wasting his tissues away like white wax, while his head on the headrest above looked down and watched; or he'd shoot an acute glance at me from out of the hunching amalgam of pricks, jactitation and drug-induced torpor. Death tickled him in a gradual crescendo, taking its time, and, with his ironic attorney's mind, he was amused. His two satisfactions were that he was privy to its most intimate preparations, everything just-so and fussy, and that at last the long spiky battling within the family was over and done. The new summer blossomed. In mid-June I saw what is meant by "a widow's tears." They flow in a flood of tremulous vulnerability, so that one thinks they will never stop.

12   Most severe on the physiologists' scale of pain is that of childbirth. It's also the worst that I've seen. A year had gone by since I'd left the

Army and quit visiting my Philadelphia friend. She came to New York, looked me up, discovered me vomiting, thin as a rail because of girl trouble, and moved in with me on the Upper West Side, spooning in food and mothering me. Then, at about the time I perked up, she told me that she had got pregnant by a chap back in Philadelphia.

13   We drew out our savings and started for San Francisco, that vainglorious, clam-colored city. In her yellow convertible, with my English setter and her cocker spaniel, we drove through the South and through Texas, taking Highway 80 because it was the autumn and cold. I remember that whenever we stopped by the side of the road in Mississippi to let the dogs pee, and I shouted if one of them dawdled, any black woman or man who happened to be close by would turn to see what I wanted, quite naturally, as if I had called. It was a grueling trip. I'd begun vomiting again after my friend told me she was pregnant, and she was suffering mysterious pains in that region between her legs, which no druggist would touch. But we reached Russian Hill and established ourselves in one of the local apartment hotels. For a while during the seven-month wait this living arrangement didn't work out and she moved to a Florence Crittenton Home and I went to the beach, but we ended the period together. At six one morning I drove her up to a whelk-pink hospital on a breezy hill and sat in the labor room for eight hours, watching the blue grid of stretch marks on her anguished stomach: awful pain. She jolted and screamed, sucking gas from a cup, squeezing my hand and falling asleep between the throes. It took me three days to stop shaking, though it was a normal delivery throughout, and she, by the mental safety catch which women have, had blocked off most of the memory by the time she was wheeled to her room asleep. I'm ashamed to say that I'd spanked her a little the night before, not realizing it was the night before; I never spanked her again.

14   The contract she'd signed obliged my friend to relinquish the baby girl to the Home for three weeks, after which she could appropriate her completely as her own. I was privileged to keep her breasts flowing during those weeks, a luxury that would have been fitting for Zeus; and, to the astonishment of the Home, as soon as the interval expired we showed up for the child. This was so rare that they wondered whether we were kidnappers. Then we drove East. The baby acquired a stepfather before she was out of her infancy and is now about ten.

15   So, pain is a packet of chiseling tools. Women in labor make no bones about protesting its severity. Neither does a dying man once he

has stopped lingering with the living—thinking of the memories of his behavior which he is leaving his children, for instance. It's when we have no imperative purpose in front of our sufferings that we think about "bearing up"; "bearing up" is converted to serve as a purpose. Pain, love, boredom, and glee, and anticipation or anxiety—these are the pilings we build our lives from. In love we beget more love and in pain we beget more pain. Since we must like it or lump it, we like it. And why not, indeed?

QUESTIONS

Ideas

1. What kinds of pain does Hoagland discuss? What examples does he use to illustrate them?
2. Hoagland suggests that "pain probably makes us a bit godly. . . . It makes us rue and summarize; it makes us bend and yield up ourselves." What do you think he means?
3. Why does he include an account of his stuttering? How does he help us to better understand the lot of the stutterer, the stutterer's pain?
4. Is this an honest essay? Does Hoagland gloss over his weaknesses, failures, and inadequacies?

Organization

5. Mark off what you take to be the introduction, body, and conclusion of the essay. Where does it shift direction, alter its focus? Why?
6. One clue to the essay's structure is the break between paragraphs 11 and 12. Is this break necessary? How is the second part related to the much longer first part? Could this second part have been omitted? Why or why not?
7. In paragraphs 4–10, Hoagland describes his stuttering—or his "stammering," as he calls it. How does he lead into this discussion? (What was he discussing immediately before he introduced the subject of stuttering?)
8. What asides or digressions does Hoagland introduce into his discussion of stuttering? Can any of them be omitted? Why or why not?

Sentences

9. Examine one of Hoagland's paragraphs, paying particular attention to the way his sentences begin, to the variety of sentence openings. Reread the paragraph paying attention to how Hoagland achieves coherence, how one sentence follows from and leads into another. (Paragraphs 1 and 9 are especially worth analyzing this way.)

10. Hoagland uses parentheses twice in the essay—in paragraphs 4 and 8. Why? How would the sentences differ either if the parentheses were omitted and the interpolated information deleted, or if dashes or commas were substituted for the parentheses?

11. Here is an unpunctuated version of paragraph 7. Punctuate it, then compare your version with those of other students and with Hoagland's punctuation. Discuss the differences in effect created by the differences in punctuation.

> As a stutterer I learned not to write notes you put yourself at someone's mercy more when you write him a note than if you just stand there like a rhinoceros and snort I could write a Stutterer's Guide to Europe too the titters in old Vienna the knowing English remembering their King the raw scorching baitings I met with in Greece surrounded sometimes like a muzzled bear the fourth means of effecting a cure I heard about was based on the fact that stutterers are able to sing without stuttering hence the victim should swing one of his arms like a big pendulum and talk in time to this which again was obviously a worse fate than the impediment though I didn't try it I was sent to a lady voice teacher who laid my hand on her conspicuous chest so that I could feel her breathe for just that moment the lessons worked wonderfully if I wasn't speechless I spoke in a rush.

Words

12. In describing his stuttering Hoagland uses a number of different words to label, classify, and define it. What are they, and what is their cumulative effect? In paragraph 7, for example, Hoagland compares a stutterer to a snorting rhinoceros and to a muzzled bear. What do these and the other terms for stutterers and stuttering convey?

13. Compare the tone and language of paragraphs 12 and 15 with the tone and language of paragraphs 10 and 11.

14. Hoagland uses comparison throughout the essay, but with particular abundance and force in paragraphs 9, 10, and 11. Examine each of the following similes and metaphors. Explain what Hoagland compares in each instance and how he uses the comparisons to advance his ideas.

[He] bawled like a half-butchered bull for an hour. (9)

[His divorce was] the most painful splinter in [his] life. (9)

Pain is a watchdog medically, telling us when to consult a doctor, and then it's the true-blue dog at the bedside who rivals the relatives for fidelity. (10)

What I remember, therefore, of death's salutation to my father was that it came as a tickler, making his withered body twitch, touching him here and touching him there, wasting his tissues away like white wax, while his head on the headrest above looked down and watched. . . .

Death tickled him in a gradual crescendo. (11)

Suggestions for Writing

A. Write an essay describing different kinds of pain that you have endured. Or focus on one kind of pain and one cause of it.

B. Write an essay about a limitation, weakness, or handicap you have. It need not be a physical limitation. Explain what it means to have the affliction or limitation, and how it affects you.

C. Write an imitation of paragraph 1 or of paragraph 9.

D. Read Didion's essay on migraine headaches—"In Bed"—and compare the discussion of her malady with Hoagland's discussion of stuttering. Consider the point, purpose, language, style, and tone of each.

FIVE

Tom Wolfe
(1931–   )

Tom Wolfe is one of the most famous of the New Journalists, a group of writers who imported the techniques of fiction into journalism. Wolfe's account of how he wrote his essay on custom cars, "The Kandy-Kolored Tangerine-Flake Streamline Baby," provides an insight into both his working habits and the new style he was unwittingly developing.

With an abundance of material about his subject and with too little time to organize, write, revise, and edit in the conventional manner, Wolfe began typing his notes in a letter to his editor at *Esquire,* where the piece was to be published. His letter took the form of a long memorandum, Wolfe supposing that somebody at the magazine would be responsible for shaping his rambling notes and writing the story. Wolfe describes the experience of writing the piece this way: "I just recorded it all, and inside a couple of hours, typing along like a madman, I could tell that something was beginning to happen. By midnight this memorandum was . . . twenty pages long and I was still typing like a maniac. . . . about 6:15 A.M. . . . it was 49 pages long." *Esquire* published it as written, inaugurating thereby an alternate writing style that was later named the "New Journalism."

In an introduction to an anthology of new-journalistic essays entitled, appropriately enough, *The New Journalism,* Wolfe singles out four techniques as being especially important for this new style. The basic device, he notes, is "scene-by-scene construction, telling the story by moving from scene to scene and resorting as little as possible to sheer historical narrative." Another technique is to rely heavily on dialogue since, as Wolfe has pointed out, "realistic dialogue involves the reader more completely than any other single device. It also establishes and defines character more quickly than any other single device." The third device involves manipulating the point of view, the angle of vision, the perspective from which a scene is presented. New Journalists will interview someone at the center of a scene, then import into their write-ups the thoughts and emotions of those interviewed. The purpose of this strategy, as Wolfe notes, is to "give the reader the feeling of being inside the character's mind and experiencing the emotional reality of the scene as he experiences it." The fourth technique concerns what Wolfe describes as "the recording of everyday gestures, habits, manners, customs . . . looks, glances, poses, styles of walking and other symbolic details. . . ."

To these can be added what Winston Weathers in his fine book *An Alternate Style* calls the *crot*—an obsolete word meaning "bit" or "fragment": "an autonomous unit, characterized by the absence of any transitional devices . . . in its most intense form . . . by a certain abruptness in its termination." Crots are something like snapshots, something like vignettes. Putting them together without transitions can make for effects of montage, collage, surprise—and sometimes confusion. They challenge the reader and involve him by inviting him to figure out how the fragments are related to one another. Besides the crot, about which Wolfe has said, "it will have you making crazy leaps of logic, leaps you never dreamed of before," Weathers singles out other devices frequently used by Wolfe and his new-journalistic colleagues: the labyrinthine sentence, the fragment, and the use of repetitions, lists, and refrains.

Wolfe began his career as an academic, earning a doctorate in American Studies at Yale. But his inclination was more journalistic than academic, and he worked for *The Washington Post* as a reporter and then as a magazine writer for *The New York Herald-Tribune*. Since 1968 he has been a contributing editor to *New York Magazine*. He has written articles on trends in American popular culture, primarily essays that have been published first in magazines and later in books. Following his first collection, *The Kandy-*

Kolored Tangerine-Flake Streamline Baby (1965), came a series of books with such zany titles as *The Electric Kool-Aid Acid Test* (1968)—on pot; *The Pump House Gang* (1968)—on California surfers (among other things); *Radical Chic and Mau-Mauing the Flak Catchers* (1970)—on rich New Yorkers vis-à-vis the Black Panthers; *Mauve Gloves and Madmen, Clutter and Vine* (1976)—on miscellaneous subjects; *The Right Stuff* (1979)—on the astronauts; *In Our Time* (1980), a collection of satirical pictorial sketches with brief notes and comments; and *From Bauhaus to Our House* (1981), a critique of modern architecture.

Wolfe takes great risks in his writing: his style is daring, flamboyant, energetic, humorous, and satirical. Reading him is like listening to a talented raconteur who reenacts the scenes and situations he describes, who comments on them in a free-wheeling style filled with digressions and associative ramblings, with less concern to instruct and moralize than to entertain and delight. His essays tend to be long and steeped in detail. He seems to need room to present the various facets of his subjects, time to amass details, and space to allow his characters to reveal, even display themselves. The masses of detail, the loose structure, the transcriptions of dialogue, the crots, lists, repetitions, and refrains cumulatively create a sense of immediacy and authenticity which suggests the reality of "This is how it is; this is what it's like."

The Right Stuff, Wolfe's longest and most ambitious work, has drawn wide critical acclaim, as well as becoming a best seller. Early in the book Wolfe describes just what the right stuff is that men need to become successful test pilots and astronauts. His comments relate as much to his own style and performance as a writer as they do to the astronauts. The right stuff, Wolfe explains, is "an amalgam of stamina, guts, fast neural synapses and old-fashioned hell raising." These elements, along with nerve, exhilaration, and a satirically edged humor, suggest something of Wolfe's tone and voice.

The four essays included here span Wolfe's new-journalistic career. "Clean Fun at Riverhead," taken from *The Kandy-Kolored Tangerine-Flake Streamline Baby,* is about a demolition derby. In this piece Wolfe reflects on the importance of the automobile in American culture, especially on its symbolic value. "Only One Life" is excerpted from a long essay, "The Me Decade and the Third Great Awakening," which appeared in *Mauve Gloves and Madmen, Clutter and Vine*. The essay satirizes the self-centered manias of people looking out for and looking into themselves. "The Lab Rat" and "The Right Stuff" are both taken from *The Right Stuff*. "The Lab Rat" depicts in comic terms the intensive and extensive physical examinations the astronauts and test pilots are put through; "The Right Stuff" shows what it takes to make it as a test pilot, defining the ineffable quality through illustration and description, anecdote and analysis.

Wolfe has been interviewed frequently and has commented extensively on writing. On one occasion he noted that "writing, unlike painting or drawing, is a process in which you *can't* tell right away whether it's successful or not. Some nights you go to bed thinking you've written some brilliant stuff, and you wake up the next morning and you realize it *is* just pure bullshit." And in response to a question about why he writes, Wolfe noted that he doesn't have a ready answer, but that if pressed he thinks that he writes out of a concern for his own glory, with more concern for *how* he handles the materials of his craft than for the issues he writes about. The challenge in writing, thus, for Wolfe, seems to reside in the compositional problem that confronts him. Aesthetic and linguistic challenges excite him more than the subjects he writes about. But this subjective priority of form over content hasn't prevented Wolfe from offering acutely intelligent analyses of contemporary fads, fashions, and mores. He is one of our best cultural critics and one of our most innovative and entertaining writers.

Clean Fun at Riverhead

1   **T**he inspiration for the demolition derby came to Lawrence Mendelsohn one night in 1958 when he was nothing but a spare-

ribbed twenty-eight-year-old stock-car driver halfway through his 10th lap around the Islip, L.I., Speedway and taking a curve too wide. A lubberly young man with a Chicago boxcar haircut came up on the inside in a 1949 Ford and caromed him 12 rows up into the grandstand, but Lawrence Mendelsohn and his entire car did not hit one spectator.

2 "That was what got me," he said, "I remember I was hanging upside down from my seat belt like a side of Jersey bacon and wondering why no one was sitting where I hit. 'Lousy promotion,' I said to myself.

3 "Not only that, but everybody who *was* in the stands forgot about the race and came running over to look at me gift-wrapped upside down in a fresh pile of junk."

4 At that moment occurred the transformation of Lawrence Mendelsohn, racing driver, into Lawrence Mendelsohn, promoter, and, a few transactions later, owner of the Islip Speedway, where he kept seeing more of this same underside of stock car racing that everyone in the industry avoids putting into words. Namely, that for every purist who comes to see the fine points of the race, such as who is going to win, there are probably five waiting for the wrecks to which stock car racing is so gloriously prone.

5 The pack will be going into a curve when suddenly two cars, three cars, four cars tangle, spinning and splattering all over each other and the retaining walls, upside down, right side up, inside out and in pieces, with the seams bursting open and discs, rods, wires and gasoline spewing out and yards of sheet metal shearing off like Reynolds Wrap and crumpling into the most baroque shapes, after which an ash-blue smoke starts seeping up from the ruins and a thrill begins to spread over the stands like Newburg sauce.

6 So why put up with the monotony between crashes?

7 Such, in brief, is the early history of what is culturally the most important sport ever originated in the United States, a sport that ranks with the gladiatorial games of Rome as a piece of national symbolism. Lawrence Mendelsohn had a vision of an automobile sport that would be all crashes. Not two cars, not three cars, not four cars, but 100 cars would be out in an arena doing nothing but smashing each other into shrapnel. The car that outrammed and outdodged all the rest, the last car that could still move amid the smoking heap, would take the prize money.

8 So at 8:15 at night at the Riverhead Raceway, just west of Riverhead, L.I., on Route 25, amid the quaint tranquility of the duck and

turkey farm flatlands of eastern Long Island, Lawrence Mendelsohn stood up on the back of a flat truck in his red neon warmup jacket and lectured his 100 drivers on the rules and niceties of the new game, the "demolition derby." And so at 8:30 the first 25 cars moved out onto the raceway's quarter-mile stock car track. There was not enough room for 100 cars to mangle each other. Lawrence Mendelsohn's dream would require four heats. Now the 25 cars were placed at intervals all about the circumference of the track, making flatulent revving noises, all headed not around the track but toward a point in the center of the infield.

9   Then the entire crowd, about 4,000, started chanting a countdown, "Ten, nine, eight, seven, six, five, four, three, two," but it was impossible to hear the rest, because right after "two" half the crowd went into a strange whinnying wail. The starter's flag went up, and the 25 cars took off, roaring into second gear with no mufflers, all headed toward that same point in the center of the infield, converging nose on nose.

10   The effect was exactly what one expects that many simultaneous crashes to produce: the unmistakable tympany of automobiles colliding and cheap-gauge sheet metal buckling; front ends folding together at the same cockeyed angles police photographs of night-time wreck scenes capture so well on grainy paper; smoke pouring from under the hoods and hanging over the infield like a howitzer cloud; a few of the surviving cars lurching eccentrically on bent axles. At last, after four heats, there were only two cars moving through the junk, a 1953 Chrysler and a 1958 Cadillac. In the Chrysler a small fascia of muscles named Spider Ligon, who smoked a cigar while he drove, had the Cadillac cornered up against a guard rail in front of the main grandstand. He dispatched it by swinging around and backing full throttle through the left side of its grille and radiator.

11   By now the crowd was quite beside itself. Spectators broke through a gate in the retaining screen. Some rushed to Spider Ligon's car, hoisted him to their shoulders and marched off the field, howling. Others clambered over the stricken cars of the defeated, enjoying the details of their ruin, and howling. The good, full cry of triumph and annihilation rose from Riverhead Raceway, and the demolition derby was over.

12   That was the 154th demolition derby in two years. Since Lawrence Mendelsohn staged the first one at Islip Speedway in 1961, they have

been held throughout the United States at the rate of one every five days, resulting in the destruction of about 15,000 cars. The figures alone indicate a gluttonous appetite for the sport. Sports writers, of course, have managed to ignore demolition derbies even more successfully than they have ignored stock car racing and drag racing. All in all, the new automobile sports have shown that the sports pages, which on the surface appear to hum with life and earthiness, are at bottom pillars of gentility. This drag racing and demolition derbies and things, well, there are too many kids in it with sideburns, tight Levis and winkle-picker boots.

13   Yet the demolition derbies keep growing on word-of-mouth publicity. The "nationals" were held last month at Langhorne, Pa., with 50 cars in the finals, and demolition derby fans everywhere know that Don McTavish, of Dover, Mass., is the new world's champion. About 1,250,000 spectators have come to the 154 contests held so far. More than 75 per cent of the derbies have drawn full houses.

14   The nature of their appeal is clear enough. Since the onset of the Christian era, i.e., since about 500 A.D., no game has come along to fill the gap left by the abolition of the purest of all sports, gladiatorial combat. As late as 300 A.D. these bloody duels, usually between men but sometimes between women and dwarfs, were enormously popular not only in Rome but throughout the Roman Empire. Since then no game, not even boxing, has successfully acted out the underlying motifs of most sport, that is, aggression and destruction.

15   Boxing, of course, is an aggressive sport, but one contestant has actually destroyed the other in a relatively small percentage of matches. Other games are progressively more sublimated forms of sport. Often, as in the case of football, they are encrusted with oddments of passive theology and metaphysics to the effect that the real purpose of the game is to foster character, teamwork, stamina, physical fitness and the ability to "give-and-take."

16   But not even those wonderful clergymen who pray in behalf of Congress, expressway ribbon-cuttings, urban renewal projects and testimonial dinners for ethnic aldermen would pray for a demolition derby. The demolition derby is, pure and simple, a form of gladiatorial combat for our times.

17   As hand-to-hand combat has gradually disappeared from our civilization, even in wartime, and competition has become more and more sophisticated and abstract, Americans have turned to the automobile

to satisfy their love of direct aggression. The mild-mannered man who turns into a bear behind the wheel of a car—i.e., who finds in the power of the automobile a vehicle for the release of his inhibitions—is part of American folklore. Among teen-agers the automobile has become the symbol, and in part the physical means, of triumph over family and community restrictions. Seventy-five per cent of all car thefts in the United States are by teen-agers out for "joy rides."

18   The symbolic meaning of the automobile tones down but by no means vanishes in adulthood. Police traffic investigators have long been convinced that far more accidents are purposeful crashes by belligerent drivers than they could ever prove. One of the heroes of the era was the Middle Eastern diplomat who rammed a magazine writer's car from behind in the Kalorama embassy district of Washington two years ago. When the American bellowed out the window at him, he backed up and smashed his car again. When the fellow leaped out of his car to pick a fight, he backed up and smashed his car a third time, then drove off. He was recalled home for having "gone native."

19   The unabashed, undisguised, quite purposeful sense of destruction of the demolition derby is its unique contribution. The aggression, the battering, the ruination are there to be enjoyed. The crowd at a demolition derby seldom gasps and often laughs. It enjoys the same full-throated participation as Romans at the Colosseum. After each trial or heat at a demolition derby, two drivers go into the finals. One is the driver whose car was still going at the end. The other is the driver the crowd selects from among the 24 vanquished on the basis of his courage, showmanship or simply the awesomeness of his crashes. The numbers of the cars are read over loudspeakers, and the crowd chooses one with its cheers. By the same token, the crowd may force a driver out of competition if he appears cowardly or merely cunning. This is the sort of driver who drifts around the edge of the battle avoiding crashes with the hope that the other cars will eliminate one another. The umpire waves a yellow flag at him and he must crash into someone within 30 seconds or run the risk of being booed off the field in dishonor and disgrace.

20   The frank relish of the crowd is nothing, however, compared to the kick the contestants get out of the game. It costs a man an average of $50 to retrieve a car from a junk yard and get it running for a derby. He will only get his money back—$50—for winning a heat. The chance of being smashed up in the madhouse first 30 seconds of a round are

so great, even the best of drivers faces long odds in his shot at the $500 first prize. None of that matters to them.

21   Tommy Fox, who is nineteen, said he entered the demolition derby because, "You know, it's fun. I like it. You know what I mean?" What was fun about it? Tommy Fox had a way of speaking that was much like the early Marlon Brando. Much of what he had to say came from the trapezii, which he rolled quite a bit, and the forehead, which he cocked, and the eyebrows, which he could bring together expressively from time to time. "Well," he said, "you know, like when you hit 'em, and all that. It's fun."

22   Tommy Fox had a lot of fun in the first heat. Nobody was bashing around quite like he was in his old green Hudson. He did not win, chiefly because he took too many chances, but the crowd voted him into the finals as the best showman.

23   "I got my brother," said Tommy. "I came in from the side and he didn't even see me."

24   His brother is Don Fox, thirty-two, who owns the junk yard where they both got their cars. Don likes to hit them, too, only he likes it almost too much. Don drives with such abandon, smashing into the first car he can get a shot at and leaving himself wide open, he does not stand much chance of finishing the first three minutes.

25   For years now sociologists have been calling upon one another to undertake a serious study of America's "car culture." No small part of it is the way the automobile has, for one very large segment of the population, become the focus of the same sort of quasi-religious dedication as art is currently for another large segment of a higher social order. Tommy Fox is unemployed, Don Fox runs a junk yard, Spider Ligon is a maintenance man for Brookhaven Naval Laboratory, but to categorize them as such is getting no closer to the truth than to have categorized William Faulkner in 1926 as a clerk at Lord & Taylor, although he was.

26   Tommy Fox, Don Fox and Spider Ligon are acolytes of the car culture, an often esoteric world of arts and sciences that came into its own after World War II and now has believers of two generations. Charlie Turbush, thirty-five, and his son, Buddy, seventeen, were two more contestants, and by no stretch of the imagination can they be characterized as bizarre figures or cultists of the death wish. As for the dangers of driving in a demolition derby, they are quite real by all physical laws. The drivers are protected only by crash helmets, seat

belts and the fact that all glass, interior handles, knobs and fixtures have been removed. Yet Lawrence Mendelsohn claims that there have been no serious injuries in 154 demolition derbies and now gets his insurance at a rate below that of stock car racing.

27   The sport's future may depend in part on word getting around about its relative safety. Already it is beginning to draw contestants here and there from social levels that could give the demolition derby the cachet of respectability. In eastern derbies so far two doctors and three young men of more than passable connections in eastern society have entered under whimsical *noms de combat* and emerged neither scarred nor victorious. Bull fighting had to win the same social combat.

28   All of which brings to mind that fine afternoon when some high-born Roman women were out in Nero's box at the Colosseum watching this sexy Thracian carve an ugly little Samnite up into prime cuts, and one said, darling, she had an inspiration, and Nero, needless to say, was all for it. Thus began the new vogue of Roman socialites fighting as gladiators themselves, for kicks. By the second century A.D. even the Emperor Commodus was out there with a tiger's head as a helmet hacking away at some poor dazed fall guy. He did a lot for the sport. Arenas sprang up all over the empire like shopping center bowling alleys.

29   The future of the demolition derby, then, stretches out over the face of America. The sport draws no lines of gender, and post-debs may reach Lawrence Mendelsohn at his office in Deer Park.

QUESTIONS

Ideas

1. Why does Wolfe say that the demolition derby is "culturally the most important sport ever originated in the United States"? (7) What does the sport symbolize for Wolfe?

2. What is Wolfe's attitude toward the demolition drivers themselves? Where is it most clearly expressed? How is Wolfe's attitude revealed?

3. What is the point of the opening anecdote? What sense is given of the fans of car racing? Can the same point be made about fans of other sports—hockey or boxing or football, for instance? Why or why not?

Organization

4. Wolfe alternates between description of the races and explanation of his ideas about them. Trace this pattern through the essay, labeling each paragraph as either descriptive or explanatory. Where does Wolfe rely most heavily and thoroughly on explanation? Is there an advantage to this alternating method of organizing, or would a simple two-part form have worked just as well (with the description first and the explanation afterward)?

5. Paragraphs 1–11 describe a typical demolition derby and also explain how the sport began. What is the function of paragraphs 12 and 13? Of paragraphs 14–19?

6. Can this essay be divided into the conventional three-part format—introduction, body, and conclusion? Why or why not?

Sentences

7. Why do sentences in paragraphs 5 and 6 exist as independent paragraphs? Would the sentence in paragraph 5 be better as three or four short sentences? Why or why not?

8. What is the function of the colon and the semicolons in the opening sentence of paragraph 10? How do they help you to organize and process the information in the sentence?

Words

9. In paragraphs 2 and 3, and later in paragraph 21, Wolfe quotes directly the words of Lawrence Mendelsohn and Tommy Fox. Why are their comments quoted directly instead of reported indirectly? What does each man's comment reveal about him?

10. In his descriptive paragraphs Wolfe makes occasional use of simile. Examine the similes in paragraphs 5 and 10. What is the point of each?

11. Examine the verbs in paragraphs 5, 10, and 11. Why are there so many? What common feature of form do the verbs of paragraphs 5 and 10 share? What is the cumulative effect of these verbs?

Suggestions for Writing

A. Write an essay arguing that demolition driving is or is not a sport. Consider Wolfe's notion that it is the "purest" modern sport, the closest to the purest of all sports ever—gladiatorial combat.

B. Write an essay explaining the appeal of the automobile. You may want to develop the ideas Wolfe mentions in paragraphs 17–18 and 25–26. Or you may want to develop some other idea about cars, perhaps their connection with status, sex, self-image.
C. Look through a few issues of a popular car magazine like *Car and Driver* or *Road and Track*. On the basis of the articles, advertisements, editorials, letters to the editor, write an essay explaining why such a magazine exists, who it appeals to and why.
D. Look through any popular magazine that contains automobile ads. Select one ad and analyze its purpose, audience, appeals, strategies of persuasion, and language.
E. Write an essay about one kind of sports fan—or about the fans of one sport. Or compare the fans of two sports—football fans and baseball fans, for instance.

Only One Life

1   In 1961 a copy writer named Shirley Polykoff was working for the Foote, Cone & Belding advertising agency on the Clairol hair-dye account when she came up with the line: "If I've only one life, let me live it as a blonde!" In a single slogan she had summed up what might be described as the secular side of the Me Decade. "If I've only one life, let me live it as a _____!" (You have only to fill in the blank.)

2   This formula accounts for much of the popularity of the women's liberation or feminist movement. "What does a woman want?" said Freud. Perhaps there are women who want to humble men or reduce their power or achieve equality or even superiority for themselves and their sisters. But for every one such woman, there are nine who simply want to *fill in the blank* as they see fit. "If I've only one life, let me live it as . . . a free spirit!" (Instead of . . . a house slave: a cleaning woman, a cook, a nursemaid, a station-wagon hacker, and an occasional household sex aid.) But even that may be overstating it, because often the unconscious desire is nothing more than: *Let's talk about Me.* The great unexpected dividend of the feminist movement has been to elevate an ordinary status—woman, housewife—to the level of drama. One's

very existence as *a woman* . . . as *Me* . . . becomes something all the world analyzes, agonizes over, draws cosmic conclusions from, or, in any event, takes seriously. Every woman becomes Emma Bovary, Cousin Bette, or Nora . . . or Erica Jong or Consuelo Saah Baehr.

3   Among men the formula becomes: "If I've only one life, let me live it as a . . . Casanova or a Henry VIII! (instead of a humdrum workadaddy, eternally faithful, except perhaps for a mean little skulking episode here and there, to a woman who now looks old enough to be your aunt and needs a shave or else has electrolysis lines above her upper lip, as well as atrophied calves, and is an embarrassment to be seen with when you take her on trips). The right to shuck overripe wives and take on fresh ones was once seen as the prerogative of kings only, and even then it was scandalous. In the 1950's and 1960's it began to be seen as the prerogative of the rich, the powerful, and the celebrated (Nelson Rockefeller, Henry Ford, and Show Business figures), although it retained the odor of scandal. Wife-shucking damaged Adlai Stevenson's chances of becoming President in 1952 and 1956 and Rockefeller's chances of becoming the Republican nominee in 1964 and 1968. Until the 1970's wife-shucking made it impossible for an astronaut to be chosen to go into space. Today, in the Me Decade, it becomes *normal behavior*, one of the factors that has pushed the divorce rate above 50 percent.

4   When Eugene McCarthy filled in the blank in 1972 and shucked his wife, it was hardly noticed. Likewise in the case of several astronauts. When Wayne Hays filled in the blank in 1976 and shucked his wife of thirty-eight years, it did not hurt his career in the slightest. Copulating with the girl in the office, however, was still regarded as scandalous. (Elizabeth Ray filled in the blank in another popular fashion: If I've only one life, let me live it as a . . . Celebrity!" As did Arthur Bremer, who kept a diary during his stalking of Nixon and, later, George Wallace . . . with an eye toward a book contract. Which he got.) Some wiseacre has remarked, supposedly with levity, that the federal government may in time have to create reservations for women over thirty-five, to take care of the swarms of shucked wives and widows. In fact, women in precisely those categories have begun setting up communes or "extended families" to provide one another support and companionship in a world without workadaddies. ("If I've only one life, why live it as an anachronism?")

5   Much of what is now known as the "sexual revolution" has con-

sisted of both women and men filling in the blank this way: "If I've only one life, let me live it as . . . a Swinger!" (Instead of a frustrated, bored monogamist.) In "swinging," a husband and wife give each other license to copulate with other people. There are no statistics on the subject that mean anything, but I do know that it pops up in conversation today in the most unexpected corners of the country. It is an odd experience to be in De Kalb, Illinois, in the very corncrib of America, and have some conventional-looking housewife (not *housewife*, damn it!) come up to you and ask: "Is there much tripling going on in New York?"

6   *"Tripling?"*

7   Tripling turns out to be a practice, in De Kalb, anyway, in which a husband and wife invite a third party—male or female, but more often female—over for an evening of whatever, including polymorphous perversity, even the practices written of in the one-hand magazines, such as *Hustler*, all the things involving tubes and hoses and tourniquets and cups and double-jointed sailors.

8   One of the satisfactions of this sort of life, quite in addition to the groin spasms, is talk: *Let's talk about Me.* Sexual adventurers are given to the most relentless and deadly serious talk . . . about Me. They quickly succeed in placing themselves onstage in the sexual drama whose outlines were sketched by Freud and then elaborated by Wilhelm Reich. Men and women of all sorts, not merely swingers, are given just now to the most earnest sort of talk about the Sexual Me. A key drama of our own day is Ingmar Bergman's movie *Scenes from a Marriage*. In it we see a husband and wife who have good jobs and a well-furnished home but who are unable to "communicate"—to cite one of the signature words of the Me Decade. Then they begin to communicate, and thereupon their marriage breaks up and they start divorce proceedings. For the rest of the picture they communicate endlessly, with great candor, but the "relationship"—another signature word—remains doomed. Ironically, the lesson that people seem to draw from this movie has to do with . . ."the need to communicate."

9   *Scenes from a Marriage* is one of those rare works of art, like *The Sun Also Rises*, that not only succeed in capturing a certain mental atmosphere in fictional form . . . but also turn around and help radiate it throughout real life. I personally know of two instances in which couples, after years of marriage, went to see *Scenes from a Marriage* and came home convinced of the "need to communicate." The dis-

cussions began with one of the two saying, Let's try to be completely candid for once. You tell me exactly what you don't like about me, and I'll do the same for you. At this, the starting point, the whole notion is exciting. We're going to talk about *Me!* (And I can take it.) I'm going to find out what he (or she) really thinks about me! (Of course, I have my faults, but they're minor . . . or else exciting.)

10   She says, "Go ahead. What don't you like about me?"

11   They're both under the Bergman spell. Nevertheless, a certain sixth sense tells him that they're on dangerous ground. So he decides to pick something that doesn't seem too terrible.

12   "Well," he says, "one thing that bothers me is that when we meet people for the first time, you never know what to say. Or else you get nervous and start chattering away, and it's all so banal, it makes me look bad."

13   Consciously she's still telling herself, "I can take it." But what he has just said begins to seep through her brain like scalding water. What's he talking about?—makes *him* look bad? *He's saying I'm unsophisticated, a social liability and an embarrassment. All those times we've gone out, he's been ashamed of me!* (And what makes it worse—it's the sort of disease for which there's no cure!) She always knew she was awkward. His crime is: he *noticed!* He's known it, too, all along. He's had *contempt* for me.

14   Out loud she says, "Well, I'm afraid there's nothing I can do about that."

15   He detects the petulant note. "Look," he says, "you're the one who said to be candid."

16   She says, "I know. I *want* you to be."

17   He says, "Well, it's your turn."

18   "Well," she says, "I'll tell *you* something about when we meet people and when we go places. You never clean yourself properly—you don't know how to wipe yourself. Sometimes we're standing there talking to people, and there's . . . a smell. And I'll tell you something else: People can tell it's you."

19   And he's still telling *him*self, "I can take it"—but what inna namea Christ is *this?*

20   He says, "But you've never said anything—about anything like that."

21   She says, "But I *tried* to. How many times have I told you about your dirty drawers when you were taking them off at night?"

22   Somehow this really makes him angry . . . All those times
. . . and his mind immediately fastens on Harley Thatcher and his
wife, whom he has always wanted to impress . . . From underneath
my $350 suits I smelled of *shit!* What infuriates him is that this is a
humiliation from which there's no recovery. *How often have they snig-
gered about it later?—or not invited me places? Is it something people
say every time my name comes up?* And all at once he is intensely
annoyed with his wife, not because she never told him all these years,
but simply because she *knows* about his disgrace—and she was the one
who *brought him the bad news!*

23   From that moment on they're ready to get the skewers in. It's
only a few minutes before they've begun trying to sting each other with
confessions about their little affairs, their little slipping around, their
little coitus on the sly—"Remember that time I told you my flight from
Buffalo was canceled?"—and at that juncture the ranks of those *who
can take it* become very thin indeed. So they communicate with great
candor! and break up! and keep on communicating! and they find the
relationship hopelessly doomed.

24   One couple went into group therapy. The other went to a marriage
counselor. Both types of therapy are very popular forms, currently, of
Let's talk about Me. This phase of the breakup always provides a rush
of exhilaration—for what more exhilarating topic is there than . . . *Me?*
Through group therapy, marriage counseling, and other forms of "psychological consultation" they can enjoy that same *Me* euphoria that
the very rich have enjoyed for years in psychoanalysis. The cost of the
new Me sessions is only $10 to $30 an hour, whereas psychoanalysis
runs from $50 to $125. The woman's exhilaration, however, is soon
complicated by the fact that she is (in the typical case) near or beyond
the cutoff age of thirty-five and will have to retire to the reservation.

25   Well, my dear Mature Moderns . . . Ingmar never promised you
a rose garden!

QUESTIONS

Ideas

1. What is Wolfe's subject here? Women's Liberation? Talk Therapy? Selfishness? Something else? And what is the predominant tone of the essay?
   How does this tone reveal and carry Wolfe's attitude toward his subject?

2. What is Wolfe's purpose, and who is his implied audience? Consider the literary allusions in paragraph 2, the historical and political allusions in paragraph 3, and the contemporary allusions in paragraph 4.

Organization

3. "Only One Life" falls into two major parts: paragraphs 1–8 and paragraphs 9–23—with paragraphs 24 and 25 as a wrap-up. Identify the subject and point of the two main parts and explain how Wolfe moves, in paragraphs 8 and 9, from the subject of the first part to the subject of the second.
4. Paragraphs 1 and 2 are about women, 3 and 4 about men, and 5–8 about both. What ties all eight paragraphs together?
5. Examine the transitions Wolfe uses to link his first eight paragraphs. How does the first sentence of each paragraph tie it to the preceding paragraph? What specific words and phrases form the links? And why are transitions sparse in paragraphs 9–25?

Sentences

6. Wolfe uses a slogan, which he repeats throughout the first part of the essay: "If I've only one life, let me live it as a *blonde!*" Examine the variations he works on this slogan. What is the point of the variations?
7. He uses another repeated sentence as well, this one without variation: "Let's talk about Me" (paragraphs 2, 8, and 24). What tone is established with this repeated sentence?
8. What are the function and the effect of the parenthetical sentences in paragraphs 1, 2, 4, 9, and 13? Of the ellipses in sentences in paragraphs 2, 3, 4, 5, 8, 9, and 24?

Words

9. Reread the dialogue in paragraphs 9–23. Explain why some words are italicized. What is the effect of this?
10. Wolfe's diction ranges from the colloquial and the familiar to the unusual and the recondite. Find examples of different kinds of words and phrases showing evidence of Wolfe's range and diversity of language.

Suggestions for Writing

A. Write an essay responding to the comments from paragraph 2 that follow:
(1) "The great unexpected dividend of the feminist movement has been to elevate an ordinary status—woman, housewife—to the level of drama."

(2) "One's very existence as a *woman* . . . as *Me* . . . becomes something all the world analyzes, agonizes over, draws conclusions from, or, in any event, takes seriously."

B. Imitate the second part of this essay by writing a dialogue that includes not only what the speakers say, but also what they think. You will have, then, an inner-outer dialogue, which gains effect by the discrepancy between what is said and what is thought. You may include, as Wolfe does, a narrator to explain the conversation, perhaps to comment on it.

C. Take a popular slogan from advertising or from a contemporary issue. Write an essay examining its implications and ramifications. Explain how the slogan sums up and epitomizes important attitudes, ideals, and values of whoever uses it, believes in it, or lives by it.

The Lab Rat

---

1   **A**lbuquerque, home of the Lovelace Clinic, was a dirty red sod-hut tortilla highway desert city that was remarkably short on charm, despite the Mexican touch here and there. But career officers were used to dreary real estate. That was what they inhabited in America, especially if they were fliers. No, it was Lovelace itself that began to get everybody's back up. Lovelace was a fairly new private diagnostic clinic, somewhat like the Mayo Clinic, doing "aerospace-medical" work for the government, among other things. Lovelace had been founded by Randy Lovelace—W. Randolph Lovelace II—who had served along with Crossfield and Flickinger on the committee on "human factors" in space flight. The chief of the medical staff at Lovelace was a recently retired general of the Air Force medical corps, Dr. A. H. Schwichten-berg. He was General Schwichtenberg to everybody at Lovelace. The operation took itself very seriously. The candidates for astronaut would be given their physical testing here. Then they would go to Wright-Patterson Air Force Base in Dayton for psychological and stress testing. It was all very hush-hush. Conrad went to Lovelace in a group of only six men, once more in their ill-fitting mufti and terrific watches, apparently so that they would blend in with the clinic's civilian patients. They had been warned that the tests at Lovelace and Wright-Patterson

would be more exacting and strenuous than any they had ever taken. It was not the tests *per se*, however, that made every self-respecting fighter jock, early in the game, begin to hate Lovelace.

2   Military pilots were veterans of physical examinations, but in addition to all the usual components of "the complete physical," the Lovelace doctors had devised a series of novel tests involving straps, tubes, hoses, and needles. They would put a strap around your head, clamp some sort of instrument over your eyes—and then stick a hose in your ear and pump cold water into your ear canal. It would make your eyeballs flutter. It was an unpleasant, disorienting sensation, although not painful. If you wanted to know what it was all about, the Lovelace doctors and technicians, in their uncompromising white smocks, indicated that you really didn't need to know, and that was that.

3   What really made Conrad feel that something *eccentric* was going on here, however, was the business of the electrode in the thumb muscle. They brought him into a room and strapped his hand down to a table, palm up. Then they brought out an ugly-looking needle attached to an electrical wire. Conrad didn't like needles in the first place, and this looked like a monster. *Hannh?*—they drove the needle into the big muscle at the base of his thumb. It hurt like a bastard. Conrad looked up as if to say, "What the hell's going on?" But they weren't even looking at him. They were looking—at the meter. The wire from the needle led to what looked like a doorbell. They pushed the buzzer. Conrad looked down, and his hand—his own goddamned hand!—was balling up into a fist and springing open and balling up into a fist and springing open and balling up into a fist and springing open and balling up into a fist and springing open at an absolutely furious rate, faster than he could have ever made it do so on its own, and there seemed to be nothing that he, with his own mind and his own central nervous system, could do to stop his own hand or even slow it down. The Lovelace doctors in their white smocks, with their reflectors on their heads, were having a hell of a time for themselves . . . with *his* hand . . . They were reading the meter and scribbling away on their clipboards at a jolly rate.

4   Afterward Conrad said, "What was that for?"

5   A doctor looked up, distractedly, as if Conrad were interrupting an important train of thought.

6   "I'm afraid there's no simple way to explain it to you," he said. "There's nothing for you to worry about."

7   It was then that it began to dawn on Conrad, first as a feeling rather than as a fully formed thought: "Lab rats."

8   It went on like that. The White Smocks gave each of them a test tube and said they wanted a sperm count. *What do you mean?* Place your sperm in the tube. *How?* Through ejaculation. *Just like that?* Masturbation is the customary procedure. *What!* The best results seem to be obtained through fantasization, accompanied by masturbation, followed by ejaculation. *Where, f'r chrissake?* Use the bathroom. A couple of the boys said things such as, "Well, okay, I'll do it if you'll send a nurse in with me—to help me along if I get stuck." The White Smocks looked at them as if they were schoolboys making obscene noises. This got the pilots' back up, and a couple of them refused, flat out. But by and by they gave in, and so now you had the ennobling prospect of half a dozen test pilots padding off one by one to the head in their skivvies to jack off for the Lovelace Clinic, Project Mercury, and America's battle for the heavens. Sperm counts were supposed to determine the density and motility of the sperm. What this had to do with a man's fitness to fly on top of a rocket or anywhere else was incomprehensible. Conrad began to get the feeling that it wasn't just him and his brother lab rats who didn't know what was going on. He now had the suspicion that the Reflector Heads didn't know, either. They had somehow gotten *carte blanche* to try out any goddamned thing they could think up—and that was what they were doing, whether there was any logic to it or not.

9   Each candidate was to deliver two stool specimens to the Lovelace laboratory in Dixie cups, and days were going by and Conrad had been unable to egest even one, and the staff kept getting after him about it. Finally he managed to produce a single bolus, a mean hard little ball no more than an inch in diameter and shot through with some kind of seeds, whole seeds, undigested. Then he remembered. The first night in Albuquerque he had gone to a Mexican restaurant and eaten a lot of jalapeño peppers. They were jalapeño seeds. Even in the turd world this was a pretty miserable-looking *objet*. So Conrad tied a red ribbon around the goddamned thing, with a bow and all, and put it in the Dixie cup and delivered it to the lab. Curious about the ribbons that flopped out over the lip of the cup, the technicians all peered in. Conrad broke into his full cackle of mirth, much the way Wally might have.

No one was swept up in the joke, however. The Lovelace staffers looked at the beribboned bolus, and then they looked at Conrad . . . as if he were a bug on the windshield of the pace car of medical progress.

10   One of the tests at Lovelace was an examination of the prostate gland. There was nothing exotic about this, of course; it was a standard part of the complete physical for men. The doctor puts a rubber sleeve on a finger and slips the finger up the subject's rectum and presses the prostate, looking for signs of swelling, infection, and so on. But several men in Conrad's group had come back from the prostate examination gasping with pain and calling the doctor a sadistic little pervert and worse. He had prodded the prostate with such force a couple of them had passed blood.

11   Conrad goes into the room, and sure enough, the man reams him so hard the pain brings him to his knees.

12   "What the hell!—"

13   Conrad comes up swinging, but an orderly, a huge monster, immediately grabs him, and Conrad can't move. The doctor looks at him blankly, as if he's a vet and Conrad's a barking dog.

14   The probings of the bowels seemed to be endless, full proctosigmoidoscope examinations, the works. These things were never pleasant; in fact, they were a bit humiliating, involving, as they did, various things being shoved up your tail. The Lovelace Clinic specialty seemed to be the exacting of maximum indignity from each procedure. The pilots had never run into anything like this before. Not only that, before each ream-out you had to report to the clinic at seven o'clock in the morning and give yourself an enema. *Up yours!* seemed to be the motto of the Lovelace Clinic—and they even made you do it to yourself. So Conrad reports at seven one morning and gives himself the enema. He's supposed to undergo a lower gastrointestinal tract examination that morning. In the so-called lower G.I. examination, barium is pumped into the subject's bowels; then a little hose with a balloon on the end of it is inserted in the rectum, and the balloon is inflated, blocking the canal to keep the barium from forcing its way out before the radiologist can complete his examination. After the examination, like everyone who has ever been through the procedure, Conrad now feels as if there are eighty-five pounds of barium in his intestines and they are about to explode. The Smocks inform him that there is no john on this floor. He's supposed to pick up the tube that is coming out of his rectum and follow an orderly, who will lead him to a john two floors below. On

the tube there is a clamp, and he can release the clamp, deflating the balloon, at the proper time. *It's unbelievable!* To try to walk, with this explosive load sloshing about in your pelvic saddle, is agony. Nevertheless, Conrad picks up the tube and follows the orderly. Conrad has on only the standard bed patient's tunic, the angel robes, open up the back. The tube leading out of his tail to the balloon gizmo is so short that he has to hunch over to about two feet off the floor to carry it in front of him. His tail is now, as the saying goes, flapping in the breeze, with a tube coming out of it. The orderly has on red cowboy boots. Conrad is intensely aware of that fact, because he is now hunched over so far that his eyes hit the orderly at about calf level. He's hunched over, with his tail in the breeze, scuttling like a crab after a pair of red cowboy boots. Out into the corridor they go, an ordinary public corridor, the full-moon hunchback and the red cowboy boots, amid men, women, children, nurses, nuns, the lot. The red cowboy boots are beginning to trot along like mad. The orderly is no fool. He's been through this before. He's been through the whole disaster. He's seen the explosions. Time is of the essence. There's a hunchback stick of dynamite behind him. To Conrad it becomes more incredible every step of the way. They actually have to go down an elevator—full of sane people—and do their crazy tango through another public hallway—agog with normal human beings—before finally reaching the goddamned john.

15   Later that day Conrad received, once more, instructions to report to the clinic at seven the next morning to give himself an enema. The next thing the people in the administrative office of the clinic knew, a small but enraged young man was storming into the office of General Schwichtenberg himself, waving a great flaccid flamingo-pink enema bag and hose like some sort of obese whip. As he waved it, it gurgled.

16   The enema bag came slamming down on the general's desk. It landed with a tremendous *plop* and then began gurgling and sighing.

17   "General Schwichtenberg," said Conrad, "you're looking at a man who has given himself his last enema. If you want enemas from me, from now on you can come get 'em yourself. You can take this bag and give it to a nurse and send her over—"

18   Just you—

19   "—and let her do the honors. I've given myself my last enema. Either things shape up around here, or I ship out."

20   The general stared at the great flamingo bag, which lay there heaving and wheezing on his desk, and then he stared at Conrad. The general seemed appalled . . . All the same it wouldn't do anybody any good, least of all the Lovelace Clinic, if one of the candidates pulled out, firing broadsides at the operation. The general started trying to mollify this vision of enema rage.

21   "Now, Lieutenant," he said, "I know this hasn't been pleasant. This is probably the toughest examination you'll ever have to go through in your life, but as you know, it's for a project of utmost importance. The project needs men like yourself. You have a compact build, and every pound saved in Project Mercury can be critical."

22   And so forth and so on. He kept spraying Conrad's fire.

23   "All the same, General, I've given myself my last enema."

24   Word of the Enema Bag Showdown spread rapidly among the other candidates, and they were delighted to hear about it. Practically all of them had wanted to do something of the sort. It wasn't just that the testing procedures were unpleasant; the entire atmosphere of the testing constituted an affront. There was something . . . decidedly *out of joint* about it. Pilots and doctors were natural enemies, of course, at least as pilots saw it. The flight surgeon was pretty much kept *in his place* in the service. His only real purpose was to tend to pilots and keep 'em flying. He was an attendant to the pilots' vital stuff. In fact, flight surgeons were encouraged to fly backseat with fighter pilots from time to time, so as to understand what stresses and righteous stuff the job entailed. Regardless of how much he thought of himself, no flight surgeon dared position himself *above* the pilots in his squadron in the way he conducted himself before them: i.e., it was hard for him to be a consummate panjandrum, the way the typical civilian doctor was.

25   But at Lovelace, in the testing for Project Mercury, the natural order was turned upside down. These people not only did not treat them as righteous pilots, they did not treat them as pilots of any sort. They never even alluded to the fact that they were pilots. An irksome thought was beginning to intrude. In the competition for *astronaut* the kind of stuff you were made of as a *pilot* didn't count for a goddamned thing. They were looking for a certain type of animal who registered bingo on the meter. You wouldn't win this competition in the air. If you won it, it would be right here on the examination table in the land of the rubber tubes.

26   Yes, the boys were delighted when Conrad finally told off General
Schwichtenberg. Attaboy, Pete! At the same time, they were quite
content to let the credit for the Lab Rat Revolt fall to Conrad and to
him alone.

QUESTIONS

Ideas

1. What is Wolfe's purpose in presenting the details of the physical examinations? What point does he make about the relationship between pilots
   and doctors?
2. What is the dominant tone of the piece? Does the tone shift at any point?

Organization

3. "Lab Rat" breaks into three main sections: paragraphs 1–14 (1, 2–13, 14),
   paragraphs 15–23, and paragraphs 24–25. Explain what Wolfe is showing
   in each section and how the sections are related. In which section is Wolfe's
   writing primarily explanatory? Primarily descriptive? Primarily narrative-
   dramatic?
4. Could paragraphs 15–23 be omitted? What does Wolfe gain by including
   them?

Sentences

5. In paragraph 3 Wolfe includes a long sentence that contains repeated
   elements. Could or should this long sentence have been condensed and
   its repeated words excised? It begins: "Conrad looked down . . ."
6. About two-thirds of the way through paragraph 14, the sentences become
   shorter. In addition, the final sentence of paragraph 14 is interrupted twice
   by pairs of dashes. What is the effect of each of these changes of sentence
   style, and why are these changes appropriate?

Words

7. Wolfe employs colloquial language in a number of places in "Lab Rat":
   "jack off" (8), "get everybody's back up" (1), "shoved up your tail" (14),
   "with his tail between his legs" (14). What are the tone and effect of such
   language? Why do you think Wolfe uses it?

8. Compare the language of the pilots with the language of the doctors. See especially paragraphs 8 and 10. What is the point of the different kinds of talk?

9. The major image of this essay, is, of course, the pilot as test animal—as laboratory rat. How does Wolfe initiate, sustain, and develop this analogy? Where is it most emphatic?

10. Discuss the effectiveness of the comparisons in paragraphs 9, 13, and 14.

11. In paragraphs 10–14 Wolfe uses present-tense verbs. Would it make any difference if these verbs were in the past tense? Why or why not?

Suggestions for Writing

A. Describe an experience in which you were put through a series of tests without knowing what was happening or what the tests were for. Try to give the reader a sense of what it was like to have this happen to you.

B. Write imitations of Wolfe's long sentence in paragraph 3 and of the entire final paragraph.

C. Write a paragraph in which you focus on, sustain, and develop an analogy.

The Right Stuff

---

1   **A** young man might go into military flight training believing that he was entering some sort of technical school in which he was simply going to acquire a certain set of skills. Instead, he found himself all at once enclosed in a fraternity. And in this fraternity, even though it was military, men were not rated by their outward rank as ensigns, lieutenants, commanders, or whatever. No, herein the world was divided into those who had it and those who did not. This quality, this *it*, was never named, however, nor was it talked about in any way.

2   As to just what this ineffable quality was . . . well, it obviously involved bravery. But it was not bravery in the simple sense of being willing to risk your life. The idea seemed to be that any fool could do that, if that was all that was required, just as any fool could throw away his life in the process. No, the idea here (in the all-enclosing fraternity)

seemed to be that a man should have the ability to go up in a hurtling piece of machinery and put his hide on the line and then have the moxie, the reflexes, the experience, the coolness, to pull it back in the last yawning moment—and then to go up again *the next day*, and the next day, and every next day, even if the series should prove infinite— and, ultimately, in its best expression, do so in a cause that means something to thousands, to a people, a nation, to humanity, to God. Nor was there *a test* to show whether or not a pilot had this righteous quality. There was, instead, a seemingly infinite series of tests. A career in flying was like climbing one of those ancient Babylonian pyramids made up of a dizzy progression of steps and ledges, a ziggurat, a pyramid extraordinarily high and steep; and the idea was to prove at every foot of the way up that pyramid that you were one of the elected and anointed ones who had *the right stuff* and could move higher and higher and even—ultimately, God willing, one day—that you might be able to join that special few at the very top, that elite who had the capacity to bring tears to men's eyes, the very Brotherhood of the Right Stuff itself.

3   None of this was to be mentioned, and yet it was acted out in a way that a young man could not fail to understand. When a new flight (i.e., a class) of trainees arrived at Pensacola, they were brought into an auditorium for a little lecture. An officer would tell them: "Take a look at the man on either side of you." Quite a few actually swiveled their heads this way and that, in the interest of appearing diligent. Then the officer would say: "One of the three of you is not going to make it!"—meaning, not get his wings. That was the opening theme, the *motif* of primary training. We already know that one-third of you do not have the right stuff—it only remains to find out who.

4   Furthermore, that was the way it turned out. At every level in one's progress up that staggeringly high pyramid, the world was once more divided into those men who had the right stuff to continue the climb and those who had to be *left behind* in the most obvious way. Some were eliminated in the course of the opening classroom work, as either not smart enough or not hardworking enough, and were left behind. Then came the basic flight instruction, in single-engine, pro- peller-driven trainers, and a few more—even though the military tried to make this stage easy—were washed out and left behind. Then came more demanding levels, one after the other, formation flying, instru- ment flying, jet training, all-weather flying, gunnery, and at each level more were washed out and left behind. By this point easily a third of

the original candidates had been, indeed, eliminated . . . from the ranks of those who might prove to have the right stuff.

5 In the Navy, in addition to the stages that Air Force trainees went through, the neophyte always had waiting for him, out in the ocean, a certain grim gray slab; namely, the deck of an aircraft carrier; and with it perhaps the most difficult routine in military flying, carrier landings. He was shown films about it, he heard lectures about it, and he knew that carrier landings were hazardous. He first practiced touching down on the shape of a flight deck painted on an airfield. He was instructed to touch down and gun right off. This was safe enough—the shape didn't move, at least—but it could do terrible things to, let us say, the gyroscope of the soul. *That shape!—it's so damned small!* And more candidates were washed out and left behind. Then came the day, without warning, when those who remained were sent out over the ocean for the first of many days of reckoning with the slab. The first day was always a clear day with little wind and a calm sea. The carrier was so steady that it seemed, from up there in the air, to be resting on pilings, and the candidate usually made his first carrier landing successfully, with relief and even *élan*. Many young candidates looked like terrific aviators up to that very point—and it was not until they were actually standing on the carrier deck that they first began to wonder if they had the proper stuff, after all. In the training film the flight deck was a grand piece of gray geometry, perilous, to be sure, but an amazing abstract shape as one looks down upon it on the screen. And yet once the newcomer's two feet were on it . . . *Geometry—my God, man, this is a . . . skillet!* It *heaved*, it moved up and down underneath his feet, it pitched up, it pitched down, it rolled to port (this great beast *rolled!*) and it rolled to starboard, as the ship moved into the wind and, therefore, into the waves, and the wind kept sweeping across, sixty feet up in the air out in the open sea, and there were no railings whatsoever. This was a *skillet!*—a frying pan!—a short-order grill!—not gray but black, smeared with skid marks from one end to the other and glistening with pools of hydraulic fluid and the occasional jet-fuel slick, all of it still hot, sticky, greasy, runny, virulent from God knows what traumas—still ablaze!—consumed in detonations, explosions, flames, combustion, roars, shrieks, whines, blasts, horrible shudders, fracturing impacts, as little men in screaming red and yellow and purple and green shirts with black Mickey Mouse helmets over their ears skittered about on the surface as if for their very lives (you've said

it now!), hooking fighter planes onto the catapult shuttles so that they can explode their afterburners and be slung off the deck in a red-mad fury with a *kaboom!* that pounds through the entire deck—a procedure that seems absolutely controlled, orderly, sublime, however, compared to what he is about to watch as aircraft return to the ship for what is known in the engineering stoicisms of the military as "recovery and arrest." To say that an F-4 was coming back onto this heaving barbecue from out of the sky at a speed of 135 knots . . . that might have been the truth in the training lecture, but it did not begin to get across the idea of what the newcomer saw from the deck itself, because it created the notion that perhaps the plane was gliding in. On the deck one knew differently! As the aircraft came closer and the carrier heaved on into the waves and the plane's speed did not diminish and the deck did not grow steady—indeed, it pitched up and down five or ten feet per greasy heave—one experienced a neural alarm that no lecture could have prepared him for: This is not an *airplane* coming toward me, it is a brick with some poor sonofabitch riding it *(someone much like myself!)*, and it is not *gliding*, it is *falling*, a fifty-thousand-pound brick, headed not for a stripe on the deck but for *me*—and with a horrible *smash!* it hits the skillet, and with a blur of momentum as big as a freight train's it hurtles toward the far end of the deck—another blinding storm!— another roar as the pilot pushes the throttle up to full military power and another smear of rubber screams out over the skillet—and this is nominal!—quite okay!—for a wire stretched across the deck has grabbed the hook on the end of the plane as it hit the deck tail down, and the smash was the rest of the fifteen-ton brute slamming onto the deck, as it tripped up, so that it is now straining against the wire at full throttle, in case it hadn't held and the plane had "boltered" off the end of the deck and had to struggle up into the air again. And already the Mickey Mouse helmets are running toward the fiery monster . . .

6   And the candidate, looking on, begins to *feel* that great heaving sun-blazing deathboard of a deck wallowing in his own vestibular system—and suddenly he finds himself backed up against his own limits. He ends up going to the flight surgeon with so-called conversion symptoms. Overnight he develops blurred vision or numbness in his hands and feet or sinusitis so severe that he cannot tolerate changes in altitude. On one level the symptom is real. He really cannot see too well or use his fingers or stand the pain. But somewhere in his subconscious he knows it is a plea and a beg-off; he shows not the slightest concern (the

flight surgeon notes) that the condition might be permanent and affect him in whatever life awaits him outside the arena of the right stuff.

7   Those who remained, those who qualified for carrier duty—and even more so those who later on qualified for *night* carrier duty—began to feel a bit like Gideon's warriors. *So many have been left behind!* The young warriors were now treated to a deathly sweet and quite unmentionable sight. They could gaze at length upon the crushed and wilted pariahs who had washed out. They could inspect those who did not have that righteous stuff.

8   The military did not have very merciful instincts. Rather than packing up these poor souls and sending them home, the Navy, like the Air Force and the Marines, would try to make use of them in some other role, such as flight controller. So the washout has to keep taking classes with the rest of his group, even though he can no longer touch an airplane. He sits there in the classes staring at sheets of paper with cataracts of sheer human mortification over his eyes while the rest steal looks at him . . . this man reduced to an ant, this untouchable, this poor sonofabitch. And in what test had he been found wanting? Why, it seemed to be nothing less than *manhood* itself. Naturally, this was never mentioned, either. Yet there it was. *Manliness, manhood, manly courage* . . . there was something ancient, primordial, irresistible about the challenge of this stuff, no matter what a sophisticated and rational age one might think he lived in.

9   Perhaps because it could not be talked about, the subject began to take on superstitious and even mystical outlines. A man either had it or he didn't! There was no such thing as having *most* of it. Moreover, it could blow at any seam. One day a man would be ascending the pyramid at a terrific clip, and the next—bingo!—he would reach his own limits in the most unexpected way. Conrad and Schirra met an Air Force pilot who had had a great pal at Tyndall Air Force Base in Florida. This man had been the budding ace of the training class; he had flown the hottest fighter-style trainer, the T-38, like a dream; and then he began the routine step of being checked out in the T-33. The T-33 was not nearly as hot an aircraft as the T-38; it was essentially the old P-80 jet fighter. It had an exceedingly small cockpit. The pilot could barely move his shoulders. It was the sort of airplane of which everybody said, "You don't get into it, you *wear* it." Once inside a T-33 cockpit this man, this budding ace, developed claustrophobia of the most paralyzing sort. He tried everything to overcome it. He even went to a

psychiatrist, which was a serious mistake for a military officer if his superiors learned of it. But nothing worked. He was shifted over to flying jet transports, such as the C-135. Very demanding and necessary aircraft they were, too, and he was still spoken of as an excellent pilot. But as everyone knew—and, again, it was never explained in so many words—only those who were assigned to fighter squadrons, the "fighter jocks," as they called each other with a self-satisfied irony, remained in the true fraternity. Those assigned to transports were not humiliated like washouts—*somebody* had to fly those planes—nevertheless, they, too, had been *left behind* for lack of the right stuff.

10 Or a man could go for a routine physical one fine day, feeling like a million dollars, and be grounded for *fallen arches*. It happened!— just like that! (And try raising them.) Or for breaking his wrist and losing only *part* of its mobility. Or for a minor deterioration of eyesight, or for any of hundreds of reasons that would make no difference to a man in an ordinary occupation. As a result all fighter jocks began looking upon doctors as their natural enemies. Going to see a flight surgeon was a no-gain proposition; a pilot could only hold his own or lose in the doctor's office. To be grounded for a medical reason was no humiliation, looked at objectively. But it was a humiliation, nonetheless!—for it meant you no longer had that indefinable, unutterable, integral stuff. (It could blow at *any* seam.)

11 All the hot young fighter jocks began trying to test the limits themselves in a superstitious way. They were like believing Presbyterians of a century before who used to probe their own experience to see if they were truly among *the elect*. When a fighter pilot was in training, whether in the Navy or the Air Force, his superiors were continually spelling out strict rules for him, about the use of the aircraft and conduct in the sky. They repeatedly forbade so-called hot-dog stunts, such as outside loops, buzzing, flat-hatting, hedgehopping and flying under bridges. But somehow one got the message that the man who truly *had* it could ignore those rules—not that he should make a point of it, but that he *could*—and that after all there was only one way to find out— and that in some strange unofficial way, peeking through his fingers, his instructor halfway expected him to challenge all the limits. They would give a lecture about how a pilot should never fly without a good solid breakfast—eggs, bacon, toast, and so forth—because if he tried to fly with his blood-sugar level too low, it could impair his alertness. Naturally, the next day every hot dog in the unit would get up and

have a breakfast consisting of one cup of black coffee and take off and go up into a vertical climb until the weight of the ship exactly canceled out the upward pull of the engine and his air speed was zero, and he would hang there for one thick adrenal instant—and then fall like a rock, until one of three things happened: he keeled over nose first and regained his aerodynamics and all was well, he went into a spin and fought his way out of it, or he went into a spin and had to eject or crunch it, which was always supremely possible.

12   Likewise, "hassling"—mock dogfighting—was strictly forbidden, and so naturally young fighter jocks could hardly wait to go up in, say, a pair of F-100s and start the duel by making a pass at each other at 800 miles an hour, the winner being the pilot who could slip in behind the other one and get locked in on his tail ("wax his tail"), and it was not uncommon for some eager jock to try too tight an outside turn and have his engine flame out, whereupon, unable to restart it, he has to eject . . . and he shakes his fist at the victor as he floats down by parachute and his half-a-million-dollar aircraft goes *kaboom!* on the palmetto grass or the desert floor, and he starts thinking about how he can get together with the other guy back at the base in time for the two of them to get their stories straight before the investigation: "I don't know what happened, sir. I was pulling up after a target run, and it just flamed out on me." Hassling was forbidden, and hassling that led to the destruction of an aircraft was a serious court-martial offense, and the man's superiors knew that the engine hadn't *just flamed out*, but every unofficial impulse on the base seemed to be saying: "Hell, we wouldn't give you a nickel for a pilot who hasn't done some crazy rat-racing like that. It's all part of the right stuff."

13   The other side of this impulse showed up in the reluctance of the young jocks to admit it when they had maneuvered themselves into a bad corner they couldn't get out of. There were two reasons why a fighter pilot hated to declare an emergency. First, it triggered a complex and very public chain of events at the field: all other incoming flights were held up, including many of one's comrades who were probably low on fuel; the fire trucks came trundling out to the runway like yellow toys (as seen from way up there), the better to illustrate one's hapless state; and the bureaucracy began to crank up the paper monster for the investigation that always followed. And second, to declare an emergency, one first had to reach that conclusion in his own mind, which to the young pilot was the same as saying: "A minute ago I still *had* it—

now I need your help!" To have a bunch of young fighter pilots up in the air thinking this way used to drive flight controllers crazy. They would see a ship beginning to drift off the radar, and they couldn't rouse the pilot on the microphone for anything other than a few meaningless mumbles, and they would know he was probably out there with engine failure at a low altitude, trying to reignite by lowering his auxiliary generator rig, which had a little propeller that was supposed to spin in the slipstream like a child's pinwheel.

14 "Whiskey Kilo Two Eight, do you want to declare an emergency?"

15 *This* would rouse him!—to say: "Negative, negative, Whiskey Kilo Two Eight is not declaring an emergency."

16 Kaboom. Believers in the right stuff would rather crash and burn.

17 One fine day, after he had joined a fighter squadron, it would dawn on the young pilot exactly how the losers in the great fraternal competition were now being left behind. Which is to say, not by instructors or other superiors or by failures at prescribed levels of competence, but by death. At this point the essence of the enterprise would begin to dawn on him. Slowly, step by step, the ante had been raised until he was now involved in what was surely the grimmest and grandest gamble of manhood. Being a fighter pilot—for that matter, simply taking off in a single-engine jet fighter of the Century series, such as an F-102, or any of the military's other marvelous bricks with fins on them—presented a man, on a perfectly sunny day, with more ways to get himself killed than his wife and children could imagine in their wildest fears. If he was barreling down the runway at two hundred miles an hour, completing the takeoff run, and the board started lighting up red, should he (a) abort the takeoff (and try to wrestle with the monster, which was gorged with jet fuel, out in the sand beyond the end of the runway) or (b) eject (and hope that the goddamned human cannonball trick works at zero altitude and he doesn't shatter an elbow or a kneecap on the way out) or (c) continue the takeoff and deal with the problem aloft (knowing full well that the ship may be on fire and therefore seconds away from exploding)? He would have one second to sort out the options and act, and this kind of little workaday decision came up all the time. Occasionally a man would look coldly at the binary problem he was now confronting every day—Right Stuff/Death—and decide it wasn't worth it and voluntarily shift over to transports or reconnaissance or whatever. And his comrades would wonder, for a day or so, what evil virus had invaded his soul . . . as they left him behind. More often,

however, the reverse would happen. Some college graduate would enter Navy aviation through the Reserves, simply as an alternative to the Army draft, fully intending to return to civilian life, to some waiting profession or family business; would become involved in the obsessive business of ascending the ziggurat pyramid of flying; and, at the end of his enlistment, would astound everyone back home and very likely himself as well by signing up for another one. What on earth got into him? He couldn't explain it. After all, the very words for it had been amputated. A Navy study showed that two-thirds of the fighter pilots who were rated in the top rungs of their groups—i.e., the hottest young pilots—reenlisted when the time came, and practically all were college graduates. By this point, a young fighter jock was like the preacher in *Moby Dick* who climbs up into the pulpit on a rope ladder and then pulls the ladder up behind him; except the pilot could not use the words necessary to express the vital lessons. Civilian life, and even home and hearth, now seemed not only far away but far *below*, back down many levels of the pyramid of the right stuff.

18   A fighter pilot soon found he wanted to associate only with other fighter pilots. Who else could understand the nature of the little proposition (right stuff/death) they were all dealing with? And what other subject could compare with it? It was riveting! To talk about it in so many words was forbidden, of course. The very words *death, danger, bravery, fear* were not to be uttered except in the occasional specific instance or for ironic effect. Nevertheless, the subject could be adumbrated in *code* or *by example*. Hence the endless evenings of pilots huddled together talking about flying. On these long and drunken evenings (the bane of their family life) certain theorems would be propounded and demonstrated—and all by *code* and *example*. One theorem was: There are no *accidents* and no fatal flaws in the machines; there are only pilots with the wrong stuff. (I.e., blind Fate can't kill me.) When Bud Jennings crashed and burned in the swamps at Jacksonville, the other pilots in Pete Conrad's squadron said: *How could he have been so stupid?* It turned out that Jennings had gone up in the SNJ with his cockpit canopy opened in a way that was expressly forbidden in the manual, and carbon monoxide had been sucked in from the exhaust, and he passed out and crashed. All agreed that Bud Jennings was a good guy and a good pilot, but his epitaph on the ziggurat was: *How could he have been so stupid?* This seemed shocking at first, but by the time Conrad had reached the end of that bad string at Pax River, he

was capable of his own corollary to the theorem: viz., no single factor
ever killed a pilot; there was always a chain of mistakes. But what about
Ted Whelan, who fell like a rock from 8,100 feet when his parachute
failed? Well, the parachute was merely part of the chain: first, someone
should have caught the structural defect that resulted in the hydraulic
leak that triggered the emergency; second, Whelan did not check out
his seat-parachute rig, and the drogue failed to separate the main parachute from the seat; but even after those two mistakes, Whelan had
fifteen or twenty seconds, as he fell, to disengage himself from the seat
and open the parachute manually. Why just stare at the scenery coming
up to smack you in the face! And everyone nodded. (He failed—but I
wouldn't have!) Once the theorem and the corollary were understood,
the Navy's statistics about one in every four Navy aviators dying meant
nothing. The figures were averages, and averages applied to those with
average stuff.

19   A riveting subject, especially if it were one's own hide that was
on the line. Every evening at bases all over America, there were military
pilots huddled in officers clubs eagerly cutting the right stuff up in coded
slices so they could talk about it. What more compelling topic of conversation was there in the world? In the Air Force there were even pilots
who would ask the tower for priority landing clearance so that they
could make the beer call on time, at 4 p.m. sharp, at the Officers Club.
They would come right out and state the reason. The drunken rambles
began at four and sometimes went on for ten or twelve hours. Such
conversations! They diced that righteous stuff up into little bits, bowed
ironically to it, stumbled blindfolded around it, groped, lurched,
belched, staggered, bawled, sang, roared, and feinted at it with self-
deprecating humor. Nevertheless!—they never mentioned it by name.
No, they used the approved codes, such as: "Like a jerk I got myself
into a hell of a corner today." They told of how they "lucked out of it."
To get across the extreme peril of his exploit, one would use certain
oblique cues. He would say, "I looked over at Robinson"—who would
be known to the listeners as a non-com who sometimes rode backseat
to read radar—"and he wasn't talking any more, he was just staring at
the radar, like this, giving it that *zombie* look. Then I *knew* I was in
trouble!" Beautiful! Just right! For it would also be known to the listeners
that the non-coms advised one another: "*Never* fly with a lieutenant.
Avoid captains and majors. Hell, man, do yourself a favor: don't fly
with anybody below colonel." Which in turn said: "Those young bucks

shoot dice with death!" And yet once in the air the non-com had his own standards. He was determined to remain as outwardly cool as the pilot, so that when the pilot did something that truly petrified him, he would say nothing; instead, he would turn silent, catatonic, like a zombie. Perfect! *Zombie.* There you had it, compressed into a single word all of the foregoing. I'm a hell of a pilot! I shoot dice with death! And now all you fellows know it! And I haven't spoken of that unspoken stuff even once!

20   The talking and drinking began at the beer call, and then the boys would break for dinner and come back afterward and get more wasted and more garrulous or else more quietly fried, drinking good cheap PX booze until 2 a.m. The night was young! Why not get the cars and go out for a little proficiency run? It seemed that every fighter jock thought himself an ace driver, and he would do anything to obtain a hot car, especially a sports car, and the drunker he was, the more convinced he would be about his driving skills, as if the right stuff, being indivisible, carried over into any enterprise whatsoever, under any conditions. A little proficiency run, boys! (There's only one way to find out!) And they would roar off in close formation from, say, Nellis Air Force Base, down Route 15, into Las Vegas, barreling down the highway, rat-racing, sometimes four abreast, jockeying for position, piling into the most listless curve in the desert flats as if they were trying to root each other out of the groove at the Rebel 500—and then bursting into downtown Las Vegas with a rude fraternal roar like the Hell's Angels—and the natives chalked it up to youth and drink and the bad element that the Air Force attracted. They knew nothing about the right stuff, of course.

21   More fighter pilots died in automobiles than in airplanes. Fortunately, there was always some kindly soul up the chain to certify the papers "line of duty," so that the widow could get a better break on the insurance. That was okay and only proper because somehow the system itself had long ago said *Skol!* and *Quite right!* to the military cycle of Flying & Drinking and Drinking & Driving, as if there were no other way. Every young fighter jock knew the feeling of getting two or three hours' sleep and then waking up at 5:30 a.m. and having a few cups of coffee, a few cigarettes, and then carting his poor quivering liver out to the field for another day of flying. There were those who arrived not merely hungover but still drunk, slapping oxygen tank cones over their faces and trying to burn the alcohol out of their systems, and then going

up, remarking later: "I don't *advise* it, you understand, but it *can* be done." (Provided you have the right stuff, you miserable pudknocker.)
22   Air Force and Navy airfields were usually on barren or marginal stretches of land and would have looked especially bleak and Low Rent to an ordinary individual in the chilly light of dawn. But to a young pilot there was an inexplicable bliss to coming out to the flight line while the sun was just beginning to cook up behind the rim of the horizon, so that the whole field was still in shadow and the ridges in the distance were in silhouette and the flight line was a monochrome of Exhaust Fume Blue, and every little red light on top of the water towers or power stanchions looked dull, shriveled, congealed, and the runway lights, which were still on, looked faded, and even the landing lights on a fighter that had just landed and was taxiing in were no longer dazzling, as they would be at night, and looked instead like shriveled gobs of candlepower out there—and yet it was beautiful, exhilarating!— for he was revved up with adrenalin, anxious to take off before the day broke, to burst up into the sunlight over the ridges before all those thousands of comatose souls down there, still dead to the world, snug in home and hearth, even came to their senses. To take off in an F-100F at dawn and cut on the afterburner and hurtle twenty-five thousand feet up into the sky in thirty seconds, so suddenly that you felt not like a bird but like a trajectory, yet with full control, full control of *four tons* of thrust, all of which flowed from your will and through your fingertips, with the huge engine right beneath you, so close that it was as if you were riding it bareback, until all at once you were supersonic, an event registered on earth by a tremendous cracking boom that shook windows, but up here only by the fact that you now felt utterly free of the earth—to describe it, even to wife, child, near ones and dear ones, seemed impossible. So the pilot kept it to himself, along with an even more indescribable . . . an even more sinfully inconfessable . . . feeling of superiority, appropriate to him and to his kind, lone bearers of the right stuff.
23   From *up here* at dawn the pilot looked down upon poor hopeless Las Vegas (or Yuma, Corpus Christi, Meridian, San Bernardino, or Dayton) and began to wonder: How can all of them down there, those poor souls who will soon be waking up and trudging out of their minute rectangles and inching along their little noodle highways toward whatever slots and grooves make up their everyday lives—how could they

live like that, with such earnestness, if they had the faintest idea of what it was like up here in this righteous zone?

24 But of course! Not only the washed-out, grounded, and dead pilots had been left behind—but also all of those millions of sleepwalking souls who never even attempted the great gamble. The entire world below . . . *left behind.* Only at this point can one begin to understand just how big, how titanic, the ego of the military pilot could be. The world was used to enormous egos in artists, actors, entertainers of all sorts, in politicians, sports figures, and even journalists, because they had such familiar and convenient ways to show them off. But that slim young man over there in uniform, with the enormous watch on his wrist and the withdrawn look on his face, that young officer who is so shy that he can't even open his mouth unless the subject is flying— that young pilot—well, my friends, his ego is even *bigger!*—so big, it's *breathtaking!* Even in the 1950's it was difficult for civilians to comprehend such a thing, but *all* military officers and many enlisted men tended to feel superior to civilians. It was really quite ironic, given the fact that for a good thirty years the rising business classes in the cities had been steering their sons away from the military, as if from a bad smell, and the officer corps had never been held in lower esteem. Well, career officers returned the contempt in trumps. They looked upon themselves as men who lived by higher standards of behavior than civilians, as men who were the bearers and protectors of the most important values of American life, who maintained a sense of discipline while civilians abandoned themselves to hedonism, who maintained a sense of honor while civilians lived by opportunism and greed. Opportunism and greed: there you had your much-vaunted corporate business world. Khrushchev was right about one thing: when it came time to hang the capitalist West, an American businessman would sell him the rope. When the showdown came—and the showdowns always came— not all the wealth in the world or all the sophisticated nuclear weapons and radar and missile systems it could buy would take the place of those who had the uncritical willingness to face danger, those who, in short, had the right stuff.

25 In fact, the feeling was so righteous, so exalted, it could become religious. Civilians seldom understood this, either. There was no one to teach them. It was no longer the fashion for serious writers to describe the glories of war. Instead, they dwelt upon its horrors, often with

cynicism or disgust. It was left to the occasional pilot with a literary
flair to provide a glimpse of the pilot's self-conception in its heavenly
or spiritual aspect. When a pilot named Robert Scott flew his P-43 over
Mount Everest, quite a feat at the time, he brought his hand up and
snapped a salute to his fallen adversary. He thought he had *defeated*
the mountain, surmounting all the forces of nature that had made it
formidable. And why not? "God is my co-pilot," he said—that became
the title of his book—and he meant it. So did the most gifted of all the
pilot authors, the Frenchman Antoine de Saint-Exupéry. As he gazed
down upon the world . . . from up there . . . during transcontinental
flights, the good Saint-Ex saw civilization as a series of tiny fragile
patches clinging to the otherwise barren rock of Earth. He felt like a
lonely sentinel, a protector of those vulnerable little oases, ready to lay
down his life in their behalf, if necessary; a saint, in short, true to his
name, flying up here at the right hand of God. The good Saint-Ex!
And he was not the only one. He was merely the one who put it into
words most beautifully and anointed himself before the altar of the right
stuff.

QUESTIONS

Ideas

1. While recognizing and allowing for differences among individuals, Wolfe
   presents a generalized profile of a military test pilot. He suggests that to
   succeed, a test pilot needs "the right stuff." What is "the right stuff"? What
   qualities and attributes are necessary for success as a military test pilot?

2. What does Wolfe mean when he says that the men were in "an enclosing
   fraternity"? How does that fact affect their view of themselves and their
   behavior? Is such isolation necessary?

3. In paragraphs 11 and 12, Wolfe presents two sides of the test pilots—the
   official and the unofficial. Why is it important for us to see both sides?
   What effect does Wolfe create with these contrasted views?

4. Paragraphs 22 and 23 are written from the point of view of the pilot. We
   are taken up with him into the sky, and we enter into and read his thoughts.
   Can Wolfe legitimately include such details even though he himself never
   piloted a jet?

5. What point is made at the end of paragraph 21? In paragraphs 24–25? In paragraph 9?

Organization

6. The overall structure of this selection breaks down into something like this: paragraphs 1–4; 5; 6–10; 11–16; 17–25. Explain what unifies the paragraphs in each grouping. And explain how each section is related to the one before. (Why is paragraph 5 a self-contained unit?)

7. Paragraph 5—the odd one in the structure of the whole—is extremely long. Is there a reason for this? What would be the effect of breaking it into two or three or even more parts? What is the purpose of this paragraph?

8. Read the first two paragraphs for coherence. Note how within each paragraph Wolfe joins one sentence to another, and also how he links one paragraph to another.

9. Wolfe doesn't bother with interparagraph transitions in paragraphs 14–17. Why not?

10. What do you notice about the final sentence of each paragraph? Are there any differences among the various repetitions and variations? Consider, for example, the final words of paragraphs 6 and 7.

11. In paragraphs 17 and 18 Wolfe makes different points at the beginning and at the end. Explain how, in each paragraph, Wolfe gets from his opening idea to his concluding one.

Sentences

12. In paragraph 5 Wolfe uses an extraordinarily long sentence beginning "This was a skillet. . . ." What would be lost or gained if this sentence were divided into three or four parts?

13. What is the effect of the two long sentences of paragraph 22? Should these two sentences be converted to a series of shorter ones? Why or why not?

14. In the last sentence of paragraph 2 Wolfe stacks a series of parallel phrases:

> a dizzy progression of steps
> a ziggurat
> a pyramid

and again:

> that special few
> that elite
> the very Brotherhood

What would be lost if in each of these series there were not three items, but only two? (Or only one?)

15. Explain which version of the following sentence you prefer.

Wolfe: In the Navy, in addition to the stages that Air Force trainees went through, the neophyte always had waiting for him, out in the ocean, a certain grim gray slab! (5)

Revision: In addition to the stages that Air Force trainees went through, in the Navy the neophyte always had a grim gray slab waiting for him out in the ocean.

16. Wolfe mixes the lengths of his sentences effectively throughout "The Right Stuff." Look closely at paragraph 2, attending both to the variety of sentence lengths and to the long sentence with its series of parallel pieces:

the moxie, the reflexes, the experience, the coolness:

and later:

> to go up, to go up again the next day
> and the next day
> and every next day
> in a cause that means something to thousands,
> to a people,
> a nation,
> to humanity,
> to God.

What is the effect of this elaboration and repetition? Why does Wolfe mix in some short sentences as well?

Words

17. Throughout "The Right Stuff" Wolfe mixes idiomatic, colloquial language with formal, technical diction. Find passages where one or the other predominates.

18. In paragraph 5 Wolfe compares the slab, the aircraft carrier, to a skillet, a frying pan, a short-order grill. Does that comparison in its three variations seem appropriate? Farfetched? What is Wolfe's point in making it? What details does he use to elaborate and extend the analogy?

19. How do the quoted remarks in paragraph 19 help us understand what Wolfe means by "the right stuff"? Why don't the pilots use the words Wolfe uses in paragraph 18: "death," "danger," "bravery," "fear"?

20. Wolfe makes frequent use of triplets—groups of three words, phrases or details. He often uses them at the ends of paragraphs, as in the following examples:

    ancient, primordial, irresistible (8)

    manliness, manhood, manly courage (8)

    indefinable, unutterable, integral (10)

    Find two more examples. Try mentally eliminating one of the three terms from each set, as in this revised version of the triplet from paragraph 8: "ancient and primordial" or "ancient and irresistible." What is different about the triplet?

21. What is the effect of the direct speech, the dialogue, that Wolfe uses in paragraphs 12–15?

22. What is the effect of Wolfe's repetitions and variations of the term "the right stuff"? Why is the term capitalized at the end of paragraph 2?

23. Wolfe frequently italicizes words and phrases. Explain the effect of each of the following:

    it (1)
    the next day; the right stuff; a test (2)
    left behind (4)
    that shape—it's so damned small; heaved; rolled (5)

Suggestions for Writing

A. Write an essay explaining what field you will go into—what kind of work you expect to do, and why. Explain what "the right stuff" is that you think necessary for success in whatever you expect to do.

B. Interview three or four athletes, teachers, musicians, scholars, students, who have what you think of as "the right stuff." Write an essay presenting a composite picture of a _____ with the right stuff.

C. Write imitations of the sentences discussed in questions 13–16.

SIX

John McPhee

(1931–   )

John McPhee is a master of detail, a poet of information, an artist of the factual. His passion for getting it right is almost obsessive. If he were a painter, he would probably be a photo-realist; if a filmmaker, he would broaden the artistic possibilities of the documentary. In fact, according to one critic, he has already "stretched the artistic dimensions of reportage." His book *Oranges* (1967) is typical of his literary nonfiction. Although we learn an enormous amount about citrus botany and history, about international customs and economic realities, we are also aesthetically entertained by the craft and photographic precision of his prose—by the clarity of his accurate and authentic details.

Unlike Tom Wolfe and Joan Didion, John McPhee is not a New Journalist: his presence is barely noticeable in the events he is describing, and he almost never tells the reader what he is thinking. He is self-effacing. The persona he adopts as a narrator reveals little; instead he usually lets his carefully arranged details convey his feelings. In a traditional sense, he tries for objectivity. However, because writing is a process of selecting, rejecting, and arranging information, a writer cannot possibly be completely objective. McPhee has to leave some material out; he has to put other material in. All writers have to choose. In McPhee's case it is easy enough to infer his attitude. He leaves many traces.

He clearly admires the finesse and dedication of the basketball player Bill Bradley and likes the independence and pluck of Fred Brown, a piney backwoodsman. McPhee is interested in the values that people live by, and he usually writes about people he likes. They can be basketball players, scientists, headmasters, or canoe makers. Very often his heroes possess competence, self-assurance, modesty, and self-discipline. Many critics attribute these same qualities to McPhee.

But he is more interested in giving the reader a precisely rendered account of the people he writes about than in extolling them. When we encounter the people of the Pine Barrens, we find out about their lives and the codes they live by through details that have been meticulously researched and verified. McPhee gains authority through fact and layers of details. We trust his persona because he has mastered his material. He has done his homework. His scholarly attention to creating a particular atmosphere makes his nonfiction as complex as a novel. His refined, economically controlled portraits make his characters breathe. McPhee once said that "factual characters can live as much on the page as any fictional character . . . writing is more than just the delivery of information per se."

None of this comes easy, of course. In fact, McPhee says that writing "gets harder and harder the older you get. Not easier." He claims that as a young writer he "would thread my bathrobe sash through the spokes of the chair and tie myself in." Even today McPhee finds the life of a writer difficult. Although he is a staff writer for *The New Yorker* and has an office there, he does all his writing in a study on Main Street in Princeton, New Jersey. He arrives at 8:30 in the morning and doesn't leave until 8:30 at night. He maintains, however, that he gets only two or three hours of good writing done. "The rest of the time I wander around in here going nuts—trying to bring it all into focus."

To make the process of composing easier, McPhee tries to follow a pattern that he feels comfortable with, one that fits his personality. He does not use a tape recorder, preferring instead to fill up notebooks in longhand with the results of interviews, observations, and library research. After reading and rereading these notes, he looks for gaps that will need future research. Then he jots down possible structures, later trying possible opening paragraphs. He then arranges his notes according to a tentative structure.

Unlike many writers, McPhee does most of his planning in his head instead of on paper. He decides whether to use a prearranged pattern or to let the material suggest an organic pattern. Generally he prefers a logical, simple form. Then he writes his first draft. A critic described his composing processes: "Some authors overwrite and later boil down; he culls before ever typing a phrase."

McPhee's first draft is for him the most difficult. After that he edits, pruning and polishing his sentences. Because of the "laborious planning and composing" that McPhee goes through in the early stages of his writing, he can concentrate on style in the closing stages.

Although he doesn't begin to write until the end of his planning stage, his overall composing sequence is comparable to that of many other experienced writers who spend up to 80 percent of their composing effort in preparation for the first good draft. For most writers, revising that draft involves a good deal of rearranging, refocusing, and reseeing. However, McPhee feels he has already laid a solid foundation and so makes few changes in the original structure. His purpose in choosing an organization is to create an unobtrusive design, one so logical and simple that the reader's attention will be drawn only to meaning, to content; not to the window, but to the scene beyond.

His style is as unaffected as his organization. His prose is strong, direct, and economical. His most characteristic sentence pattern is the straightforward assertion: "Bradley is not an innovator" or "Bradley's graceful hook shot is a masterpiece of eclecticism." These sentences are often placed first in a paragraph so that he can follow them with supporting details. And these specifics are concrete and knowledgeable. He achieves some of his authority by absorbing the vocabulary, the "sound" of whatever he is writing about. If it is pinballs, he will use the right jargon: "Ballys" and "Gottliebs," "reinforcing" and "death channels." If it is oranges, we will hear about "Maltese Ovals" and "Lue Gim Gongs," "zygotic seedlings" and "pomologists." His use of the concrete suggests a writer deeply involved in his subject, a person totally in touch with his surroundings. Readers trust a writer who sounds as if he knows what he is talking about.

John McPhee uses disciplined hard work to let readers see, to make us understand. With *The Pine Barrens* (1968) and *Coming Into the Country* (1979), he earned a reputation

as the most versatile and literate journalist in America, a
reporter who creates living art out of inert information.
Through a patient and textured prose he shows us how it
was to be there. He stands back and lets his sentences and
paragraphs evoke special people, special places.

In "Brigade de Cuisine," an essay from *Giving Good
Weight* about a dedicated, superb chef, McPhee could be
describing himself:

He is a very honest person. Basically. In his bones. And that is
what the food is all about. He is so good with flavor because he
looks for arrows to point to the essence of the material. His tastes
are very fresh and bouncy. He has honor, idealism, a lack of guile.
I don't know how he puts them together. I don't know his likes
and dislikes. I can't even buy him a birthday present. He has
intelligence. He has education. He has character. He has integrity.
He applies all these to this manual task. His hands follow what
he is.

Bradley

Bradley is one of the few basketball players who have ever
been appreciatively cheered by a disinterested away-from-home crowd
while warming up. This curious event occurred last March, just before
Princeton eliminated the Virginia Military Institute, the year's Southern
Conference champion, from the N.C.A.A. championships. The game
was played in Philadelphia and was the last of a tripleheader. The people
there were worn out, because most of them were emotionally committed
to either Villanova or Temple—two local teams that had just been
involved in enervating battles with Providence and Connecticut, re-
spectively, scrambling for a chance at the rest of the country. A group
of Princeton boys shooting basketballs miscellaneously in preparation
for still another game hardly promised to be a high point of the evening,
but Bradley, whose routine in the warmup time is a gradual crescendo
of activity, is more interesting to watch before a game than most players

are in play. In Philadelphia that night, what he did was, for him, anything but unusual. As he does before all games, he began by shooting set shots close to the basket, gradually moving back until he was shooting long sets from twenty feet out, and nearly all of them dropped into the net with an almost mechanical rhythm of accuracy. Then he began a series of expandingly difficult jump shots, and one jumper after another went cleanly through the basket with so few exceptions that the crowd began to murmur. Then he started to perform whirling reverse moves before another cadence of almost steadily accurate jump shots, and the murmur increased. Then he began to sweep hook shots into the air. He moved in a semicircle around the court. First with his right hand, then with his left, he tried seven of these long, graceful shots—the most difficult ones in the orthodoxy of basketball—and ambidextrously made them all. The game had not even begun, but the presumably unimpressible Philadelphians were applauding like an audience at an opera.

QUESTIONS

Ideas

1. Why do the crowds react to Bradley so enthusiastically?
2. What kind of person does Bradley seem to be? Would Magic Johnson warm up like this? How about Daryl Dawkins?
3. Although McPhee is reporting objectively, we somehow get a clear sense of his attitude toward Bradley. What is McPhee's reaction and how do we know it?

Organization

4. If you were going to divide this paragraph into a beginning, middle, and end, how would you defend your partitioning?
5. In what way is the first sentence related to what follows?
6. How is the last sentence connected to the first?

Sentences

7. Some critics have praised McPhee's style as "unaffected and strong." Read this paragraph aloud; does it sound that way to you? Why?

8. Probably the most basic sentence structure is the simple declaration, e.g., McPhee's first sentence. Are there other examples here? What is the effect of stringing these assertions together?

Words

9. Why does McPhee say "like an audience at an opera"? Why not at another sporting event? Has McPhee prepared us for this simile?

Suggestions for Writing

10. Sit someplace on campus and observe people interacting. Write a brief sketch that follows McPhee's tight organization of supporting a simple assertion with concrete detail.

11. Write a brief portrait of someone you admire, but don't tell the reader why directly: let the details of his or her actions convey your admiration.

Grizzly

I

Fatal encounters with bears are as rare as they are memorable. Some people reject the rifle as cumbersome extra baggage, not worth toting, given the minimal risk. And, finally, there are a few people who feel that it is wrong to carry a gun, in part because the risk is low and well worth taking, but most emphatically because they see the gun as an affront to the wild country of which the bear is sign and symbol. This, while strongly felt, is a somewhat novel attitude. When Robert Marshall explored the Brooks Range half a century ago, he and his companions fired at almost every bear they saw, without pausing for philosophical reflection. The reaction was automatic. They were expressing mankind's immemorial fear of this beast—man and rattlesnake, man and bear. Among modern environmentalists, to whom a figure like Marshall is otherwise a hero, fear of the bear has been exceeded by reverence. A notable example, in his own past and present, is Andy Russell, author of a book called "Grizzly Country." Russell was once a professional hunter, but he gave that up to become a photographer, specializing in grizzlies. He says that he has given up not only shooting bears but even carrying a gun. On rare instances when grizzlies charge toward him, he shouts at them and stands his ground. The worst thing to do, he says, is to run, because anything that runs on open tundra suggests game to a bear. Game does not tend to stand its ground in the presence of grizzlies. Therefore, when the bear comes at you, just stand there. Charging something that does not move, the bear will theoretically stop and reconsider. (Says Russell.) More important, Russell believes that the bear will *know* if you have a gun, even if the gun is concealed:

> Reviewing our experiences, we had become more and more convinced that carrying arms was not only unnecessary in most grizzly country but was certainly no good for the desired atmosphere and proper protocol in obtaining good film records. If we were to obtain such film and fraternize successfully with the big bears, it would be better to go unarmed in most places. The mere fact of having a gun within reach, cached somewhere in a pack or a hidden holster, causes a man to act with unconscious arrogance and thus maybe to smell different or to transmit some kind of signal objectionable to bears. The armed man does not assume his proper role in association with the wild ones, a fact of which they seem instantly aware at some distance. He, being wilder than they, whether he likes to admit it or not, is instantly under even more suspicion than he would encounter if unarmed.

> One must follow the role of an uninvited visitor—an intruder—rather than that of an aggressive hunter, and one should go unarmed to insure this attitude.

Like pictures from pages riffled with a thumb, all of these things went through my mind there on the mountainside above the grazing bear. I will confess that in one instant I asked myself, "What the hell am I doing *here?*" There was nothing more to the question, though, than a hint of panic. I knew why I had come, and therefore what I was doing there. That I was frightened was incidental. I just hoped the fright would not rise beyond a relatively decorous level. I sensed that Fedeler and Hession were somewhat frightened, too. I would have been troubled if they had not been. Meanwhile, the sight of the bear stirred me like nothing else the country could contain. What mattered was not so much the bear himself as what the bear implied. He was the predominant thing in that country, and for him to be in it at all meant that there had to be more country like it in every direction and more of the same kind of country all around that. He implied a world. He was an affirmation to the rest of the earth that his kind of place was extant. There had been a time when his race was everywhere in North America, but it had been hunted down and pushed away in favor of something else. For example, the grizzly bear is the state animal of California, whose country was once his kind of place; and in California now the grizzly is extinct.

The animals I have encountered in my wilderness wanderings have been reluctant to reveal all the things about them I would like to know. The animal that impresses me most, the one I find myself liking more and more, is the grizzly. No sight encountered in the wilds is quite so stirring as those massive, clawed tracks pressed into mud or snow. No sight is quite so impressive as that of the great bear stalking across some mountain slope with the fur of his silvery robe rippling over his mighty muscles. His is a dignity and power matched by no other in the North American wilderness. To share a mountain with him for a while is a privilege and an adventure like no other.

I have followed his tracks into an alder hell to see what he had been doing and come to the abrupt end of them, when the maker stood up thirty feet away with a sudden snort to face me.

To see a mother grizzly ambling and loafing with her cubs across the broad, hospitable bosom of a flower-spangled mountain meadow is to see life in true wilderness at its best.

If a wolf kills a caribou, and a grizzly comes along while the wolf is feeding on the kill, the wolf puts its tail between its legs and hurries away. A black bear will run from a grizzly, too. Grizzlies sometimes kill and eat black bears. The grizzly takes what he happens upon. He is an opportunistic eater. The predominance of the grizzly in his terrain is challenged by nothing but men and ravens. To frustrate ravens from stealing his food, he will lie down and sleep on top of a carcass, occasionally swatting the birds as if they were big black flies. He prefers a vegetable diet. He can pulp a moosehead with a single blow, but he is not lusting always to kill, and when he moves through his country he can be something munificent, going into copses of willow among unfleeing moose and their calves, touching nothing, letting it all breathe as before. He may, though, get the head of a cow moose between his legs and rake her flanks with the five-inch knives that protrude from the ends of his paws. Opportunistic. He removes and eats her entrails. He likes porcupines, too, and when one turns and presents to him a pygal bouquet of quills, he will leap into the air, land on the other side, chuck the fretful porcupine beneath the chin, flip it over, and, with a swift ventral incision, neatly remove its body from its skin, leaving something like a sea urchin behind him on the ground. He is nothing if not athletic. Before he dens, or just after he emerges, if his mountains are covered with snow he will climb to the brink of some impossible schuss, sit down on his butt, and shove off. Thirty-two, sixty-four, ninety-six feet per second, he plummets down the mountainside, spray snow flying to either side, as he approaches collision with boulders and trees. Just short of catastrophe, still going at bonecrushing speed, he flips to his feet and walks sedately onward as if his ride had not occurred.

His population density is thin on the Arctic barren ground. He needs for his forage at least fifty and perhaps a hundred square miles that are all his own—sixty-four thousand acres, his home range. Within it, he will move, typically, eight miles a summer day, doing his travelling through the twilight hours of the dead of night. To scratch his belly he walks over a tree—where forest exists. The tree bends beneath him as he passes. He forages in the morning, generally; and he rests a great deal, particularly after he eats. He rests fourteen hours a day. If he becomes hot in the sun, he lies down in a pool in the river. He sleeps on the tundra—restlessly tossing and turning, forever changing position. What he could be worrying about I cannot imagine.

II

What had struck me most in the isolation of this wilderness was an abiding sense of paradox. In its raw, convincing emphasis on the irrelevance of the visitor, it was forcefully, importantly repellent. It was no less strongly attractive—with a beauty of nowhere else, composed in turning circles. If the wild land was indifferent, it gave a sense of difference. If at moments it was frightening, requiring an effort to put down the conflagrationary imagination, it also augmented the touch of life. This was not a dare with nature. This was nature.

The bottoms of the Kleppers were now trellised with tape. Pourchot was smoothing down a final end. Until recently, he had been an avocational parachutist, patterning the sky in star formation with others as he fell. He had fifty-one jumps, all of them in Colorado. But he had started waking up in the night with cold sweats, so—with two small sons now—he had sold his jumping gear. With the money, he bought a white-water kayak and climbing rope. "You're kind of on your own, really. You run the risk," he was saying. "I haven't seen any bear incidents, for example. I've never had any bear problems. I've never carried a gun. Talk to ten people and you get ten different bear-approach theories. Some carry flares. Ed Bailey, in Fish and Wildlife, shoots pencil flares into the ground before approaching bears. They go away. Bear attacks generally occur in road-system areas anyway. Two, maybe four people die a year. Some years more than others. Rarely will a bear attack a person in a complete wilderness like this."

Kauffmann said, "Give a grizzly half a chance and he'll avoid you."

Fedeler had picked cups of blueberries to mix into our breakfast pancakes. Finishing them, we prepared to go. The sun was coming through. The rain was gone. The morning grew bright and warm. Pourchot and I got into the canoe, which, for all its heavy load, felt light. Twenty minutes downriver, we had to stop for more repairs to the Kleppers, but afterward the patchwork held. With higher banks, longer pools, the river was running deeper. The sun began to blaze.

Rounding bends, we saw sculpins, a pair of great horned owls, mergansers, Taverner's geese. We saw ravens and a gray jay. Coming down a long, deep, green pool, we looked toward the riffle at the lower end and saw an approaching grizzly. He was young, possibly four years old, and not much over four hundred pounds. He crossed the river. He studied the salmon in the riffle. He did not see, hear, or smell us. Our three boats were close together, and down the light current on the flat water we drifted toward the fishing bear.

He picked up a salmon, roughly ten pounds of fish, and, holding it with one paw, he began to whirl it around his head. Apparently, he was not hungry, and this was a form of play. He played sling-the-salmon. With his claws embedded near the tail, he whirled the salmon and then tossed it high, end over end. As it fell, he scooped it up and slung it around his head again, lariat salmon, and again he tossed it into the air. He caught it and heaved it high once more. The fish flopped to the ground. The bear turned away, bored. He began to move upstream by the edge of the river. Behind his big head his hump projected. His brown fur rippled like a field under wind. He kept coming. The breeze was behind him. He had not yet seen us. He was romping along at an easy walk. As he came closer to us, we drifted slowly toward him. The single Klepper, with John Kauffmann in it, moved up against a snagged stick and broke it off. The snap was light, but enough to stop the bear. Instantly, he was motionless and alert, remaining on his four feet and straining his eyes to see. We drifted on toward him. At last, we arrived in his focus. If we were looking at something we had rarely seen before, God help him so was he. If he was a tenth as awed as I was, he could not have moved a muscle, which he did, now, in a hurry that was not pronounced but nonetheless seemed inappropriate to his status in the situation. He crossed low ground and went up a bank toward a copse of willow. He stopped there and faced us again. Then, breaking stems to pieces, he went into the willows.

We drifted to the rip, and down it past the mutilated salmon. Then we came to another long flat surface, spraying up the light of the sun. My bandanna, around my head, was nearly dry. I took it off, and trailed it in the river.

QUESTIONS

Ideas

1. Within a few pages, McPhee writes about two encounters with grizzly bears. In the first one, what image of the bear do you get from McPhee's details? Do you get a different impression of the bear in section II?

2. What is the effect of the last sentence in section I? How does the impact of this sentence compare to the concluding sentence of section II?

3. In the second excerpt from *Coming Into the Country*, McPhee uses a classic deductive pattern: a generalization followed by support; in this case he uses a narrative. In your own words, what idea is McPhee illustrating in this second bear narrative?

4. What would be an appropriate thesis statement for section I?

Organization

5. Section I is obviously more loosely structured than II. How would you describe McPhee's organizational strategies in I? Is McPhee's purpose in I different from his goal in II?

Sentences

6. In section II, when McPhee finally sees the bear, he begins his next four sentences with "He." Why does he do this? Is this technique effective?
7. Describe the mix of sentence lengths in the next-to-last paragraph of section I. Does McPhee vary the typical subject-verb-object pattern? Why?

Words

8. Give your own definitions of the difficult words in the first paragraph of section II. Do your choices make the paragraph more or less effective?
9. Make a list of the verbs McPhee uses to describe the grizzly in the next-to-last paragraph of section I. What impression do these words create for you?

Suggestions for Writing

A. Recall an incident from your experience when you were afraid, nervous, or excited. Write an essay describing these circumstances by beginning with a generalization that you then support with concrete, specific details.
B. Write an informal sketch of an animal. Include generalizations based on your direct observations.

Oranges

---

1   The custom of drinking orange juice with breakfast is not very widespread, taking the world as a whole, and it is thought by many peoples to be a distinctly American habit. But many Danes drink it regularly with breakfast, and so do Hondurans, Filipinos, Jamaicans, and the wealthier citizens of Trinidad and Tobago. The day is started

with orange juice in the Colombian Andes, and, to some extent, in Kuwait. Bolivians don't touch it at breakfast time, but they drink it steadily for the rest of the day. The "play lunch," or morning tea, that Australian children carry with them to school is usually an orange, peeled spirally halfway down, with the peel replaced around the fruit. The child unwinds the peel and holds the orange as if it were an ice-cream cone. People in Nepal almost never peel oranges, preferring to eat them in cut quarters, the way American athletes do. The sour oranges of Afghanistan customarily appear as seasoning agents on Afghan dinner tables. Squeezed over Afghan food, they cut the grease. The Shamouti Orange, of Israel, is seedless and sweet, has a thick skin, and grows in Hadera, Gaza, Tiberias, Jericho, the Jordan Valley, and Jaffa; it is exported from Jaffa, and for that reason is known universally beyond Israel as the Jaffa Orange. The Jaffa Orange is the variety that British people consider superior to all others, possibly because Richard the Lionhearted spent the winter of 1191–92 in the citrus groves of Jaffa. Citrus trees are spread across the North African coast from Alexandria to Tangier, the city whose name was given to tangerines. Oranges tend to become less tart the closer they are grown to the equator, and in Brazil there is one kind of orange that has virtually no acid in it at all. In the principal towns of Trinidad and Tobago, oranges are sold on street corners. The vendor cuts them in half and sprinkles salt on them. In Jamaica, people halve oranges, get down on their hands and knees and clean floors with one half in each hand. Jamaican mechanics use oranges to clear away grease and oil. The blood orange of Spain, its flesh streaked with red, is prized throughout Europe. Blood oranges grow well in Florida, but they frighten American women. Spain has about thirty-five million orange trees, grows six billion oranges a year, and exports more oranges than any other country, including the United States. In the Campania region of Italy, land is scarce; on a typical small patch, set on a steep slope, orange trees are interspersed with olive and walnut trees, grapes are trained to cover trellises overhead, and as many as five different vegetables are grown on the ground below. The over-all effect is that a greengrocer's shop is springing out of the hillside. Italy produces more than four billion oranges a year, but most of its citrus industry is scattered in gardens of one or two acres. A Frenchman sits at the dinner table, and, as the finishing flourish of the meal, slowly and gently disrobes an orange. In France, peeling the fruit is not yet considered an inconvenience. French preferences run to the blood oranges and the Thomson Navels of Spain, and to the thick-skinned, bland *Maltaises*, which the French import not from Malta but from Tunisia. France itself only grows about four hundred thousand oranges each year, almost wholly in the Department of the *Alpes Maritimes*. Sometimes, Europeans eat oranges with knives and forks. On occasion, they serve a dessert orange that has previously been peeled with such extraordinary care that strips of the peel arc outward like the petals of a flower from the separated and reassembled segments in the center. The Swiss sometimes serve oranges under a smothering of sugar and whipped cream; on a hot day in a Swiss garden, orange juice with ice is a luxurious drink. Norwegian children like to remove the top of an orange, make a little hole, push a lump of sugar into it, and then suck out the juice. English children make orange-peel teeth and wedge them over their gums on Halloween. Irish children take oranges to the movies, where they eat them while they watch the show, tossing the peels at each other and at the people on the screen. In Reykjavik, Iceland, in greenhouses that are heated by volcanic springs, orange trees yearly bear fruit. In the New York Botanical Garden, six mature orange trees are growing in the soil of the Bronx. Their trunks are six inches in diameter, and they bear well every year. The oranges are for viewing and are not supposed to be picked. When people walk past them, however, they sometimes find them irresistible.

•••

2   Oranges and orange blossoms have long been symbols of love. Boccaccio's *Decameron*, written in the fourteenth century, is redolent with the scent of oranges and orange blossoms, with lovers who wash in orange-flower water, a courtesan who sprinkles her sheets with orange perfume, and the mournful Isabella, who cuts off the head of her dead lover, buries it in an ample pot, plants sweet basil above it, and irrigates the herbs exclusively with rosewater, orange-flower water, and tears. In the fifteenth century, the Countess Mathilda of Württemberg received from her impassioned admirer, Dr. Heinrich Steinbowel, a declaration of love in the form of a gift of two dozen oranges. Before long, titled German girls were throwing oranges down from their balconies in the way that girls in Italy or Spain were dropping handkerchiefs. After Francis I dramatically saved Marseilles from a Spanish siege, a great

feast was held for him at the city's harborside, and Marseillaise ladies, in token of their love and gratitude, pelted him with oranges. Even Nostradamus was sufficiently impressed with the sensual power of oranges to publish, in 1556, a book on how to prepare various cosmetics from oranges and orange blossoms. Limes were also used cosmetically, by ladies of the French court in the seventeenth century, who kept them on their persons and bit into them from time to time in order to redden their lips. In the nineteenth century, orange blossoms were regularly shipped to Paris in salted barrels from Provence, for no French bride wanted to be married without wearing or holding them.

• • •

3   The color of an orange has no absolute correlation with the maturity of the flesh and juice inside. An orange can be as sweet and ripe as it will ever be and still glisten like an emerald in the tree. Cold—coolness, rather—is what makes an orange orange. In some parts of the world, the weather never gets cold enough to change the color; in Thailand, for example, an orange is a green fruit, and traveling Thais often blink with wonder at the sight of oranges the color of flame. The ideal nighttime temperature in an orange grove is forty degrees. Some of the most beautiful oranges in the world are grown in Bermuda, where the temperature, night after night, falls consistently to that level. Andrew Marvell's poem wherein the "remote Bermudas ride in the ocean's bosom unespied" was written in the sixteen-fifties, and contains a description, from hearsay, of Bermuda's remarkable oranges, set against their dark foliage like "golden lamps in a green night." Cool air comes down every night into the San Joaquin Valley in California, which is formed by the Coast Range to the west and the Sierra Nevadas to the east. The tops of the Sierras are usually covered with snow, and before dawn the temperature in the valley edges down to the frost point. In such cosmetic surroundings, it is no wonder that growers have heavily implanted the San Joaquin Valley with the Washington Navel Orange, which is the most beautiful orange grown in any quantity in the United States, and is certainly as attractive to the eye as any orange grown in the world. Its color will go to a deep, flaring cadmium orange, and its surface has a suggestion of coarseness, which complements its perfect ellipsoid shape.

QUESTIONS

Ideas

1. Can you think of a generalization that would cover all the facts in paragraph 1; on what basis do they all hang together? Look carefully at the first two sentences.
2. Even though the last sentences in paragraph 1 refer specifically to the trees in the Bronx, could they serve as indirect topic sentences?
3. How would you describe the persona McPhee is using in all three paragraphs (which appear at the beginning of his book)?
4. For his opening, McPhee has decided to jump right into the uses of oranges around the world. How does this technique affect you?
5. Can you explain why oranges were used as symbols of love?

Organization

6. Should McPhee have used a more traditional introduction, stating explicitly what he intends to do?
7. After reading the first paragraph—and after catching your breath—what is your impression of how McPhee ordered his notes?
8. Is McPhee breaking the rules of paragraphing here? Are there hard-and-fast rules for professional writers or do you think they make up their own?
9. If you turned paragraph 1 in to one of your high school English teachers, what might have been the response?
10. Paragraphs 2 and 3 seem more traditional than paragraph 1. How are they organized and developed? What is the relation between the first sentence and those that follow?

Sentences

11. Typically, paragraphs cohere, that is, sentences are connected to preceding and succeeding sentences. Sometimes a writer will use explicit connecting chains, such as repeated words, synonyms, and transitional terms ("however," "but," "next," "this"). Sometimes the connections are less direct: an extension of a previous idea, a more specific example of a general notion. Pick any six consecutive sentences in "Oranges" and explain how they are bound together.

Words

12. McPhee occasionally uses metaphors and similes (direct and indirect comparisons). Find as many of these devices as you can. What is their effect? Why do writers decide to make these comparisons?

Suggestions for Writing

A. Using the information in these three paragraphs, rewrite the piece, using a conventional beginning, middle, and end. Use an explicit topic sentence and arrange your details to support this generalization.
B. Pick another fruit, or a vegetable, and after doing library research, write an essay that develops in some details an aspect (use, history, etc.) of this food.

The Pineys

---

1   While isolation in the woods was bringing out self-reliance, it was also contributing to other developments that eventually attracted more attention. After the pine towns lost touch, to a large extent, with the outside world, some of the people slid into illiteracy, and a number slid further than that. Marriages were pretty casual in the pines late in the nineteenth century and early in the twentieth. For lawful weddings, people had to travel beyond the woods, to a place like Mt. Holly. Many went to native "squires," who performed weddings for a fee of one dollar. No questions were asked, even if the squires recognized the brides and the grooms as people they had married to other people a week or a month before. Given the small population of the pines, the extreme rarity of new people coming in, and the long span of time that most families had been there, some relationships were extraordinarily complicated and a few were simply incestuous. To varying degrees, there was a relatively high incidence in the pines of what in the terms of the era was called degeneracy, feeblemindedness, or mental deficiency.

2   In 1913, startling publicity was given to the most unfortunate stratum of the pine society, and the effects have not yet faded. In that year, Elizabeth Kite, a psychological researcher, published a report called "The Pineys," which had resulted from two years of visits to cabins in the pines. Miss Kite worked for the Vineland Training School, on the southern edge of the Pine Barrens, where important early work was being done with people of subnormal intelligence, and she was a fearless young woman who wore spotless white dresses as she rode in a horse-drawn wagon through the woods. Her concern for the people there became obvious to the people themselves, who grew fond of her, and even dependent upon her, and a colony for the care of the "feebleminded" was founded in the northern part of the Pine Barrens as a result of her work. Her report told of children who shared their bedrooms with pigs, of men who could not count beyond three, of a mother who walked nine miles with her children almost every day to get whiskey, of a couple who took a wheelbarrow with them when they went out drinking, so that one could wheel the other home. "In the heart of the region, scattered in widely separated huts over miles of territory, exists today a group of human beings as distinct in morals and manners as to excite curiosity and wonder in the mind of any outsider brought into contact with them," Miss Kite wrote. "They are recognized as a distinct people by the normal communities living on the borders of their forests." The report included some extremely gnarled family trees, such as one headed by Sam Bender, who conceived a child with his daughter, Mollie Bender Brooks, whose husband, Billie Brooks, sometimes said the child had been fathered by his wife's brother rather than her father, both possibilities being strong ones. When a district nurse was sent around to help clean up Mollie's house, chickens and a pig were found in the kitchen, and the first implement used in cleaning the house was a hoe. Mollie, according to Miss Kite, was "good-looking and sprightly, which fact, coupled with an utter lack of sense of decency, made her attractive even to men of otherwise normal intelligence." When Billie and all of their children were killed in a fire, Mollie said cheerfully, "Well, they was all insured. I'm still young and can easy start another family." Miss Kite reported some relationships that are almost impossible to follow. Of the occupants of another cabin, she wrote, "That May should call John 'Uncle' could be accounted for on the basis of a childish acceptance of 'no-matter-what' conditions, for the connection was that her mother was married to the brother of John's other woman's second man, and

her mother's sister had had children by John. This bond of kinship did not, however, keep the families long together." Miss Kite also told of a woman who came to ask for food at a state almshouse on a bitter winter day. The people at the almshouse gave her a large burlap sack containing a basket of potatoes, a basket of turnips, three cabbages, four pounds of pork, five pounds of rye flour, two pounds of sugar, and some tea. The woman shouldered the sack and walked home cross-country through snow. Thirty minutes after she reached her home, she had a baby. No one helped her deliver it, nor had anyone helped her with the delivery of her nine other children.

3   Miss Kite's report was made public. Newspapers printed excerpts from it. All over the state, people became alarmed about conditions in the Pine Barrens—a region most of them had never heard of. James T. Fielder, the governor of New Jersey, travelled to the pines, returned to Trenton, and sought to increase his political momentum by recommending to the legislature that the Pine Barrens be somehow segregated from the rest of New Jersey in the interest of the health and safety of the people of the state at large. "I have been shocked at the conditions I have found," he said. "Evidently these people are a serious menace to the State of New Jersey because they produce so many persons that inevitably become public charges. They have inbred, and led lawless and scandalous lives, till they have become a race of imbeciles, criminals, and defectives." Meanwhile, H. H. Goddard, director of the research laboratory at the Vineland Training School and Miss Kite's immediate superior, had taken the genealogical charts that Miss Kite had painstakingly assembled, pondered them, extrapolated a bit, and published what became a celebrated treatise on a family called Kallikak–a name that Goddard said he had invented to avoid doing harm to real people. According to the theory set forth in the treatise, nearly all pineys were descended from one man. This man, Martin Kallikak, conceived an illegitimate son with an imbecile barmaid. Martin's bastard was said to be the forebear of generations of imbeciles, prostitutes, epileptics, and drunks. Martin himself, however, married a normal girl, and among their progeny were generations of normal and intelligent people, including doctors, lawyers, politicians, and a president of Princeton University. Goddard coined the name Kallikak from the Greek *kalós* and *kakós*—"good" and "bad." Goddard's work has been discredited, but its impact, like that of Governor Fielder's proposal to segregate the Pine Barrens, was powerful in its time. Even Miss Kite

seemed to believe that there was some common flaw in the blood of all the people of the pines. Of one pinelands woman, Miss Kite wrote, "Strangely enough, this woman belonged originally to good stock. No piney blood flowed in her veins."

⁴   The result of all this was a stigma that has never worn off. A surprising number of people in New Jersey today seem to think that the Pine Barrens are dark backlands inhabited by hostile and semi-literate people who would as soon shoot an outsider as look at him. A policeman in Trenton who had never been to the pines—"only driven through on the way downa shore," as people usually say—once told me, in an anxious tone, that if I intended to spend a lot of time in the Pine Barrens I was asking for trouble. Some of the gentlest of people— botanists, canoemen, campers—spent a great deal of time in the pines, but their influence has not been sufficient to correct an impression, vivid in some parts of the state for fifty years, that the pineys are weird and sometimes dangerous barefoot people who live in caves, marry their sisters, and eat snakes. Pineys are, for the most part, mild and shy, but their resentment is deep, and they will readily and forcefully express it. The unfortunate people that Miss Kite described in her report were a minor fraction of the total population of the Pine Barrens, and the larger number suffered from it, and are still suffering from it. This appalled Elizabeth Kite, who said to an interviewer in 1940, some years before her death, "Nothing would give me greater pleasure than to correct the idea that has unfortunately been given by the newspapers regarding the pines. Anybody who lived in the pines was a piney. I think it a most terrible calamity that the newspapers publicly took the term and gave it the degenerate sting. Those families who were not potential state cases did not interest me as far as my study was concerned. I have no language in which I can express my admiration for the pines and the people who live there."

⁵   The people of the Pine Barrens turn cold when they hear the word "piney" spoken by anyone who is not a native. Over the years since 1913, in many places outside the pines, the stigma of degeneracy has been concentrated in that word. A part of what hurts them is that they themselves are fond of the word. They refer to one another freely, and frequently, as pineys. They have a strong regional pride, and, in a way that is not at all unflattering to them, they *are* different from the run of the people of the state. A visitor who stays awhile in the Pine

Barrens soon feels that he is in another country, where attitudes and ambitions are at variance with the American norm. People who drive around in the pines and see houses like Fred Brown's, with tarpaper peeling from the walls, and automobiles overturned in the front yard, often decide, as they drive on, that they have just looked destitution in the face. I wouldn't call it that. I have yet to meet anyone living in the Pine Barrens who has in any way indicated envy of people who live elsewhere. One reason there are so many unpainted houses in the Pine Barrens is that the pineys believe, correctly, that their real-estate assessments would be higher if their houses were painted. Some pineys who make good money in blueberries or cranberries or in jobs on the outside would never think of painting their houses. People from other parts of New Jersey will say of Pine Barrens people, "They don't like to work. They can't seem to hold jobs." This, too, is a judgment based on outside values. What the piney usually says is "I hate to be tied down long to any one job." That remark is made so often in the pines that it is almost a local slogan. It expresses an attitude born of the old pines cycle—sphagnum in the spring, berries in the summer, coaling when the weather is cold. With the plenitude of the woodland around them—and, historically, behind them—pineys are bored with the idea of doing the same thing all year long, in every weather. Many of them have to, of course. Many work at regular jobs outside the woods. But many try that and give it up, preferring part-time labor—always at rest in the knowledge that no one who knows the woods and is willing to do a little work on his own is ever going to go hungry. The people have no difficulty articulating what it is that gives them a special feeling about the landscape they live in; they know that their environment is unusual and they know why they value it. Some, of course, put it with more finesse than others do. "I'm just a woods boy," a fellow named Jim Leek said to me one day. "There ain't nobody bothers you here. You can be alone. I'm just a woods boy. I wouldn't want to live in a town." When he said "town," he meant one of the small communities in the pines; he preferred living in the woods to living in a Pine Barrens town. When pineys talk about going to "the city," they usually mean Mt. Holly or the Moorestown Mall or the Two Guys from Harrison store on Route 206. When Jim Leek said "nobody bothers you" and "you can be alone," he was sounding two primary themes of the pines. Bill Wasovwich said one day, "The woods just look nice and it's more

quieter. It's quiet anywhere in the pines. That's why I like it here."
Another man, Scorchy Jones, who works for the state Fish and Game
Division, said this to an interviewer from a small New Jersey radio
station: "A sense of security is high among us. We were from pioneers.
We know how to survive in the woods. Here in these woods areas, you
have a reputation. A dishonest person can't survive in the community.
You have to maintain your reputation, or you would have to jump
from place to place. A man lives by his reputation and by his honesty
and by his ambition to work. If he doesn't have it, he would be an
outcast. These people have the reputations of their parents and grandparents ahead of them—and they are proud of them, and they want to
maintain that same standard. They don't worship gold. All they want
is necessities. They would rather live than make a lot of money. They
live by this code. They're the best citizens in this country." Later in the
interview, Jones said, "Unless these wild areas are preserved, we're going
to get to the point where dense population is going to work on the
nervous systems of the people, and the more that takes place, the poorer
neighbors they become. Eventually, like birds or animals confined to
too small an area, they will fight among themselves. Man is an animal
as well." People known in the pines as "the old-time pineys"—those
who lived wholly by the cycle, and seldom, if ever, saw an outsider—
are gone now. When the United States Army built Camp Dix on the
northwestern edge of the Pine Barrens during the First World War,
civilian jobs were created, and many people of the pines first got to
know what money was and how to use it. Paved roads first crossed the
pines in the nineteen-twenties. Electrical lines, the Second World War,
and television successively brought an end to the utter isolation of the
pineys. But so far all this has not materially changed their attitudes.
They are apparently a tolerant people, with an attractive spirit of live
and let live. They seem to like hard work, if not steady work, and they
like to brag about working hard. When they say they will do something,
they do it. They seem shy, like the people who went before them, but
when they get to know an outsider they are not shy and will generously
share their tables, which often include new-potato stews and cranberry
potpies. I have met Pine Barrens people who have, at one time or
another, moved to other parts of the country. Most of them tried other
lives for a while, only to return unreluctantly to the pines. One of them
explained to me, "It's a privilege to live in these woods."

QUESTIONS

Ideas

1. How do you explain the behavior of the pineys?
2. What function does Miss Kite serve in this piece?
3. Do you think Mollie is amoral? What principles do the pineys operate on? Do they have a morality or a code that they follow?
4. Do you think it was unusual for the newspapers to have given the pineys such negative publicity?
5. What do you think McPhee thinks about the pineys? How can you tell? Look especially at the extended quotes he uses.
6. If you regarded this piece as a research essay (which, of course, it is), you might find it profitable to examine McPhee's way of integrating facts, details, quotes, dialogue, narration, and commentary into a seamless whole. At the end of this piece the reader knows a good deal. Jot down in phrases what you remember from a first reading, then go back and read the piece again, noting the amount of information McPhee is able to blend almost unnoticed into his account.

Organization

7. As Aristotle perceptively noted, effective pieces of writing tend to have a beginning, a middle, and an end. Composition textbooks often say an introduction, a body, and a conclusion. What kind of pattern is being used here?
8. Can you point to a thematic sentence that suggests the focus of this piece?
9. Look at the first sentence in each paragraph. What function does it serve?

Sentences

10. Is the first sentence in each paragraph shorter than the others, on the average? What might be a reason for this?
11. Notice how McPhee weaves quotes into his sentences to give them authority and force. Based on the second paragraph, write some general rules for using quotes. Include the use of commas, capital letters, and quote marks, and note especially McPhee's technique of using a quote as part of his sentence.

Words

12. What emotional association do you have to these words: "feebleminded-ness," "mental deficiency," "imbeciles," and "degenerate." Can such con-notations be changed?

Suggestions for Writing

A. Interview someone in class on a specific topic (favorite guitar player, sports hero, whatever). Copy down exact quotes and indirect quotes (exact mean-ing but not the specific words used). Now write up the interview using the quotes. Blend as many of the quotes as you can into your own sentences.
B. Do some focused research on a group that typically gets bad publicity. In writing your brief research essay arrange your facts and quotes so as to convey your attitude toward the group. (It can, of course, be positive or negative.)

SEVEN

Joan Didion

(1934–   )

Joan Didion writes to understand herself and her culture. For her writing is a tool, a way to overcome the randomness of life and to create order and clarity. Writing can do that. It can help us give shape to experience. In fact, one cognitive skill that separates us from primitive cultures is our ability to create an identity, a special voice for ourself by writing down what we think about things.

If you lived in a traditional culture, your identity would be given to you. You would not think of shaping and interpreting your experience, and you would not even imagine that you could create new and important ways of looking at the world. In highly literate societies, however, writers do just that. Didion is often striving for greater self-knowledge through her essays. She does not accept what is given to her by the media, her parents, or school. She is exploring and searching for her own understanding of the world through language. In advanced societies, like ours, writing can be a powerful tool for knowing.

But Didion goes even further than that. She begins one of her essays, "The White Album" (after the famous 1968 Beatles double album), with this provocative sentence: "We tell ourselves stories in order to live." Isn't she implying that giving shape and meaning to our lives through writing is necessary and vital? When we see and read about events, we can impose a structure and significance on them through writing. As a result, we really begin to know them. This is what E. M. Forster meant when he said, "How do I know what I think until I see what I say?" Our experiences and ideas exist as shapeless, half-articulated thoughts and

151

impressions until we impose order on them through writing. Didion continues: "We interpret what we see, select the most workable of the multiple choices. We live entirely, especially if we are writers, by the imposition of a narrative line upon disparate images, by the 'ideas' with which we have learned to freeze the shifting phantasmagoria which is our actual experience."

That sounds positive and encouraging. Writing, unlike speech, freezes our experiences and our ideas and helps us to see, to understand, to contemplate what we have written. Then we can look back and revise; we can get to the center of things, the heart of the matter. And in doing so, Didion refines and strengthens her voice and her sense of self.

Although Didion is a reporter, she is not strictly a journalist. In *The White Album*, for example, she gives us vivid and representative snapshots of life in the 1960s. But these are subjective reports, usually offered without commentary. She does not tie things together in neat bundles, and she is clearly not trying to be objective. She wants readers to fit the pieces together to form their own pictures, their own understanding, their own theme. She is a witness to important truths about our culture, but she does not usually present her findings explicitly. In "The White Album" and "Marrying Absurd" she makes her points by carefully selecting details and placing them in precisely the right place. The reader must do the rest.

Didion's prose style is also understated, almost indirect. She gives the impression of being in control, of withholding strong emotion. And she can be direct "without being trivial or colloquial." The following two sentences from "Goodbye to All That" are typical of her spare, elegant prose: "All I know is that it was very bad when I was twenty-eight. Everything that was said to me I seemed to have heard before, and I could no longer listen." The directness of these lines makes a promise to the reader. Didion is not hiding behind elaborately complex sentences or difficult vocabulary. Such clear, strong writing does not come naturally to anyone. Didion had to work at it, long and hard. Like all writers, regardless of ability or success, Didion worries about her ability to "get it right." Her solution is both simple and rigorous: revise, cut, rearrange, rework—again and again. The hard work pays off in the bite and authority of her exact prose.

Some of this concern for stylistic precision she learned as a student, from reading Hemingway:

> I learned a lot about how sentences worked. How a short sentence worked. How they worked in a paragraph. Where the commas worked. How every word had to matter. It made me excited about words. . . . When I was fifteen or sixteen I would type out his stories . . . I mean they're perfect sentences. Very direct sentences, smooth rivers, clear water over granite, no sinkholes.

After she graduated from the University of California, Berkeley, in 1956 with a degree in English, she wrote for such national magazines as *Mademoiselle, Saturday Evening Post,* and *Life.* Early in her career she worked on *Vogue's* editorial staff. Later, she commented that she learned how verbs work from a senior editor there: "Every day I would go into her office with eight lines of copy or a caption or something. She would sit there and mark it up with a pencil and get very angry about extra words, about verbs not working. . . . In an eight-line caption everything had to work, every word, every comma."

She went on to publish a novel, *Run River,* in 1963. Then, after having spent about eight years in New York, she moved back to California, where she still lives with her husband, the novelist John Gregory Dunne. She wrote about the move: "We took an afternoon flight back to Los Angeles, and on the way home from the airport that night I could see the moon on the Pacific and smell jasmine all around and we both knew that there was no longer any point in keeping the apartment we still kept in New York." Although she continued to write interesting novels (*Play It As It Lays* and *The Book of Common Prayer*), she has received most acclaim for her two nonfiction collections, *Slouching Towards Bethlehem* (1968) and *The White Album* (1979).

Probably because her family has lived in Sacramento for generations, Didion is concerned with traditional values in conflict with modern life-styles, with what we've lost and what we still have in America. She is afraid that "the children of the aerospace engineers" who "have never met a great-aunt" will "have lost the real past and gained a man-

ufactured one, and there will be no way for them to know,
no way at all." But even this nostalgia cannot withstand her
passion for a deeper, more personal truth. She continues:
"But perhaps it is presumptuous of me to assume that they
will be missing something. Perhaps in retrospect this has
been a story not about Sacramento at all, but about the
things we lose and the promises we break as we grow older;
perhaps I have been playing out unawares the Margaret in
the poem:

Margaret, are you grieving
Over Goldengrove unleaving? . . .
It is the blight man was born for,
It is Margaret you mourn for.

There is no doubt that Didion often despairs about
the fragmentation and banality of contemporary American
life, but the clarity and energy of her writing suggest that
she has found an antidote to inconclusiveness and plastic
values.

In Bed

1   Three, four, sometimes five times a month, I spend the
day in bed with a migraine headache, insensible to the world around
me. Almost every day of every month, between these attacks, I feel the
sudden irrational irritation and the flush of blood into the cerebral
arteries which tell me that migraine is on its way, and I take certain
drugs to avert its arrival. If I did not take the drugs, I would be able to
function perhaps one day in four. The physiological error called migraine is, in brief, central to the given of my life. When I was 15, 16,
even 25, I used to think that I could rid myself of this error by simply
denying it, character over chemistry. "Do you have headaches *sometimes? frequently? never?*" the application forms would demand. "Check
one." Wary of the trap, wanting whatever it was that the successful
circumnavigation of that particular form could bring (a job, a schol-

arship, the respect of mankind and the grace of God), I would check one. "*Sometimes,*" I would lie. That in fact I spent one or two days a week almost unconscious with pain seemed a shameful secret, evidence not merely of some chemical inferiority but of all my bad attitudes, unpleasant tempers, wrongthink.

2   For I had no brain tumor, no eyestrain, no high blood pressure, nothing wrong with me at all: I simply had migraine headaches, and migraine headaches were, as everyone who did not have them knew, imaginary. I fought migraine then, ignored the warnings it sent, went to school and later to work in spite of it, sat through lectures in Middle English and presentations to advertisers with involuntary tears running down the right side of my face, threw up in washrooms, stumbled home by instinct, emptied ice trays onto my bed and tried to freeze the pain in my right temple, wished only for a neurosurgeon who would do a lobotomy on house call, and cursed my imagination.

3   It was a long time before I began thinking mechanistically enough to accept migraine for what it was: something with which I would be living, the way some people live with diabetes. Migraine is something more than the fancy of a neurotic imagination. It is an essentially hereditary complex of symptoms, the most frequently noted but by no means the most unpleasant of which is a vascular headache of blinding severity, suffered by a surprising number of women, a fair number of men (Thomas Jefferson had migraine, and so did Ulysses S. Grant, the day he accepted Lee's surrender), and by some unfortunate children as young as two years old. (I had my first when I was eight. It came on during a fire drill at the Columbia School in Colorado Springs, Colorado. I was taken first home and then to the infirmary at Peterson Field, where my father was stationed. The Air Corps doctor prescribed an enema.) Almost anything can trigger a specific attack of migraine: stress, allergy, fatigue, an abrupt change in barometric pressure, a contretemps over a parking ticket. A flashing light. A fire drill. One inherits, of course, only the predisposition. In other words I spent yesterday in bed with a headache not merely because of my bad attitudes, unpleasant tempers and wrongthink, but because both my grandmothers had migraine, my father has migraine and my mother has migraine.

4   No one knows precisely what it is that is inherited. The chemistry of migraine, however, seems to have some connection with the nerve hormone named serotonin, which is naturally present in the brain. The amount of serotonin in the blood falls sharply at the onset of migraine,

and one migraine drug, methysergide, or Sansert, seems to have some effect on serotonin. Methysergide is a derivative of lysergic acid (in fact Sandoz Pharmaceuticals first synthesized LSD-25 while looking for a migraine cure), and its use is hemmed about with so many contraindications and side effects that most doctors prescribe it only in the most incapacitating cases. Methysergide, when it is prescribed, is taken daily, as a preventive; another preventive which works for some people is old-fashioned ergotamine tartrate, which helps to constrict the swelling blood vessels during the "aura," the period which in most cases precedes the actual headache.

5   Once an attack is under way, however, no drug touches it. Migraine gives some people mild hallucinations, temporarily blinds others, shows up not only as a headache but as a gastrointestinal disturbance, a painful sensitivity to all sensory stimuli, an abrupt overpowering fatigue, a strokelike aphasia, and a crippling inability to make even the most routine connections. When I am in a migraine aura (for some people the aura lasts fifteen minutes, for others several hours), I will drive through red lights, lose the house keys, spill whatever I am holding, lose the ability to focus my eyes or frame coherent sentences, and generally give the appearance of being on drugs, or drunk. The actual headache, when it comes, brings with it chills, sweating, nausea, a debility that seems to stretch the very limits of endurance. That no one dies of migraine seems, to someone deep into an attack, an ambiguous blessing.

6   My husband also has migraine, which is unfortunate for him but fortunate for me: perhaps nothing so tends to prolong an attack as the accusing eye of someone who has never had a headache. "Why not take a couple of aspirin," the unafflicted will say from the doorway, or "I'd have a headache, too, spending a beautiful day like this inside with all the shades drawn." All of us who have migraine suffer not only from the attacks themselves but from this common conviction that we are perversely refusing to cure ourselves by taking a couple of aspirin, that we are making ourselves sick, that we "bring it on ourselves." And in the most immediate sense, the sense of why we have a headache this Tuesday and not last Thursday, of course we often do. There certainly is what doctors call a "migraine personality," and that personality tends to be ambitious, inward, intolerant of error, rather rigidly organized, perfectionist. "You don't look like a migraine personality," a doctor once said to me. "Your hair's messy. But I suppose you're a compulsive

housekeeper." Actually my house is kept even more negligently than my hair, but the doctor was right nonetheless: perfectionism can also take the form of spending most of a week writing and rewriting and not writing a single paragraph.

7   But not all perfectionists have migraine, and not all migrainous people have migraine personalities. We do not escape heredity. I have tried in most of the available ways to escape my own migrainous heredity (at one point I learned to give myself two daily injections of histamine with a hypodermic needle, even though the needle so frightened me that I had to close my eyes when I did it), but I still have migraine. And I have learned now to live with it, learned when to expect it, how to outwit it, even how to regard it, when it does come, as more friend than lodger. We have reached a certain understanding, my migraine and I. It never comes when I am in real trouble. Tell me that my house is burned down, my husband has left me, that there is gunfighting in the streets and panic in the banks, and I will not respond by getting a headache. It comes instead when I am fighting not an open but a guerrilla war with my own life, during weeks of small household confusions, lost laundry, unhappy help, canceled appointments, on days when the telephone rings too much and I get no work done and the wind is coming up. On days like that my friend comes uninvited.

8   And once it comes, now that I am wise in its ways, I no longer fight it. I lie down and let it happen. At first every small apprehension is magnified, every anxiety a pounding terror. Then the pain comes, and I concentrate only on that. Right there is the usefulness of migraine, there in that imposed yoga, the concentration on the pain. For when the pain recedes, ten or twelve hours later, everything goes with it, all the hidden resentments, all the vain anxieties. The migraine has acted as a circuit breaker, and the fuses have emerged intact. There is a pleasant convalescent euphoria. I open the windows and feel the air, eat gratefully, sleep well. I notice the particular nature of a flower in a glass on the stair landing. I count my blessings.

QUESTIONS

Ideas

1. What has Didion learned from her experiences with migraine headaches? What is the theme, the point of the last paragraph?

2. Why does she "eat gratefully," and why does she count her blessings? What does the last sentence imply about suffering? Are we wiser because of difficulty and illness?

3. Has Didion's essay changed your attitude about people who complain about migraine headaches? Has it made you more sympathetic toward them? Why or why not?

Organization

4. What is Didion trying to do in each paragraph? Look carefully at the last sentence in each paragraph and the first one in the next. What transitional device does she use to blend them together? Does she repeat words or ideas? Does she use pronouns or synonyms?

5. In the last paragraph, what coherence relationship ("and," "but," "for," "so," "or," and the colon) exists between each sentence? Count the number of words in each sentence. Is there a pattern?

Sentences

6. How many sentences begin with "and" or "but"? Why? Are those sentences clear and effective? Are there sentences here that do not contain a subject and a verb? What effect is Didion trying for by doing this? Does it work?

7. In paragraph 2, sentence 3, Didion uses a compound sentence (two clauses that can be used separately as sentences). Are there other examples of sentences like this, joined by a conjunction and a comma?

8. Didion begins a definition of migraine in paragraph 3 and continues for two more paragraphs. What kinds of details does she include in each paragraph? Why?

9. How useful and how important are the personal details she includes?

10. Paragraph 6 makes extensive use of quotation—of casual remarks heard in conversation. Why are those quoted comments included? How effective are they?

11. What is the purpose of the contrasting examples in paragraph 9? How well do they illustrate Didion's point?

Words

12. Look up the definition of migraine in a dictionary, then in a medical encyclopedia. What is the purpose of each definition? How do they compare with Didion's definition? What is involved in defining a word? What part

does the purpose of the writer play? How does the audience change the way you define something?

13. Look up three of the scientific words that Didion uses. How would you redefine them for a fifth-grade student?

Suggestions for Writing

A. Write a brief sentence outline for this eight-paragraph essay, using one generalization for each paragraph.

B. Rewrite a compound sentence as a simple sentence, then as a complex sentence with an independent and a dependent clause.

C. The final sentence of the first paragraph uses a long clause beginning with "That." Write an imitation, using your own vocabulary. Do the same for the last sentence of paragraph 5.

D. Paragraph 2 contains only two sentences, but the second sentence is quite long. It contains ten clauses with verbs carrying the action. Rewrite the sentence as four or five short sentences. What is different about the rewritten passage? Then try an imitation of this verb-stacked sentence.

E. Write an essay about a difficulty or problem you lived through. Like Didion, try to be specific about what happened to you, how others reacted to you, and what that difficulty or problem told you about yourself or about others.

F. How would you define migraine for a second grader, for a high school biology student, for a psychology student in college?

G. Write an essay in which you try to explain something about yourself that others just don't understand. Try to get your readers to see your side of the issue and to come away with a better understanding of some facet of your personality or some element of your behavior.

Marrying Absurd

1   To be married in Las Vegas, Clark County, Nevada, a bride must swear that she is eighteen or has parental permission and a bridegroom that he is twenty-one or has parental permission. Someone

must put up five dollars for the license. (On Sundays and holidays, fifteen dollars. The Clark County Courthouse issues marriage licenses at any time of the day or night except between noon and one in the afternoon, between eight and nine in the evening, and between four and five in the morning.) Nothing else is required. The State of Nevada, alone among these United States, demands neither a premarital blood test nor a waiting period before or after the issuance of a marriage license. Driving in across the Mojave from Los Angeles, one sees the signs way out on the desert, looming up from that moonscape of rattlesnakes and mesquite, even before the Las Vegas lights appear like a mirage on the horizon: "GETTING MARRIED? Free License Information First Strip Exit." Perhaps the Las Vegas wedding industry achieved its peak operational efficiency between 9:00 p.m. and midnight of August 26, 1965, an otherwise unremarkable Thursday which happened to be, by Presidential order, the last day on which anyone could improve his draft status merely by getting married. One hundred and seventy-one couples were pronounced man and wife in the name of Clark County and the State of Nevada that night, sixty-seven of them by a single justice of the peace, Mr. James A. Brennan. Mr. Brennan did one wedding at the Dunes and the other sixty-six in his office, and charged each couple eight dollars. One bride lent her veil to six others. "I got it down from five to three minutes," Mr. Brennan said later of his feat. "I could've married them *en masse*, but they're people, not cattle. People expect more when they get married."

2   What people who get married in Las Vegas actually do expect—what, in the largest sense, their "expectations" are—strikes one as a curious and self-contradictory business. Las Vegas is the most extreme and allegorical of American settlements, bizarre and beautiful in its venality and in its devotion to immediate gratification, a place the tone of which is set by mobsters and call girls and ladies' room attendants with amyl nitrite poppers in their uniform pockets. Almost everyone notes that there is no "time" in Las Vegas, no night and no day and no past and no future (no Las Vegas casino, however, has taken the obliteration of the ordinary time sense quite so far as Harold's Club in Reno, which for a while issued, at odd intervals in the day and night, mimeographed "bulletins" carrying news from the world outside); neither is there any logical sense of where one is. One is standing on a highway in the middle of a vast hostile desert looking at an eighty-foot sign which blinks "STARDUST" or "CAESAR'S PALACE." Yes, but what

does that explain? This geographical implausibility reinforces the sense that what happens there has no connection with "real" life; Nevada cities like Reno and Carson are ranch towns, Western towns, places behind which there is some historical imperative. But Las Vegas seems to exist only in the eye of the beholder. All of which makes it an extraordinarily stimulating and interesting place, but an odd one in which to want to wear a candlelight satin Priscilla of Boston wedding dress with Chantilly lace insets, tapered sleeves and a detachable modified train.

3   And yet the Las Vegas wedding business seems to appeal to precisely that impulse. "Sincere and Dignified Since 1954," one wedding chapel advertises. There are nineteen such wedding chapels in Las Vegas, intensely competitive, each offering better, faster, and, by implication, more sincere services than the next: Our Photos Best Anywhere, Your Wedding on A Phonograph Record, Candlelight with Your Ceremony, Honeymoon Accommodations, Free Transportation from Your Motel to Courthouse to Chapel and Return to Motel, Religious or Civil Ceremonies, Dressing Rooms, Flowers, Rings, Announcements, Witnesses Available, and Ample Parking. All of these services, like most others in Las Vegas (sauna baths, payroll-check cashing, chinchilla coats for sale or rent) are offered twenty-four hours a day, seven days a week, presumably on the premise that marriage, like craps, is a game to be played when the table seems hot.

4   But what strikes one most about the Strip chapels, with their wishing wells and stained-glass paper windows and their artificial bouvardia, is that so much of their business is by no means a matter of simple convenience, of late-night liaisons between show girls and baby Crosbys. Of course there is some of that. (One night about eleven o'clock in Las Vegas I watched a bride in an orange minidress and masses of flame-colored hair stumble from a Strip chapel on the arm of her bridegroom, who looked the part of the expendable nephew in movies like *Miami Syndicate*. "I gotta get the kids," the bride whimpered. "I gotta pick up the sitter, I gotta get to the midnight show." "What you gotta get," the bridegroom said, opening the door of a Cadillac Coupe de Ville and watching her crumple on the seat, "is sober.") But Las Vegas seems to offer something other than "convenience"; it is merchandising "niceness," the facsimile of proper ritual, to children who do not know how else to find it, how to make the arrangements, how to do it "right." All day and evening long on the

Strip, one sees actual wedding parties, waiting under the harsh lights
at a crosswalk, standing uneasily in the parking lot of the Frontier while
the photographer hired by The Little Church of the West ("Wedding
Place of the Stars") certifies the occasion, takes the picture: the bride
in a veil and white satin pumps, the bridegroom usually in a white
dinner jacket, and even an attendant or two, a sister or a best friend in
hot-pink *peau de soie*, a flirtation veil, a carnation nosegay. "When I
Fall in Love It Will Be Forever," the organist plays, and then a few
bars of Lohengrin. The mother cries; the stepfather, awkward in his
role, invites the chapel hostess to join them for a drink at the Sands.
The hostess declines with a professional smile; she has already transferred
her interest to the group waiting outside. One bride out, another in,
and again the sign goes up on the chapel door: "One moment please—
Wedding."

5   I sat next to one such wedding party in a Strip restaurant the last
time I was in Las Vegas. The marriage had just taken place; the bride
still wore her dress, the mother her corsage. A bored waiter poured out
a few swallows of pink champagne ("on the house") for everyone but
the bride, who was too young to be served. "You'll need something
with more kick than that," the bride's father said with heavy jocularity
to his new son-in-law; the ritual jokes about the wedding night had a
certain Panglossian character, since the bride was clearly several months
pregnant. Another round of pink champagne, this time not on the
house, and the bride began to cry. "It was just as nice," she sobbed,
"as I hoped and dreamed it would be."

QUESTIONS

Ideas

1. Didion jumps into this essay without the usual introductory announcement
   of the theme. Does she, in fact, give us one later on? What is it, in your
   own words?

2. What contrast does Didion hope the reader will see between the "candlelight
   satin . . . wedding dress" and the Las Vegas chapels? Just what does Las
   Vegas have to offer these young people? Is it false or real? Does that matter
   to them? To Didion? To you? You need to consider the implications of
   the title, of course.

3. What is Didion's purpose in the essay? To entertain? To persuade? To ridicule? What is she suggesting about Las Vegas marriages and about the cast of characters involved in them? On a more general level, what does the contrast between the traditional "Norman Rockwell" wedding and the chapels in Las Vegas suggest about America? Is this the same theme Didion develops in "On Going Home"?

4. Are we meant to laugh at the scene in the last paragraph?

5. On a more abstract level, what is the function of ritual in our lives? Can we do without it? Should we?

Organization

6. Didion organized this piece as a blend of description, narration, and exposition. She provides the essay with a narrative frame: we begin with Mr. Brennan, then comes the show girl section, and then the final paragraph. How effective is this structure? Could Didion have organized the essay differently? How?

7. Notice the connecting devices between each of the paragraphs. What is the connection between the first and last sentences of paragraph 2? Between the first sentence of paragraph 2 and the last sentence of paragraph 1?

8. Paragraph 2 has a different function than paragraphs 1 and 3. And it contains a different kind of information. How does that information help us to understand the details of the first and third paragraphs?

Sentences

9. Didion makes extensive use of direct quotation in this essay. Three paragraphs, in fact, end with a direct statement (1, 4, and 5). What is the effect of these quotations?

10. Do the sentences in the second paragraph seem more complicated than those in either the first or last? What might be the reason for this?

Words

11. When Didion uses a simile in comparing marriage in Las Vegas to playing craps (paragraph 3), what does the use of that device suggest about her attitude toward the Strip chapels? What other comparisons does she use, and what is she implying by the comparisons?

12. Is the title effective? Can you think of an alternate title? How about "Marriage in Las Vegas"? Is Didion's title better? Why or why not?

13. Irony is often conveyed by writing one thing but meaning another. We are not, it seems, meant to be impressed by Mr. Brennan's concern for the individual just because he doesn't marry people en masse. Didion uses irony throughout her essay for a variety of purposes. What are some other examples of Didion's use of irony? Look especially at the last paragraph. What effect is she trying to achieve? Does she assume you will agree with her view of the people in Las Vegas? Do you? Would the bride of the last paragraph agree with the thesis of this essay? Why does she cry? Does the last sentence surprise you?

Suggestions for Writing

A. Try rewriting one or two quotations (from paragraphs 1, 4, or 5), converting the direct speech into an indirectly reported statement without quotation marks. Which do you prefer? What is different about them?

B. Write an essay combining narration and description about a place you have a strong feeling about. Try to let the details indicate what your attitude is, i.e., avoid stating an explicit theme while still communicating a central impression.

C. Write an essay about something you are critical of—violent sports, TV game shows, political conventions, shopping centers, fast-food eateries, commercials, whatever. Try to describe your subject without explicitly stating your viewpoint and attitude. Carefully select specific details to convey your point by implication. When you read your essay to a friend, ask him or her to state your attitude. See how close it comes to your intentions. Perhaps you will want to select new details or add to those you have after receiving this feedback.

On Self-Respect

1 Once, in a dry season, I wrote in large letters across two pages of a notebook that innocence ends when one is stripped of the delusion that one likes oneself. Although now, some years later, I marvel that a mind on the outs with itself should have nonetheless made

painstaking record of its every tremor, I recall with embarrassing clarity the flavor of those particular ashes. It was a matter of misplaced self-respect.

2   I had not been elected to Phi Beta Kappa. This failure could scarcely have been more predictable or less ambiguous (I simply did not have the grades), but I was unnerved by it; I had somehow thought myself a kind of academic Raskolnikov, curiously exempt from the cause-effect relationships which hampered others. Although even the humorless nineteen-year-old that I was must have recognized that the situation lacked real tragic stature, the day that I did not make Phi Beta Kappa nonetheless marked the end of something, and innocence may well be the word for it. I lost the conviction that lights would always turn green for me, the pleasant certainty that those rather passive virtues which had won me approval as a child automatically guaranteed me not only Phi Beta Kappa keys but happiness, honor, and the love of a good man; lost a certain touching faith in the totem power of good manners, clean hair, and proven competence on the Stanford-Binet scale. To such doubtful amulets had my self-respect been pinned, and I faced myself that day with the nonplused apprehension of someone who has come across a vampire and has no crucifix at hand.

3   Although to be driven back upon oneself is an uneasy affair at best, rather like trying to cross a border with borrowed credentials, it seems to me now the one condition necessary to the beginnings of real self-respect. Most of our platitudes notwithstanding, self-deception remains the most difficult deception. The tricks that work on others count for nothing in that very well-lit back alley where one keeps assignations with oneself: no winning smiles will do here, no prettily drawn lists of good intentions. One shuffles flashily but in vain through one's marked cards—the kindness done for the wrong reason, the apparent triumph which involved no real effort, the seemingly heroic act into which one had been shamed. The dismal fact is that self-respect has nothing to do with the approval of others—who are, after all, deceived easily enough; has nothing to do with reputation, which, as Rhett Butler told Scarlett O'Hara, is something people with courage can do without.

4   To do without self-respect, on the other hand, is to be an unwilling audience of one to an interminable documentary that details one's failings, both real and imagined, with fresh footage spliced in for every screening. *There's the glass you broke in anger, there's the hurt on X's*

*face; watch now, this next scene, the night Y came back from Houston,
see how you muff this one.* To live without self-respect is to lie awake
some night, beyond the reach of warm milk, phenobarbital, and the
sleeping hand on the coverlet, counting up the sins of commission
and omission, the trusts betrayed, the promises subtly broken, the gifts
irrevocably wasted through sloth or cowardice or carelessness. However long we postpone it, we eventually lie down alone in that notori-
ously uncomfortable bed, the one we make ourselves. Whether or
not we sleep in it depends, of course, on whether or not we respect ourselves.

5   To protest that some fairly improbable people, some people who
could not possibly respect themselves, seem to sleep easily enough is to
miss the point entirely, as surely as those people miss it who think that
self-respect has necessarily to do with not having safety pins in one's
underwear. There is a common superstition that "self-respect" is a kind
of charm against snakes, something that keeps those who have it locked
in some unblighted Eden, out of strange beds, ambivalent conversations, and trouble in general. It does not at all. It has nothing to do
with the face of things, but concerns instead a separate peace, a private
reconciliation. Although the careless, suicidal Julian English in *Ap-
pointment in Samarra* and the careless, incurably dishonest Jordan
Baker in *The Great Gatsby* seem equally improbable candidates for self-
respect, Jordan Baker had it, Julian English did not. With that genius
for accommodation more often seen in women than in men, Jordan
took her own measure, made her own peace, avoided threats to that
peace: "I hate careless people," she told Nick Carraway. "It takes two
to make an accident."

6   Like Jordan Baker, people with self-respect have the courage of
their mistakes. They know the price of things. If they choose to commit
adultery, they do not then go running, in an access of bad conscience,
to receive absolution from the wronged parties; nor do they complain
unduly of the unfairness, the undeserved embarrassment, of being
named co-respondent. In brief, people with self-respect exhibit a certain
toughness, a kind of moral nerve; they display what was once called
character, a quality which, although approved in the abstract, sometimes
loses ground to other, more instantly negotiable virtues. The measure
of its slipping prestige is that one tends to think of it only in connection

with homely children and United States senators who have been defeated, preferably in the primary, for reelection. Nonetheless, character—the willingness to accept responsibility for one's own life—is the source from which self-respect springs.

7   Self-respect is something that our grandparents, whether or not they had it, knew all about. They had instilled in them, young, a certain discipline, the sense that one lives by doing things one does not particularly want to do, by putting fears and doubts to one side, by weighing immediate comforts against the possibility of larger, even intangible, comforts. It seemed to the nineteenth century admirable, but not remarkable, that Chinese Gordon put on a clean white suit and held Khartoum against the Mahdi; it did not seem unjust that the way to free land in California involved death and difficulty and dirt. In a diary kept during the winter of 1846, an emigrating twelve-year-old named Narcissa Cornwall noted coolly: "Father was busy reading and did not notice that the house was being filled with strange Indians until Mother spoke about it." Even lacking any clue as to what Mother said, one can scarcely fail to be impressed by the entire incident: the father reading, the Indians filing in, the mother choosing the words that would not alarm, the child duly recording the event and noting further that those particular Indians were not, "fortunately for us," hostile. Indians were simply part of the *donnée*.

8   In one guise or another, Indians always are. Again, it is a question of recognizing that anything worth having has its price. People who respect themselves are willing to accept the risk that the Indians will be hostile, that the venture will go bankrupt, that the liaison may not turn out to be one in which *every day is a holiday because you're married to me*. They are willing to invest something of themselves; they may not play at all, but when they do play, they know the odds.

9   That kind of self-respect is a discipline, a habit of mind that can never be faked but can be developed, trained, coaxed forth. It was once suggested to me that, as an antidote to crying, I put my head in a paper bag. As it happens, there is a sound physiological reason, something to do with oxygen, for doing exactly that, but the psychological effect alone is incalculable: it is difficult in the extreme to continue fancying oneself Cathy in *Wuthering Heights* with one's head in a Food Fair bag. There is a similar case for all the small disciplines, unimportant

in themselves; imagine maintaining any kind of swoon, commiserative or carnal, in a cold shower.

10 But those small disciplines are valuable only insofar as they represent larger ones. To say that Waterloo was won on the playing fields of Eton is not to say that Napoleon might have been saved by a crash program in cricket; to give formal dinners in the rain forest would be pointless did not the candlelight flickering on the liana call forth deeper, stronger disciplines, values instilled long before. It is a kind of ritual, helping us to remember who and what we are. In order to remember it, one must have known it.

11 To have that sense of one's intrinsic worth which constitutes self-respect is potentially to have everything: the ability to discriminate, to love and to remain indifferent. To lack it is to be locked within oneself, paradoxically incapable of either love or indifference. If we do not respect ourselves, we are on the one hand forced to despise those who have so few resources as to consort with us, so little perception as to remain blind to our fatal weaknesses. On the other, we are peculiarly in thrall to everyone we see, curiously determined to live out—since our self-image is untenable—their false notions of us. We flatter ourselves by thinking this compulsion to please others an attractive trait: a gist for imaginative empathy, evidence of our willingness to give. *Of course* I will play Francesca to your Paolo, Helen Keller to anyone's Annie Sullivan: no expectation is too misplaced, no role too ludicrous. At the mercy of those we cannot but hold in contempt, we play roles doomed to failure before they are begun, each defeat generating fresh despair at the urgency of divining and meeting the next demand made upon us.

12 It is the phenomenon sometimes called "alienation from self." In its advanced stages, we no longer answer the telephone, because someone might want something; that we could say *no* without drowning in self-reproach is an idea alien to this game. Every encounter demands too much, tears the nerves, drains the will, and the specter of something as small as an unanswered letter arouses such disproportionate guilt that answering it becomes out of the question. To assign unanswered letters their proper weight, to free us from the expectations of others, to give us back to ourselves—there lies the great, the singular power of self-respect. Without it, one eventually discovers the final turn of the screw: one runs away to find oneself, and finds no one at home.

QUESTIONS

Ideas

1. Essentially, this essay works toward a definition, an extended personal definition of self-respect. What are the essential characteristics of self-respect in Didion's view? Did she leave anything out? Is any one of these elements of her definition more important than the others? Which one? Why?

2. Do you like Didion's definition? Did it surprise you? Is it too subjective, embedded as it is in her own emotional life, or does it seem objective enough to apply to many people?

3. Can you underline a generalization, a broad statement that might serve as the theme or thesis of the essay? Then try to state, in your words, the central idea of the essay.

4. Why, according to Didion, is self-respect so important? Do you agree?

Organization

5. Take another look at how this piece is put together. Does it have a clear plan?

6. Why does Didion begin so personally? Where does the essay become more objective? How did you decide this?

7. Why are there three divisions in the essay? What is the purpose of each section? What is the relationship of each part to the other two?

8. Look at paragraph 6. What device does Didion use to provide a transition (a bridge) from paragraph 5? How does she link the following pairs of paragraphs: 7-8, 8-9, 9-10, and 11-12? Can you think of a general rule or guideline that would cover these five cases?

9. According to a writing theorist, there are five grammatical markers for the relationships that exist between sentences: "and," "but," "for," "so," and the colon. How do the sentences in paragraphs 6 and 10 conform to this observation?

10. How does Didion support her ideas about self-respect? Make a brief list of the specifics she uses, the concrete details, the illustrations, the facts.

11. One kind of detail Didion uses in this essay is the allusion (a reference to a person, place, or thing, often historical or literary). Didion alludes to Raskolnikov, Scarlett O'Hara, Jordan Baker, and others. Why? Are these allusions helpful, or do they confuse you? What do such allusions suggest about the audience Didion assumes she is writing for?

Sentences

12. Didion's sentences seem disciplined and controlled. They are varied and resilient. Read the first paragraph slowly, noting the blend of long and short sentences and the way each begins differently. Look also at the words that are placed between commas at the beginning of the first and second sentences. We might call these phrases "interrupters" because they break the straightforward movement of the sentence. Try reading the sentences without their interrupters. What is different about the sentences this way?

13. What are the threads running through and binding together the sentences in paragraph 11?

14. Count the number of words in each sentence in paragraphs 5 and 7. Is there a pattern? How many sentences in paragraph 5 follow the basic subject-verb-object pattern? Which sentences are simple, compound, complex? Which use subordination? Why does Didion choose to subordinate one part of a sentence to another? Is this just arbitrary; could you reverse what she does and subordinate differently?

15. Look at how the colon is used in paragraphs 3, 7, 11, and 12. What functions does it perform? Find the semicolons in paragraphs 2, 3, and 6. Based on the use of the semicolon here, what general rule might you write about it?

16. The final sentence of paragraph 6 uses the double dash. What information is embedded between the dashes? How is it related to the rest of the information in the sentence? What would be lost without the central part of the sentence—the part within the dashes?

Words

17. The essay makes extensive use of imagery, metaphors, and similes—often in a rapidly shifting sequence. Consider, for example, paragraphs 3 and 4. What are the one or two major images used in each paragraph? How is each extended and developed? What does each image contribute to Didion's meaning?

18. Didion's vocabulary in this essay, as in her others, is varied. It often surprises. What are the meaning and effect of the following words and phrases: "the totem power of good manners" (2); "doubtful amulets" (2); "private reconciliation" (5); "imaginative empathy" (11); "alienation from self" (12). What are some other unusual words or phrases? Why does she choose these rather than other, more usual terms?

Suggestions for Writing

A. Write a short sentence about the purpose of each of the twelve paragraphs.
B. Look at the way the sentences begin in paragraphs 4 and 5. Consider especially the sentences starting with infinitive phrases ("To live," "To protest that," "To do without self-respect is . . ."). Try to write two sentences that begin this way.
C. Try to imitate the general organizational pattern of this essay, at least by starting with a personal anecdote and moving to a more objective definition; try for concrete, specific details to illustrate what your abstraction is and is not. Some possibilities: success, failure, morality, self-fulfillment, deception, wisdom, charisma, masculinity, femininity, courage, soul, friendship.
D. Think about some quality, virtue, or personal characteristic that is important to you, perhaps something you possess. But it might be something you wish you had, maybe something you are trying hard to achieve or acquire. Write an essay exploring its characteristics and explaining its importance.

Bureaucrats

1   The closed door upstairs at 120 South Spring Street in downtown Los Angeles is marked OPERATIONS CENTER. In the windowless room beyond the closed door a reverential hush prevails. From six A.M. until seven P.M. in this windowless room men sit at consoles watching a huge board flash colored lights. "There's the heart attack," someone will murmur, or "we're getting the gawk effect." 120 South Spring is the Los Angeles office of Caltrans, or the California Department of Transportation, and the Operations Center is where Caltrans engineers monitor what they call "the 42-Mile Loop." The 42-Mile Loop is simply the rough triangle formed by the intersections of the Santa Monica, the San Diego and the Harbor freeways, and 42 miles represents less than ten percent of freeway mileage in Los Angeles County alone, but these particular 42 miles are regarded around 120 South Spring with a special veneration. The Loop is a "demonstration system," a phrase much favored by everyone at Caltrans, and is part of

a "pilot project," another two words carrying totemic weight on South Spring.

2   The Loop has electronic sensors embedded every half-mile out there in the pavement itself, each sensor counting the crossing cars every twenty seconds. The Loop has its own mind, a Xerox Sigma V computer which prints out, all day and night, twenty-second readings on what is and is not moving in each of the Loop's eight lanes. It is the Xerox Sigma V that makes the big board flash red when traffic out there drops below fifteen miles an hour. It is the Xerox Sigma V that tells the Operations crew when they have an "incident" out there. An "incident" is the heart attack on the San Diego, the jackknifed truck on the Harbor, the Camaro just now tearing out the Cyclone fence on the Santa Monica. "Out there" is where incidents happen. The windowless room at 120 South Spring is where incidents get "verified." "Incident verification" is turning on the closed-circuit TV on the console and watching the traffic slow down to see (this is "the gawk effect") where the Camaro tore out the fence.

3   As a matter of fact there is a certain closed-circuit aspect to the entire mood of the Operations Center. "Verifying" the incident does not after all "prevent" the incident, which lends the enterprise a kind of tranced distance, and on the day recently when I visited 120 South Spring it took considerable effort to remember what I had come to talk about, which was that particular part of the Loop called the Santa Monica Freeway. The Santa Monica Freeway is 16.2 miles long, runs from the Pacific Ocean to downtown Los Angeles through what is referred to at Caltrans as "the East-West Corridor," carries more traffic every day than any other freeway in California, has what connoisseurs of freeways concede to be the most beautiful access ramps in the world, and appeared to have been transformed by Caltrans, during the several weeks before I went downtown to talk about it, into a 16.2-mile parking lot.

4   The problem seemed to be another Caltrans "demonstration," or "pilot," a foray into bureaucratic terrorism they were calling "The Diamond Lane" in their promotional literature and "The Project" among themselves. That the promotional literature consisted largely of schedules for buses (or "Diamond Lane Expresses") and invitations to join a car pool via computer ("Commuter Computer") made clear not only the putative point of The Project, which was to encourage travel by car pool and bus, but also the actual point, which was to eradicate a central

Southern California illusion, that of individual mobility, without any-
one really noticing. This had not exactly worked out. "FREEWAY
FIASCO," the *Los Angeles Times* was headlining page-one stories.
"THE DIAMOND LANE: ANOTHER BUST BY CALTRANS."
"CALTRANS PILOT EFFORT ANOTHER IN LONG LIST OF
FAILURES." "OFFICIAL DIAMOND LANE STANCE: LET
THEM HOWL."

5   All "The Diamond Lane" theoretically involved was reserving the
fast inside lanes on the Santa Monica for vehicles carrying three or
more people, but in practice this meant that 25 per cent of the freeway
was reserved for 3 per cent of the cars, and there were other odd wrinkles
here and there suggesting that Caltrans had dedicated itself to making
all movement around Los Angeles as arduous as possible. There was
for example the matter of surface streets. A "surface street" is anything
around Los Angeles that is not a freeway ("going surface" from one part
of town to another is generally regarded as idiosyncratic), and surface
streets do not fall directly within the Caltrans domain, but now the
engineer in charge of surface streets was accusing Caltrans of threatening
and intimidating him. It appeared that Caltrans wanted him to create
a "confused and congested situation" on his surface streets, so as to
force drivers back to the freeway, where they would meet a still more
confused and congested situation and decide to stay home, or take a
bus. "We are beginning a process of deliberately making it harder for
drivers to use freeways," a Caltrans director had in fact said at a transit
conference some months before. "We are prepared to endure considerable public outcry in order to pry John Q. Public out of his car. . . . I
would emphasize that this is a political decision, and one that can be
reversed if the public gets sufficiently enraged to throw us rascals out."

6   Of course this political decision was in the name of the greater
good, was in the interests of "environmental improvement" and "con-
servation of resources," but even there the figures had about them a
certain Caltrans opacity. The Santa Monica normally carried 240,000
cars and trucks every day. These 240,000 cars and trucks normally
carried 260,000 people. What Caltrans described as its ultimate goal
on the Santa Monica was to carry the same 260,000 people, "but in
7,800 fewer, or 232,200 vehicles." The figure "232,200" had a visionary
precision to it that did not automatically create confidence, especially
since the only effect so far had been to disrupt traffic throughout the
Los Angeles basin, triple the number of daily accidents on the Santa

Monica, prompt the initiation of two lawsuits against Caltrans, and cause large numbers of Los Angeles County residents to behave, most uncharacteristically, as an ignited and conscious proletariat. Citizen guerrillas splashed paint and scattered nails in the Diamond Lanes. Diamond Lane maintenance crews expressed fear of hurled objects. Down at 120 South Spring the architects of the Diamond Lane had taken to regarding "the media" as the architects of their embarrassment, and Caltrans statements in the press had been cryptic and contradictory, reminiscent only of old communiqués out of Vietnam.

7   To understand what was going on it is perhaps necessary to have participated in the freeway experience, which is the only secular communion Los Angeles has. Mere driving on the freeway is in no way the same as participating in it. Anyone can "drive" on the freeway, and many people with no vocation for it do, hestitating here and resisting there, losing the rhythm of the lane change, thinking about where they came from and where they are going. Actual participants think only about where they are. Actual participation requires a total surrender, a concentration so intense as to seem a kind of narcosis, a rapture-of-the-freeway. The mind goes clean. The rhythm takes over. A distortion of time occurs, the same distortion that characterizes the instant before an accident. It takes only a few seconds to get off the Santa Monica Freeway at National-Overland, which is a difficult exit requiring the driver to cross two new lanes of traffic streamed in from the San Diego Freeway, but those few seconds always seem to me the longest part of the trip. The moment is dangerous. The exhilaration is in doing it. "As you acquire the special skills involved," Reyner Banham observed in an extraordinary chapter about the freeways in his 1971 *Los Angeles: The Architecture of Four Ecologies*, "the freeways become a special way of being alive . . . the extreme concentration required in Los Angeles seems to bring on a state of heightened awareness that some locals find mystical."

8   Indeed some locals do, and some nonlocals too. Reducing the number of lone souls careering around the East-West Corridor in a state of mechanized rapture may or may not have seemed socially desirable, but what it was definitely not going to seem was easy. "We're only seeing an initial period of unfamiliarity," I was assured the day I visited Caltrans. I was talking to a woman named Eleanor Wood and she was thoroughly and professionally grounded in the diction of "planning" and it did not seem likely that I could interest her in considering

the freeway as regional mystery. "Any time you try to rearrange people's daily habits, they're apt to react impetuously. All this project requires is a certain rearrangement of people's daily planning. That's really all we want."

9 It occurred to me that a certain rearrangement of people's daily planning might seem, in less rarefied air than is breathed at 120 South Spring, rather a great deal to want, but so impenetrable was the sense of higher social purpose there in the Operations Center that I did not express this reservation. Instead I changed the subject, mentioned an earlier "pilot project" on the Santa Monica: the big electronic message boards that Caltrans had installed a year or two before. The idea was that traffic information transmitted from the Santa Monica to the Xerox Sigma V could be translated, here in the Operations Center, into suggestions to the driver, and flashed right back out to the Santa Monica. This operation, in that it involved telling drivers electronically what they already knew empirically, had the rather spectral circularity that seemed to mark a great many Caltrans schemes, and I was interested in how Caltrans thought it worked.

10 "Actually the message boards were part of a larger pilot project," Mrs. Wood said. "An ongoing project in incident management. With the message boards we hoped to learn if motorists would modify their behavior according to what we told them on the boards."

11 I asked if the motorists had.

12 "Actually no," Mrs. Wood said finally. "They didn't react to the signs exactly as we'd hypothesized they would, no. *But.* If we'd *known* what the motorist would do . . . then we wouldn't have needed a pilot project in the first place, would we."

13 The circle seemed intact. Mrs. Wood and I smiled, and shook hands. I watched the big board until all lights turned green on the Santa Monica and then I left and drove home on it, all 16.2 miles of it. All the way I remembered that I was watched by the Xerox Sigma V. All the way the message boards gave me the number to call for CAR POOL INFO. As I left the freeway it occurred to me that they might have their own rapture down at 120 South Spring, and it could be called Perpetuating the Department. Today the California Highway Patrol reported that, during the first six weeks of the Diamond Lane, accidents on the Santa Monica, which normally range between 49 and 72 during a six-week period, totaled 204. Yesterday plans were announced to extend the Diamond Lane to other freeways at a cost of $42,500,000.

QUESTIONS

Ideas

1. Why do you think Didion chose such a broad title?
2. Even though Didion appears to be objective in the opening paragraphs, what clues to her attitude about Caltrans does she provide?
3. How does she prevent the impression that she is merely a crank? That is, how does she establish authority?
4. In the last paragraph, what does Didion mean by "the circle seemed intact" and "Perpetuating the Department"?

Organization

5. Describe Didion's strategy for arranging her evidence against Caltrans. Why doesn't she begin with an explicit generalization explaining her point?
6. Writers sometimes fully develop an idea in a single paragraph but rely on groups of paragraphs for further elaboration. With this in mind, how can this essay be divided?

Sentences

7. After a couple of silent readings, read paragraphs 1 and 7 out loud, with expression. What differences do you notice? What is Didion's purpose in each? How are style and meaning related here?

Words

8. Why are so many words and phrases in quotes? What kinds of words are they?
9. Why is "windowless" repeated in the first two sentences? What is the tone of "reverential," "veneration," and "totemic" in this first paragraph?
10. In paragraph 7 what words and phrases does Didion use to reinforce her "freeway as communion" metaphor?

Suggestions for Writing

A. Write an explicit introduction and conclusion; let the last sentence in the introduction be the thesis sentence.
B. Write an essay criticizing some organization—your high school, the post office, a branch of the government, etc. However, instead of stating your

opinions directly, let a sequence of concrete incidents make your point. Let your evidence do the work of abstractions.

Why I Write

1   Of course I stole the title for this talk, from George Orwell. One reason I stole it was that I like the sound of the words: *Why I Write.* There you have three short unambiguous words that share a sound, and the sound they share is this:

I

I

I

2   In many ways writing is the act of saying *I*, of imposing oneself upon other people, of saying *listen to me, see it my way, change your mind.* It's an aggressive, even a hostile act. You can disguise its aggressiveness all you want with veils of subordinate clauses and qualifiers and tentative subjunctives, with ellipses and evasions—with the whole manner of intimating rather than claiming, of alluding rather than stating—but there's no getting around the fact that setting words on paper is the tactic of a secret bully, an invasion, an imposition of the writer's sensibility on the reader's most private space.

3   I stole the title not only because the words sounded right but because they seemed to sum up, in a no-nonsense way, all I have to tell you. Like many writers I have only this one "subject," this one "area": the act of writing. I can bring you no reports from any other front. I may have other interests: I am "interested," for example, in marine biology, but I don't flatter myself that you would come out to hear me talk about it. I am not a scholar. I am not in the least an intellectual, which is not to say that when I hear the word "intellectual" I reach for my gun, but only to say that I do not think in abstracts. During the years when I was an undergraduate at Berkeley I tried, with a kind of hopeless late-adolescent energy, to buy some temporary visa into the world of ideas, to forge for myself a mind that could deal with the abstract.

4   In short I tried to think. I failed. My attention veered inexorably back to the specific, to the tangible, to what was generally considered, by everyone I knew then and for that matter have known since, the peripheral. I would try to contemplate the Hegelian dialectic and would find myself concentrating instead on a flowering pear tree outside my window and the particular way the petals fell on my floor. I would try to read linguistic theory and would find myself wondering instead if the lights were on in the bevatron up the hill. When I say that I was wondering if the lights were on in the bevatron you might immediately suspect, if you deal in ideas at all, that I was registering the bevatron as a political symbol, thinking in shorthand about the military-industrial complex and its role in the university community, but you would be wrong. I was only wondering if the lights were on in the bevatron, and how they looked. A physical fact.

5   I had trouble graduating from Berkeley, not because of this inability to deal with ideas—I was majoring in English, and I could locate the house-and-garden imagery in "The Portrait of a Lady" as well as the next person, "imagery" being by definition the kind of specific that got my attention—but simply because I had neglected to take a course in Milton. For reasons which now sound baroque I needed a degree by the end of that summer, and the English department finally agreed, if I would come down from Sacramento every Friday and talk about the cosmology of "Paradise Lost," to certify me proficient in Milton. I did this. Some Fridays I took the Greyhound bus, other Fridays I caught the Southern Pacific's City of San Francisco on the last leg of its transcontinental trip. I can no longer tell you whether Milton put the sun or the earth at the center of his universe in "Paradise Lost," the central question of at least one century and a topic about which I wrote 10,000 words that summer, but I can still recall the exact rancidity of the butter in the City of San Francisco's dining car, and the way the tinted windows on the Greyhound bus cast the oil refineries around Carquinez Straits into a grayed and obscurely sinister light. In short my attention was always on the periphery, on what I could see and taste and touch, on the butter, and the Greyhound bus. During those years I was traveling on what I knew to be a very shaky passport, forged papers: I knew that I was no legitimate resident in any world of ideas. I knew I couldn't think. All I knew then was what I couldn't do. All I knew then was what I wasn't, and it took me some years to discover what I was.

6   Which was a writer.

7   By which I mean not a "good" writer or a "bad" writer but simply a writer, a person whose most absorbed and passionate hours are spent arranging words on pieces of paper. Had my credentials been in order I would never have become a writer. Had I been blessed with even limited access to my own mind there would have been no reason to write. I write entirely to find out what I'm thinking, what I'm looking at, what I see and what it means. What I want and what I fear. Why did the oil refineries around Carquinez Straits seem sinister to me in the summer of 1956? Why have the night lights in the bevatron burned in my mind for twenty years? *What is going on in these pictures in my mind?*

8   When I talk about pictures in my mind I am talking, quite specifically, about images that shimmer around the edges. There used to be an illustration in every elementary psychology book showing a cat drawn by a patient in varying stages of schizophrenia. This cat had a shimmer around it. You could see the molecular structure breaking down at the very edges of the cat: the cat became the background and the background the cat, everything interacting, exchanging ions. People on hallucinogens describe the same perception of objects. I'm not a schizophrenic, nor do I take hallucinogens, but certain images do shimmer for me. Look hard enough, and you can't miss the shimmer. It's there. You can't think too much about these pictures that shimmer. You just lie low and let them develop. You stay quiet. You don't talk to many people and you keep your nervous system from shorting out and you try to locate the cat in the shimmer, the grammar in the picture.

9   Just as I meant "shimmer" literally I mean "grammar" literally. Grammar is a piano I play by ear, since I seem to have been out of school the year the rules were mentioned. All I know about grammar is its infinite power. To shift the structure of a sentence alters the meaning of that sentence, as definitely and inflexibly as the position of a camera alters the meaning of the object photographed. Many people know about camera angles now, but not so many know about sentences. The arrangement of the words matters, and the arrangement you want can be found in the picture in your mind. The picture dictates the arrangement. The picture dictates whether this will be a sentence with or without clauses, a sentence that ends hard or a dying-fall sentence, long or short, active or passive. The picture tells you how to arrange

the words and the arrangement of the words tells you, or tells me, what's going on in the picture. *Nota bene:*

10 It tells you.

11 You don't tell it.

12 Let me show you what I mean by pictures in the mind. I began "Play It As It Lays" just as I have begun each of my novels, with no notion of "character" or "plot" or even "incident." I had only two pictures in my mind, more about which later, and a technical intention, which was to write a novel so elliptical and fast that it would be over before you noticed it, a novel so fast that it would scarcely exist on the page at all. About the pictures: the first was of white space. Empty space. This was clearly the picture that dictated the narrative intention of the book—a book in which anything that happened would happen off the page, a "white" book to which the reader would have to bring his or her own bad dreams—and yet this picture told me no "story," suggested no situation. The second picture did. This second picture was of something actually witnessed. A young woman with long hair and a short white halter dress walks through the casino at the Riviera in Las Vegas at one in the morning. She crosses the casino alone and picks up a house telephone. I watch her because I have heard her paged, and recognize her name: she is a minor actress I see around Los Angeles from time to time, in places like Jax and once in a gynecologist's office in the Beverly Hills Clinic, but have never met. I know nothing about her. Who is paging her? Why is she here to be paged? How exactly did she come to this? It was precisely this moment in Las Vegas that made "Play It As It Lays" begin to tell itself to me, but the moment appears in the novel only obliquely, in a chapter which begins:

13 "Maria made a list of things she would never do. She would never: walk through the Sands or Caesar's alone after midnight. She would never: ball at a party, do S-M unless she wanted to, borrow furs from Abe Lipsey, deal. She would never: carry a Yorkshire in Beverly Hills."

14 That is the beginning of the chapter and that is also the end of the chapter, which may suggest what I meant by "white space."

15 I recall having a number of pictures in my mind when I began the novel I just finished, "A Book of Common Prayer." As a matter of fact one of these pictures was of that bevatron I mentioned, although I would be hard put to tell you a story in which nuclear energy figured. Another was a newspaper photograph of a hijacked 707 burning on the desert in the Middle East. Another was the night view from a room in

which I once spent a week with paratyphoid, a hotel room on the Colombian coast. My husband and I seemed to be on the Colombian coast representing the United States of America at a film festival (I recall invoking the name "Jack Valenti" a lot, as if its reiteration could make me well), and it was a bad place to have fever, not only because my indisposition offended our hosts but because every night in this hotel the generator failed. The lights went out. The elevator stopped. My husband would go to the event of the evening and make excuses for me and I would stay alone in this hotel room, in the dark. I remember standing at the window trying to call Bogotá (the telephone seemed to work on the same principle as the generator) and watching the night wind come up and wondering what I was doing eleven degrees off the equator with a fever of 103. The view from that window definitely figures in "A Book of Common Prayer," as does the burning 707, and yet none of these pictures told me the story I needed.

16   The picture that did, the picture that shimmered and made these other images coalesce, was the Panama airport at 6 A.M. I was in this airport only once, on a plane to Bogotá that stopped for an hour to refuel, but the way it looked that morning remained superimposed on everything I saw until the day I finished "A Book of Common Prayer." I lived in that airport for several years. I can still feel the hot air when I step off the plane, can see the heat already rising off the tarmac at 6 A.M. I can feel my skirt damp and wrinkled on my legs. I can feel the asphalt stick to my sandals. I remember the big tail of a Pan American plane floating motionless down at the end of the tarmac. I remember the sound of a slot machine in the waiting room. I could tell you that I remember a particular woman in the airport, an American woman, a *norteamericana*, a thin *norteamericana* about 40 who wore a big square emerald in lieu of a wedding ring, but there was no such woman there.

17   I put this woman in the airport later. I made this woman up, just as I later made up a country to put the airport in, and a family to run the country. This woman in the airport is neither catching a plane nor meeting one. She is ordering tea in the airport coffee shop. In fact she is not simply "ordering" tea but insisting that the water be boiled, in front of her, for twenty minutes. Why is this woman in this airport? Why is she going nowhere, where has she been? Where did she get that big emerald? What derangement, or disassociation, makes her believe that her will to see the water boiled can possibly prevail?

18   "She had been going to one airport or another for four months,
one could see it, looking at the visas on her passport. All those airports
where Charlotte Douglas's passport had been stamped would have looked
alike. Sometimes the sign on the tower would say 'Bienvenidos' and
sometimes the sign on the tower would say 'Bienvenue,' some places
were wet and hot and others dry and hot, but at each of these airports
the pastel concrete walls would rust and stain and the swamp off the
runway would be littered with the fuselages of cannibalized Fairchild
F-227's and the water would need boiling.

19   "I knew why Charlotte went to the airport even if Victor did not.

20   "I knew about airports."

21   These lines appear about halfway through "A Book of Common
Prayer," but I wrote them during the second week I worked on the
book, long before I had any idea where Charlotte Douglas had been or
why she went to airports. Until I wrote these lines I had no character
called "Victor" in mind: the necessity for mentioning a name, and the
name "Victor," occurred to me as I wrote the sentence. *I knew why
Charlotte went to the airport* sounded incomplete. *I knew why Charlotte
went to the airport even if Victor did not* carried a little more narrative
drive. Most important of all, until I wrote these lines I did not know
who "I" was, who was telling the story. I had intended until that moment
that the "I" be no more than the voice of the author, a 19th-century
omniscient narrator. But there it was:

22   "I knew why Charlotte went to the airport even if Victor did not.

23   "I knew about airports."

24   This "I" was the voice of no author in my house. This "I" was
someone who not only knew why Charlotte went to the airport but also
knew someone called "Victor." Who was Victor? Who was this narrator?
Why was this narrator telling me this story? Let me tell you one thing
about why writers write: had I known the answer to any of these questions
I would never have needed to write a novel.

QUESTIONS

  1. Why does Didion write? Do her reasons make sense to you? What reason
     for writing is suggested in the last paragraph? How does that reason tie in
     with the ones given in paragraph 7?

2. How does Didion begin the process of writing? What does she start with and from? What do you think of her method? Of her compulsion? Are there any advantages to starting this way? Any disadvantages?

3. Didion says she stole her title from George Orwell. Is her theft legitimate? Can one writer steal from another? How far can any writer, including you, legitimately go in this kind of stealing?

4. Didion likes her title because she says it's no-nonsense. What does she mean? Are her first three paragraphs also no-nonsense paragraphs?

5. In the second paragraph Didion says writers are bullies, and in the first paragraph she suggests that they are egocentric. Is she convincing here? Do you feel this way? Compare this with what E. B. White says about writers in "The Essayist."

6. In paragraphs 4 and 5 Didion makes a lot of her alleged inability to think—abstractly and generally. Reread these paragraphs carefully and make a list of the general ideas she includes and of the specific details she sets up as counters to them and illustrations of them.

7. What does Didion mean when she says: "To shift the structure of a sentence alters the meaning of that sentence." Can you provide an example either by altering the structure of one of Didion's sentences or by altering one of your own? How does the analogy that follows this statement help to clarify her meaning: "as the position of a camera alters the meaning of the object photographed"?

Suggestions for Writing

A. Explain, in an essay, why you write. Has writing helped you to see or to think in ways you wouldn't without writing? Has it hindered or hurt you in any way? You might describe your own composing process—that is, exactly what you do from the time you first sit down to write until you turn your essay in. Or you might write an essay about why you don't write, and how and why you avoid it.

B. In another essay, "On Keeping a Notebook," Didion says that "the point of my keeping a notebook has never been, nor is it now, to have an accurate factual record of what I have been doing or thinking." Her instinct, as she explains it, is neither for reality nor for history. It is rather, she insists, a personal impulse—a desire to remember who she was at different points in her life, an urge to recall how things felt, what they seemed like then. "It is a good idea, then," she continues, "to keep in touch, and I suppose that keeping in touch is what notebooks are all about." Try for a week, a month, or longer if you like, to keep some kind of notebook or journal of responses to things you do, see, hear, encounter. Avoid making it either a diary so private you'd want no one to read it, or simply a record of trivial and uninteresting actions ("I got up, ate, and went to work"). Instead, make it a re-acting notebook, literally a book of notes on your thoughts and feelings, your ideas and attitudes about any and every thing.

EIGHT

E. B. White

(1899–)

E. B. White is generally recognized as one of America's finest writers. Long associated with *The New Yorker*, for which he wrote stories, sketches, essays, and editorials, White has also contributed to another prominent magazine, *Harper's*, writing a monthly column, "One Man's Meat," from 1938 to 1943. These columns were collected and published with a few additional pieces from *The New Yorker* as *One Man's Meat* (1944). This book was followed by two other collections of miscellany, *The Second Tree from the Corner* (1954) and *The Points of My Compass* (1962). Besides these collections, White published, over a slightly longer span of years, three children's books: *Stuart Little* (1945), *Charlotte's Web* (1952), and *The Trumpet of the Swan* (1970). In 1976, White published a selection of his best essays, those, as he says, which had "an odor of durability clinging to them." *The Essays of E. B. White* were followed a year later by a selection of White's letters, entitled simply enough, *Letters of E. B. White. Poems and Sketches of E. B. White* appeared in 1981.

Though not a complete bibliography of White's published work, this list does suggest something of White's range and versatility, as well as something about the way writing has been for him steady work over a long stretch of time. And the steadiest of White's work, in both senses of the word, has been his essays. In fact, it is as an essayist that White is best known and most highly acclaimed. And it is as an essayist that he identifies himself in the introduction to the *Essays*, defining an essayist as "a self-liberated man sustained by the childish belief that everything he thinks about, everything that happens to him, is of general interest." And again, as one who is "content with living a free life and enjoying the satisfactions of a somewhat undisciplined existence."

Edward Hoagland has recently noted that White's name has become almost synonymous with "essay." And for good reason, we might add, since it is the form most congenial to his temperament, a form that allows him the latitude he needs to roam freely in thought, a form that he has been able to stamp with his own imprint. This imprint is reflected in the following elements: a scrupulous respect for his readers; an uncanny accuracy in the use of language; and an uncommon delight in common, everyday things. White sees the extraordinary in the ordinary, noticing and valuing what most of us either overlook or take for granted. And from his repeated and respectful acts of attention flow reminiscences, speculations, explorations, and questions about our common humanity, about our relationships with one another, with the past, with the worlds of technology and nature.

White is a writer whose insights derive directly from his literal observations, from what he sees. Thoreau, one of White's favorite writers—and one with whom White has much in common—once remarked that "you can't say more than you can see." White's writing bears this out. The relationship between sight and insight, between observation and speculation, is evident in essays such as "The Ring of Time," which begins with a description of a circus act and ends with speculations about time and change, and "Once More to the Lake," in which White reminisces about his boyhood summer holidays in Maine, both describing the place with startling vividness and offering unsettling speculations about the meaning of his memories. In these and in other essays, White's writing is rooted in the crucial act of vision, a vision which sees into and beyond the surface of his subjects.

White's best writing, however, is more than a record of what he has seen and thought. It is also art, literature. His best work is crafted, shaped, formed with the same attention to details of structure, texture, image, and tone

that a poet or painter, sculptor or novelist gives his work.
In "The Ring of Time" and "Once More to the Lake,"
matters of fact, details of time, place, and circumstance give
way to larger concerns. The circus is more than a circus
ring: it becomes an emblem of time and change; the lake
is more than a summer vacation place: it becomes an image
of serenity and a reminder of time, change, even death.
The images of light and water, the symbolism of circus ring
and lake, along with a concern for understanding the present
in relation to the past and the future—these lift their re-
spective essays beyond the merely personal and reminiscent,
beyond the ordinary and the everyday into the extraordinary
universality of art.

About writing itself White has said a good deal, and
said it well. In the chapter he contributed to the now famous
Elements of Style, White notes that when we speak of a
writer's style we mean "the sound his words make on paper."
The voice that we hear is what distinguishes one writer from
another; and it is one good reason why, to get a good sense
of a writer's style, we should read his work aloud. Beyond
this concern for hearing what language can do, White notes
that a writer's style "reveals something of his spirit, his habits, his capacities, his bias . . . it is the Self escaping into
the open." And, as White suggests, this Self cannot be
hidden, for a writer's style "reveals his identity as surely as
would his fingerprints."

Recognizing that writing is hard work requiring endurance, thought, and revision ("revising is part of writing"),
White advises that the beginning writer let his ear be his
guide, that he avoid all tricks and mannerisms, that he see
writing as "one way to go about thinking," and, finally, that
he achieve style both by affecting none and by believing
"in the truth and worth of the scrawl."

Throughout his years as a writing man, White has
often been asked for advice about writing. To one seeker
he wrote: "Remember that writing is translation, and the
opus to be translated is yourself." On another occasion he
responded to a seventeen-year-old girl this way:

You asked me about writing—how I did it. There is no trick to
it. If you like to write and want to write, you write, no matter

where you are or what else you are doing or whether anyone pays any heed. . . . If you want to write about feelings, about the end of summer, about growing, write about it. A great deal of writing is not "plotted"—most of my essays have no plot structure, they are a ramble in the woods, or a ramble in the basement of my mind.

There is a naturalness, an ease about White's writing, both in these offhand remarks from his letters and in his more elaborately plotted essays. It is an ease that derives in part from a refusal to be either pompous or pedantic; it is an ease that derives also from a consistent attempt to be honest, to achieve the candor he admires in Montaigne; and it is a naturalness that is reflected in his style, a style that mingles the high subject and the low, the big word and the small, without flamboyance or ostentation. White's style, in short, is a badge of his character—intelligent, honest, witty, exact, and fundamentally endearing.

The Essayist

1   The essayist is a self-liberated man, sustained by the childish belief that everything he thinks about, everything that happens to him, is of general interest. He is a fellow who thoroughly enjoys his work, just as people who take bird walks enjoy theirs. Each new excursion of the essayist, each new "attempt," differs from the last and takes him into new country. This delights him. Only a person who is congenitally self-centered has the effrontery and the stamina to write essays.

2   There are as many kinds of essays as there are human attitudes or poses, as many essay flavors as there are Howard Johnson ice creams.

The essayist arises in the morning and, if he has work to do, selects his garb from an unusually extensive wardrobe: he can pull on any sort of shirt, be any sort of person, according to his mood or his subject matter—philosopher, scold, jester, raconteur, confidant, pundit, devil's advocate, enthusiast. I like the essay, have always liked it, and even as a child was at work, attempting to inflict my young thoughts and experiences on others by putting them on paper. I early broke into print in the pages of *St. Nicholas*. I tend still to fall back on the essay form (or lack of form) when an idea strikes me, but I am not fooled about the place of the essay in twentieth-century American letters—it stands a short distance down the line. The essayist, unlike the novelist, the poet, and the playwright, must be content in his self-imposed role of second-class citizen. A writer who has his sights trained on the Nobel Prize or other earthly triumphs had best write a novel, a poem, or a play, and leave the essayist to ramble about, content with living a free life and enjoying the satisfactions of a somewhat undisciplined existence. (Dr. Johnson called the essay "an irregular, undigested piece"; this happy practitioner has no wish to quarrel with the good doctor's characterization.)

3   There is one thing the essayist cannot do, though—he cannot indulge himself in deceit or in concealment, for he will be found out in no time. Desmond MacCarthy, in his introductory remarks to the 1928 E. P. Dutton & Company edition of Montaigne, observes that Montaigne "had the gift of natural candour. . . ." It is the basic ingredient. And even the essayist's escape from discipline is only a partial escape: the essay, although a relaxed form, imposes its own disciplines, raises its own problems, and these disciplines and problems soon become apparent and (we all hope) act as a deterrent to anyone wielding a pen merely because he entertains random thoughts or is in a happy or wandering mood.

4   I think some people find the essay the last resort of the egoist, a much too self-conscious and self-serving form for their taste; they feel that it is presumptuous of a writer to assume that his little excursions or his small observations will interest the reader. There is some justice in their complaint. I have always been aware that I am by nature self-absorbed and egoistical; to write of myself to the extent I have done indicates a too great attention to my own life, not enough to the lives

of others. I have worn many shirts, and not all of them have been a good fit. But when I am discouraged or downcast I need only fling open the door of my closet, and there, hidden behind everything else, hangs the mantle of Michel de Montaigne, smelling slightly of camphor.

5   The essays in this collection cover a long expanse of time, a wide variety of subjects. I have chosen the ones that have amused me in the rereading, along with a few that seemed to have the odor of durability clinging to them. Some, like "Here Is New York," have been seriously affected by the passage of time and now stand as period pieces. I wrote about New York in the summer of 1948, during a hot spell. The city I described has disappeared, and another city has emerged in its place— one that I'm not familiar with. But I remember the former one, with longing and with love. David McCord, in his book *About Boston* tells of a journalist from abroad visiting this country and seeing New York for the first time. He reported that it was "inspiring but temporary in appearance." I know what he means. The last time I visited New York, it seemed to have suffered a personality change, as though it had a brain tumor as yet undetected.

6   Two of the Florida pieces have likewise experienced a sea change. My remarks about the condition of the black race in the South have happily been nullified, and the pieces are merely prophetic, not definitive.

7   To assemble these essays I have rifled my other books and have added a number of pieces that are appearing for the first time between covers. Except for extracting three chapters, I have let "One Man's Meat" alone, since it is a sustained report of about five years of country living—a report I prefer not to tamper with. The arrangement of the book is by subject matter or by mood or by place, not by chronology. Some of the pieces in the book carry a dateline, some do not. Chronology enters into the scheme, but neither the book nor its sections are perfectly chronological. Sometimes the reader will find me in the city when he thinks I am in the country, and the other way round. This may cause a mild confusion; it is unavoidable and easily explained. I spent a large part of the first half of my life as a city dweller, a large part of the second half as a countryman. In between, there were periods when nobody, including myself, quite knew (or cared) where I was: I thrashed back and forth between Maine and New York for reasons that

seemed compelling at the time. Money entered into it, affection for *The New Yorker* magazine entered in. And affection for the city.

8   I have finally come to rest.

QUESTIONS

1. Why does White write? What image of the writer does he present? Why do you write, and more generally, why does anybody write?
2. What does White enjoy about being an essayist? What does he mean when he says that the essayist is "self-liberated"? Liberated from what and for what?
3. White defines an essay as an "attempt" and an "excursion." An attempt at what and an excursion where? And for what purpose?
4. What, according to White, distinguishes the essay from the novel, the story, and the poem? Do you agree with White's (and Dr. Johnson's) characterization of the essay as "an irregular undigested piece"? Why or why not?
5. At more than one point in this essay, White suggests that essayists are egoists. Is White an egocentric writer? Are you? Explain.
6. Explain the point of White's comparisons in paragraph 2, the comparisons between essays and ice cream, and between essays and clothes.
7. "The Essayist" can be divided into two parts: paragraphs 1–4 and paragraphs 5–8. What are the purpose and the point of each part?

Suggestions for Writing

A. White mentions that the essential characteristic of any essayist must be "candor." Discuss why you think this is or is not an essential quality of good writing. Include some discussion of other qualities you think a good essayist ought to possess, and why.
B. Examine the writing of one of the authors in this book for one or more of the following qualities: candor, humor, wit, subtlety, charm, egoism, arrogance, irony, satire, mystery, power.
C. White identifies himself as an essayist, a writer of essays. This is an important aspect of his self-image. Think of some aspect of your identity, or think of something you do that is important to your sense of who and what you are. Write an essay on the meaning and value of this—whatever it is.

D. White mentions two great essayists—Samuel Johnson and Michel de Montaigne. Read an essay by either (or essays by both) and explain how it is characterized by "candor."

To Katharine S. White

[New York]
31 May [1937]

My dear Mrs. White:

1 It has occurred to me that perhaps I should attempt to clarify, for your benefit, the whole subject of my year of grace—or, as I call it, My Year. Whenever the subject has come up, I have noticed an ever so slight chill seize you, as though you felt a draught and wished someone would shut a door. I look upon this delicate spiritual tremor as completely natural, under the circumstances, and suggestive only of affectionate regard, tinged with womanly suspicion. In the world as now constituted, anybody who resigns a paying job is suspect; furthermore, in a well-ordered family, any departure from routine is cause for alarm. Having signified my intention to quit my accustomed ways, I shall do you the service of sketching, roughly, what is in my heart and mind—so that you may know in a general way what to expect of me and what not to expect. It is much easier for me to do this in a letter, typing away, word after word, than to try to tell you over a cup of coffee, when I would only stutter and grow angry at myself for inexactitudes of meanings (and probably at you, too, for misinterpreting my muddy speech).

2 First, there is the question of *why* I am giving up my job. This is easy to answer. I am quitting partly because I am not satisfied with the use I am making of my talents, such as they are; partly because I am not having fun working at my job—and am in a rut there; partly because I long to recapture something which everyone loses when he agrees to perform certain creative miracles on specified dates for a

particular sum. (I don't know whether you know what this thing is, but you'll just have to take my word that it is real. To you it may be just another Loch Ness monster, but to me it is as real as a dachshund.)

3   Now there comes the question of *what* I am going to do, having given up the job. I suppose this is a fair question—also the question of what I intend to use for money. These matters naturally concern you, and Esposito [grocer], and everybody. Dozens of people have asked: "What are you going to do?" so strong is their faith in the herb activity. I know better what I am *not* going to do. But I won't try to pretend (to you, anyway) that that is the whole story either. In the main, my plan is to have none. But everyone has secret projects, and I am no exception. Writing is a secret vice, like self abuse. A person afflicted with poetic longings of one sort or another searches for a kind of intellectual and spiritual privacy in which to indulge his strange excesses. To achieve this sort of privacy—this aerial suspension of the lyrical spirit—he does not necessarily have to wrench himself away, physically, from everybody and everything in his life (this, I suspect, often defeats him at his own game), but he *does* have to forswear certain easy rituals, such as earning a living and running the world's errands. That is what I intend to "do" in my year. I am quitting my job. In a sense, I am also quitting my family—which is a much more serious matter, and which is why I am taking the trouble to write this letter. For a long time I have been taking notes—sometimes on bits of paper, sometimes on the mind's disordered pad—on a theme which engrosses me. I intend to devote my year to assembling these notes, if I can, and possibly putting them on paper of the standard typewriter size. In short, a simple literary project. I am not particularly hopeful of it, but I am willing to meet it half way. If at the end of the year, I have nothing but a bowlful of cigarette stubs to show for my time, I shall not begrudge a moment of it and I hope you won't. They say a dirigible, after it has been in the air for a while, becomes charged with static electricity, which is not discharged till the landing ropes touch the field and ground it. I have been storing up an inner turbulence, during my long apprenticeship in the weekly gaiety field, and it is time I came down to earth.

4   I am not telling people, when they ask, that I am proposing to write anything during My Year. As I said above, nothing may come of it, and it is easier to make a simple denial at the start, than to invent

excuses and explanations at the end. I wish you would please do the same. Say I am taking a Sabbatical and doing nothing much of anything—which will come perilously near the truth, probably.

5   When I say I am quitting my family, I do not mean I am not going to be around. I simply mean that I shall invoke Man's ancient privilege of going and coming in a whimsical, rather than a reasonable, manner. I have some pilgrimages to make. To the zoo. To Mount Vernon. To Belgrade, and Bellport,[1] and other places where my spoor is still to be found. I shall probably spend a good deal of time in parks, libraries, and the waiting rooms of railway stations—which is where I hung out before I espoused this more congenial life. My attendance at meals may be a little spotty—for a twelvemonth I shall not adjust my steps to a soufflé. I hope this doesn't sound ungrateful, or like a declaration of independence—I intend it merely to inform you of a new allegiance—to a routine of my own spirit rather than to a fixed household & office routine. I seek the important privilege of not coming home to supper unless I happen to. I plan no absences, I plan no attendances. No plans.

6   The financial aspect of this escapade does not seem portentous, or ominous. I'm going to have Arty send me the money which comes in from my securities.[2] I'm going to sell the P.A. [Pierce Arrow], which should bring $2,000, of which you get $1500. My taxes are paid, and I have enough money in the bank to continue in the same fifty-fifty arrangement with you in all matters of maintenance, recreation, and love. My luncheons will be 50 centers, instead of the dollar and a quarter number, and I will be riding common carriers, not Sunshine cabs. Instead of keeping a car on service at a garage, I would like your permission to keep the Plymouth nearby at some cheap lodging. I don't anticipate laying in a cellar of wine, or buying any new broadloom carpets. I think if I pull in my ears and you watch your artichokes, we can still stay solvent. I think it is better to do it this way than to try some possibly abortive rearrangement of our way of living, such as letting out the top floor to a Bingo society, or going to France to take advantage of the cheap wines. I notice Joe is already starting to sell his paintings.

---

1. Bellport, Long Island. White had spent summers there.
2. Arthur Illian had guided White in investing his savings.

7   Well, this about covers my Year. I urge you not to take it too seriously, or me. I am the same old fellow. I hope I shall give and receive the same old attentions and trifles. I don't want you tiptoeing around the halls telling people not to annoy me—the chances are I won't be doing anything anyway, except changing a bird's water. But I do want you to have some general conception of my internal processes during this odd term of grace. I want you to be able to face my departure for Bellport on a rainy Thursday afternoon with an equanimity of spirit bordering on coma.

Yrs with love and grace,
Mr. White

P.S. This letter is rather long, but I didn't have time to make it shorter, such are the many demands on me these days from so many points of the compass. I realize, too, that the whole plan sounds selfish and not much fun for you; but that's the way art goes. You let yourself in for this, marrying a man who is supposed to write something, even though he never does.

P.P.S. Unnecessary to answer this communication. Would be a drain on your valuable time. Just signify your good will with a package of Beemans—one if by land, two if by sea.

PPPPPS. Will be glad to answer any questions, or argue the whole matter out if it fails to meet with your approval or pleasure. I do not, however, want to discuss the literary nature of the project: for altho you are my b.f. and s.c.,[3] I will just have to do my own writing, as always.

QUESTIONS

Ideas

1. Why did White write this letter? Do you think there is any advantage for White in presenting his explanation this way rather than doing it orally?

2. Do White's reasons for taking a year off seem legitimate and his plans worthwhile? Why or why not?

---

3. Best friend and severest critic.

Organization

3. How is the letter organized? Does White stick to one idea per paragraph or does he pack in more?
4. What do the postscripts add? Are they necessary? How would the letter be different without them?

Sentences

5. In paragraph 5 White includes some very short sentences, even some fragments. What tone is established with these short and fragmentary sentences? Would the paragraph be better with longer sentences and with no fragments?
6. Throughout the letter White uses dashes and parentheses. What is the cumulative effect of this punctuation on the tone of the letter?

Words

7. White's diction is a mix of the familiar and the strange, of casual informality and studied formality. Paragraph 5 is a good example of such a blend. The first sentence combines an unusual expression, "quitting my family," with a more familiar one, "I do not mean I am not going to be around." The sentence that follows it offers a similar combination, with the informal expressions alternating with more formal ones:

> I simply mean that   I shall invoke Man's ancient privilege
> of going and coming   in a whimsical, rather than a reasonable
>   manner.

8. One of the charming features of White's letter (and of his style in general) is the kind of detail he includes as his points of reference, his touchstones of reality. In paragraph 5, for example, he writes: "for a twelvemonth I shall not adjust my steps to a soufflé." What does he mean? Can you make the point in a more general way? What is the advantage of the way White puts it?
9. Throughout the letter, White uses comparisons and analogies. Explain how each of the following clarifies White's meaning or communicates his feeling.

> Whenever the subject has come up, I have noticed an ever so slight chill seize you, as though you felt a draught and wished someone would shut a door. (1)

To you it may be just another Loch Ness monster, but to me it is as real as a dachshund. (2)

Writing is a secret vice, like self abuse. (3)

Suggestions for Writing

A. Imagine that you are Katharine S. White. Write a letter in reply to E. B. White.

B. Write a letter to a parent, spouse, friend, teacher, boss, explaining why you want a week, month, or year off—or why you have already decided on (and what provisions you have made for) taking off the time. Explain what, if anything, you will do with the free time—or what you won't do and why.

C. Rewrite paragraph 5, combining the short sentences to create longer ones and converting the fragments to grammatically complete sentences. Which version do you prefer and why?

D. Write an imitation of paragraph 5, using your own subject but following the sequence, structure, and length of White's sentences.

Good-bye to Forty-eighth Street

Turtle Bay, November 12, 1957

1   For some weeks now I have been engaged in dispersing the contents of this apartment, trying to persuade hundreds of inanimate objects to scatter and leave me alone. It is not a simple matter. I am impressed by the reluctance of one's worldly goods to go out again into the world. During September I kept hoping that some morning, as by magic, all books, pictures, records, chairs, beds, curtains, lamps, china, glass, utensils, keepsakes would drain away from around my feet, like the outgoing tide, leaving me standing silent on a bare beach. But this did not happen. My wife and I diligently sorted and discarded things

from day to day, and packed other objects for the movers, but a six-room apartment holds as much paraphernalia as an aircraft carrier. You can whittle away at it, but to empty the place completely takes real ingenuity and great staying power. On one of the mornings of disposal, a man from a secondhand bookstore visited us, bought several hundred books, and told us of the death of his brother, the word "cancer" exploding in the living room like a time bomb detonated by his grief. Even after he had departed with his heavy load, there seemed to be almost as many books as before, and twice as much sorrow.

2   Every morning, when I left for work, I would take something in my hand and walk off with it, for deposit in the big municipal wire trash basket at the corner of Third, on the theory that the physical act of disposal was the real key to the problem. My wife, a strategist, knew better and began quietly mobilizing the forces that would eventually put our goods to rout. A man could walk away for a thousand mornings carrying something with him to the corner and there would still be a home full of stuff. It is not possible to keep abreast of the normal tides of acquisition. A home is like a reservoir equipped with a check valve: the valve permits influx but prevents outflow. Acquisition goes on night and day—smoothly, subtly, imperceptibly. I have no sharp taste for acquiring things, but it is not necessary to desire things in order to acquire them. Goods and chattels seek a man out; they find him even though his guard is up. Books and oddities arrive in the mail. Gifts arrive on anniversaries and fête days. Veterans send ballpoint pens. Banks send memo books. If you happen to be a writer, readers send whatever may be cluttering up their own lives; I had a man once send me a chip of wood that showed the marks of a beaver's teeth. Someone dies, and a little trickle of indestructible keepsakes appears, to swell the flood. This steady influx is not counterbalanced by any comparable outgo. Under ordinary circumstances, the only stuff that leaves a home is paper trash and garbage; everything else stays on and digs in.

3   Lately we haven't spent our nights in the apartment; we are bivouacked in a hotel and just come here mornings to continue the work. Each of us has a costume. My wife steps into a cotton dress while I shift into midnight-blue tropical pants and bowling shoes. Then we buckle down again to the unending task.

4   All sorts of special problems arise during the days of disposal. Anyone who is willing to put his mind to it can get rid of a chair, say, but what about a trophy? Trophies are like leeches. The ones made of

paper, such as a diploma from a school or a college, can be burned if
you have the guts to light the match, but the ones made of bronze not
only are indestructible but are almost impossible to throw away, because
they usually carry your name, and a man doesn't like to throw away
his good name, or even his bad one. Some busybody might find it.
People differ in their approach to trophies, of course. In watching
Edward R. Murrow's "Person to Person" program on television, I have
seen several homes that contained a "trophy room," in which the celebrated pack rat of the house had assembled all his awards, so that they
could give out the concentrated aroma of achievement whenever he
wished to loiter in such an atmosphere. This is all very well if you enjoy
the stale smell of success, but if a man doesn't care for that air he is
in a real fix when disposal time comes up. One day a couple of weeks
ago, I sat for a while staring moodily at a plaque that had entered my
life largely as a result of some company's zest for promotion. It was
bronze on walnut, heavy enough to make an anchor for a rowboat, but
I didn't need a rowboat anchor, and this thing had my name on it. By
deft work with a screwdriver, I finally succeeded in prying the nameplate
off; I pocketed this, and carried the mutilated remains to the corner,
where the wire basket waited. The work exhausted me more than did
the labor for which the award was presented.

5   Another day, I found myself on a sofa between the chip of wood
gnawed by the beaver and an honorary hood I had once worn in an
academic procession. What I really needed at the moment was the
beaver himself, to eat the hood. I shall never wear the hood again, but
I have too weak a character to throw it away, and I do not doubt that
it will tag along with me to the end of my days, not keeping me either
warm or happy but occupying a bit of my attic space.

6   Right in the middle of the dispersal, while the mournful rooms
were still loaded with loot, I had a wonderful idea: we would shut the
apartment, leave everything to soak for a while, and go to the Fryeburg
Fair, in Maine, where we could sit under a tent at a cattle auction and
watch somebody else trying to dispose of something. A fair, of course,
is a dangerous spot if a man is hoping to avoid acquisition, and the
truth is I came close to acquiring a very pretty whiteface heifer, safe in
calf—which would have proved easily as burdensome as a chip of wood
gnawed by a beaver. But Fryeburg is where some of my wife's ancestors
lived, and is in the valley of the Saco, looking west to the mountains,
and the weather promised to be perfect, and the premium list of the

Agricultural Society said, "Should Any Day Be Stormy, the Exercises for That Day Will Be Postponed to the First Fair Day," and I would rather have a ringside seat at a cattle sale than a box at the opera, so we picked up and left town, deliberately overshooting Fryeburg by 175 miles in order to sleep one night at home.

7   The day we spent at the Fryeburg Fair was the day the first little moon was launched by the new race of moon-makers. Had I known in advance that a satellite was about to be added to my world, in this age of additives, I might have stayed in New York and sulked instead of going to the Fair, but in my innocence I was able to enjoy a day watching the orbiting of trotting horses—an ancient terrestrial phenomenon that has given pleasure to unnumbered thousands. We attended the calf scramble, the pig scramble, and the baby-beef auction; we ate lunch in the back seat of our flashy old 1949 automobile, parked in the infield; and then I found myself a ringside seat with my feet in the shavings at the Hereford sale, under the rattling tongue and inexorable hammer of auctioneer Dick Murray, enjoying the wild look in the whites of a cow's eyes.

8   The day had begun under the gray blanket of a fall overcast, but the sky soon cleared. Nobody had heard of the Russian moon. The wheels wheeled, the chairs spun, the cotton candy tinted the faces of children, the bright leaves tinted the woods and hills. A cluster of amplifiers spread the theme of love over everything and everybody; the mild breeze spread the dust over everything and everybody. Next morning, in the Lafayette Hotel in Portland, I went down to breakfast and found May Craig looking solemn at one of the tables and Mr. Murray, the auctioneer, looking cheerful at another. The newspaper headlines told of the moon. At that hour of the morning, I could not take in the exact significance, if any, of a national heavenly body. But I was glad I had spent the last day of the natural firmament at the One Hundred and Seventh Annual Exhibition of the West Oxford Agricultural Society. I see nothing in space as promising as the view from a Ferris wheel.

9   But that was weeks ago. As I sit here this afternoon in this disheveled room, surrounded by the boxes and bales that hold my undisposable treasure, I feel the onset of melancholy. I look out onto Forty-eighth Street; one out of every ten passers-by is familiar to me. After a dozen years of gazing idly at the passing show, I have assembled,

quite unbeknownst to them, a cast of characters that I depend on. They are the nameless actors who have a daily walk-on part in my play—the greatest of dramas. I shall miss them all, them and their dogs. Even more, I think, I shall miss the garden out back—the wolf whistle of the starling, the summer-night murmur of the fountain; the cat, the vine, the sky, the willow. And the visiting birds of spring and fall—the small, shy birds that drop in for one drink and stay two weeks. Over a period of thirty years, I have occupied eight caves in New York, eight digs—four in the Village, one on Murray Hill, three in Turtle Bay. In New York, a citizen is likely to keep on the move, shopping for the perfect arrangement of rooms and vistas, changing his habitation according to fortune, whim, and need. And in every place he abandons he leaves something vital, it seems to me, and starts his new life somewhat less encrusted, like a lobster that has shed its skin and is for a time soft and vulnerable.

QUESTIONS

Ideas

1. What is White's purpose in this essay? Is he trying to convince us of something? Is he concerned with amusing us? With something else?
2. Why does White find it so hard to throw things away? Why does he find it so difficult to leave? Are you convinced of these difficulties? Why or why not?
3. What does White mean by saying that when a person moves he leaves something vital behind?

Organization

4. How is this essay organized? And how does White help us keep our bearings as we read?
5. Paragraphs 6, 7, and 8 form a digression from the main business of the essay. Are these paragraphs necessary? How would the essay read if you cut them out, connecting paragraph 5 directly with paragraph 9?
6. Reread paragraph 4 carefully. The first sentence is the controlling sentence: it contains the main point and provides a center of gravity. Explain how the rest of the paragraph opens out of and develops the opening sentence.

Sentences

7. Throughout "Good-bye to Forty-eighth Street," White writes sentences with balanced phrasing. In paragraph 2, for example, he writes:

   The valve permits influx
         but prevents outflow.

   and

   It is not necessary to desire things
         in order to acquire them.

   What advantage does such balanced phrasing provide? (Note also the parallels of sound in each example.)

8. Paragraph 2 is noteworthy for another kind of balance—the balance of long and short sentences. The first three sentences are loose and expansive; the next three are shorter, more cryptic. What is the tone of each set of sentences? Is there any advantage in using the two kinds of sentences together?

9. In the following sentences White splits the information he wants to convey, using a colon. What is the effect of the colon in these sentences, and what is the relationship of the right-hand part of each sentence to the left-hand side?

   A home is like a reservoir equipped with a check valve: the valve permits influx but prevents outflow.

   Right in the middle of the dispersal, while the mournful rooms were still loaded with loot, I had a wonderful idea: we would shut the apartment, leave everything to soak for a while, and go to the Fryeburg Fair, in Maine, where we could sit under a tent at a cattle auction and watch somebody else trying to dispose of something.

10. In paragraph 2 White uses a sentence that contains a dash:

   Acquisition goes on night and day—smoothly, subtly, imperceptibly.

   If we make one small change in the sentence—substitute a comma for the dash—there is a difference.

   Acquisition goes on night and day, smoothly, subtly, imperceptibly.

   And if we take the comma out we get this:

   Acquisition goes on night and day smoothly, subtly, imperceptibly.

   Which version do you prefer and why?

11. Examine in paragraphs 6 and 9 sentences that contain a dash. What generalizations can you make about the use of the dash based on the ways White uses it?

Words

12. In the first sentence of the essay, White remarks that he tries to "persuade" the objects to leave him alone. Isn't that rather strange language for talking about the contents of an apartment? How is that kind of animating and personifying language carried through and modified in the remainder of the essay? Look, for example, at paragraph 2, where White says that his wife, a "strategist," began "mobilizing the forces that would eventually put our goods to rout." What other imagery is used to describe the various items to be discarded and the way they remain undiscarded?

13. White's diction in "Good-bye to Forty-eighth Street" is a mix of the everyday with the occasional, the common with the recondite. Big words jostle small; words of Latin derivation sit alongside native, Saxon words. In paragraph 1, for example, "dispersing," "inanimate," and "reluctance" exist beside "leave me alone," "go out again into the world," and "It is not a simple matter." Later (paragraphs 2 and 4) "home full of stuff" occurs alongside "tides of acquisition," and "if you have the guts" is followed a bit later by "the concentrated aroma of achievement." What effect is achieved by balancing and combining the two kinds of language in this way?

14. Throughout the essay White repeats varied forms of two words that establish the focus and center of gravity of the piece. These words, "acquisition" and "disposal," reappear as "acquire" and "acquiring"; "dispose," "undisposable," "dispersal," and "dispersing." Would White have been better off substituting different words—synonyms—for disposal and acquisition? Or is there an advantage to repeating related forms of a word?

15. In paragraph 4 White uses the following phrases:

> the concentrated aroma of achievement
> the stale smell of success

What is the difference between them? What would be gained or lost if you switched the final word of each?

> the concentrated aroma of success
> the stale smell of achievement

Suggestions for Writing

A. Discuss the idea White mentions in his final paragraph: that you leave a part of yourself when you move from a place you love.

B. Describe something that has been hard for you to give up, to let go of. Explain why this separation was difficult for you, how it affected you.

C. Describe a time when you had to move from a place where you felt at home. Try to give the reader a sense of how you felt and why. Explain what you were leaving and what you thought you were heading for. You might compare what you left to what you found.

D. Write a paragraph that balances long and short sentences.

E. Write imitations of the sentences discussed in questions 7, 9, and 10.

The Ring of Time

Fiddler Bayou, March 22, 1956

1   **A**fter the lions had returned to their cages, creeping angrily through the chutes, a little bunch of us drifted away and into an open doorway nearby, where we stood for a while in semidarkness, watching a big brown circus horse go harumphing around the practice ring. His trainer was a woman of about forty, and the two of them, horse and woman, seemed caught up in one of those desultory treadmills of afternoon from which there is no apparent escape. The day was hot, and we kibitzers were grateful to be briefly out of the sun's glare. The long rein, or tape, by which the woman guided her charge counterclockwise in his dull career formed the radius of their private circle, of which she was the revolving center; and she, too, stepped a tiny circumference of her own, in order to accommodate the horse and allow him his maximum scope. She had on a short-skirted costume and a conical straw hat. Her legs were bare and she wore high heels, which probed deep into the loose tanbark and kept her ankles in a state of constant turmoil. The great size and meekness of the horse, the repetitious exercise, the heat of the afternoon, all exerted a hypnotic charm that invited boredom; we spectators were experiencing a languor—we neither expected relief nor felt entitled to any. We had paid a dollar to get into the grounds,

to be sure, but we had got our dollar's worth a few minutes before, when the lion trainer's whiplash had got caught around a toe of one of the lions. What more did we want for a dollar?

2   Behind me I heard someone say, "Excuse me, please," in a low voice. She was halfway into the building when I turned and saw her— a girl of sixteen or seventeen, politely threading her way through us onlookers who blocked the entrance. As she emerged in front of us, I saw that she was barefoot, her dirty little feet fighting the uneven ground. In most respects she was like any of two or three dozen showgirls you encounter if you wander about the winter quarters of Mr. John Ringling North's circus, in Sarasota—cleverly proportioned, deeply browned by the sun, dusty, eager, and almost naked. But her grave face and the naturalness of her manner gave her a sort of quick distinction and brought a new note into the gloomy octagonal building where we had all cast our lot for a few moments. As soon as she had squeezed through the crowd, she spoke a word or two to the older woman, whom I took to be her mother, stepped to the ring, and waited while the horse coasted to a stop in front of her. She gave the animal a couple of affectionate swipes on his enormous neck and then swung herself aboard. The horse immediately resumed his rocking canter, the woman goading him on, chanting something that sounded like "Hop! Hop!"

3   In attempting to recapture this mild spectacle, I am merely acting as recording secretary for one of the oldest of societies—the society of those who, at one time or another, have surrendered, without even a show of resistance, to the bedazzlement of a circus rider. As a writing man, or secretary, I have always felt charged with the safekeeping of all unexpected items of worldly or unworldly enchantment, as though I might be held personally responsible if even a small one were to be lost. But it is not easy to communicate anything of this nature. The circus comes as close to being the world in microcosm as anything I know; in a way, it puts all the rest of show business in the shade. Its magic is universal and complex. Out of its wild disorder comes order; from its rank smell rises the good aroma of courage and daring; out of its preliminary shabbiness comes the final splendor. And buried in the familiar boasts of its advance agents lies the modesty of most of its people. For me the circus is at its best before it has been put together. It is at its best at certain moments when it comes to a point, as through a burning glass, in the activity and destiny of a single performer out of so many. One ring is always bigger than three. One rider, one aerialist,

is always greater than six. In short, a man has to catch the circus unawares to experience its full impact and share its gaudy dream.

4   The ten-minute ride the girl took achieved—as far as I was concerned, who wasn't looking for it, and quite unbeknownst to her, who wasn't even striving for it—the thing that is sought by performers everywhere, on whatever stage, whether struggling in the tidal currents of Shakespeare or bucking the difficult motion of a horse. I somehow got the idea she was just cadging a ride, improving a shining ten minutes in the diligent way all serious artists seize free moments to hone the blade of their talent and keep themselves in trim. Her brief tour included only elementary postures and tricks, perhaps because they were all she was capable of, perhaps because her warmup at this hour was unscheduled and the ring was not rigged for a real practice session. She swung herself off and on the horse several times, gripping his mane. She did a few knee-stands—or whatever they are called—dropping to her knees and quickly bouncing back up on her feet again. Most of the time she simply rode in a standing position, well aft on the beast, her hands hanging easily at her sides, her head erect, her straw-colored ponytail lightly brushing her shoulders, the blood of exertion showing faintly through the tan of her skin. Twice she managed a one-foot stance—a sort of ballet pose, with arms outstretched. At one point the neck strap of her bathing suit broke and she went twice around the ring in the classic attitude of a woman making minor repairs to a garment. The fact that she was standing on the back of a moving horse while doing this invested the matter with a clownish significance that perfectly fitted the spirit of the circus—jocund, yet charming. She just rolled the strap into a neat ball and stowed it inside her bodice while the horse rocked and rolled beneath her in dutiful innocence. The bathing suit proved as self-reliant as its owner and stood up well enough without benefit of strap.

5   The richness of the scene was in its plainness, its natural condition—of horse, of ring, of girl, even to the girl's bare feet that gripped the bare back of her proud and ridiculous mount. The enchantment grew not out of anything that happened or was performed but out of something that seemed to go round and around and around with the girl, attending her, a steady gleam in the shape of a circle—a ring of ambition, of happiness, of youth. (And the positive pleasures of equilibrium under difficulties.) In a week or two, all would be changed, all

(or almost all) lost: the girl would wear makeup, the horse would wear gold, the ring would be painted, the bark would be clean for the feet of the horse, the girl's feet would be clean for the slippers that she'd wear. All, all would be lost.

6   As I watched with the others, our jaws adroop, our eyes alight, I became painfully conscious of the element of time. Everything in the hideous old building seemed to take the shape of a circle, conforming to the course of the horse. The rider's gaze, as she peered straight ahead, seemed to be circular, as though bent by force of circumstance; then time itself began running in circles, and so the beginning was where the end was, and the two were the same, and one thing ran into the next and time went round and around and got nowhere. The girl wasn't so young that she did not know the delicious satisfaction of having a perfectly behaved body and the fun of using it to do a trick most people can't do, but she was too young to know that time does not really move in a circle at all. I thought: "She will never be as beautiful as this again"—a thought that made me acutely unhappy—and in a flash my mind (which is too much of a busybody to suit me) had projected her twenty-five years ahead, and she was now in the center of the ring, on foot, wearing a conical hat and high-heeled shoes, the image of the older woman, holding the long rein, caught in the treadmill of an afternoon long in the future. "She is at that enviable moment in life [I thought] when she believes she can go once around the ring, make one complete circuit, and at the end be exactly the same age as at the start." Everything in her movements, her expression, told you that for her the ring of time was perfectly formed, changeless, predictable, without beginning or end, like the ring in which she was traveling at this moment with the horse that wallowed under her. And then I slipped back into my trance, and time was circular again—time, pausing quietly with the rest of us, so as not to disturb the balance of a performer.

7   Her ride ended as casually as it had begun. The older woman stopped the horse, and the girl slid to the ground. As she walked toward us to leave, there was a quick, small burst of applause. She smiled broadly, in surpise and pleasure; then her face suddenly regained its gravity and she disappeared through the door.

8   It has been ambitious and plucky of me to attempt to describe what is indescribable, and I have failed, as I knew I would. But I have discharged my duty to my society; and besides, a writer, like an acrobat,

must occasionally try a stunt that is too much for him. At any rate, it is worth reporting that long before the circus comes to town, its most notable performances have already been given. Under the bright lights of the finished show, a performer need only reflect the electric candle power that is directed upon him; but in the dark and dirty old training rings and in the makeshift cages, whatever light is generated, whatever excitement, whatever beauty, must come from original sources—from internal fires of professional hunger and delight, from the exuberance and gravity of youth. It is the difference between planetary light and the combustion of stars.

QUESTIONS

Ideas

1. What does White mean by his suggestion in paragraph 3 that the circus is "the world in microcosm"?
2. In what sense is this an essay about the circus, about performance, about time?
3. Has White failed to accomplish what he set out to do (paragraph 8)? What seems to be his purpose in "The Ring of Time"?
4. Twice in the essay White refers to his task and responsibility as a writer. What is his point?

Organization

5. In the opening paragraph White locates and describes the scene. Later, he moves from that initial description to speculation about what he has seen. As you read, or reread, the essay, note which sections are descriptive and which speculative. Explain how the essay as a whole is structured.
6. Try reorganizing the essay by ordering its paragraphs another way: 1, 2, 4, 7, 3, 5, 6, 8. Is there any advantage to reading (and writing) the essay this way? Any disadvantage?
7. What connections exist between the end of the essay and the beginning? Explain why paragraph 8 does or does not sound like a conclusion, an ending.

Sentences

8. The following sentence appears in paragraph 3:

   (1) Out of its wild disorder comes order;
   (2) from its rank smell rises the good aroma of courage and daring;
   (3) out of its preliminary shabbiness comes its final splendor.

   Read the sentence aloud as it is written. Then read it aloud as you reorder its three parts. Try a few different combinations (2, 3, 1; 2, 1, 3; 1, 3, 2; 3, 2, 1; 3, 1, 2. Which version(s) do you prefer and why? Besides experimenting with different arrangements of the three major parts of the sentence, you might consider different kinds of word order within each part. The first clause, for example, might be rewritten like this: "Order comes out of its wild disorder"; and the second: "the good aroma of courage and daring rises from its rank smell." How would the third section be rewritten? Which versions of each do you prefer and why?

9. The following sentence, like the sentence discussed in question 8, inverts the regular word order of the English sentence—subject, verb, object. How does the following alteration compare with the sentence as White wrote it?

   White: And buried in the familiar boasts of its advance agents lies the modesty of most of its people.

   Revised: The modesty of most of its people lies buried in the familiar boasts of its advance agents.

   Look at each version in the context in which White's original sentence appears (paragraph 3). Notice what kinds of sentences precede and follow. Then explain which version you prefer.

10. Read paragraph 5 aloud. Mark off the repeated sounds at the level of syllable, phrase, and sentence.

Words

11. Reread the opening paragraph and underline, circle, or list all the words suggesting circularity—all the "circle" words. Why does White include so many of them? And how is the notion of circularity relevant to the ideas and title of the essay?

12. Look through paragraph 6 for echoes and repetitions of the details of the opening paragraph. What is the effect of the repetitions? How are these repetitions of word and phrase related to what White is suggesting about the girl and about time?

13. If paragraph 1 is heavily saturated with "circle" words, primarily nouns, paragraph 2 is noteworthy for its use of precise, vivid verbs. Before you reread the paragraph fill in the blanks in the verb-deleted version below. Compare your choices with White's and with the choices of other students. Discuss the different effects of the various verbs used.

   Behind me I _____ someone _____, "Excuse me, please," in a low voice. She _____ halfway into the building when I turned and _____ her—a girl of sixteen or seventeen, politely _____ her way through us onlookers who _____ the entrance. As she _____ in front of us, I _____ that she _____ barefoot, her dirty little feet _____ the uneven ground. In most respects she _____ like any of two or three dozen showgirls you _____ if you _____ about the winter quarters of Mr. John Ringling North's circus in Sarasota—cleverly proportioned, deeply browned by the sun, dusty, eager, and almost naked. But her grave face and the naturalness of her manner _____ her a sort of quick distinction and _____ a new note into the gloomy octagonal building where we had all _____ our lot for a few moments. As soon as she had _____ through the crowd, she _____ a word or two to the older woman, whom I _____ to be her mother, _____ to the ring, and _____ while the horse _____ to a stop in front of her. She _____ the animal a couple of affectionate swipes on his enormous neck and then _____ herself aboard. The horse immediately _____ his rocking canter, the woman _____ him on, _____ something that sounded like "Hop! Hop!"

14. Paragraph 3 introduces the language of light, which burns so brilliantly in the essay's final sentences. List all the "light" (and "dark") words you can find in this paragraph. Explain what each of the images means, especially this one: "out of its preliminary shabbiness comes the final splendor."

15. Paragraph 8 contains a number of "light" words. Explain which are literal and which metaphorical. Explain the point of each metaphorical word, especially the following: "whatever light is generated, whatever excitement, whatever beauty, must come from original sources—from internal fires of professional hunger and delight, from the exuberance and gravity of youth. It is the difference between planetary light and the combustion of stars."

Suggestions for Writing

A. Recall an incident in your life which made you feel old, perhaps when something had passed you by, when someone else was moving into the place you once held. You might think, for example, of periods of transition or graduation—from elementary school, from high school, from Little

League, Girl Scouts, or something similar. Recreate the scene from your past, its time, place, and tone with concrete details. Weave into your description your insights and speculations on time, change, and age.

B. Write imitations of the sentences discussed in questions 8 and 9.
C. Write an imitation of paragraph 5.
D. Write an analysis of "The Ring of Time." Explain what White is saying in the essay. Discuss his strategy of organization and his use of language. Summarize his main points and paraphrase the essay's most important paragraphs.

Once More to the Lake

August 1941

1   One summer, along about 1904, my father rented a camp on a lake in Maine and took us all there for the month of August. We all got ringworm from some kittens and had to rub Pond's Extract on our arms and legs night and morning, and my father rolled over in a canoe with all his clothes on; but outside of that the vacation was a success and from then on none of us ever thought there was any place in the world like that lake in Maine. We returned summer after summer— always on August 1 for one month. I have since become a salt-water man, but sometimes in summer there are days when the restlessness of the tides and the fearful cold of the sea water and the incessant wind that blows across the afternoon and into the evening make me wish for the placidity of a lake in the woods. A few weeks ago this feeling got so strong I bought myself a couple of bass hooks and a spinner and returned to the lake where we used to go, for a week's fishing and to revisit old haunts.

2   I took along my son, who had never had any fresh water up his nose and who had seen lily pads only from train windows. On the journey over to the lake I began to wonder what it would be like. I wondered how time would have marred this unique, this holy spot— the coves and streams, the hills that the sun set behind, the camps and the paths behind the camps. I was sure that the tarred road would have

found it out, and I wondered in what other ways it would be desolated.
It is strange how much you can remember about places like that once
you allow your mind to return into the grooves that lead back. You
remember one thing, and that suddenly reminds you of another thing.
I guess I remembered clearest of all the early mornings, when the lake
was cool and motionless, remembered how the bedroom smelled of the
lumber it was made of and of the wet woods whose scent entered through
the screen. The partitions in the camp were thin and did not extend
clear to the top of the rooms, and as I was always the first up I would
dress softly so as not to wake the others, and sneak out into the sweet
outdoors and start out in the canoe, keeping close along the shore in
the long shadows of the pines. I remembered being very careful never
to rub my paddle against the gunwale for fear of disturbing the stillness
of the cathedral.

3   The lake had never been what you would call a wild lake. There
were cottages sprinkled around the shores, and it was in farming country
although the shores of the lake were quite heavily wooded. Some of
the cottages were owned by nearby farmers, and you would live at the
shore and eat your meals at the farmhouse. That's what our family did.
But although it wasn't wild, it was a fairly large and undisturbed lake
and there were places in it that, to a child at least, seemed infinitely
remote and primeval.

4   I was right about the tar: it led to within half a mile of the shore.
But when I got back there, with my boy, and we settled into a camp
near a farmhouse and into the kind of summertime I had known, I
could tell that it was going to be pretty much the same as it had been
before—I knew it, lying in bed the first morning, smelling the bedroom
and hearing the boy sneak quietly out and go off along the shore in a
boat. I began to sustain the illusion that he was I, and therefore, by
simple transposition, that I was my father. This sensation persisted, kept
cropping up all the time we were there. It was not an entirely new
feeling, but in this setting it grew much stronger. I seemed to be living
a dual existence. I would be in the middle of some simple act, I would
be picking up a bait box or laying down a table fork, or I would be
saying something, and suddenly it would be not I but my father who
was saying the words or making the gesture. It gave me a creepy sensation.

5   We went fishing the first morning. I felt the same damp moss
covering the worms in the bait can, and saw the dragonfly alight on the

the tip of my rod as it hovered a few inches from the surface of the water. It was the arrival of this fly that convinced me beyond any doubt that everything was as it always had been, that the years were a mirage and that there had been no years. The small waves were the same, chucking the rowboat under the chin as we fished at anchor, and the boat was the same boat, the same color green and the ribs broken in the same places, and under the floorboards the same fresh-water leavings and débris—the dead helgramite, the wisps of moss, the rusty discarded fishhook, the dried blood from yesterday's catch. We stared silently at the tips of our rods, at the dragonflies that came and went. I lowered the tip of mine into the water, tentatively, pensively dislodging the fly, which darted two feet away, poised, darted two feet back, and came to rest again a little farther up the rod. There had been no years between the ducking of this dragonfly and the other one—the one that was part of memory. I looked at the boy, who was silently watching his fly, and it was my hands that held his rod, my eyes watching. I felt dizzy and didn't know which rod I was at the end of.

6   We caught two bass, hauling them in briskly as though they were mackerel, pulling them over the side of the boat in a businesslike manner without any landing net, and stunning them with a blow on the back of the head. When we got back for a swim before lunch, the lake was exactly where we had left it, the same number of inches from the dock, and there was only the merest suggestion of a breeze. This seemed an utterly enchanted sea, this lake you could leave to its own devices for a few hours and come back to, and find that it had not stirred, this constant and trustworthy body of water. In the shallows, the dark, water-soaked sticks and twigs, smooth and old, were undulating in clusters on the bottom against the clean ribbed sand, and the track of the mussel was plain. A school of minnows swam by, each minnow with its small individual shadow, doubling the attendance, so clear and sharp in the sunlight. Some of the other campers were in swimming, along the shore, one of them with a cake of soap, and the water felt thin and clear and unsubstantial. Over the years there had been this person with the cake of soap, this cultist, and here he was. There had been no years.

7   Up to the farmhouse to dinner through the teeming, dusty field, the road under our sneakers was only a two-track road. The middle track was missing, the one with the marks of the hooves and the splotches of dried, flaky manure. There had always been three tracks to choose

from in choosing which track to walk in; now the choice was narrowed down to two. For a moment I missed terribly the middle alternative. But the way led past the tennis court, and something about the way it lay there in the sun reassured me; the tape had loosened along the backline, the alleys were green with plantains and other weeds, and the net (installed in June and removed in September) sagged in the dry noon, and the whole place steamed with midday heat and hunger and emptiness. There was a choice of pie for dessert, and one was blueberry and one was apple, and the waitresses were the same country girls, there having been no passage of time, only the illusion of it as in a dropped curtain—the waitresses were still fifteen; their hair had been washed, that was the only difference—they had been to the movies and seen the pretty girls with the clean hair.

8   Summertime, oh, summertime, pattern of life indelible, the fade-proof lake, the woods unshatterable, the pasture with the sweetfern and the juniper forever and ever, summer without end; this was the background, and the life along the shore was the design, the cottagers with their innocent and tranquil design, their tiny docks with the flagpole and the American flag floating against the white clouds in the blue sky, the little paths over the roots of the trees leading from camp to camp and the paths leading back to the outhouses and the can of lime for sprinkling, and at the souvenir counters at the store the miniature birch-bark canoes and the postcards that showed things looking a little better than they looked. This was the American family at play, escaping the city heat, wondering whether the newcomers in the camp at the head of the cove were "common" or "nice," wondering whether it was true that the people who drove up for Sunday dinner at the farmhouse were turned away because there wasn't enough chicken.

9   It seemed to me, as I kept remembering all this, that those times and those summers had been infinitely precious and worth saving. There had been jollity and peace and goodness. The arriving (at the beginning of August) had been so big a business in itself, at the railway station the farm wagon drawn up, the first smell of the pine-laden air, the first glimpse of the smiling farmer, and the great importance of the trunks and your father's enormous authority in such matters, and the feel of the wagon under you for the long ten-mile haul, and at the top of the last long hill catching the first view of the lake after eleven months of not seeing this cherished body of water. The shouts and cries of the other campers when they saw you, and the trunks to be unpacked, to

give up their rich burden. (Arriving was less exciting nowadays, when you sneaked up in your car and parked it under a tree near the camp and took out the bags and in five minutes it was all over, no fuss, no loud wonderful fuss about trunks.)

10   Peace and goodness and jollity. The only thing that was wrong now, really, was the sound of the place, an unfamiliar nervous sound of the outboard motors. This was the note that jarred, the one thing that would sometimes break the illusion and set the years moving. In those other summertimes all motors were inboard; and when they were at a little distance, the noise they made was a sedative, an ingredient of summer sleep. They were one-cylinder and two-cylinder engines, and some were make-and-break and some were jump-spark, but they all made a sleepy sound across the lake. The one-lungers throbbed and fluttered, and the twin-cylinder ones purred and purred, and that was a quiet sound, too. But now the campers all had outboards. In the daytime, in the hot mornings, these motors made a petulant, irritable sound; at night, in the still evening when the afterglow lit the water, they whined about one's ears like mosquitoes. My boy loved our rented outboard, and his great desire was to achieve single-handed mastery over it, and authority, and he soon learned the trick of choking it a little (but not too much), and the adjustment of the needle valve. Watching him I would remember the things you could do with the old one-cylinder engine with the heavy flywheel, how you could have it eating out of your hand if you got really close to it spiritually. Motorboats in those days didn't have clutches, and you would make a landing by shutting off the motor at the proper time and coasting in with a dead rudder. But there was a way of reversing them, if you learned the trick, by cutting the switch and putting it on again exactly on the final dying revolution of the flywheel, so that it would kick back against compression and begin reversing. Approaching a dock in a strong following breeze, it was difficult to slow up sufficiently by the ordinary coasting method, and if a boy felt he had complete mastery over his motor, he was tempted to keep it running beyond its time and then reverse it a few feet from the dock. It took a cool nerve, because if you threw the switch a twentieth of a second too soon you would catch the flywheel when it still had speed enough to go up past center, and the boat would leap ahead, charging bull-fashion at the dock.

11   We had a good week at the camp. The bass were biting well and the sun shone endlessly, day after day. We would be tired at night and

lie down in the accumulated heat of the little bedrooms after the long hot day and the breeze would stir almost imperceptibly outside and the smell of the swamp drift in through the rusty screens. Sleep would come easily and in the morning the red squirrel would be on the roof, tapping out his gay routine. I kept remembering everything, lying in bed in the mornings—the small steamboat that had a long rounded stern like the lip of a Ubangi, and how quietly she ran on the moonlight sails, when the older boys played their mandolins and the girls sang and we ate doughnuts dipped in sugar, and how sweet the music was on the water in the shining night, and what it had felt like to think about girls then. After breakfast we would go up to the store and the things were in the same place—the minnows in a bottle, the plugs and spinners disarranged and pawed over by the youngsters from the boys' camp, the Fig Newtons and the Beeman's gum. Outside, the road was tarred and cars stood in front of the store. Inside, all was just as it had always been, except there was more Coca-Cola and not so much Moxie and root beer and birch beer and sarsaparilla. We would walk out with the bottle of pop apiece and sometimes the pop would backfire up our noses and hurt. We explored the streams, quietly, where the turtles slid off the sunny logs and dug their way into the soft bottom; and we lay on the town wharf and fed worms to the tame bass. Everywhere we went I had trouble making out which was I, the one walking at my side, the one walking in my pants.

12   One afternoon while we were there at that lake a thunderstorm came up. It was like the revival of an old melodrama that I had seen long ago with childish awe. The second-act climax of the drama of the electrical disturbance over a lake in America had not changed in any important respect. This was the big scene, still the big scene. The whole thing was so familiar, the first feeling of oppression and heat and a general air around camp of not wanting to go very far away. In mid-afternoon (it was all the same) a curious darkening of the sky, and a lull in everything that had made life tick; and then the way the boats suddenly swung the other way at their moorings with the coming of a breeze out of the new quarter, and the premonitory rumble. Then the kettle drum, then the snare, then the bass drum and cymbals, then crackling light against the dark, and the gods grinning and licking their chops in the hills. Afterward the calm, the rain steadily rustling in the calm lake, the return of light and hope and spirits, and the campers running out in joy and relief to go swimming in the rain, their bright

cries perpetuating the deathless joke about how they were getting simply drenched, and the children screaming with delight at the new sensation of bathing in the rain, and the joke about getting drenched linking the generations in a strong indestructible chain. And the comedian who waded in carrying an umbrella.

13   When the others went swimming, my son said he was going in, too. He pulled his dripping trunks from the line where they had hung all through the shower and wrung them out. Languidly, and with no thought of going in, I watched him, his hard little body, skinny and bare, saw him wince slightly as he pulled up around his vitals the small, soggy, icy garment. As he buckled the swollen belt, suddenly my groin felt the chill of death.

QUESTIONS

Ideas

1. Like "The Ring of Time," "Once More to the Lake" is a lyrical and speculative essay. It is, of course, a reminiscence of a memorable summer. But it is something more: a meditation on time. What ideas about time does White suggest? Consider especially what he says in paragraphs 4, 5, and 6.

2. Explain what you think White means by the following statements:

   I seemed to be living a dual existence. (4)

   I felt dizzy and didn't know which rod I was at the end of. (5)

   I began to sustain the illusion that he was I, and therefore, by simple transposition, that I was my father. (4)

3. Besides time and change, what is this essay about?

Organization

4. Divide the essay into sections and provide titles for each part. In deciding upon your sections and titles, consider which paragraphs are primarily descriptive and which are speculative.

5. White gains emphasis by positioning his key ideas at the ends of paragraphs. Reread paragraphs 4, 5, and 6, attending to the final sentence of each paragraph. All three build toward the concluding sentence, which completes the idea in a forceful statement or embodies it in a striking image.

Find at least one other example of a final effective sentence in a paragraph. Explain how it completes the paragraph.

6. Examine paragraphs 9 and 10 to see how White uses comparison and contrast to elaborate his point about the place. Note all the words and phrases that set up and emphasize the comparisons White makes between the lake in the past and now.

Sentences

7. A number of White's sentences resonate and reverberate with repeated words and phrases. Read the following sentence aloud, noting its repetitions:

> The small waves were the same, chucking the rowboat under the chin as we fished at anchor, and the boat was the same boat, the same color green and the ribs broken in the same places, and under the floorboards the same fresh-water leavings and débris—the dead helgramite, the wisps of moss, the rusty discarded fishhook, the dried blood from yesterday's catch.

8. Another way White uses repetition in the essay is to employ the same words in different sentences. For example, the following sentences occur in different paragraphs:

> There had been jollity and peace and goodness. (9)
>
> Peace and goodness and jollity. (10)

Reread these two sentences in their context. Does the reordering of words affect the meaning? Why might White have altered the word order when he came to repeat the words "jollity and peace and goodness"?

9. In the sentences that follow, White expands his thought and accumulates details toward the end—after a brief direct statement of idea. You might think of the sentence formed this way as a string or a stack of details laid out in a series of parallel clauses or phrases.

> It was the arrival of this fly that convinced me beyond any doubt
>   that everything was as it always had been,
>   that the years were a mirage
> and that there had been no years.

> We caught two bass,
>   hauling them in briskly as though they were mackerel,
>   pulling them in over the side of the boat in a businesslike manner
>   without any landing net,
> and stunning them with a blow on the back of the head.

10. Compare the following sentence by White with the alternate form for sound and rhythm.

White: I wondered how time would have marred this unique, this holy spot—the coves and streams, the hills that the sun set behind, the camps and the paths behind the camps.

Alternate: I wondered how time would have marred this unique, holy spot—the coves, streams, hills, camps and paths.

Words

11. What words in paragraphs 1 and 2 describe the lake? What connotations does each possess? What overall impression of the lake is created by the accumulation of these words? How do the final words of paragraph 3 reinforce this impression?

12. "Once More to the Lake" is rich in sensuous detail—in images of sight, sound, smell, taste, and touch. List the visual details of paragraph 7 and the sound and sense details of paragraphs 10, 11, and 12. What is the overall effect of each paragraph?

13. White's diction in this essay and in others combines the high and the low, the common and the unusual, the formally elegant and the colloquially casual. Compare the tone, sound, and rhythm of the following remarks: (1) "the restlessness of the tides"; "the incessant wind that blows across the afternoon"; "the placidity of a lake in the woods." (2) "A few weeks ago this feeling got so strong I bought myself a couple of bass hooks and a spinner and returned to the lake where we used to go, for a week's fishing and to revisit old haunts." What is different about the second voice? Which words in particular are responsible for its feeling and tone?

14. In this essay and in others White combines factual with emotional details. He extends a literal fact into a metaphoric detail, which carries a charge of meaning and a spark of feeling. Here is an example: "the whole place steamed with midday heat and hunger and emptiness" (7). To obtain the full force of how this literal fact (the heat) is extended to a human fact of feeling (hunger and emptiness) you'll need to read the sentence in context. Try to find another example of White's shading a fact into a metaphor and explain how the literal and metaphorical meanings intersect.

Suggestions for Writing

A. Write an essay about a place you have revisited after a long absence. Try to account for what the place meant to you after the first visit and after the later visit. Give some sense of what you expected and hoped for on the later visit. Try to suggest how the place had changed and how it remained the way you remembered it.

B. Explain, in a short essay, the sources of White's appeal as a writer. Does it have something to do with his subjects? With his ideas? His attitude and tone? His style?

C. In a paragraph or short essay, explain the idea of the following poem. Consider especially the imagery of stanzas 3 and 4. Compare the ideas about time in the poem with the ideas about time in White's essay. (Note especially the last stanza of the poem and the last paragraph of the essay.)

MEN AT FORTY

Men at forty
Learn to close softly
The doors to rooms they will not be
Coming back to.

At rest on a stair landing,
They feel it moving
Beneath them now like the deck of a ship,
Though the swell is gentle.

And deep in mirrors
They rediscover
The face of the boy as he practices tying
His father's tie there in secret

And the face of that father,
Still warm with the mystery of lather.
They are more fathers than sons themselves now.
Something is filling them, something

That is like the twilight sound
Of the crickets, immense,
Filling the woods at the foot of the slope
Behind their mortgaged houses.

—DONALD JUSTICE

D. Write an essay explaining White's ideas in two of his essays. You might compare and contrast his treatment of a similar subject or discuss his treatment of a similar theme using two different subjects.

E. Write imitations of the sentences discussed in questions 7, 9, and 10.

NINE

Annie Dillard

(1945–   )

Annie Dillard writes out of an impassioned awe of the natural world. She both loves and fears it. And she reveals in prose that is by turns taut and expansive both its delights and its terrors. Something of a visionary who possesses a mystical strain, Dillard can be accorded a place in the line of American Transcendentalist writers, a line that includes Emerson, Thoreau, and Whitman in the nineteenth century and Loren Eiseley and Peter Matthiessen in our own time.

Her first book, *Pilgrim at Tinker Creek* (1974), was a best seller, and won a Pulitzer Prize. In this work Dillard describes what she saw while patiently observing nature at Tinker Creek in the Roanoke Valley in Virginia. Throughout the book, Dillard moves from a careful exploration of the natural world to the largest philosophical and theological questions, questions about the design and purpose of the universe and of man's place in it; questions about pain, cruelty, suffering, and death—unanswerable yet inescapable questions all.

Meaning and design are central not only as subjects of Dillard's writing, but also as dimensions of its substance and form as well. Her essays, that is, are attempts to explore and explain the meanings hidden in nature; however, Dillard's essays also raise questions about the meaning of life and the purpose of nature. Moreover, just as Dillard seeks to discover patterns of form and structure in nature, in her chance encounters with mystery, so too do her essays both reveal and conceal intricacies of structure and form. (Perhaps we ought to read Dillard with the same attention and deliberation she lavishes on nature.)

What is apparent from even a casual reading of her work is its intensity, its seriousness. There's nothing chatty about her tone, nothing superficial about her subjects or her ideas. In "Jest and Earnest," an excerpt from the first chapter of *Pilgrim at Tinker Creek*, Dillard describes a shocking event: a frog being drained of its internal organs, reduced to juice by a powerful enzyme of the giant water bug. This event stirs Dillard, provoking her to ask a series of questions about God, nature, beauty, and terror. The writing, highly charged with feeling, relies heavily on an accumulation of verbs in the descriptive section and on a pile-up of questions in the speculative part. This is typical of the way Dillard arranges her essays. She often starts with a close description of something she has seen or heard about—a frog, a bird, a fire, an airplane accident, a dream. From description she moves out through a series of questions and provisional answers into speculation and argument.

Her concern throughout *Pilgrim* is with seeing. Her interest, however, is less in what we see than in how we see; less in what we know than in how we come to know. Chapter Two, entitled "Seeing," is an investigation of what it means to really see something; it is an exploration of the different ways of seeing, knowing, and understanding available to us.

One of the things Dillard seeks to understand is the fixedness of nature, the way particular plants and animals are locked into what seems to be mindless, repetitive, compulsive behavior. She explores this idea in two chapters of *Pilgrim*, "The Fixed" and "Fecundity." Together they present a picture of nature that is simultaneously heartening and frightening.

In the essay "God's Tooth," excerpted from her second book of prose, *Holy the Firm* (1977), Dillard raises and responds to the difficult question of the meaning of suffering, particularly the seemingly senseless suffering of children. The essay is casual in structure, angry in tone, and passionate in its agonized quest for meaning in a chance tragic event.

Dillard has described herself as "an explorer" and "a stalker"—both of the natural world and of the meanings locked within it. Both naturalist and symbolist, Dillard searches in and through nature for transcendent truths. Though at times such an intense scrutiny of nature and such a passionate search for meaning lead her into over-reacting and overwriting, such lapses are rare. In fact it is the risks she takes that make possible her best work, writing steeped in wonder and rooted in reality, writing that moves consistently from sight to insight.

Seeing

---

1   It is still the first week in January, and I've got great plans. I've been thinking about seeing. There are lots of things to see, un-wrapped gifts and free surprises. The world is fairly studded and strewn with pennies cast broadside from a generous hand. But—and this is the point—who gets excited by a mere penny? If you follow one arrow, if you crouch motionless on a bank to watch a tremulous ripple thrill on the water and are rewarded by the sight of a muskrat kit paddling from its den, will you count that sight a chip of copper only, and go your rueful way? It is dire poverty indeed when a man is so malnourished and fatigued that he won't stoop to pick up a penny. But if you cultivate a healthy poverty and simplicity, so that finding a penny will literally make your day, then, since the world is in fact planted in pennies, you have with your poverty bought a lifetime of days. It is that simple. What you see is what you get.

2   I used to be able to see flying insects in the air. I'd look ahead and see, not the row of hemlocks across the road, but the air in front of it. My eyes would focus along that column of air, picking out flying insects. But I lost interest, I guess, for I dropped the habit. Now I can see birds. Probably some people can look at the grass at their feet and discover all the crawling creatures. I would like to know grasses and sedges—and care. Then my least journey into the world would be a field trip, a series of happy recognitions. Thoreau, in an expansive mood, exulted, "What a rich book might be made about buds, includ-

ing, perhaps, sprouts!" It would be nice to think so. I cherish mental images I have of three perfectly happy people. One collects stones. Another—an Englishman, say—watches clouds. The third lives on a coast and collects drops of seawater which he examines microscopically and mounts. But I don't see what the specialist sees, and so I cut myself off, not only from the total picture, but from the various forms of happiness.

3   Unfortunately, nature is very much a now-you-see-it, now-you-don't affair. A fish flashes, then dissolves in the water before my eyes like so much salt. Deer apparently ascend bodily into heaven; the brightest oriole fades into leaves. These disappearances stun me into stillness and concentration; they say of nature that it conceals with a grand nonchalance, and they say of vision that it is a deliberate gift, the revelation of a dancer who for my eyes only flings away her seven veils. For nature does reveal as well as conceal: now-you-don't-see-it, now-you-do. For a week last September migrating red-winged blackbirds were feeding heavily down by the creek at the back of the house. One day I went out to investigate the racket; I walked up to a tree, an Osage orange, and a hundred birds flew away. They simply materialized out of the tree. I saw a tree, then a whisk of color, then a tree again. I walked closer and another hundred blackbirds took flight. Not a branch, not a twig budged: the birds were apparently weightless as well as invisible. Or, it was as if the leaves of the Osage orange had been freed from a spell in the form of red-winged blackbirds; they flew from the tree, caught my eye in the sky, and vanished. When I looked again at the tree the leaves had reassembled as if nothing had happened. Finally I walked directly to the trunk of the tree and a final hundred, the real diehards, appeared, spread, and vanished. How could so many hide in the tree without my seeing them? The Osage orange, unruffled, looked just as it had looked from the house, when three hundred red-winged blackbirds cried from its crown. I looked downstream where they flew, and they were gone. Searching, I couldn't spot one. I wandered downstream to force them to play their hand, but they'd crossed the creek and scattered. One show to a customer. These appearances catch at my throat; they are the free gifts, the bright coppers at the roots of trees.

4   It's all a matter of keeping my eyes open. Nature is like one of those line drawings of a tree that are puzzles for children: Can you find hidden in the leaves a duck, a house, a boy, a bucket, a zebra, and a boot? Specialists can find the most incredibly well-hidden things. A

book I read when I was young recommended an easy way to find caterpillars to rear: you simply find some fresh caterpillar droppings, look up, and there's your caterpillar. More recently an author advised me to set my mind at ease about those piles of cut stems on the ground in grassy fields. Field mice make them; they cut the grass down by degrees to reach the seeds at the head. It seems that when the grass is tightly packed, as in a field of ripe grain, the blade won't topple at a single cut through the stem; instead, the cut stem simply drops vertically, held in the crush of grain. The mouse severs the bottom again and again, the stem keeps dropping an inch at a time, and finally the head is low enough for the mouse to reach the seeds. Meanwhile, the mouse is positively littering the field with its little piles of cut stems into which, presumably, the author of the book is constantly stumbling.

5   If I can't see these minutiae, I still try to keep my eyes open. I'm always on the lookout for antlion traps in sandy soil, monarch pupae near milkweed, skipper larvae in locust leaves. These things are utterly common, and I've not seen one. I bang on hollow trees near water, but so far no flying squirrels have appeared. In flat country I watch every sunset in hopes of seeing the green ray. The green ray is a seldom-seen streak of light that rises from the sun like a spurting fountain at the moment of sunset; it throbs into the sky for two seconds and disappears. One more reason to keep my eyes open. A photography professor at the University of Florida just happened to see a bird die in midflight; it jerked, died, dropped, and smashed on the ground. I squint at the wind because I read Stewart Edward White: "I have always maintained that if you look closely enough you could *see* the wind— the dim, hardly-made-out, fine débris fleeing high in the air." White was an excellent observer, and devoted an entire chapter of *The Mountains* to the subject of seeing deer: "As soon as you can forget the naturally obvious and construct an artificial obvious, then you too will see deer."

6   But the artificial obvious is hard to see. My eyes account for less than one percent of the weight of my head; I'm bony and dense; I see what I expect. I once spent a full three minutes looking at a bullfrog that was so unexpectedly large I couldn't see it even though a dozen enthusiastic campers were shouting directions. Finally I asked, "What color am I looking for?" and a fellow said, "Green." When at last I picked out the frog, I saw what painters are up against: the thing wasn't green at all, but the color of wet hickory bark.

7   The lover can see, and the knowledgeable. I visited an aunt and uncle at a quarter-horse ranch in Cody, Wyoming. I couldn't do much of anything useful, but I could, I thought, draw. So, as we all sat around the kitchen table after supper, I produced a sheet of paper and drew a horse. "That's one lame horse," my aunt volunteered. The rest of the family joined in: "Only place to saddle that one is his neck"; "Looks like we better shoot the poor thing, on account of those terrible growths." Meekly, I slid the pencil and paper down the table. Everyone in that family, including my three young cousins, could draw a horse. Beautifully. When the paper came back it looked as though five shining, real quarter horses had been corraled by mistake with a papier-mâché moose; the real horses seemed to gaze at the monster with a steady, puzzled air. I stay away from horses now, but I can do a creditable goldfish. The point is that I just don't know what the lover knows; I just can't see the artificial obvious that those in the know construct. The herpetologist asks the native, "Are there snakes in that ravine?" "Nosir." And the herpetologist comes home with, yessir, three bags full. Are there butterflies on that mountain? Are the bluets in bloom, are there arrowheads here, or fossil shells in the shale?

8   Peeping through my keyhole I see within the range of only about thirty percent of the light that comes from the sun; the rest is infrared and some little ultraviolet, perfectly apparent to many animals, but invisible to me. A nightmare network of ganglia, charged and firing without my knowledge, cuts and splices what I do see, editing it for my brain. Donald E. Carr points out that the sense impressions of one-celled animals are *not* edited for the brain: "This is philosophically interesting in a rather mournful way, since it means that only the simplest animals perceive the universe as it is."

9   A fog that won't burn away drifts and flows across my field of vision. When you see fog move against a backdrop of deep pines, you don't see the fog itself, but streaks of clearness floating across the air in dark shreds. So I see only tatters of clearness through a pervading obscurity. I can't distinguish the fog from the overcast sky; I can't be sure if the light is direct or reflected. Everywhere darkness and the presence of the unseen appalls. We estimate now that only one atom dances alone in every cubic meter of intergalactic space. I blink and squint. What planet or power yanks Halley's Comet out of orbit? We haven't seen that force yet; it's a question of distance, density, and the pallor of reflected light. We rock, cradled in the swaddling band of

darkness. Even the simple darkness of night whispers suggestions to the mind. Last summer, in August, I stayed at the creek too late. . . .

10   Seeing is of course very much a matter of verbalization. Unless I call my attention to what passes before my eyes, I simply won't see it. It is, as Ruskin says, "not merely unnoticed, but in the full, clear sense of the word, unseen." My eyes alone can't solve analogy tests using figures, the ones which show, with increasing elaborations, a big square, then a small square in a big square, then a big triangle, and expect me to find a small triangle in a big triangle. I have to say the words, describe what I'm seeing. If Tinker Mountain erupted, I'd be likely to notice. But if I want to notice the lesser cataclysms of valley life, I have to maintain in my head a running description of the present. It's not that I'm observant; it's just that I talk too much. Otherwise, especially in a strange place, I'll never know what's happening. Like a blind man at the ball game, I need a radio.

11   When I see this way I analyze and pry. I hurl over logs and roll away stones; I study the bank a square foot at a time, probing and tilting my head. Some days when a mist covers the mountains, when the muskrats won't show and the microscope's mirror shatters, I want to climb up the blank blue dome as a man would storm the inside of a circus tent, wildly, dangling, and with a steel knife claw a rent in the top, peep, and, if I must, fall.

12   But there is another kind of seeing that involves a letting go. When I see this way I sway transfixed and emptied. The difference between the two ways of seeing is the difference between walking with and without a camera. When I walk with a camera I walk from shot to shot, reading the light on a calibrated meter. When I walk without a camera, my own shutter opens, and the moment's light prints on my own silver gut. When I see this second way I am above all an unscrupulous observer.

13   It was sunny one evening last summer at Tinker Creek; the sun was low in the sky, upstream. I was sitting on the sycamore log bridge with the sunset at my back, watching the shiners the size of minnows who were feeding over the muddy sand in skittery schools. Again and again, one fish, then another, turned for a split second across the current and flash! the sun shot out from its silver side. I couldn't watch for it. It was always just happening somewhere else, and it drew my vision just as it disappeared: flash, like a sudden dazzle of the thinnest blade, a sparking over a dun and olive ground at chance intervals from every

direction. Then I noticed white specks, some sort of pale petals, small, floating from under my feet on the creek's surface, very slow and steady. So I blurred my eyes and gazed towards the brim of my hat and saw a new world. I saw the pale white circles roll up, roll up, like the world's turning, mute and perfect, and I saw the linear flashes, gleaming silver, like stars being born at random down a rolling scroll of time. Something broke and something opened. I filled up like a new wineskin. I breathed an air like light; I saw a light like water. I was the lip of a fountain the creek filled forever; I was ether, the leaf in the zephyr; I was fleshflake, feather, bone.

14   When I see this way I see truly. As Thoreau says, I return to my senses. I am the man who watches the baseball game in silence in an empty stadium. I see the game purely; I'm abstracted and dazed. When it's all over and the white-suited players lope off the green field to their shadowed dugouts, I leap to my feet; I cheer and cheer.

15   But I can't go out and try to see this way. I'll fail, I'll go mad. All I can do is try to gag the commentator, to hush the noise of useless interior babble that keeps me from seeing just as surely as a newspaper dangled before my eyes. The effort is really a discipline requiring a lifetime of dedicated struggle; it marks the literature of saints and monks of every order East and West, under every rule and no rule, discalced and shod. The world's spiritual geniuses seem to discover universally that the mind's muddy river, this ceaseless flow of trivia and trash, cannot be dammed, and that trying to dam it is a waste of effort that might lead to madness. Instead you must allow the muddy river to flow unheeded in the dim channels of consciousness; you raise your sights; you look along it, mildly, acknowledging its presence without interest and gazing beyond it into the realm of the real where subjects and objects act and rest purely, without utterance. "Launch into the deep," says Jacques Ellul, "and you shall see."

16   The secret of seeing is, then, the pearl of great price. If I thought he could teach me to find it and keep it forever I would stagger barefoot across a hundred deserts after any lunatic at all. But although the pearl may be found, it may not be sought. The literature of illumination reveals this above all: although it comes to those who wait for it, it is always, even to the most practiced and adept, a gift and a total surprise. I return from one walk knowing where the killdeer nests in the field by the creek and the hour the laurel blooms. I return from the same walk a day later scarcely knowing my own name. Litanies hum in my ears;

my tongue flaps in my mouth Ailinon, alleluia! I cannot cause light; the most I can do is try to put myself in the path of its beam. It is possible, in deep space, to sail on solar wind. Light, be it particle or wave, has force: you rig a giant sail and go. The secret of seeing is to sail on solar wind. Hone and spread your spirit till you yourself are a sail, whetted, translucent, broadside to the merest puff.

QUESTIONS

1. What is Dillard's main point about seeing? Can you learn to see in the manner she describes? And in what sense is it true that "what you see is what you get"?

2. What does Dillard mean when she suggests that nature both reveals and conceals? What are the "free gifts of nature" that "catch at the throat"? Are the mockingbird, frog, and sharks of "Jest and Earnest" such gifts? Explain.

3. How is it that, as Dillard says, many wonders of nature are "utterly common," yet go unobserved and unnoticed.

4. Explain her remark: "I see what I expect." What does she expect to see as she looks for the bullfrog. Why can't she see it? In what ways does expectation influence *what* we see? How does it also influence *how* we see?

5. In paragraph 7 Dillard says that the powers of seeing are limited to the lovers and to the knowledgeable—to specialists. Do you agree? How can knowledge of and love for something or someone help you to see that person or thing better? Can love or knowledge ever be an impediment to seeing things as they are? Explain.

6. Paragraph 10 contains a remark especially significant for writing: "Seeing is of course very much a matter of verbalization." Dillard continues: "Unless I call my attention to what passes before my eyes, I simply won't see it. . . . I have to say the words, describe what I'm seeing." Explain how saying the words either by speaking them or writing them helps you to see.

7. Dillard makes a number of distinctions: between things unnoticed and things unseen; between looking for and looking; between probing and looking without a camera. Explain what you think she means by one or more of these distinctions.

Suggestions for Writing

A. Look at something you see all the time—but don't really see. Make a list of twenty-five specific details concerning it.

B. Walk along a route you habitually travel. Try to notice at least ten things you've never noticed before. Jot them down as you notice them.
C. Think of something you are knowledgeable about—something that you love. You might be an expert camper, skater, sailor, dancer, athlete, guitarist, coin collector, model builder. Write an essay explaining the fine points of the activity. Try to describe, for example, what a layman might need to know to look at a rare coin, to understand a magic trick or clever con, to really see an art masterpiece. Or you might explain what to look for in a good performance—of whatever kind. Here, you would have to isolate the characteristics of a good skiing or skating performance, for example, as well as to describe and explain them in such a way that a non-skier or non-skater would know how to look at them and what to look for to appreciate the performance.

Jest and Earnest

1   **A** couple of summers ago I was walking along the edge of the island to see what I could see in the water, and mainly to scare frogs. Frogs have an inelegant way of taking off from invisible positions on the bank just ahead of your feet, in dire panic, emitting a froggy "Yike!" and splashing into the water. Incredibly, this amused me, and, incredibly, it amuses me still. As I walked along the grassy edge of the island, I got better and better at seeing frogs both in and out of the water. I learned to recognize, slowing down, the difference in texture of the light reflected from mudbank, water, grass, or frog. Frogs were flying all around me. At the end of the island I noticed a small green frog. He was exactly half in and half out of the water, looking like a schematic diagram of an amphibian, and he didn't jump.

2   He didn't jump; I crept closer. At last I knelt on the island's winterkilled grass, lost, dumbstruck, staring at the frog in the creek just four feet away. He was a very small frog with wide, dull eyes. And just as I looked at him, he slowly crumpled and began to sag. The spirit vanished from his eyes as if snuffed. His skin emptied and drooped; his very skull seemed to collapse and settle like a kicked tent. He was shrinking before my eyes like a deflating football. I watched the taut,

glistening skin on his shoulders ruck, and rumple, and fall. Soon, part of his skin, formless as a pricked balloon, lay in floating folds like bright scum on top of the water: it was a monstrous and terrifying thing. I gaped bewildered, appalled. An oval shadow hung in the water behind the drained frog; then the shadow glided away. The frog skin bag started to sink.

3   I had read about the giant water bug, but never seen one. "Giant water bug" is really the name of the creature, which is an enormous, heavy-bodied brown beetle. It eats insects, tadpoles, fish, and frogs. Its grasping forelegs are mighty and hooked inward. It seizes a victim with these legs, hugs it tight, and paralyzes it with enzymes injected during a vicious bite. That one bite is the only bite it ever takes. Through the puncture shoot the poisons that dissolve the victim's muscles and bones and organs—all but the skin—and through it the giant water bug sucks out the victim's body, reduced to a juice. This event is quite common in warm fresh water. The frog I saw was being sucked by a giant water bug. I had been kneeling on the island grass; when the unrecognizable flap of frog skin settled on the creek bottom, swaying, I stood up and brushed the knees of my pants. I couldn't catch my breath.

4   Of course, many carnivorous animals devour their prey alive. The usual method seems to be to subdue the victim by downing or grasping it so it can't flee, then eating it whole or in a series of bloody bites. Frogs eat everything whole, stuffing prey into their mouths with their thumbs. People have seen frogs with their wide jaws so full of live dragonflies they couldn't close them. Ants don't even have to catch their prey: in the spring they swarm over newly hatched, featherless birds in the nest and eat them tiny bite by bite.

5   That it's rough out there and chancy is no surprise. Every live thing is a survivor on a kind of extended emergency bivouac. But at the same time we are also created. In the Koran, Allah asks, "The heaven and the earth and all in between, thinkest thou I made them *in jest?"* It's a good question. What do we think of the created universe, spanning an unthinkable void with an unthinkable profusion of forms? Or what do we think of nothingness, those sickening reaches of time in either direction? If the giant water bug was not made in jest, was it then made in earnest? Pascal uses a nice term to describe the notion of the creator's, once having called forth the universe, turning his back to it: *Deus Absconditus.* Is this what we think happened? Was the sense of it there, and God absconded with it, ate it, like a wolf who disappears round the

edge of the house with the Thanksgiving turkey? "God is subtle," Einstein said, "but not malicious." Again, Einstein said that "nature conceals her mystery by means of her essential grandeur, not by her cunning." It could be that God has not absconded but spread, as our vision and understanding of the universe have spread, to a fabric of spirit and sense so grand and subtle, so powerful in a new way, that we can only feel blindly of its hem. In making the thick darkness a swaddling band for the sea, God "set bars and doors" and said, "Hitherto shalt thou come, but no further." But have we come even that far? Have we rowed out to the thick darkness, or are we all playing pinochle in the bottom of the boat?

6   Cruelty is a mystery, and the waste of pain. But if we describe a world to compass these things, a world that is a long, brute game, then we bump against another mystery: the inrush of power and light, the canary that sings on the skull. Unless all ages and races of men have been deluded by the same mass hypnotist (who?), there seems to be such a thing as beauty, a grace wholly gratuitous. About five years ago I saw a mockingbird make a straight vertical descent from the roof gutter of a four-story building. It was an act as careless and spontaneous as the curl of a stem or the kindling of a star.

7   The mockingbird took a single step into the air and dropped. His wings were still folded against his sides as though he were singing from a limb and not falling, accelerating thirty-two feet per second per second, through empty air. Just a breath before he would have been dashed to the ground, he unfurled his wings with exact, deliberate care, revealing the broad bars of white, spread his elegant, white-banded tail, and so floated onto the grass. I had just rounded a corner when his insouciant step caught my eye; there was no one else in sight. The fact of his free fall was like the old philosophical conundrum about the tree that falls in the forest. The answer must be, I think, that beauty and grace are performed whether or not we will or sense them. The least we can do is try to be there.

8   Another time I saw another wonder: sharks off the Atlantic coast of Florida. There is a way a wave rises about the ocean horizon, a triangular wedge against the sky. If you stand where the ocean breaks on a shallow beach, you see the raised water in a wave is translucent, shot with lights. One late afternoon at low tide a hundred big sharks passed the beach near the mouth of a tidal river in a feeding frenzy.

As each green wave rose from the churning water, it illuminated within itself the six- or eight-foot-long bodies of twisting sharks. The sharks disappeared as each wave rolled toward me; then a new wave would swell above the horizon, containing in it, like scorpions in amber, sharks that roiled and heaved. The sight held awesome wonders: power and beauty, grace tangled in a rapture with violence.

9   We don't know what's going on here. If these tremendous events are random combinations of matter run amok, the yield of millions of monkeys at millions of typewriters, then what is it in us, hammered out of those same typewriters, that they ignite? We don't know. Our life is a faint tracing on the surface of mystery, like the idle, curved tunnels of leaf miners on the face of a leaf. We must somehow take a wider view, look at the whole landscape, really see it, and describe what's going on here. Then we can at least wail the right question into the swaddling band of darkness, or, if it comes to that, choir the proper praise.

10   At the time of Lewis and Clark, setting the prairies on fire was a well-known signal that meant, "Come down to the water." It was an extravagant gesture, but we can't do less. If the landscape reveals one certainty, it is that the extravagant gesture is the very stuff of creation. After the one extravagant gesture of creation in the first place, the universe has continued to deal exclusively in extravagances, flinging intricacies and colossi down aeons of emptiness, heaping profusions on profligacies with ever-fresh vigor. The whole show has been on fire from the word go. I come down to the water to cool my eyes. But everywhere I look I see fire; that which isn't flint is tinder, and the whole world sparks and flames.

QUESTIONS

Ideas

1. Good writing often begins with seeing, with close observation. What does Dillard look at closely and then describe for us to see?
2. Dillard's seeing does not end with literal observation. It extends outward into thought. What ideas does Dillard develop out of her seeing?

Organization

3. The first two paragraphs present a description—a shocking one. Following this comes a pair of informative paragraphs and a paragraph that offers speculation about the information and description presented up to that point. Label paragraphs 6–10 as primarily descriptive, informative, or speculative.

4. What is the connection between paragraphs 5 and 6? Look especially at the first two sentences of paragraph 6, where a link is made. If the first sentence of paragraph 6 sums up what Dillard has been saying in the preceding paragraph, what does the second sentence do? And how do the sentences following that develop the point of paragraph 6?

5. Why does Dillard separate paragraph 7 from the one before it? Why does she bother including this paragraph at all? Does she need this mockingbird section? How does it fit in with what Dillard has shown up to that point?

6. The essay can be thought of or approached in terms of the three creatures described: frog, mockingbird, shark. Why is each included, and how are the three related in the context of Dillard's idea?

7. Is the final paragraph of the essay necessary? What does it contribute to the idea of the piece? To the effect?

Sentences

8. Most of the essay consists of declarative sentences, of statements. In paragraphs 5 and 6, however, Dillard uses many questions. What is the effect of these questions and what is the tone of the paragraphs?

9. Dillard uses participles to extend sentences in paragraphs 2 and 7. Here is one example: "At last I knelt on the island's winterkilled grass, lost, dumbstruck, staring at the frog in the creek just four feet away." If you ended the sentence after "dumbstruck," beginning a new sentence after, you might get this: At last I knelt on the island's winterkilled grass, lost, dumbstruck. I stared at the frog in the creek just four feet away. What advantage—in this instance—does the participial sentence have over the two shorter sentences?

10. In paragraph 3 Dillard writes an inverted sentence: "Through the puncture shoot the poisons that dissolve the victim's bones and muscles and organs. . . ." Here is an alternate version: The poisons that dissolve the victim's bones and muscles and organs shoot through the puncture. Which version do you prefer and why?

11. Return once more to the frog description, this time for a look at Dillard's punctuation. After examining the sentences with semicolons, try to formulate a general rule for their use. What is the relationship, in each

sentence, of the part before the semicolon to the part after it? Here are the important sentences: "He didn't jump; I crept closer." "His skin emptied and drooped; his very skull seemed to collapse and settle like a kicked tent." "An oval shadow hung in the water behind the drained frog; then the shadow glided away."

12. Dillard uses the colon in paragraphs 4, 6, and 8. For all three sentences, decide whether a period or comma could replace the colon. For each sentence, explain the relationship between the two parts—the part to the left of the colon and the part to the right.

Words

13. Examine the verbs in the first three sentences of paragraph 7. Compare the number and kind of verbs with the number and type of verbs in paragraph 2. What do you notice?
14. In the frog description Dillard uses a number of comparisons. What do they have in common? What is their purpose and what is their cumulative effect?
15. Imagery of light and darkness appears throughout the essay. Explain how the fire of paragraph 10 is related to the darkness of paragraphs 5, 6, and 9. What does Dillard mean when she writes: "But everywhere I look I see fire, that which isn't flint is tinder, and the whole world sparks and flames"?
16. In paragraph 5 Dillard alludes to and quotes from Einstein, Pascal, and the Koran. What is the purpose of each of these quotations and allusions? Could Dillard have made her point as well without quotation and allusion?

Suggestions for Writing

A. Write imitations of the sentences discussed in questions 9–12.
B. Write variations of some of the sentences discussed in questions 9–12. For example, you might change the punctuation or the word order of the sentences.
C. Look closely at something. Be attentive to details of shape, color, form, texture, background, line. If you like, observe a place with a considerable amount of action such as a restaurant, supermarket, or intersection. List the things you see. From your list select three or four items that stand out. Write freely, jotting down thoughts as they occur about each of the items on your list.
D. For each of the following poems explain what the speaker is looking at. Notice that in both poems a passage of explanation, generalization, or speculation accompanies the passage of description. What point does each

poem make? How necessary is the descriptive, "seeing" part of each to its idea? In each poem, how is what is seen related to or connected with what is thought?

DESIGN

I found a dimpled spider, fat and white,
On a white heal-all, holding up a moth
Like a white piece of rigid satin cloth—
Assorted characters of death and blight
Mixed ready to begin the morning right,
Like the ingredients of a witches' broth—
A snow-drop spider, a flower like a froth,
And dead wings carried like a paper kite.

What had that flower to do with being white,
The wayside blue and innocent heal-all?
What brought the kindred spider to that height,
Then steered the white moth thither in the night?
What but design of darkness to appall?—
If design govern in a thing so small.

—ROBERT FROST

MUSÉE DES BEAUX ARTS

About suffering they were never wrong,
The Old Masters: how well they understood
Its human position; how it takes place
While someone else is eating or opening a window or just walking
      dully along;
How, when the aged are reverently, passionately waiting
For the miraculous birth, there always must be
Children who did not specially want it to happen, skating
On a pond at the edge of the wood:
They never forgot
That even the dreadful martyrdom must run its course
Anyhow in a corner, some untidy spot
Where the dogs go on with their doggy life and the torturer's horse
Scratches its innocent behind on a tree.

In Brueghel's *Icarus*, for instance: how everything turns away
Quite leisurely from the disaster; the ploughman may
Have heard the splash, the forsaken cry,
But for him it was not an important failure; the sun shone

As it had to on the white legs disappearing into the green
Water: and the expensive delicate ship that must have seen
Something amazing, a boy falling out of the sky,
Had somewhere to get to and sailed calmly on.

—W. H. AUDEN

Fecundity

I

1   I wakened myself last night with my own shouting. It must have been that terrible yellow plant I saw pushing through the flood-damp soil near the log by Tinker Creek, the plant as fleshy and featureless as a slug, that erupted through the floor of my brain as I slept, and burgeoned into the dream of fecundity that woke me up.

2   I was watching two huge luna moths mate. Luna moths are those fragile ghost moths, fairy moths, whose five-inch wings are swallowtailed, a pastel green bordered in silken lavender. From the hairy head of the male sprouted two enormous, furry antennae that trailed down past his ethereal wings. He was on top of the female, hunching repeatedly with a horrible animal vigor.

3   It was the perfect picture of utter spirituality and utter degradation. I was fascinated and could not turn away my eyes. By watching them I in effect permitted their mating to take place and so committed myself to accepting the consequences—all because I wanted to see what would happen. I wanted in on a secret.

4   And then the eggs hatched and the bed was full of fish. I was standing across the room in the doorway, staring at the bed. The eggs hatched before my eyes, on my bed, and a thousand chunky fish swarmed there in a viscid slime. The fish were firm and fat, black and white, with triangular bodies and bulging eyes. I watched in horror as they squirmed three feet deep, swimming and oozing about in the glistening, transparent slime. Fish in the bed!—and I awoke. My ears still rang with the foreign cry that had been my own voice.

5   For nightmare you eat wild carrot, which is Queen Anne's lace, or you chew the black seeds of the male peony. But it was too late for prevention, and there is no cure. What root or seed will erase that scene from my mind? Fool, I thought: child, you child, you ignorant, innocent fool. What did you expect to see—angels? For it was understood in the dream that the bed full of fish was my own fault, that if I had turned away from the mating moths the hatching of their eggs wouldn't have happened, or at least would have happened in secret, elsewhere. I brought it upon myself, this slither, this swarm.

6   I don't know what it is about fecundity that so appalls. I suppose it is the teeming evidence that birth and growth, which we value, are ubiquitous and blind, that life itself is so astonishingly cheap, that nature is as careless as it is bountiful, and that with extravagance goes a crushing waste that will one day include our own cheap lives, Henle's loops and all. Every glistening egg is a memento mori.

7   After a natural disaster such as a flood, nature "stages a comeback." People use the optimistic expression without any real idea of the pressures and waste the comeback involves. Now, in late June, things are popping outside. Creatures extrude or vent eggs; larvae fatten, split their shells, and eat them; spores dissolve or explode; root hairs multiply, corn puffs on the stalk, grass yields seed, shoots erupt from the earth turgid and sheathed; wet muskrats, rabbits, and squirrels slide into the sunlight, mewling and blind; and everywhere watery cells divide and swell, swell and divide. I can like it and call it birth and regeneration, or I can play the devil's advocate and call it rank fecundity—and say that it's hell that's a-poppin'.

8   This is what I plan to do. Partly as a result of my terrible dream, I have been thinking that the landscape of the intricate world that I have painted is inaccurate and lopsided. It is too optimistic. For the notion of the infinite variety of detail and the multiplicity of forms is a pleasing one; in complexity are the fringes of beauty, and in variety are generosity and exuberance. But all this leaves something vital out of the picture. It is not one pine I see, but a thousand. I myself am not one, but legion. And we are all going to die.

9   In this repetition of individuals is a mindless stutter, an imbecilic fixedness that must be taken into account. The driving force behind all this fecundity is a terrible pressure I also must consider, the pressure of birth and growth, the pressure that splits the bark of trees and shoots out seeds, that squeezes out the egg and bursts the pupa, that hungers

and lusts and drives the creature relentlessly toward its own death. Fecundity, then, is what I have been thinking about, fecundity and the pressure of growth. Fecundity is an ugly word for an ugly subject. It is ugly, at least, in the eggy animal world. I don't think it is for plants.
10   I never met a man who was shaken by a field of identical blades of grass. An acre of poppies and a forest of spruce boggle no one's mind. Even ten square miles of wheat gladdens the hearts of most people, although it is really as unnatural and freakish as the Frankenstein monster; if man were to die, I read, wheat wouldn't survive him more than three years. No, in the plant world, and especially among the flowering plants, fecundity is not an assault on human values. Plants are not our competitors; they are our prey and our nesting materials. We are no more distressed at their proliferation than an owl is at a population explosion among field mice. . . .

11   But in the animal world things are different, and human feelings are different. While we're in New York, consider the cockroaches under the bed and the rats in the early morning clustered on the porch stoop. Apartment houses are hives of swarming roaches. Or again: in one sense you could think of Manhattan's land as high-rent, high-rise real estate; in another sense you could see it as an enormous breeding ground for rats, acres and acres of rats. I suppose that the rats and the cockroaches don't do so much actual damage as the roots do; nevertheless, the prospect does not please. Fecundity is anathema only in the animal. "Acres and acres of rats" has a suitably chilling ring to it that is decidedly lacking if I say, instead, "acres and acres of tulips."

12   The landscape of earth is dotted and smeared with masses of apparently identical individual animals, from the great Pleistocene herds that blanketed grasslands to the gluey gobs of bacteria that clog the lobes of lungs. The oceanic breeding grounds of pelagic birds are as teeming and cluttered as any human Calcutta. Lemmings blacken the earth and locusts the air. Grunion run thick in the ocean, corals pile on pile, and protozoans explode in a red tide stain. Ants take to the skies in swarms, mayflies hatch by the millions, and molting cicadas coat the trunks of trees. Have you seen the rivers run red and lumpy with salmon?
13   Consider the ordinary barnacle, the rock barnacle. Inside every one of those millions of hard white cones on the rocks—the kind that bruises your heel as you bruise its head—is of course a creature as alive

as you or I. Its business in life is this: when a wave washes over it, it sticks out twelve feathery feeding appendages and filters the plankton for food. As it grows, it sheds its skin like a lobster, enlarges its shell, and reproduces itself without end. The larvae "hatch into the sea in milky clouds." The barnacles encrusting a single half mile of shore can leak into the water a million million larvae. How many is that to a human mouthful? In sea water they grow, molt, change shape wildly, and eventually, after several months, settle on the rocks, turn into adults, and build shells. Inside the shells they have to shed their skins. Rachel Carson was always finding the old skins; she reported: "Almost every container of sea water that I bring up from the shore is flecked with white, semitransparent objects. . . . Seen under the microscope, every detail of structure is perfectly represented. . . . In the little cellophane-like replicas I can count the joints of the appendages; even the bristles, growing at the bases of the joints, seem to have been slipped intact out of their casings." All in all, rock barnacles may live four years.

14   My point about rock barnacles is those million million larvae "in milky clouds" and those shed flecks of skin. Sea water seems suddenly to be but a broth of barnacle bits. Can I fancy that a million million human infants are more real?

15   What if God has the same affectionate disregard for us that we have for barnacles? I don't know if each barnacle larva is of itself unique and special, or if we the people are essentially as interchangeable as bricks. My brain is full of numbers; they swell and would split my skull like a shell. I examine the trapezoids of skin covering the back of my hands like blown dust motes moistened to clay. I have hatched, too, with millions of my kind, into a milky way that spreads from an unknown shore.

16   I have seen the mantis's abdomen dribbling out eggs in wet bubbles like tapioca pudding glued to a thorn. I have seen a film of a termite queen as big as my face, dead white and featureless, glistening with slime, throbbing and pulsing out rivers of globular eggs. Termite workers, who looked like tiny longshoremen unloading the *Queen Mary*, licked each egg as fast as it was extruded to prevent mold. The whole world is an incubator for incalculable numbers of eggs, each one coded minutely and ready to burst.

17   The egg of a parasite chalcid wasp, a common small wasp, multiplies unassisted, making ever more identical eggs. The female lays a

single fertilized egg in the flaccid tissues of its live prey, and that one egg divides and divides. As many as two thousand new parasitic wasps will hatch to feed on the host's body with identical hunger. Similarly— only more so—Edwin Way Teale reports that a lone aphid, without a partner, breeding "unmolested" for one year, would produce so many living aphids that, although they are only a tenth of an inch long, together they would extend into space twenty-five hundred *light-years*. Even the average goldfish lays five thousand eggs, which she will eat as fast as she lays, if permitted. The sales manager of Ozark Fisheries in Missouri, which raises commercial goldfish for the likes of me, said, "We produce, measure, and sell our product by the ton." The intricacy of Ellery and aphids multiplied mindlessly into tons and light-years is more than extravagance; it is holocaust, parody, glut.

18   The pressure of growth among animals is a kind of terrible hunger. These billions must eat in order to fuel their surge to sexual maturity so that they may pump out more billions of eggs. And what are the fish on the bed going to eat, or the hatched mantises in the Mason jar going to eat, but each other? There is a terrible innocence in the benumbed world of the lower animals, reducing life there to a universal chomp. Edwin Way Teale, in *The Strange Lives of Familiar Insects*—a book I couldn't live without—describes several occasions of meals mouthed under the pressure of a hunger that knew no bounds.

19   You remember the dragonfly nymph, for instance, which stalks the bottom of the creek and the pond in search of live prey to snare with its hooked, unfolding lip. Dragonfly nymphs are insatiable and mighty. They clasp and devour whole minnows and fat tadpoles. Well, a dragonfly nymph, says Teale, "has even been seen climbing up out of the water on a plant to attack a helpless dragonfly emerging, soft and rumpled, from its nymphal skin." Is this where I draw the line?

20   It is between mothers and their offspring that these feedings have truly macabre overtones. Look at lacewings. Lacewings are those fragile green insects with large, rounded transparent wings. The larvae eat enormous numbers of aphids, the adults mate in a fluttering rush of instinct, lay eggs, and die by the millions in the first cold snap of fall. Sometimes, when a female lays her fertile eggs on a green leaf atop a slender stalked thread, she is hungry. She pauses in her laying, turns around, and eats her eggs one by one, then lays some more, and eats them, too.

21   Anything can happen, and anything does; what's it all about?

Valerie Eliot, T. S. Eliot's widow, wrote in a letter to the London *Times:* "My husband, T. S. Eliot, loved to recount how late one evening he stopped a taxi. As he got in the driver said: 'You're T. S. Eliot.' When asked how he knew, he replied: 'Ah, I've got an eye for a celebrity. Only the other evening I picked up Bertrand Russell, and I said to him, "Well, Lord Russell, what's it all about," and, do you know, he couldn't tell me.' " Well, Lord God, asks the delicate, dying lacewing whose mandibles are wet with the juice secreted by her own ovipositor, what's it all about? ("And do you know . . .")

22   Planarians, which live in the duck pond, behave similarly. They are those dark laboratory flatworms that can regenerate themselves from almost any severed part. Arthur Koestler writes, "during the mating season the worms become cannibals, devouring everything alive that comes their way, including their own previously discarded tails which were in the process of growing a new head." Even such sophisticated mammals as the great predator cats occasionally eat their cubs. A mother cat will be observed licking the area around the umbilical cord of the helpless newborn. She licks, she licks, she licks until something snaps in her brain, and she begins eating, starting there, at the vulnerable belly.

23   Although mothers devouring their own offspring is patently the more senseless, somehow the reverse behavior is the more appalling. In the death of the parent in the jaws of its offspring I recognize a universal drama that chance occurrence has merely telescoped, so that I can see all the players at once. Gall gnats, for instance, are common small flies. Sometimes, according to Teale, a gall gnat larva, which does not resemble the adult in the least, and which has certainly not mated, nevertheless produces within its body eggs, live eggs, which then hatch within its soft tissues. Sometimes the eggs hatch alive even within the quiescent body of the pupa. The same incredible thing occasionally occurs within the fly genus *Miastor*, again to both larvae and pupae. "These eggs hatch within their bodies and the ravenous larvae which emerge immediately begin devouring their parents." In this case, I know what it's all about, and I wish I didn't. The parents die, the next generation lives, *ad majorem gloriam*, and so it goes. If the new generation hastens the death of the old, it scarcely matters; the old has served its one purpose, and the direct processing of proteins is tidily all in the family. But think of the invisible swelling of ripe eggs inside the

pupa as wrapped and rigid as a mummified Egyptian queen! The eggs
burst, shatter her belly, and emerge alive, awake, and hungry from a
mummy case which they crawl over like worms and feed on till its
gone. And then they turn to the world.

QUESTIONS

Ideas

1. What generalization does Dillard draw from her many examples? What
   does all this fecundity mean to her, and what is her purpose in describing
   it? Can you draw other conclusions from her astonishing examples?
2. Explain the paradox at the end of paragraph 6: "Every glistening egg is a
   memento mori." Relate this to the end of paragraphs 8 and 16.
3. Explain the point of the quotations in the following paragraphs: 11, 17,
   19, 22, and 23. Would Dillard have been better off paraphrasing any of
   these quotations? Omitting any? Explain.

Organization

4. Dillard begins this essay with a dream. What is the dream's relation to what
   follows? Is it an effective opening? Why or why not?
5. "Fecundity" has been divided by the editors into three parts: paragraphs
   1–4; 5–10; 11–23. Explain the basis of this three-part division. Can you
   devise any other division?

Sentences

6. Paragraphs 6 and 9 both contain extended sentences. Here, for example,
   is the second sentence of paragraph 6:

   > I suppose it is the teeming evidence that birth and growth, which we
   > value, are ubiquitous and blind, that life itself is so astonishingly cheap,
   > that nature is as careless as it is bountiful, and that with extravagance
   > goes a crushing waste that will one day include our own cheap lives.

   The sentence, of course, makes sense only in context, only if we know
   that it follows this remark: "I don't know what it is about fecundity that
   so appalls." The long sentence provides an elaborate answer to the short
   one, an answer that could have ended with the word "blind" but continues
   through three more expansions of the point, expansions that are included

in the sentence using a series of "that" clauses: "that life is," "that nature is," "that with extravagance goes." What are the tone, feeling, and effect of such an elaborate sentence?

7. Note how the following sentence makes use of repetition and parallelism:

> The driving force behind all this fecundity is
>   a terrible pressure I also must consider,
>   the   pressure of birth and growth,
>   the   pressure
>   that splits the bark of trees
> and   shoots out seeds,
>   that squeezes out the egg
> and   bursts the pupa,
>   that hungers
>   and lusts
>   and drives the creature relentlessly toward its own death.

8. Count the words in each of the sentences in paragraphs 8, 9, and 10. What do you notice about the lengths of Dillard's sentences? Are the longer or shorter sentences "better"? Is more uniformity of length desirable in these paragraphs?

9. Sentences in paragraphs 7, 10, 11, and 15 use the semicolon. After examining these, explain some uses of the semicolon.

Words

10. Paragraphs 7 and 9 are top-heavy with verbs. What do these verbs have in common? Why are there so many? Explain how Dillard, in her accent and emphasis, imitates what she describes.

11. Paragraph 9 contains repeated words and phrases. What words are repeated and to what effect? Would Dillard have been better off to avoid this repetition? Explain.

12. Reread paragraph 12. List all the words that suggest quantity or volume. What is their cumulative effect?

Suggestions for Writing

A. Write imitations of the sentences discussed in questions 6 and 7.

B. Write an imitation of paragraph 8, 9, or 10, striving to vary and balance the length of your sentences. If you choose to imitate paragraph 9, you will also need to work in some repetition of words and phrases.

C. Write an essay in which you begin by describing a dream or a fantasy. Follow with a description of something in the external world, something outside yourself that is related to your dream. From that double description launch out into a discussion of an idea suggested by your dream or your observations. You might stress the similarities or the differences between the imagined and the real. Or you might, instead, decide to explain the significance of your dream—why you had it, what it might mean, what it might reveal about you or about someone else.

God's Tooth

1   **I**nto this world falls a plane.
2   The earth is a mineral speckle planted in trees. The plane snagged its wing on a tree, fluttered in a tiny arc, and struggled down.
3   I heard it go. The cat looked up. There was no reason: the plane's engine simply stilled after takeoff, and the light plane failed to clear the firs. It fell easily; one wing snagged on a fir top; the metal fell down the air and smashed in the thin woods where cattle browse; the fuel exploded; and Julie Norwich seven years old burnt off her face.
4   Little Julie mute in some room at St. Joe's now, drugs dissolving into the sheets. Little Julie with her eyes naked and spherical, baffled. Can you scream without lips? Yes. But do children in long pain scream?
5   It is November 19 and no wind, and no hope of heaven, and no wish for heaven, since the meanest of people show more mercy than hounding and terrorist gods.

6   The airstrip, a cleared washboard affair on the flat crest of a low hill, is a few long fields distant from my house—up the road and through the woods, or across the sheep pasture and through the woods. A flight instructor told me once that when his students get cocky, when they think they know how to fly a plane, he takes them out here and makes them land on that field. You go over the wires and down, and along the strip and up before the trees, or vice versa, vice versa, depending on the wind. But the airstrip is not unsafe. Jesse's engine failed. The FAA will cart the wreckage away, bit by bit, picking it out of the tree trunk, and try to discover just why that engine failed. In the meantime,

the emergency siren has sounded, causing everyone who didn't see the plane go down to halt—Patty at her weaving, Jonathan slicing apples, Jan washing her baby's face—to halt, in pity and terror, wondering which among us got hit, by what bad accident, and why. The volunteer firemen have mustered; the fire trucks have come—stampeding Shuller's sheep—and gone, bearing burnt Julie and Jesse her father to the emergency room in town, leaving the rest of us to gossip, fight grass fires on the airstrip, and pray, or wander from window to window, fierce.

7   So she is burnt on her face and neck, Julie Norwich. The one whose teeth are short in a row, Jesse and Ann's oldest, red-kneed, green-socked, carrying cats.

8   I saw her only once. It was two weeks ago, under an English hawthorn tree, at the farm.

9   There are many farms in this neck of the woods, but only one we call "the farm"—the old Corcoran place, where Gus grows hay and raises calves: the farm, whose abandoned frame chicken coops ply the fields like longboats, like floating war canoes; whose clay driveway and grass footpaths are a tangle of orange calendula blossoms, ropes, equipment, and seeding grasses; the farm, whose canny heifers and bull calves figure the fences, run amok to the garden, and plant themselves suddenly black and white, up to their necks in green peas.

10   Between the gray farmhouse and the barn is the green grass farmyard, suitable for all projects. That day, sixteen of us were making cider. It was cold. There were piles of apples everywhere. We had filled our trucks that morning, climbing trees and shaking their boughs, dragging tarps heavy with apples, hauling bushels and boxes and buckets of apples, and loading them all back to the farm. Jesse and Ann, who are in their thirties, with Julie and the baby, whose name I forget, had driven down from the mountains that morning with a truckload of apples, loose, to make cider with us, fill their jugs, and drive back. I had not met them before. We all drank coffee on the farmhouse porch to warm us; we hosed jugs in the yard. Now we were throwing apples into a shredder and wringing the mash through pillowcases, staining our palms and freezing our fingers, and decanting the pails into seventy one-gallon jugs. And all this long day, Julie Norwich chased my cat Small around the farmyard and played with her, manhandled her, next to the porch under the hawthorn tree.

11 She was a thin child, pointy-chinned, yellow bangs and braids. She squinted, and when you looked at her she sometimes started laughing, as if you had surprised her at using some power she wasn't yet ready to show. I kept my eye on her, wondering if she was cold with her sweater unbuttoned and bony knees bare.

12 She would hum up a little noise for half-hour stretches. In the intervals, for maybe five minutes each, she was trying, very quietly, to learn to whistle. I think. Or she was practicing a certain concentrated face. But I think she was trying to learn to whistle, because sometimes she would squeak a little falsetto note through an imitation whistle hole in her lips, as if that could fool anyone. And all day she was dressing and undressing the yellow cat, sticking it into a black dress, a black dress long and full as a nun's.

13 I was amazed at that dress. It must have been some sort of doll clothing she had dragged with her in the truck; I've never seen its kind before or since. A white collar bibbed the yoke of it like a guimpe. It had great black sleeves like wings. Julie scooped up the cat and rammed her into the cloth. I knew how she felt, exasperated, breaking her heart on a finger curl's width of skinny cat arm. I knew the many feelings she had sticking those furry arms through the sleeves. Small is not large: her limbs feel like bird bones strung in a sock. When Julie had the cat dressed in its curious habit, she would rock it like a baby doll. The cat blinked, upside down.

14 Once she whistled at it, or tried, blowing in its face; the cat poured from her arms and ran. It leapt across the driveway, lightfoot in its sleeves; its black dress pulled this way and that, dragging dust, bent up in back by its yellow tail. I was squeezing one end of a twisted pillowcase full of apple mash and looking over my shoulder. I watched the cat hurdle the driveway and vanish under the potting shed, cringing; I watched Julie dash after it without hesitation, seize it, hit its face, and drag it back to the tree, carrying it caught fast by either forepaw, so its body hung straight from its arms.

15 She saw me watching her and we exchanged a look, a very conscious and self-conscious look—because we look a bit alike and we both knew it; because she was still short and I grown; because I was stuck kneeling before the cider pail, looking at her sidewise over my shoulder; because she was carrying the cat so oddly, so that she had to walk with her long legs parted; because it was my cat, and she'd dressed it, and

it looked like a nun; and because she knew I'd been watching her, and how fondly, all along. We were laughing.

16 We *looked* a bit alike. Her face is slaughtered now, and I don't remember mine. It is the best joke there is, that we are here, and fools— that we are sown into time like so much corn, that we are souls sprinkled at random like salt into time and dissolved here, spread into matter, connected by cells right down to our feet, and those feet likely to fell us over a tree root or jam us on a stone. The joke part is that we forget it. Give the mind two seconds alone and it thinks it's Pythagoras. We wake up a hundred times a day and laugh.

17 The joke of the world is less like a banana peel than a rake, the old rake in the grass, the one you step on, foot to forehead. It all comes together. In a twinkling. You have to admire the gag for its symmetry, accomplishing all with one right angle, the same right angle which accomplishes all philosophy. One step on the rake and it's mind under matter once again. You wake up with a piece of tree in your skull. You wake up with fruit on your hands. You wake up in a clearing and see yourself, ashamed. You see your own face and it's seven years old and there's no knowing why, or where you've been since. We're tossed broadcast into time like so much grass, some ravening god's sweet hay. You wake up and a plane falls out of the sky.

18 That day was a god, too, the day we made cider and Julie played under the hawthorn tree. He must have been a heyday sort of god, a husbandman. He was spread under gardens, sleeping in time, an innocent old man scratching his head, thinking of pruning the orchard, in love with families.

19 Has he no power? Can the other gods carry time and its loves upside down like a doll in their blundering arms? As though we the people were playing house—when we are serious and do love—and not the gods? No, that day's god has no power. No gods have power to save. There are only days. The one great god abandoned us to days, to time's tumult of occasions, abandoned us to the gods of days each brute and amok in his hugeness and idiocy.

20 Jesse her father had grabbed her clear of the plane this morning, and was hauling her off when the fuel blew. A glob of flung ignited vapor hit her face, or something flaming from the plane or fir tree hit her face. No one else was burned, or hurt in any way.

21   So this is where we are. Ashes, ashes, all fall down. How could I have forgotten? Didn't I see the heavens wiped shut just yesterday, on the road walking? Didn't I fall from the dark of the stars to these senselit and noisome days? The great ridged granite millstone of time is illusion, for only the good is real; the great ridged granite millstone of space is illusion, for God is spirit and worlds his flimsiest dreams: but the illusions are almost perfect, are apparently perfect for generations on end, and the pain is also, and undeniably, real. The pain within the millstones' pitiless turning is real, for our love for each other—for world and all the products of extension—is real, vaulting, insofar as it is love, beyond the plane of the stones' sickening churn and arcing to the realm of spirit bare. And you can get caught holding one end of a love, when your father drops, and your mother; when a land is lost, or a time, and your friend blotted out, gone, your brother's body spoiled, and cold, your infant dead, and you dying: you reel out love's long line alone, stripped like a live wire loosing its sparks to a cloud, like a live wire loosed in space to longing and grief everlasting.

22   I sit at the window. It is a fool's lot, this sitting always at windows spoiling little blowy slips of paper and myself in the process. Shall I be old? Here comes Small, old sparrow-mouth, wanting my lap. Done. Do you have any earthly idea how young I am? Where's your dress, kitty? I suppose I'll outlive this wretched cat. Get another. Leave it my silver spoons, like old ladies you hear about. I prefer dogs.

23   So I read. Angels, I read, belong to nine different orders. Seraphs are the highest; they are aflame with love for God, and stand closer to him than the others. Seraphs love God; cherubs, who are second, possess perfect knowledge of him. So love is greater than knowledge; how could I have forgotten? The seraphs are born of a stream of fire issuing from under God's throne. They are, according to Dionysius the Areopagite, "all wings," having, as Isaiah noted, six wings apiece, two of which they fold over their eyes. Moving perpetually toward God, they perpetually praise him, crying Holy, Holy, Holy. . . . But, according to some rabbinic writings, they can sing only the first "Holy" before the intensity of their love ignites them again and dissolves them again, perpetually, into flames. "Abandon everything," Dionysius told his disciple. "God despises ideas."

24   God despises everything, apparently. If he abandoned us, slashing

creation loose at its base from any roots in the real; and if we in turn abandon everything—all these illusions of time and space and lives— in order to love only the real: then where are we? Thought itself is impossible, for subject can have no guaranteed connection with object, nor any object with God. Knowledge is impossible. We are precisely nowhere, sinking on an entirely imaginary ice floe, into entirely imaginary seas themselves adrift. Then we reel out love's long line alone toward a God less lovable than a grasshead, who treats us less well than we treat our lawns.

25   Of faith I have nothing, only of truth: that this one God is a brute and traitor, abandoning us to time, to necessity and the engines of matter unhinged. This is no leap; this is evidence of things seen: one Julie, one sorrow, one sensation bewildering the heart, and enraging the mind, and causing me to look at the world stuff appalled, at the blithering rock of trees in a random wind, at my hand like some gibberish sprouted, my fist opening and closing, so that I think, Have I once turned my hand in this circus, have I ever called it home?

26   Faith would be that God is self-limited utterly by his creation— a contraction of the scope of his will; that he bound himself to time and its hazards and haps as a man would lash himself to a tree for love. That God's works are as good as we make them. That God is helpless, our baby to bear, self-abandoned on the doorstep of time, wondered at by cattle and oxen. Faith would be that God moved and moves once and for all and "down," so to speak, like a diver, like a man who eternally gathers himself for a dive and eternally is diving, and eternally splitting the spread of the water, and eternally drowned.

27   Faith would be, in short, that God has any willful connection with time whatsoever, and with us. For I know it as given that God is all good. And I take it also as given that whatever he touches has meaning, if only in his mysterious terms, the which I readily grant. The question is, then, whether God touches anything. Is anything firm, or is time on the loose? Did Christ descend once and for all to no purpose, in a kind of divine and kenotic suicide, or ascend once and for all, pulling his cross up after him like a rope ladder home? Is there— even if Christ holds the tip of things fast and stretches eternity clear to the dim souls of men—is there no link at the base of things, some kernel or air deep in the matrix of matter from which universe furls like a ribbon twined into time?

28   Has God a hand in this? Then it is a good hand. But has he a

hand at all? Or is he a holy fire burning self-contained for power's sake alone? Then he knows himself blissfully as flame unconsuming, as all brilliance and beauty and power, and the rest of us can go hang. Then the accidental universe spins mute, obedient only to its own gross terms, meaningless, out of mind, and alone. The universe is neither contingent upon nor participant in the holy, in being itself, the real, the power play of fire. The universe is illusion merely, not one speck of it real, and we are not only its victims, falling always into or smashed by a planet slung by its sun—but also its captives, bound by the mineral-made ropes of our senses.

29   But how do we know—how could we know—that the real is there? By what freak chance does the skin of illusion ever split, and reveal to us the real, which seems to know us by name, and by what freak chance and why did the capacity to prehend it evolve?

30   I sit at the window, chewing the bones in my wrist. Pray for them: for Julie, for Jesse her father, for Ann her mother, pray. Who will teach us to pray? The god of today is a glacier. We live in his shifting crevasses, unheard. The god of today is delinquent, a barn-burner, a punk with a pittance of power in a match. It is late, a late time to be living. Now it is afternoon; the sky is appallingly clear. Everything in the landscape points to sea, and the sea is nothing; it is snipped from the real as a stuff without form, rising up the sides of islands and falling, mineral to mineral, salt.

31   Everything I see—the water, the log-wrecked beach, the farm on the hill, the bluff, the white church in the trees—looks overly distinct and shining. (What is the relationship of color to this sun, of sun to anything else?) It all looks staged. It all looks brittle and unreal, a skin of colors painted on glass, which if you prodded it with a finger would powder and fall. A blank sky, perfectly blended with all other sky, has sealed over the crack in the world where the plane fell, and the air has hushed the matter up.

32   If days are gods, then gods are dead, and artists pyrotechnic fools. Time is a hurdy-gurdy, a lampoon, and death's a bawd. We're beheaded by the nick of time. We're logrolling on a falling world, on time released from meaning and rolling loose, like one of Atalanta's golden apples, a bauble flung and forgotten, lapsed, and the gods on the lam.

33   And now outside the window, deep on the horizon, a new thing appears, as if we needed a new thing. It is a new land blue beyond

islands, hitherto hidden by haze and now revealed, and as dumb as the rest. I check my chart, my amateur penciled sketch of the skyline. Yes, this land is new, this spread blue spark beyond yesterday's new wrinkled line, beyond the blue veil a sailor said was Salt Spring Island. How long can this go on? But let us by all means extend the scope of our charts.

34   I draw it as I seem to see it, a blue chunk fitted just so beyond islands, a wag of graphite rising just here above another anonymous line, and here meeting the slope of Salt Spring: though whether this be headland I see or heartland, or the distance-blurred bluffs of a hundred bays, I have no way of knowing, or if it be island or main. I call it Thule, O Julialand, Time's Bad News; I name it Terror, the Farthest Limb of the Day, God's Tooth.

QUESTIONS

Ideas

1. What is Dillard getting at in this essay? Does she explicitly state her point in a sentence or two? Where? In your own words, explain the idea of "God's Tooth."

2. Does this essay affect your beliefs in any way? Is that part of Dillard's purpose? Is she trying to explain, to defend, to persuade—or something else?

3. How do you explain the tragedy—or the kind of tragedy—that Dillard describes here. How do people cope with such horrors?

Organization

4. The essay can be divided into eight sections. Provide a title for each and explain the point of each section. Which sections are primarily narrative and descriptive? Which are more speculative and expository?

5. In section IV (paragraphs 11–17) Dillard describes the child, Julie Norwich. Where in this section does Dillard shift from direct description to something else? What is that something else, and what are the purpose and point of the non-descriptive part of section IV?

Sentences

6. Reread the opening paragraphs. What do you notice about the shape and length of Dillard's sentences? Do any of the early paragraphs rely heavily on piling up short sentences and brief, staccato phrases? Where, and to what effect?

7. Look at paragraphs 19 and 21, 28 and 29, and also paragraph 4—in that order. Why does Dillard ask so many questions in these paragraphs? Are the kinds of questions similar or different in each set of paragraphs? Explain.

8. In paragraphs 26 and 27 Dillard uses repeated words and phrases at the beginning of her sentences. What advantage is there to such a procedure?

Words

9. What is the tone of paragraphs 24 and 25? Which words in particular convey that tone? What is Dillard's attitude toward God as evidenced in these paragraphs?

10. List and explain the comparisons in paragraphs 16 and 17. What do the comparisons have in common, and what point does Dillard make in using them? What is their purpose? To describe? To amuse? To explain? To persuade?

Suggestions for Writing

A. Write an essay combining description and narration with exposition. Focus on an event that disturbed you, an event that you had (or still have) trouble understanding. Try to incorporate into your essay the process you underwent in trying to understand the experience.

B. Write an essay describing how you came to lose a belief you once held or how you came to believe (in) something you formerly didn't believe (in). Why did you hold or not hold the belief in the first place? What prompted you to give up or to adopt the belief?

C. Rewrite paragraph 2, combining the short statements into longer, smoother sentences. Compare your version with that of another student, then with Dillard's version. What differences in tone and effect do you notice?

D. Write a paragraph exclusively, or almost exclusively, of questions (like paragraphs 27, 28, or 29).

E. Write a paragraph imitating the repetition of word and phrase at the beginnings of sentences that Dillard employs in paragraphs 26 and 27.

TEN

Lillian Hellman

(1906–   )

Lillian Hellman has the reputation for being a tough-minded woman, a kind of "super-literate female Humphrey Bogart." Her friend Dorothy Parker once remarked, "When Lillian gets mad, I regret to say she screams." It is no accident that her writing reflects this vigor and intensity. Her style is not poetic; instead it is rather stark and abrupt. In *Scoundrel Time*, for example, she writes about Richard Nixon and Joseph McCarthy searching in the State Department for Communists and left-wing subversives: "I do not think they believed much, if anything, of what they said: the time was ripe for a new wave in America, and they seized their political chance to lead it along each day's opportunity, spitballing whatever and with whoever came into view."

Her style has been called "laconic, reserved, unfooled." Hellman manages to blend slang and polish, the sassy and the graceful. She uses the combination to create a conversational yet serious voice. Although she wants to be lucid and cogent, *Scoundrel Time* is not an attempt at objective history. So her casual tone is appropriate: it signals the personal nature of her memoirs. Her "moral history" of the investigations by the House Un-American Activities Committee (HUAC) is, then, flinty and stylish. She writes:

It was not the first time in history that the confusions of honest people were picked up in space by cheap baddies who, hearing a few bars of popular notes, made them into an opera of public disorder, staged and sung, as much of the congressional testimony shows, in the wards of an insane asylum.

Her voice here is angry, but under control—what Hellman later called "pretend cool." And the natural rhythms of American speech together with her extended metaphor are typical of the ironic, point-blank bluntness of her style. This ironic bluntness also corresponds nicely to her sense of moral outrage at injustice and arrogance.

Although she was born and raised in New Orleans, a good deal of her childhood was spent on Riverside Drive in New York City. She tells us that she felt slightly out of place in both locations. She went to high school in New York and for a couple of years attended New York University and Columbia. For a while she worked as a manuscript reader for a prestigious publishing house, as a book reviewer for the *New York Herald-Tribune*, and as a scenario reader in Hollywood. Then, in 1934, *The Children's Hour*, Hellman's drama about the effects of lies and sexual prejudice, opened to sensational reviews. She was an immediate success. She went on to write other hits, including *The Little Foxes*, an indictment of selfishness and hypocrisy in Southern families, and *Watch on the Rhine*, about an anti-Nazi and his sacrifice of personal happiness for freedom.

Although never overtly political, Hellman has always been interested in left-wing causes, especially the Loyalists' struggle against Franco during the Spanish Civil War. Her friendship with some socialists and communists in Hollywood during the 1930s eventually aroused the suspicions of HUAC, and in 1952 she was subpoenaed to testify. She refused to do so and for years afterward was blacklisted from working in Hollywood. Columnist Murray Kempton wrote about her sense of ethics and honor when she refused to give the committee the names of acquaintances who had attended left-wing political meetings: "The most important thing is never to forget that here is someone who knew how to act when there was nothing harder on earth than knowing how to act."

Although she is still considered one of America's leading dramatists, Lillian Hellman is best known for her nonfiction. In 1969, *An Unfinished Woman*, the first memoir in her autobiographical trilogy, won the National Book Award. Two of the selections taken from that book, "In the Fig Tree" and "Wasting Time," are self-portraits. She freely admits, however, that some of the details are part memory, part imagination.

In these sketches she introduces themes that recur throughout her memoirs: her rebellious bent, her groping toward self-knowledge through rites of initiation, and her interweaving of the past and the present as a way to clarify and understand. The character portrayed in these pieces is, of course, Lillian Hellman in her youth, but we should separate that portrait from the narrator, since the voice or persona a writer creates is not meant as a literal replica of the writer.

"A Lost Passion" was written around 1978, after she reread *An Unfinished Woman*; in it, she reaffirms her rebel spirit and her frustration with the limitations of writing. "Giants" is a typical selection from that memoir, especially in its use of irony and metaphor. Her third memoir, *Scoundrel Time* (1976), recounts Hellman's "own history" of the McCarthy era (the late 1940s, and early 1950s). One critic noted the book's "understated fury." In fact, in the short coda printed here, Hellman tells us that she is still angry at the scoundrels (most intellectuals) who let McCarthyism happen. Also included here is a famous letter to John S. Wood, Chairman of HUAC, containing her much quoted line: "I cannot and will not cut my conscience to fit this year's fashions. . . ." The final selection (printed in the Questions section) was written some years after the publication of *Scoundrel Time* and represents Hellman's reaction to rereading this very controversial memoir. She is, as you can see, still convinced that she had told the truth.

Her rereading seems to have rekindled the emotional turmoil of those years: "But I am angrier now than I hope I will ever be again; more disturbed now than when it all took place." After rereading all three books, Hellman is still unsparing in her attempts to be honest with herself; she shows us how writing can be a process of searching for personal meaning. We sense in the following paragraph that she comes to know what she thinks as she is writing about it. It is the kind of moral and intellectual toughness that is characteristic of a woman who risked smuggling $50,000 into Nazi Germany to save the lives of hundreds of Jews. For Hellman, style is character.

What a word is truth. Slippery, tricky, unreliable. I tried in these books to tell the truth. I did not fool with facts. But, of course, that is a shallow definition of the truth. I see now, in rereading, that I kept much from myself, not always, but sometimes. And so sometimes in this edition I have tried to correct that. But I can be sure I still do not see it and never will. That is a common experience for all writers, I think, and I wonder, therefore, whether what I, or they, have to say about past work is worth very much. Judge for yourself, is the only answer.

In the Fig Tree

There was a heavy fig tree on the lawn where the house turned the corner into the side street, and to the front and sides of the fig tree were three live oaks that hid the fig from my aunts' boarding-house. I suppose I was eight or nine before I discovered the pleasures of the fig tree, and although I have lived in many houses since then, including a few I made for myself, I still think of it as my first and most beloved home.

I learned early, in our strange life of living half in New York and half in New Orleans, that I made my New Orleans teachers uncomfortable because I was too far ahead of my schoolmates, and my New York teachers irritable because I was too far behind. But in New Orleans, I found a solution: I skipped school at least once a week and often twice, knowing that nobody cared or would report my absence. On those days I would set out for school done up in polished strapped shoes and a prim hat against what was known as "the climate," carrying my books and a little basket filled with delicious stuff my Aunt Jenny and Carrie, the cook, had made for my school lunch. I would round the corner of the side street, move on toward St. Charles Avenue, and sit on a bench as if I were waiting for a streetcar until the boarders and the neighbors had gone to work or settled down for the post-breakfast rest that all Southern ladies thought necessary. Then I would run back to the fig tree, dodging in and out of bushes to make sure the house had no dangers for me. The fig tree was heavy, solid, comfortable, and I had, through time, convinced myself that it wanted me, missed me when I was absent, and approved all the rigging I had done for the happy days I spent in its arms: I had made a sling to hold the school books, a pulley rope for my lunch basket, a hole for the bottle of afternoon cream-soda pop, a fishing pole and a smelly little bag of elderly bait, a pillow embroidered with a picture of Henry Clay on a horse that I had stolen from Mrs. Stillman, one of my aunts' boarders, and a proper nail to hold my dress and shoes to keep them neat for the return to the house.

It was in that tree that I learned to read, filled with the passions that can only come to the bookish, grasping, very young, bewildered by almost all of what I read, sweating in the attempt to understand a world of adults I fled from in real life but desperately wanted to join in books. (I did not connect the grown men and women in literature with the grown men and women I saw around me. They were, to me, another species.)

It was in the fig tree that I learned that anything alive in water was of enormous excitement to me. True, the water was gutter water and the fishing could hardly be called that: sometimes the things that swam in New Orleans gutters were not pretty, but I didn't know what was pretty and I liked them all. After lunch—the men boarders returned for a large lunch and a siesta—the street would be safe again, with only the noise from Carrie and her helpers in the kitchen, and they could be counted on never to move past the back porch, or the chicken coop. Then I would come down from my tree to sit on the side street gutter with my pole and bait. Often I would catch a crab that had wandered in from the Gulf, more often I would catch my favorite, the crayfish, and sometimes I would, in that safe hour, have at least six of them for my basket. Then, about 2:30, when house and street would stir again, I would go back to my tree for another few hours of reading or dozing or having what I called the ill hour. It is too long ago for me to know why I thought the hour "ill," but certainly I did not mean sick. I think I meant an intimation of sadness, a first recognition that there was so much to understand that one might never find one's way and the first signs, perhaps, that for a nature like mine, the way would not be easy. I cannot be sure that I felt all that then, although I can be sure that it was in the fig tree, a few years later, that I was first puzzled by the conflict which would haunt me, harm me, and benefit me the rest of my life: simply, the stubborn, relentless, driving desire to be alone as it came into conflict with the desire not to be alone when I wanted not to be. I already guessed that other people wouldn't allow that, although, as an only child, I pretended for the rest of my life that they would and must allow it to me.

QUESTIONS

Ideas

1. Hellman seems to be building toward a theme. The momentum picks up as she remembers the "ill" hour. How does this word lead her into a larger meaning? How would you paraphrase the last two sentences?

2. What do you make of Hellman's belief that the fig tree missed her? Does this fantasy seem unusual? Is it connected to her central concern about being alone?

3. This essay is part description, part narrative, and part exposition. Hellman mixes these modes to discover something about herself from her childhood. What does she learn? Is this consistent with her thoughts about herself in the first two paragraphs?

Organization

4. There are only four paragraphs in this selection. Briefly state the purpose of each.

5. Does each paragraph have an explicit or implicit topic sentence?

6. The last paragraph seems rather long. Is the first sentence related to the last? How does this paragraph develop? Is there a clear and logical sequence from one thought to the next?

7. An inductive pattern moves from details to a general observation. A deductive arrangement starts with a thesis and then supports it with particulars. Which pattern does Hellman use here? Would it matter if she worked the other way?

Sentences

8. What kind of voice do you hear in the second paragraph? Do you think it is true that "nobody cared"? Could this be an indication that she felt abandoned? Might that explain her behavior here?

9. Look at the last sentence in the second paragraph: Why does she choose to write such a long sentence? Should she have? Would a sentence as long as this one work in informational or scientific prose? Why?

10. Compare this sentence with the penultimate sentence in the last paragraph. What is the purpose of each? Why does she use the colon in both of these sentences?

Words

11. What does the phrase "intimation of sadness" mean to you?
12. Hellman doesn't seem to use polysyllabic words. Why do you think this is?

Suggestions for Writing

A. Think of a place from your childhood that has significance for you. Using specific details, try to recapture that time and place, describing what you did and what it means to you now.
B. Can you see continuity in your life? Write an essay that traces some characteristic of your personality from childhood to the present. Blend narration and exposition in either an inductive or deductive pattern.
C. Rewrite the last two sentences using polysyllabic or Latinate words. Which version do you prefer?
D. Rewrite the last sentence in the second paragraph using a series of short sentences.

Wasting Time

1   **M**y mother had gone to Sophie Newcomb College in New Orleans, and although the experience had left little on the memory except a fire in her dormitory, she felt it was the right place for me. (My aunts Jenny and Hannah could keep an eye on me.) But I had had enough of Southern education and wanted to go to Smith. A few months before the autumn entrance term, when I thought the matter had been settled, my mother and father held out for Goucher on the strange ground that it was closer to New York. But a month before I was to leave for Goucher, my mother became ill and it was obvious that I was meant to stay at home. I do not remember any sharp words about these changes and that in itself is odd, because sharp words came

often in those years, but I do remember a feeling of what difference did it make. I knew, without rancor, that my parents were worried about a wild and headstrong girl; and then, too, a defeat for an only child can always be turned into a later victory.

2   New York University had started its Washington Square branch only a few years before, with an excellent small faculty and high requirements for the students it could put into one unattractive building. I was, of course, not where I wanted to be and I envied those of my friends who were. And yet I knew that in another place I might have been lost, because the old story was still true: I was sometimes more advanced but often less educated than other students and I had little desire to be shown up. And by seventeen, I was openly rebellious against almost everything. I knew that the seeds of the rebellion were scattered and aimless in a nature that was wild to be finished with something-or-other and to find something-else-or-other, and I had sense enough to know that I was overproud, oversensitive, overdaring because I was shy and frightened. Ah, what a case can be made for vanity in the shy. (And what a losing game is self-description in the long ago.)

3   It was thus in the cards that college would mean very little to me, although one professor opened up a slit into another kind of literature: I began an exciting period of Kant and Hegel, a little, very little, of Karl Marx and Engels. In a time when students didn't leave classes or even skip them very often, I would slip away from a class conducted by a famous editor, annoyed at the glimpses of his well-bred life, and would slam my seat as I left in the middle of a lecture by the famous Alexander Woollcott whenever he paraded the gibe-wit and shabby literary taste of his world. (My bad manners interested Woollcott. He went out of his way, on several occasions, to find me after class and to offer a ride uptown. But the kindness or interest made me resentful and guilty, and I remember a tart exchange about a novel written by a friend of his. Years later, because Woollcott admired Hammett, who did not admire him, I was to meet him again. And after that, when I wrote plays, he was pleasant to me—if saying that I looked like a prow head on a whaling ship is pleasant.)

4   A good deal of the college day I spent in a Greenwich Village restaurant called Lee Chumley's curled up on a dark bench with a book, or arguing with a brilliant girl called Marie-Louise and her extraordinary, foppish brother, up very often from Princeton, carrying a Paris

copy of *Ulysses* when he wasn't carrying Verlaine. (Hal was a handsome, strange young man and we all hoped to be noticed by him. A few years later he married one of our group and a few years after that he killed himself and a male companion in a Zurich hotel room.)

5   In my junior year, I knew I was wasting time. My mother took me on a long tour to the Midwest and the South, almost as a reward for leaving college. We returned to New York for my nineteenth birthday and the day after I began what was then called an "affair." It was an accident: the young man pressed me into it partly because it satisfied the tinkering malice that has gone through the rest of his life, mostly because it pained his best friend. The few months it lasted did not mean much to me, but I have often asked myself whether I underestimated the damage that so loveless an arrangement made on my future. But my generation did not often deal with the idea of love—we were ashamed of the word, and scornful of the misuse that had been made of it—and I suppose that the cool currency of the time carried me past the pain of finding nastiness in what I had hoped would be a moving adventure.

QUESTIONS

Ideas

1. In an attempt to define who she is, Hellman narrates events from her youth. Do you find the young woman pictured here "rebellious" and "headstrong"?

2. Even though Lillian Hellman is a writer from an earlier generation, is there evidence that "Wasting Time" applies to college students of today?

3. If you ever read the whole of Hellman's autobiography, you will notice many sentences like the one in parentheses at the end of paragraph 2. What do you think she means by this?

4. What do you make of the "thus" in the first sentence of paragraph 3? What connection between "overproud, oversensitive, overdaring" and college is she making? Do you agree?

5. Does Hellman's attitude toward her affair fit into your image of her?

6. Does your generation have a different view of love than that expressed in the last sentence?

Organization

7. Of the five paragraphs in this piece, which ones are narrative, which expository?
8. Although "Wasting Time" is excerpted from one chapter of a book, it reads like a unified piece. What holds it together?
9. Does the first sentence of the last paragraph "cover" the details of this piece?

Sentences

10. Find the sentences that begin with "and" or "but." What relation does each have to the sentence before?
11. What is the purpose of the sentences in parentheses. Can you generalize about Hellman's use of parentheses?

Words

12. Although Hellman tries to avoid "big" words, she does like to use phrases like "tinkering malice," "cool currency," and "gibe-wit." Do you think her blend of strong basic words and literary phrases works well?

Suggestions for Writing

A. What were your parents' reactions to your college choice? Write a list of their reasons for approving or disapproving your choice and then a list of your own reasons for your choice. In a paragraph or two, compare the lists.
B. Hellman offers some complicated reasons for her affair. From your experiences and observations, write a short essay that tries to develop reasons why students have affairs.

A Lost Passion

1   **W**orld War I, for many intelligent people, ended in a revulsion against the high-toned rhetoric that could not hide a dislocated world and a dangerous future. World War II was, in the first years,

fought in Europe in a bewildered, half-crazed confusion of inefficient defense, and then, too late, in patriotic protection of homeland. The strength of the patriotism came only after the Germans had started their long, terrible and triumphant march toward the north, south and east.

2   Many people here who were neither callous nor cowards remembered the palaver of Woodrow Wilson, and while they were revolted by Hitler and Mussolini, they fought the war in good-natured consent only because they had been conscripted, and you fought for your country when your country said it needed you. We forget that it took us a long time to believe in the German death camps for Jews and political dissenters because it took us a long time to stop the dismissive talk about the little Austrian house painter and the Italian clown with the frown.

3   There wasn't much to say about the Korean War and almost nobody said it. There is much to say about the dirty Vietnam War and some good stuff has been said, but it remains a puzzling time out, and one still wants to turn one's face away from the memory of American kids doing murder, being murdered, and from those of them who remain in our hospitals, crippled forever by the Washington loonies and the boys who tell the loonies how to think.

4   But among these wars, tucked away, there was a so-called little war in Spain, a minute of history that caught the imagination not only of the generation that is old enough to remember it, but of the present young who, in every college where I have ever taught, know more of the Spanish Civil War and ask more questions than they do about World War II or even Vietnam, about which they are surprisingly ignorant. (Where are history departments now and what do they teach?)

5   The Spanish Republicans, politically denouncing each other every minute of the way, managed to fight with extraordinary force for nothing more radical than the right to continue free elections. We approved of that, and so did the French, but approval did not mean guns or planes. Only the Russians supplied those and then not enough, and under such accusations from the squabbling political parties of the Left that even that amount driveled down to almost nothing towards the end.

6   But the Spanish were fighting for their country, as we all would, given an enemy of danger. The International Brigades, however, were made up of strangers to Spain, men from all over Europe and America who came to fight against Fascism: middle-aged Germans; Yugoslavs,

including Tito; young Englishmen from Oxford and Cambridge. And us. And us was something of a sight. Young men came from the Middle West who had been auto mechanics and were sudden geniuses with planes and tanks. And boys like Jim Lardner just out of Harvard. (I will remember all my life the night before Lardner left Paris, only a short time before he was killed in Spain, when I tried all during dinner to persuade him not to go. He listened politely and then asked me if I wanted to see a puzzle he had just invented.) And slum kids who had never been out of their own neighborhoods in the giant cities of their birth. They were an extraordinary bunch: strangers in a country with an unattractive history, often wounded and sent to inadequate hospitals, many of them dying without recognition or honors or enough pain-killers to make death anything but weeks of agony.

7   In the Abraham Lincoln Brigade, the American section of the International Brigades, there were a large number of Jewish kids. Ernest Hemingway said three or four times to me and to other people, "God damn it, these little Jews fight fine." I do not believe he meant anything anti-Semitic. I think he never could understand that lower middle class kids could fight as well as his sporting types raised on fine guns and rods. A basic conviction of Hemingway's life was shaken, but not so shaken as to alter the nature of his war heroes or his personal taste ever.

8   Any form of the word "ideal" has suspect meanings, but the foreigners in the Brigades were more than idealists. You become more, I think, when you lay yourself on the line. That must, has to be, a very pure state of being and I think the cleanness and clarity of it is what the present generation recognizes, envies, or wants for itself.

9   And yet and yet. My pieces here about Spain do not say all or even much of what I wanted to say. I knew it when I first wrote them, I knew it when I included them in this book, and I knew it last week when I read them again. I wish I understood why. Somehow they do not include the passion that I felt, my absolute conviction that when the Spanish War was lost, we were all going to be caught in a storm of murder and destruction in another, larger war. It does not console me that almost nothing that has been written about Spain includes what I missed. Certainly not "For Whom the Bell Tolls," nor the brilliant but limited political stuff of Orwell's. Certainly some of Malraux, but not enough, and on and on. Maybe passion, passion on paper, takes more than most of us have.

QUESTIONS

Ideas

1. This piece blends Hellman's very personal historical view of several wars with anecdotes and remembrances, all as a context for her main concern, the Spanish Civil War. Why do you think this war was so important for her?

2. How does she characterize the men of the Abraham Lincoln Brigade?

3. How do you respond to the Hemingway quote in paragraph 7? What do you think Hellman's last sentence means here? What is she implying about Hemingway's biases?

4. What do you think she means by "You become more . . . when you lay yourself on the line"?

5. What is the meaning of "And yet and yet"?

6. What do you think she means by the last sentence? Is she referring to the inadequacies of memory, language, or skill?

7. What does paragraph 3 tell you about her political views?

Organization

8. How would you group the nine paragraphs in this piece? Why do certain ones belong together?

9. What is the relationship between paragraphs 5 and 6? Between 7 and 8?

10. Several sentences in paragraph 6 begin with conjunctions. Do you think this is an effective device?

Sentences

11. Hellman often connects a series of independent clauses by using "and" or "but." Look especially at paragraphs 3 and 4. Is this better than writing them as separate sentences? How do you decide to do either?

12. Are there any irregular sentences in paragraphs 3 and 4? What is their purpose?

Words

13. Why did Hellman choose the word "palaver"? What is the meaning of this term? What might have been some alternatives?

14. Connotation is the emotional association a word carries. "Die" has such
    unpleasant connotations that we often substitute other, less harsh words
    such as "passed away" or "deceased." What connotation do these words
    have (from paragraph 3): "loonies," "boys," "stuff," "dirty." Why do you
    think Hellman chose them?

Suggestions for Writing

A. Read the first sentence of paragraph 4. What do you think of its structure
   and its length? Rewrite it into several shorter sentences and compare yours
   with hers. Which is easier to read?
B. Write a sketch of your remembrances of some public event that you have
   some feeling about.
C. Do you agree with Hellman's idea that your generation "recognizes, envies,
   or wants for itself" the "cleanness and clarity" of laying yourselves on the
   line? Write an essay in which you discuss what you think your generation's
   "commitments" are.

Scoundrel Time

---

1   I have tried twice before to write about what has come to
be known as the McCarthy period but I didn't much like what I wrote.
My reasons for not being able to write about my part in this sad, comic,
miserable time of our history were simple to me, although some people
thought I had avoided it for mysterious reasons. There was no mystery.
I had strange hangups and they are always hard to explain. Now I tell
myself that if I face them, maybe I can manage.

2   The prevailing eccentricity was and is my inability to feel much
against the leading figures of the period, the men who punished me.
Senators McCarthy and McCarran, Representatives Nixon, Walter and
Wood, all of them, were what they were: men who invented when
necessary, maligned even when it wasn't necessary. I do not think they
believed much, if anything, of what they said: the time was ripe for a
new wave in America, and they seized their political chance to lead it

along each day's opportunity, spitballing whatever and with whoever came into view.

3   But the new wave was not so new. It began with the Russian Revolution of 1917. The victory of the revolution, and thus its menace, had haunted us through the years that followed, then twisted the tail of history when Russia was our ally in the Second World War and, just because that had been such an unnatural connection, the fears came back in fuller force after the war when it looked to many people as if Russia would overrun Western Europe. Then the revolution in China caused an enormous convulsion in capitalist societies and somewhere along the line gave us the conviction that we could have prevented it if only. If only was never explained with any sense, but the times had very little need of sense.

4   The fear of Communism did not begin that year, but the new China, allied in those days with Russia, had a more substantial base and there were many honest men and women who were, understandably, frightened that their pleasant way of life could end in a day.

5   It was not the first time in history that the confusions of honest people were picked up in space by cheap baddies who, hearing a few bars of popular notes, made them into an opera of public disorder, staged and sung, as much of the congressional testimony shows, in the wards of an insane asylum.

6   A theme is always necessary, a plain, simple, unadorned theme to confuse the ignorant. The anti-Red theme was easily chosen from the grab bag, not alone because we were frightened of socialism, but chiefly, I think, to destroy the remains of Roosevelt and his sometimes advanced work. The McCarthy group—a loose term for all the boys, lobbyists, Congressmen, State Department bureaucrats, CIA operators—chose the anti-Red scare with perhaps more cynicism than Hitler picked anti-Semitism. He, history can no longer deny, deeply believed in the impurity of the Jew. But it is impossible to remember the drunken face of McCarthy, merry often with a kind of worldly malice, as if he were mocking those who took him seriously, and believe that he himself could take seriously anything but his boozed-up nightmares. And if all the rumors were true the nightmares could have concerned more than the fear of a Red tank on Pennsylvania Avenue, although it is possible that in his case a tank could have turned him on. Mr. Nixon's beliefs, if indeed they ever existed, are best left to jolly quarter-historians like Theodore White. But one has a right to believe that if Whittaker Cham-

bers* was capable of thinking up a pumpkin, and he was, Mr. Nixon seized upon this strange hiding place with the eagerness of a man who already felt deep contempt for public intelligence. And he was right.

7   But none of them, even on the bad morning of my hearing before the House Un-American Activities Committee, interested me or disturbed me at a serious level. They didn't and they don't. They are what they are, or were, and are no relation to me by blood or background. (My own family held more interesting villains of another, wittier nature.)

8   I have written before that my shock and my anger came against what I thought had been the people of my world, although in many cases, of course, I did not know the men and women of that world except by name. I had, up to the late 1940's, believed that the educated, the intellectual, lived by what they claimed to believe: freedom of thought and speech, the right of each man to his own convictions, a more than implied promise, therefore, of aid to those who might be persecuted. But only a very few raised a finger when McCarthy and the boys appeared. Almost all, either by what they did or did not do, contributed to McCarthyism, running after a bandwagon which hadn't bothered to stop to pick them up.

9   Simply, then and now, I feel betrayed by the nonsense I had believed. I had no right to think that American intellectuals were people who would fight for anything if doing so would injure them; they have very little history that would lead to that conclusion. Many of them found in the sins of Stalin Communism—and there were plenty of sins and plenty that for a long time I mistakenly denied—the excuse to join those who should have been their hereditary enemies. Perhaps that, in part, was the penalty of nineteenth-century immigration. The children of timid immigrants are often remarkable people: energetic, intelligent, hardworking; and often they make it so good that they are determined

---

*In August 1948 Whittaker Chambers appeared before the House Un-American Activities Committee. Chambers, a senior editor of *Time* magazine, told the Committee that he had once been a Communist and an underground courier. He named ten men as his former associates, the best known being Alger Hiss, formerly a high official of the State Department. Chambers accused Hiss of giving him secret government material, which Chambers preserved by placing it in a pumpkin at his farm in Maryland. Hiss was indicted, tried twice, and sent to jail for almost four years. In 1975 the secret pumpkin papers were found to contain nothing secret, nothing confidential. They were, in fact, nonclassified, which is Washington's way of saying anybody who says please can have them.

to keep it at any cost. The native grandees, of course, were glad to have them as companions on the conservative ship: they wrote better English, had read more books, talked louder and with greater fluency.

10   But I don't want to write about my historical conclusions—it isn't my game. I tell myself that this third time out, if I stick to what I know, what happened to me, and a few others, I have a chance to write my own history of the time.

QUESTIONS

Ideas

1. What do you think of Hellman's reason for waiting over twenty years to write about this critical period in her life?
2. Although Hellman makes no pretense at objectivity, she does try to understand what motivated "the men who punished me." What do you think of her explanation?
3. How does Hellman's tone change from paragraph 4 to paragraph 5?
4. Objectivity and subjectivity are rarely absolute, rather are they points on a continuum. What sentences seem most obviously subjective, personal? Which ones seem closer to our traditional notions of "facts"?
5. What is the effect of the last paragraph? Is she trying to soften her previous accusations?
6. How would you characterize Hellman's attitude here? Is she bitter? Do you think she is trying to control herself? Should she?
7. Who are the scoundrels? Why? Do you agree with Hellman?
8. The following two paragraphs conclude *Scoundrel Time*. How would you compare her attitude here toward the McCarthy followers and the intellectuals with her opening ten paragraphs?

Epilogue

I have written here that I have recovered. I mean it only in a worldly sense because I do not believe in recovery. The past, with its pleasures, its rewards, its foolishness, its punishments, is there for each of us forever, and it should be.

   As I finish writing about this unpleasant part of my life, I tell myself that was then, and there is now, and the years between then and now, and the then and now are one.

9. The following piece was written five or six years after Hellman wrote
Scoundrel Time. Has the meaning of the McCarthy era changed for her?
In what ways? Be specific about attitude, tone, and persona.

It is six thirty on a bright August morning. I finished reading "Scoundrel
Time" again an hour ago. I made myself a cup of coffee, carried it to
the beach, and watched some minnows moving about. I do not now see
as well as I once did and so, leaning over to look at them more closely,
I couldn't find them again. I spilled the coffee and thought, O.K., watch
yourself, sit down, be still. I don't know how long I stayed, but when
I got up the memory of a small dinner party last year in San Francisco
had come back and with it the reason for my occasional discomfort
during last night's reading of this book.

The dinner was with a few old friends, most pleasant and easy
until the host, a distinguished scientist, announced that one of my critics
who also happened to be in town from New York—the crankiest, in
fact—would join us. I believe that the host had really forgotten this man's
strangely based, oddly personal case against the book and me. (Who can
be expected to remember other people's book fights?) We were polite to
each other, the new arrival and I, and I said nothing throughout his
almost manic long speeches. The speeches were, in any case, not meant
for me, but for a famous French visitor. When my critic left early, not
because of me, but because the Frenchman was not responding with
proper admiration or interest, the hostess, for her own reasons, was
annoyed with me.

She said, "You must really learn to be more tolerant and forgiving."

Many people have more than a distaste for certain words. My
great-uncle, who was a corrupt man, would cover his face and make a
sound at the use of the word "toilet." My hostess could not be expected
to know that I feel strongly about "tolerance." It is, to me, an arrogant
conception. Who am I to forgive? To forget, not to punish, is one thing,
but forgiveness is for God if you believe in him and maybe even if you
don't. I wanted to tell my hostess that, couldn't, couldn't even say that
it is not pleasant to correct people for what they haven't done.

So I said, "Yes, and that's a long story."

"No," she said, "I mean it. You do not forgive people. You must
learn to forgive. The time has come in your life when you must learn
to be tolerant and forgive."

Wine makes for repetition, and the fourth time she said it I was
in the elevator. But I was not thinking of her, the evening or my critic.
I was thinking of something else and the something else only came clear
this morning on the beach.

For years before "Scoundrel Time" was written I had many offers
to publish such a book. But I believed I had to wait until I could reach
a view, make a "tone" that was not a jumble, not chaotic with judgments
and weary storms that were meaningless to anybody but me. I was waiting

for a period of what my hostess would have called "tolerance," what I called "calm." It came, I thought; I wrote the book and I misrepresented myself in the book. I am, of course, sorry for that. I am not cool about those days, I am not tolerant about them and I never wish to be.

This book seemed to me last night too restrained. All those years I had waited for a view that came only because of time and recovery from pain and disorder. Or maybe I didn't have the final nerve—an accusation made by Tolstoi against Chekhov in another context, but coming out the same place here—to say that my mistakes and the political commitments of other more radical people were no excuse for the disgraceful conduct of intellectuals no matter how much they disagreed.

I believe that I am telling the truth, not the survivors' consolation, when I say that the disasters of the McCarthy period were, in many ways, good for me: I learned things, I got rid of much I didn't need. But I am angrier now than I hope I will ever be again; more disturbed now than when it all took place. I tried to avoid, when I wrote this book, what is called a moral stand. I'd like to take that stand now. I never want to live again to watch people turn into liars and cowards and others into frightened, silent collaborators. And to hell with the fancy reasons they give for what they did.

Organization

10. What is the function of the first and last paragraphs of this piece?
11. What is the function of the first sentence of paragraph 3? Is that sentence supported?
12. Some theorists believe that paragraphs cluster together, to form a stadium of discourse. What paragraphs would you group together? Why?
13. How is the first sentence of paragraph 6 supported?

Sentences

14. Compare the voice and imagery of paragraphs 4 and 5. Is there a reason for this difference?
15. In paragraph 9, how are the sentences related to one another: with words? ideas? Can you explain Hellman's use of the dash, the colon, the comma, and the semicolon in this paragraph?

Words

16. What is the effect of the following words and phrases: "spitballing" (2); "cheap buddies" (5); "boozed-up nightmares" and "quarter-historians" (6)?

17. What do the following phrases mean in context: "prevailing eccentricity" (2); "pleasant way of life" (4); "opera of public disorder" (5)?

Suggestions for Writing

A. Do you agree with Hellman's last sentence in paragraph 6? Begin an essay with a sentence that agrees or disagrees with her assessment of the public's intelligence. Use reasons and examples to support your thesis.

B. Do you think that educated intellectuals have a responsibility to aid those who are persecuted? Take a position on this issue and write an editorial for the college newspaper. Use a current controversial topic as your focus.

Letter to John S. Wood

May 19, 1952

Honorable John S. Wood
Chairman
House Committee on Un-American Activities
Room 226 Old House Office Building
Washington 25, D.C.

Dear Mr. Wood:

1   As you know, I am under subpoena to appear before your Committee on May 21, 1952.

2   I am most willing to answer all questions about myself. I have nothing to hide from your Committee and there is nothing in my life of which I am ashamed. I have been advised by counsel that under the Fifth Amendment I have a constitutional privilege to decline to answer any questions about my political opinions, activities and associations,

on the grounds of self-incrimination. I do not wish to claim this privilege. I am ready and willing to testify before the representatives of our Government as to my own opinions and my own actions, regardless of any risks or consequences to myself.

3   But I am advised by counsel that if I answer the Committee's questions about myself, I must also answer questions about other people and that if I refuse to do so, I can be cited for contempt. My counsel tells me that if I answer questions about myself, I will have waived my rights under the Fifth Amendment and could be forced legally to answer questions about others. This is very difficult for a layman to understand. But there is one principle that I do understand: I am not willing, now or in the future, to bring bad trouble to people who, in my past association with them, were completely innocent of any talk or any action that was disloyal or subversive. I do not like subversion or disloyalty in any form and if I had ever seen any I would have considered it my duty to have reported it to the proper authorities. But to hurt innocent people whom I knew many years ago in order to save myself is, to me, inhuman and indecent and dishonorable. I cannot and will not cut my conscience to fit this year's fashions, even though I long ago came to the conclusion that I was not a political person and could have no comfortable place in any political group.

4   I was raised in an old-fashioned American tradition and there were certain homely things that were taught to me: to try to tell the truth, not to bear false witness, not to harm my neighbor, to be loyal to my country, and so on. In general, I respected these ideals of Christian honor and did as well with them as I knew how. It is my belief that you will agree with these simple rules of human decency and will not expect me to violate the good American tradition from which they spring. I would, therefore, like to come before you and speak of myself.

5   I am prepared to waive the privilege against self-incrimination and to tell you anything you wish to know about my views or actions if your Committee will agree to refrain from asking me to name other people. If the Committee is unwilling to give me this assurance, I will be forced to plead the privilege of the Fifth Amendment at the hearing.

6   A reply to this letter would be appreciated.

Sincerely yours,
Lillian Hellman

QUESTIONS

Ideas

1. Hellman knows that millions of people will read this letter. What, then, are her purposes? In analyzing the needs of her audience, what techniques of persuasion does she assume will work?
2. What traditional American values does she imply the committee is violating?

Organization

3. Why does Hellman begin with a cooperative statement? What do you think Hellman's best argument is? Is it effectively placed?
4. What is the purpose of each paragraph?

Sentences/Words

5. How would you compare the tone of this letter to that of the selection from *Scoundrel Time?* How does Hellman's sentence structure contribute to her tone?
6. What words and phrases does Hellman hope will have a salubrious effect? Notice especially words that have strong emotional overtones—"decency," for example.

Suggestions for Writing

A. Write a letter to Hellman agreeing or disagreeing with the principle of her defense.
B. Write an analysis of this letter as a piece of persuasion. Include audience, persona, arguments, and organization.

Giants

Moscow was always an ugly city except for the Kremlin Red Square and a few rich merchant sections, but now it is much uglier, as if Los Angeles had no sun and no grass. The city sprawls around, is inconvenient and haphazard with brash new buildings pushing against the old, as if bright mail order teeth were fitted next to yellowed fangs. There is a brutality about modern architecture in America, but in Moscow the brutality is mixed with something idiot-minded, as if their architects could loll about, giggling, poking at each other at a tipsy party given in honor of nothing.

There are still some fine nineteenth-century houses in Moscow—it has very few from the eighteenth century—and while they never could have compared to the great houses of London or Paris, now they seem lovely and soft, often in pinks and fading yellows, next to the new shabbiness on the next block. More churches are open, more have been restored since I was last here during the war, and St. Basil's, opposite my window at the hotel, is a wonderful building, as if wild bands of children had painted the brilliant onion domes and put the cheerful blocks into rounded shape. The light comes up late in Moscow in November, but there is never a morning that I don't want to walk across Red Square to look at St. Basil's. But you can't walk across Red Square anymore: I guess it was smart to allow no dangerous foot traffic in the giant spaces of the Square, but it is a tiring nuisance to go down the subway steps through the long corridors, up again and down, pushed and shoved, simply to find yourself across the street. True, it is very nice when you get there: nice to see the crowds all day, every day, waiting to look in religious reverence at Lenin's body, nice that the grounds of the Kremlin are now open to the public, wonderful to be able to go inside the exquisite small churches. Greek Catholicism, Russian form, has a warmth and coziness unlike other architectural church forms, as if God needed only brilliance of color and carving to feel praised.

The Palace of Congresses, the new building inside the walls of the Kremlin, is less bad than most, but it was vanity to put it so close to the wonderful old Kremlin buildings and ask it to compete. The new apartment buildings, spread out in all directions in the flat, ugly land, have no color and no form. The new hotels are imitations, I guess, of Abramovitz, or maybe men of the same time share the same vulgarities. The Danes and the Swedes have done some decent modern design, but the Russians have ignored their close neighbors and seem to be intent on imitating the mess we have made of our cities. But then everybody who has been in the Soviet Union for any length of time has noticed their concern with the United States: we may be the enemy, but we are the admired enemy, and the so-called good life for us is the to-be-good life for them. During the war, the Russian combination of dislike and grudging admiration for us, and ours for them, seemed to me like the innocent rivalry of two men proud of being large, handsome and successful. But I was wrong. They have chosen to imitate and compete with the most vulgar aspects of American life, and we have chosen, as in the revelations of the CIA bribery of intellectuals and scholars, to say, "But the Russians do the same thing," as if honor were a mask that you put on and took off at a costume ball. They condemn Vietnam, we condemn Hungary. But the moral tone of giants with swollen heads, fat fingers pressed over the atom bomb, staring at each other across the forests of the world, is monstrously comic.

QUESTIONS

Ideas

1. What impact does this essay have on you? Are you shocked, annoyed, sympathetic?
2. Hellman starts off talking about architecture in Moscow. In her judgment, what is wrong with Moscow's buildings?
3. Somewhere in that long third paragraph Hellman gradually shifts her analysis from the Kremlin's buildings to the Soviet Union and the United States. Have we been prepared for this?
4. About what was she wrong? How does her tone change after this sentence? Can nations be monstrously comic? How?
5. Now that you have read the last four or five sentences, does this piece seem more or less focused?

Organization

6. Assume that this piece is all one paragraph; where would you break it for new paragraphs?
7. Can you defend the organization of Hellman's last paragraph? Try to see reasons why all these sentences belong together.
8. Explain how the three paragraphs of the essay cohere, i.e., stick together, one sentence with the next.

Sentences

9. Notice how many times Hellman uses the phrase "as if." It appears, in fact, in the first sentence and links Los Angeles and Moscow. What is her purpose in doing this and what effect does it have on you?

10. Why do you think Hellman decided to use so much coordination ("and" and "but") in the last section of the essay?

Words

11. Each sentence in the first paragraph is structured similarly. What is the pattern? Is it effective?

12. After using similes throughout this piece, Hellman abandons them for the directness of metaphor in the last sentence. Why?

Suggestions for Writing

A. Compare and contrast the USSR and the USA around one specific focus. Hellman suggests architecture and morality, but you might want to try others, for example, sports, culture, foreign affairs, or space exploration. Try to come to some conclusions as a result of your comparison.

B. Write a letter to Lillian Hellman agreeing or disagreeing with those last half dozen sentences.

C. Describe in some detail a particularly ugly scene. What makes it so? Can you see how others might see it differently? Notice the details and Hellman's personal reaction in the second paragraph and see if you can use this approach.

ELEVEN

Loren Eiseley
(1907–1977)

Many critics bemoan the increasingly narrow focus of both scientists and humanists. Unfortunately, the age of specialization asks us to probe deep but not wide. Loren Eiseley is different. He is the rare individual who can range far, wide, and deep in both cultures. He is a renowned anthropologist and archeologist, a naturalist and a philosopher, an essayist and poet. Eiseley bridges the gulf between science and the humanities by returning to nature the wonder and mystery that reason often takes away. Although gifted with a mature and acute perception of nature's secrets, he is able in his nonfiction to maintain the child's capacity for wonder and surprise. He feels that the man of science needs balance, needs both analysis and intuition. At the end of his scientific career as a museum curator and university professor, he wrote: "When the human mind exists in the light of reason and no more than reason, we may say with absolute certainty that man and all that made him will be in that instant gone."

Eiseley did not even realize that he wanted to be a scientist until graduate school. Until then he felt he was rootless: spending his childhood on the plains of western Nebraska, attending college, riding the freight trains during the Depression, recuperating from an illness in a cabin in Colorado. For much of this time he was unhappy and lonely. In his autobiography, *All the Strange Hours* (1975), he recounts the frustration and pain of growing up in poverty in a tumultuous, neurotic family. Specifically, in "The Running Man" he tries to understand how several encounters from his childhood shaped the man he has become.

He is especially obsessed with his mother and his awkward, scarring relationship with her. His description of one dramatic and public episode forms the center of this essay. It is painful and honest, haunting and lyrical.

Even though Eiseley's reputation as a scientist was firmly established through his articles in scholarly journals, it was not until his collection of popular essays, *The Immense Journey* (1957), was published that he became known to the general public.

This book marked the beginning of a new career for Eiseley as a writer of the "concealed essay," a form in which personal observations lead to thoughts of a more general, objective nature. Eiseley, like Annie Dillard, is willing to read cosmic significance into small incidents—in the flight of birds, the web of a spider, in a run-in with a neighborhood bully, and in a chance encounter with a young fox. In these essays Eiseley, as narrator, is a knowing and helpful presence, but he is also there with the reader as an observer, questioning and puzzling over the inexplicable. In "The Judgment of the Birds," for example, he comes across an improbable and transitory web, built by a spider who refuses to succumb to the weather. He observes the spider carefully, then speculates: "Maybe man himself will fight like this in the end." The everyday event reverberates in the scientist's mind until it awakens the artist. This is characteristic of Eiseley's vision: the mundane is "refracted, transmuted and clarified through the prism of his poetic imagination." In this way, the scientist looks beyond logic to beauty and mystery that defy explanation. And so wonder is returned to nature.

One of Eiseley's most persistent themes is the mystery and complexity of time—an appropriate topic for an archeologist. Eiseley treats it with the intellectual rigor and curiosity of a scientist, without neglecting eloquence and sensitivity. In "Charles Darwin" he reflects on evolution as an expert, but his style and tone are filled with poetic sensibility and an amateur's sense of wonder and reverence. Somehow he can simultaneously observe, speculate, and dream. In "The Time of Man," an early essay on evolution (1962), the following passages are characteristic of Eiseley's incantatory, lyrical prose:

A strange animal, indeed: so very quiet when one turns over the mineral-hardened skull in a gravel bed, or peers into that little dark space which has housed so much cruelty and delight. One feels that something should be there still, some indefinable essence, some jinni to be evoked out of this little space which may contain at the same time the words of Jesus and the blasphemous megatons of modern physics. They are all in there together, inextricably intermixed. . . .

Those ancient bestial stirrings which still claw at sanity are part, also, of that dark continent we long chose to forget. But we do not forget, because man in contemplation reveals something that is characteristic of no other form of life known to us: he suffers because of what he is, and wishes to become something else. The moment we cease to hunger to be otherwise, our soul is dead. Long ago we began that hunger: long ago we painted on the walls of caverns and buried the revered dead. More and more, because our brain lays hold upon and seeks to shape the future, we are conscious of what we are, and what we might be. "No man," wrote John Donne, "doth exalt Nature to the height it would beare." He saw the great discrepancy between the dream and the reality.

Loren Eiseley learned not just to study nature but to participate in it. His essays are written in the same spirit: the reader is urged to be an active voyager. Eiseley once wrote that animals understand their roles, but that man, "bereft of instinct, must search continually for meanings." These essays are a rich source for such a journey.

Charles Darwin

I

1   In the autumn of 1831 the past and the future met and dined in London—in the guise of two young men who little realized

where the years ahead would take them. One, Robert Fitzroy, was a sea captain who at twenty-six had already charted the remote, sea-beaten edges of the world and now proposed another long voyage. A religious man with a strong animosity toward the new-fangled geology, Captain Fitzroy wanted a naturalist who would share his experience of wild lands and refute those who used rocks to promote heretical whisperings. The young man who faced him across the table hesitated. Charles Darwin, four years Fitzroy's junior, was a gentleman idler after hounds who had failed at medicine and whose family, in desperation, hoped he might still succeed as a country parson. His mind shifted uncertainly from fox hunting in Shropshire to the thought of shooting llamas in South America. Did he really want to go? While he fumbled for a decision and the future hung irresolute, Captain Fitzroy took command.

2   "Fitzroy," wrote Darwin later to his sister Susan, "says the stormy sea is exaggerated; that if I do not choose to remain with them, I can at any time get home to England; and that if I like, I shall be left in some healthy, safe and nice country; that I shall always have assistance; that he has many books, all instruments, guns, at my service. . . . There is indeed a tide in the affairs of men, and I have experienced it. Dearest Susan, Goodbye."

3   They sailed from Devonport December 27, 1831, in H.M.S. *Beagle*, a ten-gun brig. Their plan was to survey the South American coastline and to carry a string of chronometrical measurements around the world. The voyage almost ended before it began, for they at once encountered a violent storm. "The sea ran very high," young Darwin recorded in his diary, "and the vessel pitched bows under and suffered most dreadfully; such a night I never passed, on every side nothing but misery; such a whistling of the wind and roar of the sea, the hoarse screams of the officers and shouts of the men, made a concert that I shall not soon forget." Captain Fitzroy and his officers held the ship on the sea by the grace of God and the cat-o'-nine-tails. With an almost irrational stubborness Darwin decided, in spite of his uncomfortable discovery of his susceptibility to seasickness, that "I did right to accept the offer." When the *Beagle* was buffeted back into Plymouth Harbor, Darwin did not resign. His mind was made up. "If it is desirable to see the world," he wrote in his journal, "what a rare and excellent opportunity this is. Perhaps I may have the same opportunity of drilling my mind that I threw away at Cambridge."

4   So began the journey in which a great mind untouched by an old-fashioned classical education was to feed its hunger upon rocks and broken bits of bone at the world's end, and eventually was to shape from such diverse things as bird beaks and the fused wing-cases of island beetles a theory that would shake the foundations of scientific thought in all the countries of the earth.

II

5   The intellectual climate from which Darwin set forth on his historic voyage was predominantly conservative. Insular England had been horrified by the excesses of the French Revolution and was extremely wary of emerging new ideas which it attributed to "French atheists." Religious dogma still held its powerful influence over natural science. True, the seventeenth-century notion that the world had been created in 4004 B.C. was beginning to weaken in the face of naturalists' studies of the rocks and their succession of life forms. But the conception of a truly ancient and evolving planet was still unformed. No one could dream that the age of the earth was as vast as we now know it to be. And the notion of a continuity of events—of one animal changing by degrees into another—seemed to fly in the face not only of religious beliefs but also of common sense. Many of the greatest biologists of the time—men like Louis Agassiz and Richard Owen—tended to the belief that the successive forms of life in the geological record were all separate creations, some of which had simply been extinguished by historic accidents.

6   Yet Darwin did not compose the theory of evolution out of thin air. Like so many great scientific generalizations, the theory with which his name is associated had already had premonitory beginnings. All of the elements which were to enter into the theory were in men's minds and were being widely discussed during Darwin's college years. His own grandfather, Erasmus Darwin, who died seven years before Charles was born, had boldly proposed a theory of the "transmutation" of living forms. Jean Baptiste Lamarck had glimpsed a vision of evolutionary continuity. And Sir Charles Lyell—later to become Darwin's confidant—had opened the way for the evolutionary point of view by demonstrating that the planet must be very old—old enough to allow ex-

tremely slow organic change. Lyell dismissed the notion of catastrophic extinction of animal forms on a world-wide scale as impossible, and he made plain that natural forces—the work of wind and frost and water—were sufficient to explain most of the phenomena found in the rocks, provided these forces were seen as operating over enormous periods. Without Lyell's gift of time in immense quantities, Darwin would not have been able to devise the theory of natural selection.

7   If all the essential elements of the Darwinian scheme of nature were known prior to Darwin, why is he accorded so important a place in biological history? The answer is simple: Almost every great scientific generalization is a supreme act of creative synthesis. There comes a time when an accumulation of smaller discoveries and observations can be combined in some great and comprehensive view of nature. At this point the need is not so much for increased numbers of facts as for a mind of great insight capable of taking the assembled information and rendering it intelligible. Such a synthesis represents the scientific mind at its highest point of achievement. The stature of the discoverer is not diminished by the fact that he has slid into place the last piece of a tremendous puzzle on which many others have worked. To finish the task he must see correctly over a vast and diverse array of data.

8   Still it must be recognized that Darwin came at a fortunate time. The fact that another man, Alfred Russel Wallace, conceived the Darwinian theory independently before Darwin published it shows clearly that the principle which came to be called natural selection was in the air—was in a sense demanding to be born. Darwin himself pointed out in his autobiography that "innumerable well-observed facts were stored in the minds of naturalists ready to take their proper places as soon as any theory which would receive them was sufficiently explained."

III

9   Darwin, then, set out on his voyage with a mind both inquisitive to see and receptive to what he saw. No detail was too small to be fascinating and provocative. Sailing down the South American coast, he notes the octopus changing its color angrily in the waters of a cove. In the dry arroyos of the pampas he observes great bones and shrewdly seeks to relate them to animals of the present. The local inhabitants insist that the fossil bones grew after death, and also that

certain rivers have the power of "changing small bones into large."
Everywhere men wonder, but they are deceived through their thirst for
easy explanations. Darwin, by contrast, is a working dreamer. He rides,
climbs, spends long days on the Indian-haunted pampas in constant
peril of his life. Asking at a house whether robbers are numerous, he
receives the cryptic reply: "The thistles are not up yet." The huge thistles,
high as a horse's back at their full growth, provide ecological cover for
bandits. Darwin notes the fact and rides on. The thistles are overrunning
the pampas; the whole aspect of the vegetation is altering under the
impact of man. Wild dogs howl in the brakes; the common cat, run
wild, has grown large and fierce. All is struggle, mutability, change.
Staring into the face of an evil relative of the rattlesnake, he observes
a fact "which appears to me very curious and instructive, as showing
how every character, even though it may be in some degree independent
of structure . . . has a tendency to vary by slow degrees."

10   He pays great attention to strange animals existing in difficult
environments. A queer little toad with a scarlet belly he whimsically
nicknames *diabolicus* because it is "a fit toad to preach in the ear of
Eve." He notes it lives among sand dunes under the burning sun, and
unlike its brethren, cannot swim. From toads to grasshoppers, from
pebbles to mountain ranges, nothing escapes his attention. The wearing
away of stone, the downstream travel of rock fragments and boulders,
the great crevices and upthrusts of the Andes, an earthquake—all confirm the dynamic character of the earth and its great age.

11   Captain Fitzroy by now is anxious to voyage on. The sails are
set. With the towering Andes on their right flank they run north for the
Galápagos Islands, lying directly on the Equator 600 miles off the west
coast of South America. A one-time refuge of buccaneers, these islands
are essentially chimneys of burned-out volcanoes. Darwin remarks that
they remind him of huge iron foundries surrounded by piles of waste.
"A little world in itself," he marvels, "with inhabitants such as are found
nowhere else." Giant armored tortoises clank through the undergrowth
like prehistoric monsters, feeding upon the cacti. Birds in this tiny Eden
do not fear men: "One day a mocking bird alighted on the edge of a
pitcher which I held in my hand. It began very quietly to sip the water,
and allowed me to lift it with the vessel from the ground." Big sea lizards
three feet long drowse on the beaches, and feed, fantastically, upon the
seaweed. Surveying these "imps of darkness, black as the porous rocks
over which they crawl," Darwin is led to comment that "there is no

other quarter of the world, where this order replaces the herbivorous mammalia in so extraordinary a manner."

12   Yet only by degrees did Darwin awake to the fact that he had stumbled by chance into one of the most marvelous evolutionary laboratories on the planet. Here in the Galápagos was a wealth of variations from island to island—among the big tortoises, among plants and especially among the famous finches with remarkably diverse beaks. Dwellers on the islands, notably Vice Governor Lawson, called Darwin's attention to these strange variations, but as he confessed later, with typical Darwinian lack of pretense, "I did not for some time pay sufficient attention to this statement."

13   As one surveys the long and tangled course that led to Darwin's great discovery, one cannot but be struck by the part played in it by oceanic islands.

14   Until Darwin turned his attention to them, it appears to have been generally assumed that island plants and animals were simply marooned evidences of a past connection with the nearest continent. Darwin, however, noted that whole classes of continental life were absent from the island; that certain plants which were herbaceous (nonwoody) on the mainland had developed into trees on the islands; that island animals often differed from their counterparts on the mainland.

15   Above all, the fantastically varied finches of the Galápagos amazed and puzzled him. There were parrot-beaks, curved beaks for probing flowers, straight beaks, small beaks—beaks for every conceivable purpose. These beak variations existed nowhere but on the islands; they must have evolved there. Darwin had early observed: "One might really fancy that, from an original paucity of birds in this archipelago, one species had been taken and modified for different ends." The birds had become transformed, through the struggle for existence on their little islets, into a series of types suited to particular environmental niches where, properly adapted, they could obtain food and survive. As the ornithologist David Lack has remarked, "Darwin's finches form a little world of their own, but one which intimately reflects the world as a whole."

16   Darwin's recognition of the significance of this miniature world, where the forces operating to create new beings could be plainly seen, was indispensable to his discovery of the origin of species. The island worlds reduced the confusion of continental life to more simple proportions; one could separate the factors involved with greater success.

Over and over Darwin emphasized the importance of islands in his thinking. Nothing would aid natural history more, he contended to Lyell, "than careful collecting and investigating of *all the productions* of the most isolated islands. . . . Every sea shell and insect and plant is of value from such spots."

17 Darwin was born in precisely the right age even in terms of the great scientific voyages. A little earlier, the story the islands had to tell could not have been read; a little later much of it began to be erased. Today all over the globe the populations of these little worlds are vanishing, many without ever having been seriously investigated. Man, breaking into their isolation, has brought with him cats, rats, pigs, goats, weeds and insects from the continents. In the face of these hardier, tougher, more aggressive competitors, the island faunas—the rare, the antique, the strange, the beautiful—are vanishing without a trace. The giant Galápagos tortoises are almost extinct, as is the land lizard with which Darwin played. Some of the odd little finches and rare plants have gone or will go. On the island of Madagascar our own remote relatives, the lemurs, which have radiated into many curious forms, are now being exterminated through the destruction of the forests. Even that continental island Australia is suffering from the decimation wrought by man. The Robinson Crusoe worlds where small castaways could create existences idyllically remote from the ravening slaughter of man and his associates are about to pass away forever. Every such spot is now a potential air base where the cries of birds are drowned in the roar of jets, and the crevices once frequented by bird life are flattened into the long runways of the bombers. All this would not have surprised Darwin, one would guess.

IV

18 When Darwin reached home after the voyage of the *Beagle*, he was an ailing man, and he remained so to the end of his life. Today we know that this illness was in some degree psychosomatic, that he was anxiety-ridden, subject to mysterious headaches and nausea. Shortly after his voyage Darwin married his cousin Emma Wedgwood, granddaughter of the founder of the great pottery works, and isolated himself and his family in the little village of Down, in Kent. He avoided travel,

save for brief trips to watering places for his health. For twenty-two years after the *Beagle*'s return he published not one word beyond the bare journal of his trip (later titled A *Naturalist's Voyage around the World*) and technical monographs on his observations.

19   Darwin's gardener is said to have responded once to a visitor who inquired about his master's health: "Poor man, he just stands and stares at a yellow flower for minutes at a time. He would be better off with something to do." Darwin's work was of an intangible nature which eluded people around him. Much of it consisted in just such standing and staring as his gardener reported. On a visit to the Isle of Wight he watched thistle seed wafted about on offshore winds and formulated theories of plant dispersal. Sometimes he engaged in activities which his good wife must surely have struggled to keep from reaching the neighbors. When a friend sent him a half ounce of locust dung from Africa, Darwin triumphantly grew seven plants from the specimen. "There is no error," he assured Lyell, "for I dissected the seeds out of the middle of the pellets." To discover how plant seeds traveled, Darwin would go all the way down a grasshopper's gullet, or worse, without embarrassment. His eldest son Francis spoke amusedly of his father's botanical experiments: "I think he personified each seed as a small demon trying to elude him by getting into the wrong heap, or jumping away all together; and this gave to the work the excitement of a game."

20   The point of his game Darwin kept largely to himself, waiting until it should be completely finished. He piled up vast stores of data and dreamed of presenting his evolution theory in a definitive, monumental book, so large that it would certainly have fallen dead and unreadable from the press. In the meantime, Robert Chambers, a bookseller and journalist, wrote and brought out anonymously a modified version of Lamarckian evolution, under the title *Vestiges of the Natural History of Creation*. Amateurish in some degree, the book drew savage onslaughts from the critics, including Thomas Huxley, but it caught the public fancy and was widely read. It passed through numerous editions in both England and America—evidence that *sub rosa* there was a good deal more interest on the part of the public in the "development hypothesis," as evolution was then called, than the fulminations of critics would have suggested.

21   Throughout this period Darwin remained stonily silent. Many explanations of his silence have been ventured by his biographers: that

he was busy accumulating materials; that he did not wish to affront Fitzroy; that the attack on the *Vestiges* had intimidated him; that he thought it wise not to write upon so controversial a subject until he had first acquired a reputation as a professional naturalist of the first rank. A primary reason lay in his personality—a nature reluctant to face the storm that publication would bring about his ears. It was pleasanter to procrastinate, to talk of the secret to a few chosen companions such as Lyell and the great botanist Joseph Hooker.

22   The Darwin family had been well-to-do since the time of grandfather Erasmus. Charles was independent, in a position to devote all his energies to research and under no academic pressure to publish in haste.

23   "You will be anticipated," Lyell warned him. "You had better publish." That was in the spring of 1856. Darwin promised, but again delayed. We know that he left instructions for his wife to see to the publication of his notes in the event of his death. It was almost as if present fame or notoriety were more than he could bear. At all events he continued to delay, and this situation might very well have continued to the end of his life, had not Lyell's warning suddenly come true and broken his pleasant dream.

24   Alfred Russel Wallace, a comparatively unknown, youthful naturalist, had divined Darwin's great secret in a moment of fever-ridden insight while on a collecting trip in Indonesia. He, too, had put together the pieces and gained a clear conception of the scheme of evolution. Ironically enough, it was to Darwin, in all innocence, that he sent his manuscript for criticism in June of 1858.

25   Darwin, understandably shaken, turned to his friends Lyell and Hooker, who knew the many years he had been laboring upon his *magnum opus*. The two distinguished scientists arranged for the delivery of a short summary by Darwin to accompany Wallace's paper before the Linnean Society. Thus the theory was announced by the two men simultaneously.

26   The papers drew little comment at the meeting but set in motion a mild undercurrent of excitement. Darwin, though upset by the death of his son Charles, went to work to explain his views more fully in a book. Ironically he called it *An Abstract of an Essay on the Origin of Species* and insisted it would be only a kind of preview of a much larger work. Anxiety and devotion to his great hoard of data still possessed

him. He did not like to put all his hopes in this volume, which must now be written at top speed. He bolstered himself by references to the "real" book—that Utopian volume in which all that could not be made clear in his abstract would be clarified.

27   His timidity and his fears were totally groundless. When the *Origin of Species* (the title distilled by his astute publisher from Darwin's cumbersome and half-hearted one) was published in the fall of 1859, the first edition was sold in a single day. The book which Darwin had so apologetically bowed into existence was, of course, soon to be recognized as one of the great books of all time. It would not be long before its author would sigh happily and think no more of that huge, ideal volume which he had imagined would be necessary to convince the public. The public and his brother scientists would find the *Origin* quite heavy going enough. His book to end all books would never be written. It did not need to be. The world of science in the end could only agree with the sharp-minded Huxley, whose immediate reaction upon reading the *Origin* was: "How extremely stupid not to have thought of that!" And so it frequently seems in science, once the great synthesizer has done his work. The ideas were not new, but the synthesis was. Men would never again look upon the world in the same manner as before.

28   No great philosophic conception ever entered the world more fortunately. Though it is customary to emphasize the religious and scientific storm the book aroused—epitomized by the famous debate at Oxford between Bishop Wilberforce and Thomas Huxley—the truth is that Darwinism found relatively easy acceptance among scientists and most of the public. The way had been prepared by the long labors of Lyell and the wide popularity of Chambers' book, the *Vestiges*. Moreover, Darwin had won the support of Hooker and of Huxley, the most formidable scientific debater of all time. Lyell, though more cautious, helped to publicize Darwin and at no time attacked him. Asa Gray, one of America's leading botanists, came to his defense. His co-discoverer, Wallace, generously advanced the word "Darwinism" for the theory, and minimized his own part in the elaboration of the theory as "one week to twenty years."

29   This sturdy band of converts assumed the defense of Darwin before the public, while Charles remained aloof. Sequestered in his estate at Down, he calmly answered letters and listened, but not too much, to the tumult over the horizon. "It is something unintelligible to me how

anyone can argue in public like orators do," he confessed to Hooker. Hewett Watson, another botanist of note, wrote to him shortly after the publication of the *Origin:* "Your leading idea will assuredly become recognized as an established truth in science, i.e., 'Natural Selection.' It has the characteristics of all great natural truths, clarifying what was obscure, simplifying what was intricate, adding greatly to previous knowledge. You are the greatest revolutionist in natural history of this century, if not of all centuries."

30   Watson's statement was clairvoyant. Within ten years the *Origin* and its author were known all over the globe, and evolution had beome the guiding motif in all biological studies.

QUESTIONS

Ideas

1. How does Eiseley support the topic sentence of paragraph 5: "Yet Darwin did not compose the theory of evolution out of thin air"?
2. What is meant by "creative synthesis"? How does this apply to Darwin?
3. What is Eiseley's attitude toward man in the last paragraph of part III?
4. Eiseley is obviously interested in Darwin as a man and a scientist. How would you characterize the personality of Darwin?
5. What point is Eiseley making about great scientific advances?

Organization

6. What is the purpose of each of the four parts?
7. In informational discourse, paragraphs are usually more tightly structured than in narrative or personal writing. Eiseley therefore uses several formula paragraphs. He often begins with an assertion and then supports it with reasons, examples, and details. Look, for example, at paragraphs 1, 5, 6, and 9. What is the organizational pattern of the following paragraphs: 7, 14, 16, 26?

Sentences

8. Eiseley's style here is not as lyrical or subjective as in his other pieces. It serves a different function—to inform. Compare, for example, the sen-

tences in paragraphs 6 and 7 with the last three paragraphs of "The Running Man." What differences do you see in tone, length, syntax, and purpose?

Words

9. Make a list of a dozen scientific terms used in this essay and define them in your own words.
10. In the last paragraph what does "clairvoyant" mean? Does Eiseley mean this literally?

Suggestions for Writing

A. Based on your experiences, write an essay that focuses on Huxley's reaction: "How extremely stupid not to have thought of that!"
B. Write an extended definition of Darwin's leading idea, "Natural Selection."

The Judgment of the Birds

---

1   It is a commonplace of all religious thought, even the most primitive, that the man seeking visions and insight must go apart from his fellows and live for a time in the wilderness. If he is of the proper sort, he will return with a message. It may not be a message from the god he set out to seek, but even if he has failed in that particular, he will have had a vision or seen a marvel, and these are always worth listening to and thinking about.

2   The world, I have come to believe, is a very queer place, but we have been part of this queerness for so long that we tend to take it for granted. We rush to and fro like Mad Hatters upon our peculiar errands, all the time imagining our surroundings to be dull and ourselves quite ordinary creatures. Actually, there is nothing in the world to encourage this idea, but such is the mind of man, and this is why he finds it necessary from time to time to send emissaries into the wilderness in the hope of learning of great events, or plans in store for him, that will resuscitate his waning taste for life. His great news services, his world-wide radio network, he knows with a last remnant of healthy distrust

will be of no use to him in this matter. No miracle can withstand a radio broadcast, and it is certain that it would be no miracle if it could. One must seek, then, what only the solitary approach can give—a natural revelation.

3   Let it be understood that I am not the sort of man to whom is entrusted direct knowledge of great events or prophecies. A naturalist, however, spends much of his life alone, and my life is no exception. Even in New York City there are patches of wilderness, and a man by himself is bound to undergo certain experiences falling into the class of which I speak. I set mine down, therefore: a matter of pigeons, a flight of chemicals, and a judgment of birds, in the hope that they will come to the eye of those who have retained a true taste for the marvelous, and who are capable of discerning in the flow of ordinary events the point at which the mundane world gives way to quite another dimension.

4   New York is not, on the whole, the best place to enjoy the downright miraculous nature of the planet. There are, I do not doubt, many remarkable stories to be heard there and many strange sights to be seen, but to grasp a marvel fully it must be savored from all aspects. This cannot be done while one is being jostled and hustled along a crowded street. Nevertheless, in any city there are true wildernesses where a man can be alone. It can happen in a hotel room, or on the high roofs at dawn.

5   One night on the twentieth floor of a midtown hotel I awoke in the dark and grew restless. On an impulse I climbed upon the broad old-fashioned window sill, opened the curtains, and peered out. It was the hour just before dawn, the hour when men sigh in their sleep or, if awake, strive to focus their wavering eyesight upon a world emerging from the shadows. I leaned out sleepily through the open window. I had expected depths, but not the sight I saw.

6   I found I was looking down from that great height into a series of curious cupolas or lofts that I could just barely make out in the darkness. As I looked, the outlines of these lofts became more distinct because the light was being reflected from the wings of pigeons who, in utter silence, were beginning to float outward upon the city. In and out through the open slits in the cupolas passed the white-winged birds on their mysterious errands. At this hour the city was theirs, and quietly, without the brush of a single wing tip against stone in that high, eerie place, they were taking over the spires of Manhattan. They were pouring

upward in a light that was not yet perceptible to human eyes, while far down in the black darkness of the alleys it was still midnight.

7   As I crouched half-asleep across the sill, I had a moment's illusion that the world had changed in the night, as in some immense snowfall, and that, if I were to leave, it would have to be as these other inhabitants were doing, by the window. I should have to launch out into that great bottomless void with the simple confidence of young birds reared high up there among the familiar chimney pots and interposed horrors of the abyss.

8   I leaned farther out. To and fro went the white wings, to and fro. There were no sounds from any of them. They knew man was asleep and this light for a little while was theirs. Or perhaps I had only dreamed about man in this city of wings—which he could surely never have built. Perhaps I, myself, was one of these birds dreaming unpleasantly a moment of old dangers far below as I teetered on a window ledge.

9   Around and around went the wings. It needed only a little courage, only a little shove from the window ledge, to enter that city of light. The muscles of my hands were already making little premonitory lunges. I wanted to enter that city and go away over the roofs in the first dawn. I wanted to enter it so badly that I drew back carefully into the room and opened the hall door. I found my coat on the chair, and it slowly became clear to me that there was a way down through the floors, that I was, after all, only a man.

10   I dressed then and went back to my own kind, and I have been rather more than usually careful ever since not to look into the city of light. I had seen, just once, man's greatest creation from a strange inverted angle, and it was not really his at all. I will never forget how those wings went round and round, and how, by the merest pressure of the fingers and a feeling for air, one might go away over the roofs. It is a knowledge, however, that is better kept to oneself. I think of it sometimes in such a way that the wings, beginning far down in the black depths of the mind, begin to rise and whirl till all the mind is lit by their spinning, and there is a sense of things passing away, but lightly, as a wing might veer over an obstacle.

11   To see from an inverted angle, however, is not a gift allotted merely to the human imagination. I have come to suspect that within their degree it is sensed by animals, though perhaps as rarely as among men. The time has to be right; one has to be, by chance or intention,

upon the border of two worlds. And sometimes these two borders may shift or interpenetrate and one sees the miraculous.

12   I once saw this happen to a crow.

13   This crow lives near my house, and though I have never injured him, he takes good care to stay up in the very highest trees and, in general, to avoid humanity. His world begins at about the limit of my eyesight.

14   On the particular morning when this episode occurred, the whole countryside was buried in one of the thickest fogs in years. The ceiling was absolutely zero. All planes were grounded, and even a pedestrian could hardly see his outstretched hand before him.

15   I was groping across a field in the general direction of the railroad station, following a dimly outlined path. Suddenly out of the fog, at about the level of my eyes, and so closely that I flinched, there flashed a pair of immense black wings and a huge beak. The whole bird rushed over my head with a frantic cawing outcry of such hideous terror as I have never heard in a crow's voice before and never expect to hear again.

16   He was lost and startled, I thought, as I recovered my poise. He ought not to have flown out in this fog. He'd knock his silly brains out.

17   All afternoon that great awkward cry rang in my head. Merely being lost in a fog seemed scarcely to account for it—especially in a tough, intelligent old bandit such as I knew that particular crow to be. I even looked once in the mirror to see what it might be about me that had so revolted him that he had cried out in protest to the very stones.

18   Finally, as I worked my way homeward along the path, the solution came to me. It should have been clear before. The borders of our worlds had shifted. It was the fog that had done it. That crow, and I knew him well, never under normal circumstances flew low near men. He had been lost all right, but it was more than that. He had thought he was high up, and when he encountered me looming gigantically through the fog, he had perceived a ghastly and, to the crow mind, unnatural sight. He had seen a man walking on air, desecrating the very heart of the crow kingdom, a harbinger of the most profound evil a crow mind could conceive of—air-walking men. The encounter, he must have thought, had taken place a hundred feet over the roofs.

19   He caws now when he sees me leaving for the station in the morning, and I fancy that in that note I catch the uncertainty of a mind

that has come to know things are not always what they seem. He has
seen a marvel in his heights of air and is no longer as other crows. He
has experienced the human world from an unlikely perspective. He and
I share a viewpoint in common: our worlds have interpenetrated, and
we both have faith in the miraculous.

20　　It is a faith that in my own case has been augmented by two
remarkable sights. I once saw some very odd chemicals fly across a waste
so dead it might have been upon the moon, and once, by an even more
fantastic piece of luck, I was present when a group of birds passed a
judgment upon life.

21　　On the maps of the old voyageurs it is called *Mauvaises Terres,*
the evil lands, and, slurred a little with the passage through many
minds, it has come down to us anglicized as the badlands. The soft
shuffle of moccasins has passed through its canyons on the grim business
of war and flight, but the last of those slight disturbances of immemorial
silences died out almost a century ago. The land, if one can call it a
land, is a waste as lifeless as that valley in which lie the kings of Egypt.
Like the Valley of the Kings, it is a mausoleum, a place of dry bones
in what once was a place of life. Now it has silences as deep as those
in the moon's airless chasms.

22　　Nothing grows among its pinnacles; there is no shade except under
great toadstools of sandstone whose bases have been eaten to the shape
of wine glasses by the wind. Everything is flaking, cracking, disinte-
grating, wearing away in the long, imperceptible weather of time. The
ash of ancient volcanic outbursts still sterilizes its soil, and its colors in
that waste are the colors that flame in the lonely sunsets on dead planets.
Men come there but rarely, and for one purpose only, the collection
of bones.

23　　It was a late hour on a cold, wind-bitten autumn day when I
climbed a great hill spined like a dinosaur's back and tried to take my
bearings. The tumbled waste fell away in waves in all directions. Blue
air was darkening into purple along the bases of the hills. I shifted my
knapsack, heavy with the petrified bones of long-vanished creatures,
and studied my compass. I wanted to be out of there by nightfall, and
already the sun was going sullenly down in the west.

24　　It was then that I saw the flight coming on. It was moving like
a little close-knit body of black specks that danced and darted and closed
again. It was pouring from the north and heading toward me with the
undeviating relentlessness of a compass needle. It streamed through the

shadows rising out of monstrous gorges. It rushed over towering pinnacles in the red light of the sun or momentarily sank from sight within their shade. Across that desert of eroding clay and wind-worn stone they came with a faint wild twittering that filled all the air about me as those tiny living bullets hurtled past into the night.

25   It may not strike you as a marvel. It would not, perhaps, unless you stood in the middle of a dead world at sunset, but that was where I stood. Fifty million years lay under my feet, fifty million years of bellowing monsters moving in a green world now gone so utterly that its very light was traveling on the farther edge of space. The chemicals of all that vanished age lay about me in the ground. Around me still lay the shearing molars of dead titanotheres, the delicate sabers of soft-stepping cats, the hollow sockets that had held the eyes of many a strange, outmoded beast. Those eyes had looked out upon a world as real as ours; dark, savage brains had roamed and roared their challenges into the steaming night.

26   Now they were still here, or, put it as you will, the chemicals that made them were here about me in the ground. The carbon that had driven them ran blackly in the eroding stone. The stain of iron was in the clays. The iron did not remember the blood it had once moved within, the phosphorus had forgot the savage brain. The little individual moment had ebbed from all those strange combinations of chemicals as it would ebb from our living bodies into the sinks and runnels of oncoming time.

27   I had lifted up a fistful of that ground. I held it while that wild flight of south-bound warblers hurtled over me into the oncoming dark. There went phosphorus, there went iron, there went carbon, there beat the calcium in those hurrying wings. Alone on a dead planet I watched that incredible miracle speeding past. It ran by some true compass over field and waste land. It cried its individual ecstasies into the air until the gullies rang. It swerved like a single body, it knew itself, and, lonely, it bunched close in the racing darkness, its individual entities feeling about them the rising night. And so, crying to each other their identity, they passed away out of my view.

28   I dropped my fistful of earth. I heard it roll inanimate back into the gully at the base of the hill: iron, carbon, the chemicals of life. Like men from those wild tribes who had haunted these hills before me seeking visions, I made my sign to the great darkness. It was not a mocking sign, and I was not mocked. As I walked into my camp late

that night, one man, rousing from his blankets beside the fire, asked sleepily, "What did you see?"

29   "I think, a miracle," I said softly, but I said it to myself. Behind me that vast waste began to glow under the rising moon.

30   I have said that I saw a judgment upon life, and that it was not passed by men. Those who stare at birds in cages or who test minds by their closeness to our own may not care for it. It comes from far away out of my past, in a place of pouring waters and green leaves. I shall never see an episode like it again if I live to be a hundred, nor do I think that one man in a million has ever seen it, because man is an intruder into such silences. The light must be right, and the observer must remain unseen. No man sets up such an experiment. What he sees, he sees by chance.

31   You may put it that I had come over a mountain, that I had slogged through fern and pine needles for half a long day, and that on the edge of a little glade with one long, crooked branch extending across it, I had sat down to rest with my back against a stump. Through accident I was concealed from the glade, although I could see into it perfectly.

32   The sun was warm there, and the murmurs of forest life blurred softly away into my sleep. When I awoke, dimly aware of some commotion and outcry in the clearing, the light was slanting down through the pines in such a way that the glade was lit like some vast cathedral. I could see the dust motes of wood pollen in the long shaft of light, and there on the extended branch sat an enormous raven with a red and squirming nestling in his beak.

33   The sound that awoke me was the outraged cries of the nestling's parents, who flew helplessly in circles about the clearing. The sleek black monster was indifferent to them. He gulped, whetted his beak on the dead branch a moment, and sat still. Up to that point the little tragedy had followed the usual pattern. But suddenly, out of all that area of woodland, a soft sound of complaint began to rise. Into the glade fluttered small birds of half a dozen varieties drawn by the anguished outcries of the tiny parents.

34   No one dared to attack the raven. But they cried there in some instinctive common misery, the bereaved and the unbereaved. The glade filled with their soft rustling and their cries. They fluttered as though to point their wings at the murderer. There was a dim intangible ethic he had violated, that they knew. He was a bird of death.

35   And he, the murderer, the black bird at the heart of life, sat on there glistening in the common light, formidable, unmoving, unperturbed, untouchable.

36   The sighing died. It was then I saw the judgment. It was the judgment of life against death. I will never see it again so forcefully presented. I will never hear it again in notes so tragically prolonged. For in the midst of protest, they forgot the violence. There, in that clearing, the crystal note of a song sparrow lifted hesitantly in the hush. And finally, after painful fluttering, another took the song, and then another, the song passing from one bird to another, doubtfully at first, as though some evil thing were being slowly forgotten. Till suddenly they took heart and sang from many throats joyously together as birds are known to sing. They sang because life is sweet and sunlight beautiful. They sang under the brooding shadow of the raven. In simple truth they had forgotten the raven, for they were the singers of life, and not of death.

37   I was not of that airy company. My limbs were the heavy limbs of an earthbound creature who could climb mountains, even the mountains of the mind, only by a great effort of will. I knew I had seen a marvel and observed a judgment, but the mind which was my human endowment was sure to question it and to be at me day by day with its heresies until I grew to doubt the meaning of what I had seen. Eventually darkness and subtleties would ring me round once more.

38   And so it proved until, on the top of a stepladder, I made one more observation upon life. It was cold that autumn evening, and, standing under a suburban street light in a spate of leaves and beginning snow, I was suddenly conscious of some huge and hairy shadows dancing over the pavement. They seemed attached to an odd, globular shape that was magnified above me. There was no mistaking it. I was standing under the shadow of an orb-weaving spider. Gigantically projected against the street, she was about her spinning when everything was going underground. Even her cables were magnified upon the sidewalk and already I was half-entangled in their shadows.

39   "Good Lord," I thought, "she has found herself a kind of minor sun and is going to upset the course of nature."

40   I procured a ladder from my yard and climbed up to inspect the situation. There she was, the universe running down around her, warmly arranged among her guy ropes attached to the lamp supports—

a great black and yellow embodiment of the life force, not giving up to either frost or stepladders. She ignored me and went on tightening and improving her web.

41   I stood over her on the ladder, a faint snow touching my cheeks, and surveyed her universe. There were a couple of iridescent green beetle cases turning slowly on a loose strand of web, a fragment of luminescent eye from a moth's wing and a large indeterminable object, perhaps a cicada, that had struggled and been wrapped in silk. There were also little bits and slivers, little red and blue flashes from the scales of anonymous wings that had crashed there.

42   Some days, I thought, they will be dull and gray and the shine will be out of them; then the dew will polish them again and drops hang on the silk until everything is gleaming and turning in the light. It is like a mind, really, where everything changes but remains, and in the end you have these eaten-out bits of experience like beetle wings.

43   I stood over her a moment longer, comprehending somewhat reluctantly that her adventure against the great blind forces of winter, her seizure of this warming globe of light, would come to nothing and was hopeless. Nevertheless it brought the birds back into my mind, and that faraway song which had traveled with growing strength around a forest clearing years ago—a kind of heroism, a world where even a spider refuses to lie down and die if a rope can still be spun on to a star. Maybe man himself will fight like this in the end, I thought, slowly realizing that the web and its threatening yellow occupant had been added to some luminous store of experience, shining for a moment in the fogbound reaches of my brain.

44   The mind, it came to me as I slowly descended the ladder, is a very remarkable thing; it has gotten itself a kind of courage by looking at a spider in a street lamp. Here was something that ought to be passed on to those who will fight our final freezing battle with the void. I thought of setting it down carefully as a message to the future: *In the days of the frost seek a minor sun.*

45   But as I hesitated, it became plain that something was wrong. The marvel was escaping—a sense of bigness beyond man's power to grasp, the essence of life in its great dealings with the universe. It was better, I decided, for the emissaries returning from the wilderness, even if they were merely descending from a stepladder, to record their marvel, not to define its meaning. In that way it would go echoing on through the minds of men, each grasping at that beyond out of which the

miracles emerge, and which, once defined, ceases to satisfy the human need for symbols.

46   In the end I merely made a mental note: One specimen of Epeira observed building a web in a street light. Late autumn and cold for spiders. Cold for men, too. I shivered and left the lamp glowing there in my mind. The last I saw of Epeira she was hauling steadily on a cable. I stepped carefully over her shadow as I walked away.

QUESTIONS

Ideas

1. Near the end of this essay, Eiseley talks about recording events without trying to define their meaning. Does he—or can you—define the meaning of the events recorded in this essay?

2. How does the following excerpt from another Eiseley essay bear on "The Judgment of the Birds"?

   It is a funny thing what the brain will do with memories and how it will treasure them and finally bring them into odd juxtapositions with other things, as though it wanted to make a design, or get some meaning out of them, whether you want it or not, or even see it.

3. In paragraph 2 Eiseley uses the term "a natural revelation." What does he mean? (Consider the meaning of the word "reveal.")

4. In this essay and in the other Eiseley essays included in this book, Eiseley calls himself a "naturalist." What is his sense of the word?

5. In paragraphs 9 and 19, Eiseley describes a peculiar feeling that he had. What is this feeling and why is it important? (Can it be compared with his impulse to dance with the frogs? Why or why not?)

6. What does Eiseley mean by "In the days of the frost seek a minor sun"? Why does he step carefully over the spider's shadow?

Organization

7. How is the essay organized? How many parts does it have and how are they related? How does Eiseley move from one section to another? How does he link them?

8. Where does the introduction end? Where does the conclusion begin? Could paragraphs 19–28 be omitted? Why or why not?

Sentences

9. Paragraph 34 is a single sentence, as is paragraph 12. Why?
10. How does the style of Eiseley's mental note in the last paragraph differ from the syntax of the previous one?
11. In paragraphs 3 and 18 Eiseley uses the colon. What is the relationship of the right-hand part of each statement to the left-hand part? Rewrite the sentences without the colon. How are the sentences different—in tone, in rhythm, in effect?
12. Notice how dashes are used in the sentences of paragraphs 2 and 17. Rewrite the sentences without the dashes. What is different about them? Compare the sentences using dashes with those using the colon. How do they differ? Can you suggest any guidelines for using the colon or the dash?

Words

13. What words and phrases indicating attentiveness appear in the first five paragraphs? What is the effect of the language of the final sentence of paragraph 5: "I had expected depths, but not the sight I saw"?
14. Near the end of the essay (paragraph 41), Eiseley describes a spider's web, comparing the human mind to the web. How is the mind like a spider's web? What does the spider represent?

Suggestions for Writing

A. Rewrite the following sentence in normal word order: "To and fro went the white wings, to and fro." What is the difference? Do the same with this sentence: "Around and around went the wings."
B. Rewrite the following sentence: "And he, the murderer, the black bird at the heart of life, sat there, glistening in the common light, formidable, unmoving, unperturbed, untouchable."
C. Write an essay in which you examine Eiseley's ideas about nature. Consider his view of himself as a naturalist. Use at least two of his essays.
D. Compare the following passages about webs with Eiseley's comparison of the mind to a spider's web. Write an essay exploring the idea implied by one or more of the web passages—including Eiseley's.

> Experience is never limited, and it is never complete; it is an immense sensibility, a kind of huge spiderweb of the finest silken threads suspended

in the chamber of consciousness, and catching every airborne particle in its tissue.

—HENRY JAMES, from "The Art of Fiction"

The world is like an enormous spider web and if you touch it, however lightly, at any point, the vibration ripples to the remotest perimeter and the drowsy spider feels the tingle and is drowsy no more but springs out to fling the gossamer coils about you who have touched the web and then inject the black, numbing poison under your hide. It does not matter whether or not you meant to brush the web of things.

—ROBERT PENN WARREN, from *All the King's Men*

The Dance of the Frogs

I

He was a member of the Explorers Club, and he had never been outside the state of Pennsylvania. Some of us who were world travelers used to smile a little about that, even though we knew his scientific reputation had been, at one time, great. It is always the way of youth to smile. I used to think of myself as something of an adventurer, but the time came when I realized that old Albert Dreyer, huddling with his drink in the shadows close to the fire, had journeyed farther into the Country of Terror than any of us would ever go, God willing, and emerge alive.

He was a morose and aging man, without family and without intimates. His membership in the club dated back into the decades when he was a zoologist famous for his remarkable experiments upon amphibians—he had recovered and actually produced the adult stage of the Mexican axolotl, as well as achieving remarkable tissue transplants in salamanders. The club had been flattered to have him then, travel or no travel, but the end was not fortunate. The brilliant scientist had become the misanthrope; the achievement lay all in the past, and Albert

Dreyer kept to his solitary room, his solitary drink, and his accustomed spot by the fire.

The reason I came to hear his story was an odd one. I had been north that year, and the club had asked me to give a little talk on the religious beliefs of the Indians of the northern forest, the Naskapi of Labrador. I had long been a student of the strange mélange of superstition and woodland wisdom that makes up the religious life of the nature peoples. Moreover, I had come to know something of the strange similarities of the "shaking tent rite" to the phenomena of the modern medium's cabinet.

"The special tent with its entranced occupant is no different from the cabinet," I contended. "The only difference is the type of voices that emerge. Many of the physical phenomena are identical—the movement of powerful forces shaking the conical hut, objects thrown, all this is familiar to Western psychical science. What is different are the voices projected. Here they are the cries of animals, the voices from the swamp and the mountain—the solitary elementals before whom the primitive man stands in awe, and from whom he begs sustenance. Here the game lords reign supreme; man himself is voiceless."

A low, halting query reached me from the back of the room. I was startled, even in the midst of my discussion, to note that it was Dreyer.

"And the game lords, what are they?"

"Each species of animal is supposed to have gigantic leaders of more than normal size," I explained. "These beings are the immaterial controllers of that particular type of animal. Legend about them is confused. Sometimes they partake of human qualities, will and intelligence, but they are of animal shape. They control the movements of game, and thus their favor may mean life or death to man."

"Are they visible?" Again Dreyer's low, troubled voice came from the back of the room.

"Native belief has it that they can be seen on rare occasions," I answered. "In a sense they remind one of the concept of the archetypes, the originals behind the petty show of our small, transitory existence. They are the immortal renewers of substance—the force behind and above animate nature."

"Do they dance?" persisted Dreyer.

At this I grew nettled. Old Dreyer in a heckling mood was some-

thing new. "I cannot answer that question," I said acidly. "My inform-
ants failed to elaborate upon it. But they believe implicitly in these
monstrous beings, talk to and propitiate them. It is their voices that
emerge from the shaking tent."

"The Indians believe it," pursued old Dreyer relentlessly, "but do
you believe it?"

"My dear fellow"—I shrugged and glanced at the smiling audience—"I have seen many strange things, many puzzling things, but I
am a scientist." Dreyer made a contemptuous sound in his throat and
went back to the shadow out of which he had crept in his interest. The
talk was over. I headed for the bar.

II

The evening passed. Men drifted homeward or went to their
rooms. I had been a year in the woods and hungered for voices and
companionship. Finally, however, I sat alone with my glass, a little
mellow, perhaps, enjoying the warmth of the fire and remembering the
blue snowfields of the North as they should be remembered—in the
comfort of warm rooms.

I think an hour must have passed. The club was silent except for
the ticking of an antiquated clock on the mantel and small night noises
from the street. I must have drowsed. At all events it was some time
before I grew aware that a chair had been drawn up opposite me. I
started.

"A damp night," I said.

"Foggy," said the man in the shadow musingly. "But not too
foggy. They like it that way."

"Eh?" I said. I knew immediately it was Dreyer speaking. Maybe
I had missed something; on second thought, maybe not.

"And spring," he said. "Spring. That's part of it. God knows why,
of course, but we feel it, why shouldn't they? And more intensely."

"Look—" I said. "I guess—" The old man was more human than
I thought. He reached out and touched my knee with the hand that
he always kept a glove over—burn, we used to speculate—and smiled
softly.

"You don't know what I'm talking about," he finished for me. "And, besides, I ruffled your feelings earlier in the evening. You must forgive me. You touched on an interest of mine, and I was perhaps overeager. I did not intend to give the appearance of heckling. It was only that . . ."

"Of course," I said. "Of course." Such a confession from Dreyer was astounding. The man might be ill. I rang for a drink and decided to shift the conversation to a safer topic, more appropriate to a scholar.

"Frogs," I said desperately, like any young ass in a china shop. "Always admired your experiments. Frogs. Yes."

I give the old man credit. He took the drink and held it up and looked at me across the rim. There was a faint stir of sardonic humor in his eyes.

"Frogs, no," he said, "or maybe yes. I've never been quite sure. Maybe yes. But there was no time to decide properly." The humor faded out of his eyes. "Maybe I should have let go," he said. "It was what they wanted. There's no doubting that at all, but it came too quick for me. What would you have done?"

"I don't know," I said honestly enough and pinched myself.

"You had better know," said Albert Dryer severely, "if you're planning to become an investigator of primitive religions. Or even not. I wasn't, you know, and the things came to me just when I least suspected—But I forget, you don't believe in them."

He shrugged and half rose, and for the first time, really, I saw the black-gloved hand and the haunted face of Albert Dreyer and knew in my heart the things he had stood for in science. I got up then, as a young man in the presence of his betters should get up, and I said, and I meant it, every word: "Please, Dr. Dreyer, sit down and tell me. I'm too young to be saying what I believe or don't believe in at all. I'd be obliged if you'd tell me." ·

Just at that moment a strange, wonderful dignity shone out of the countenance of Albert Dreyer, and I knew the man he was. He bowed and sat down, and there were no longer the barriers of age and youthful ego between us. There were just too men under a lamp, and around them a great waiting silence. Out to the ends of the universe, I thought fleetingly, that's the way with man and his lamps. One has to huddle in, there's so little light and so much space. One—

III

"It could happen to anyone," said Albert Dreyer. "And especially in the spring. Remember that. And all I did was to skip. Just a few feet, mark you, but I skipped. Remember that, too.

"You wouldn't remember the place at all. At least not as it was then." He paused and shook the ice in his glass and spoke more easily.

"It was a road that came out finally in a marsh along the Schuykill River. Probably all industrial now. But I had a little house out there with a laboratory thrown in. It was convenient to the marsh, and that helped me with my studies of amphibia. Moreover, it was a wild, lonely road, and I wanted solitude. It is always the demand of the naturalist. You understand that?"

"Of course," I said. I knew he had gone there, after the death of his young wife, in grief and loneliness and despair. He was not a man to mention such things. "It is best for the naturalist," I agreed.

"Exactly. My best work was done there." He held up his black-gloved hand and glanced at it meditatively. "The work on the axolotl, newt neoteny. I worked hard. I had—" he hesitated— "things to forget. There were times when I worked all night. Or diverted myself, while waiting the result of an experiment, by midnight walks. It was a strange road. Wild all right, but paved and close enough to the city that there were occasional street lamps. All uphill and downhill, with bits of forest leaning in over it, till you walked in a tunnel of trees. Then suddenly you were in the marsh, and the road ended at an old, unused wharf.

"A place to be alone. A place to walk and think. A place for shadows to stretch ahead of you from one dim lamp to another and spring back as you reached the next. I have seen them get tall, tall, but never like that night. It was like a road into space."

"Cold?" I asked.

"No. I shouldn't have said 'space.' It gives the wrong effect. Not cold. Spring. Frog time. The first warmth, and the leaves coming. A little fog in the hollows. The way they like it then in the wet leaves and bogs. No moon, though; secretive and dark, with just those street lamps wandered out from the town. I often wondered what graft had brought them there. They shone on nothing—except my walks at midnight and the journeys of toads, but still . . ."

"Yes?" I prompted, as he paused.

"I was just thinking. The web of things. A politician in town gets a rake-off for selling useless lights on a useless road. If it hadn't been for that, I might not have seen them. I might not even have skipped. Or, if I had, the effect—How can you tell about such things afterwards? Was the effect heightened? Did it magnify their power? Who is to say?"

"The skip?" I said, trying to keep things casual. "I don't understand. You mean, just skipping? Jumping?"

Something like a twinkle came into his eyes for a moment. "Just that," he said. "No more. You are a young man. Impulsive? You should understand."

"I'm afraid—" I began to counter.

"But of course," he cried pleasantly. "I forget. You were not there. So how could I expect you to feel or know about this skipping. Look, look at me now. A sober man, eh?"

I nodded. "Dignified," I said cautiously.

"Very well. But, young man, there is a time to skip. On country roads in the spring. It is not necessary that there be girls. You will skip without them. You will skip because something within you knows the time—frog time. Then you will skip."

"Then I will skip," I repeated, hypnotized. Mad or not, there was a force in Albert Dreyer. Even there under the club lights, the night damp of an unused road began to gather.

IV

"It was a late spring," he said. "Fog and mist in those hollows in a way I had never seen before. And frogs, of course. Thousands of them, and twenty species, trilling, gurgling, and grunting in as many keys. The beautiful keen silver piping of spring peepers arousing as the last ice leaves the ponds—if you have heard that after a long winter alone, you will never forget it." He paused and leaned forward, listening with such an intent inner ear that one could almost hear that far-off silver piping from the wet meadows of the man's forgotten years.

I rattled my glass uneasily, and his eyes came back to me.

"They come out then," he said more calmly. "All amphibia have to return to the water for mating and egg laying. Even toads will hop miles across country to streams and waterways. You don't see them unless you go out at night in the right places as I did, but that night—

"Well, it was unusual, put it that way, as an understatement. It was late, and the creatures seemed to know it. You could feel the forces of mighty and archaic life welling up from the very ground. The water was pulling them—not water as we know it, but the mother, the ancient life force, the thing that made us in the days of creation, and that lurks around us still, unnoticed in our sterile cities.

"I was no different from any other young fool coming home on a spring night, except that as a student of life, and of amphibia in particular, I was, shall we say, more aware of the creatures. I had performed experiments"—the black glove gestured before my eyes. "I was, as it proved, susceptible.

"It began on that lost stretch of roadway leading to the river, and it began simply enough. All around, under the street lamps, I saw little frogs and big frogs hopping steadily toward the river. They were going in my direction.

"At that time I had my whimsies, and I was spry enough to feel the tug of that great movement. I joined them. There was no mystery about it. I simply began to skip, to skip gaily, and enjoy the great bobbing shadow I created as I passed onward with that leaping host all headed for the river.

"Now skipping along a wet pavement in spring is infectious, particularly going downhill, as we were. The impulse to take mightier leaps, to soar farther, increases progressively. The madness worked into me. I bounded till my lungs labored, and my shadow, at first my own shadow, bounded and labored with me.

"It was only midway in my flight that I began to grow conscious that I was not alone. The feeling was not strong at first. Normally a sober pedestrian, I was ecstatically preoccupied with the discovery of latent stores of energy and agility which I had not suspected in my subdued existence.

"It was only as we passed under a street lamp that I noticed, beside my own bobbing shadow, another great, leaping grotesquerie that had an uncanny suggestion of the frog world about it. The shocking aspect of the thing lay in its size, and the fact that, judging from the shadow, it was soaring higher and more gaily than myself.

" 'Very well,' you will say"—and here Dreyer paused and looked at me tolerantly— " 'Why didn't you turn around? That would be the scientific thing to do.'

"It would be the scientific thing to do, young man, but let me tell you it is not done—not on an empty road at midnight—not when the shadow is already beside your shadow and is joined by another, and then another.

"No, you do not pause. You look neither to left nor right, for fear of what you might see there. Instead, you dance on madly, hopelessly. Plunging higher, higher, in the hope the shadows will be left behind, or prove to be only leaves dancing, when you reach the next street light. Or that whatever had joined you in this midnight bacchanal will take some other pathway and depart.

"You do not look—you cannot look—because to do so is to destroy the universe in which we move and exist and have our transient being. You dare not look, because, beside the shadows, there now comes to your ears the loose-limbed slap of giant batrachian feet, not loud, not loud at all, but there, definitely there, behind you at your shoulder, plunging with the utter madness of spring, their rhythm entering your bones until you too are hurtling upward in some gigantic ecstasy that it is not given to mere flesh and blood to long endure.

"I was part of it, part of some mad dance of the elementals behind the show of things. Perhaps in that night of archaic and elemental passion, that festival of the wetlands, my careless hopping passage under the street lights had called them, attracted their attention, brought them leaping down some fourth-dimensional roadway into the world of time.

"Do not suppose for a single moment I thought so coherently then. My lungs were bursting, my physical self exhausted, but I sprang, I hurtled, I flung myself onward in a company I could not see, that never outpaced me, but that swept me with the mighty ecstasies of a thousand springs, and that bore me onward exultantly past my own doorstep, toward the river, toward some pathway long forgotten, toward some unforgettable destination in the wetlands and the spring.

"Even as I leaped, I was changing. It was this, I think, that stirred the last remnants of human fear and human caution that I still possessed. My will was in abeyance; I could not stop. Furthermore, certain sensations, hypnotic or otherwise, suggested to me that my own physical shape was modifying, or about to change. I was leaping with a growing ease. I was—

"It was just then that the wharf lights began to show. We were approaching the end of the road, and the road, as I have said, ended in the river. It was this, I suppose, that startled me back into some semblance of human terror. Man is a land animal. He does not willingly plunge off wharfs at midnight in the monstrous company of amphibious shadows.

"Nevertheless their power held me. We pounded madly toward the wharf, and under the light that hung above it, and the beam that made a cross. Part of me struggled to stop, and part of me hurtled on. But in that final frenzy of terror before the water below engulfed me I shrieked, '*Help! In the name of God, help me! In the name of Jesus, stop!*' "

Dreyer paused and drew in his chair a little closer under the light. Then he went on steadily.

"I was not, I suppose, a particularly religious man, and the cries merely revealed the extremity of my terror. Nevertheless this is a strange thing, and whether it involves the crossed beam, or the appeal to a Christian deity, I will not attempt to answer.

"In one electric instant, however, I was free. It was like the release from demoniac possession. One moment I was leaping in an inhuman company of elder things, and the next moment I was a badly shaken human being on a wharf. Strangest of all, perhaps, was the sudden silence of that midnight hour. I looked down in the circle of the arc light, and there by my feet hopped feebly some tiny froglets of the great migration. There was nothing impressive about them, but you will understand that I drew back in revulsion. I have never been able to handle them for research since. My work is in the past."

He paused and drank, and then, seeing perhaps some lingering doubt and confusion in my eyes, held up his black-gloved hand and deliberately pinched off the glove.

A man should not do that to another man without warning, but I suppose he felt I demanded some proof. I turned my eyes away. One does not like a webbed batrachian hand on a human being.

As I rose embarrassedly, his voice came up to me from the depths of the chair.

"It is not the hand," Dreyer said. "It is the question of choice. Perhaps I was a coward, and ill prepared. Perhaps"—his voice searched uneasily among his memories—"perhaps I should have taken them and that springtime without question. Perhaps I should have trusted them and hopped onward. Who knows? They were gay enough, at least."

He sighed and set down his glass and stared so intently into empty space that, seeing I was forgotten, I tiptoed quietly away.

QUESTIONS

Ideas

1. Does Eiseley mean us to take this essay as fact or fiction? What might be the point of such a story?

2. Regardless of your belief, what are some possible explanations for what happens in this essay? Try to construct reasons along a continuum from fact to fantasy.

3. How would you describe the narrator's personality? How does his attitude toward Dreyer change?

4. What is the significance of the following line from part II: "Maybe I should have let go . . . it was what they wanted, there's no doubting that at all, but it came too quick for me"?

Organization

5. How are the two stories here, Eiseley's and Dreyer's, related?

6. What is the purpose of part I? Look especially at the exchange between Dreyer and Eiseley. What conflict of perspective, of viewpoint, is being shown here?

7. Part IV is the longest and most detailed. Why? What is its point?

8. What is the overall structure of the four parts? What is the purpose of each?

Sentences

9. Most of this essay is told in dialogue. Compare the narrator's voice in part I with Dreyer's in the last dozen paragraphs of part IV. What differences do you find in tone, diction, sentence structure, and so on?

Words

10. In part I, the narrator refers to Dreyer as a "misanthrope." Do you think this is accurate?
11. What does "mélange" mean? How about "propitiate," "implicitly," "nettled," "whimsies," "infectious," "uncanny"?

Suggestions for Writing

A. Write down your thoughts about each of the following questions. Write quickly on each one for about five minutes:
   1. What are the advantages and disadvantages of believing in events such as these?
   2. What are some of the things you accept on faith?
   3. Is there absolute Truth within the scientific community?
   Based on your responses, write an essay that explores the idea of belief in the supernatural.
B. Compare the theme of the following poem by Eiseley to "The Dance of the Frogs."

NOCTURNE IN SILVER

Here where the barbed wire straggles in the marsh
And alkali crusts all the weeds like frost,
I have come home, I have come home to hear
The new young frogs that cry along the lost

Wild ditches where at midnight only cows
And fools with eery marsh fire in their brains
Blunder toward midnight. Silvery and clear
Cry the new frogs; the blood runs in my veins

Coldly and clearly. I am mottled, too,
And feel a silver bubble in my throat.
Lock doors, turn keys, or follow in your fear.
My eyes are green, and warily afloat

In the June darkness. I am done with fire.
Water quicksilver-like that slips through stone
Has quenched my madness—if you find me here
My lineage squat and warty will be known.

The Running Man

1   **W**hile I endured the months in the Colorado cabin, my mother, who had been offered a safe refuge in the home of her sister, quarreled and fought with everyone. Finally, in her own inelegant way of putting things, she had "skipped town" to work as a seamstress, domestic, or housekeeper upon farms. She was stone deaf. I admired her courage, but I also knew by then that she was paranoid, neurotic and unstable. What ensued on these various short-lived adventures I neither know to this day, nor wish to know.

2   It comes to me now in retrospect that I never saw my mother weep; it was her gift to make others suffer instead. She was an untutored, talented artist and she left me, if anything, a capacity for tremendous visual impressions just as my father, a one-time itinerant actor, had in that silenced household of the stone age—a house of gestures, of daylong facial contortion—produced for me the miracle of words when he came home. My mother had once been very beautiful. It is only thus that I can explain the fatal attraction that produced me. I have never known how my parents chanced to meet.

3   There will be those to say, in this mother-worshipping culture, that I am harsh, embittered. They will be quite wrong. Why should I be embittered? It is far too late. A month ago, after a passage of many years, I stood above her grave in a place called Wyuka. We, she and I, were close to being one now, lying like the skeletons of last year's leaves in a fence corner. And it was all nothing. Nothing, do you understand? All the pain, all the anguish. Nothing. We were, both of us, merely the debris life always leaves in its passing, like the maimed, discarded chicks in the hatchery trays—no more than that. For a little longer I would see and hear, but it was nothing, and to the world it would mean nothing.

4   I murmured to myself and tried to tell her this belatedly: Nothing, mama, nothing. Rest. You could never rest. That was your burden. But now, sleep. Soon I will join you, although, forgive me, not here. Neither of us then would rest. I will go far to lie down; the time draws on; it is unlikely that I will return. Now you will understand, I said,

touching the October warmth of the gravestone. It was for nothing. It has taken me all my life to grasp this one fact.

5   I am, it is true, wandering out of time and place. This narrative is faltering. To tell the story of a life one is bound to linger above gravestones where memory blurs and doors can be pushed ajar, but never opened. Listen, or do not listen, it is all the same.

6   I am every man and no man, and will be so to the end. This is why I must tell the story as I may. Not for the nameless name upon the page, not for the trails behind me that faded or led nowhere, not for the rooms at nightfall where I slept from exhaustion or did not sleep at all, not for the confusion of where I was to go, or if I had a destiny recognizable by any star. No, in retrospect it was the loneliness of not knowing, not knowing at all.

7   I was a child of the early century, American man, if the term may still be tolerated. A creature molded of plains' dust and the seed of those who came west with the wagons. The names Corey, Hollister, Appleton, McKee lie strewn in graveyards from New England to the broken sticks that rotted quickly on the Oregon trail. That ancient contingent, with a lost memory and a gene or two from the Indian, is underscored by the final German of my own name.

8   How, among all these wanderers, should I have absorbed a code by which to live? How should I have answered in turn to the restrained Puritan, and the long hatred of the beaten hunters? How should I have curbed the flaring rages of my maternal grandfather? How should—

9   But this I remember out of deepest childhood—I remember the mad Shepards as I heard the name whispered among my mother's people. I remember the pacing, the endless pacing of my parents after midnight, while I lay shivering in the cold bed and tried to understand the words that passed between my mother and my father.

10   Once, a small toddler, I climbed from bed and seized their hands, pleading wordlessly for sleep, for peace, peace. And surprisingly they relented, even my unfortunate mother. Terror, anxiety, ostracism, shame; I did not understand the words. I learned only the feelings they represent. I repeat, I am an American whose profession, even his life, is no more than a gambler's throw by the firelight of a western wagon.

11   What have I to do with the city in which I live? Why, far to the west, does my mind still leap to great windswept vistas of grass or the

eternal snows of the Cascades? Why does the sight of wolves in cages cause me to avert my eyes?

12   I will tell you only because something like this was at war in the heart of every American at the final closing of the westward trails. One of the most vivid memories I retain from my young manhood is of the wagon ruts of the Oregon trail still visible on the unplowed short-grass prairie. They stretched half a mile in width and that was only yesterday. In his young years, my own father had carried a gun and remembered the gamblers at the green tables in the cow towns. I dream inexplicably at times of a gathering of wagons, of women in sunbonnets and black-garbed, bewhiskered men. Then I wake and the scene dissolves.

13   I have strayed from the Shepards. It was a name to fear but this I did not learn for a long time. I thought they were the people pictured in the family Bible, men with white beards and long crooks with which they guided sheep.

14   In the house, when my father was away and my mother's people came to visit, the Shepards were spoken of in whispers. They were the mad Shepards, I slowly gathered, and they lay somewhere in my line of descent. When I was recalcitrant the Shepards were spoken of and linked with my name.

15   In that house there was no peace, yet we loved each other fiercely. Perhaps the adults were so far on into the midcountry that mistakes were never rectifiable, flight disreputable. We were Americans of the middle border where the East was forgotten and the one great western road no longer crawled with wagons.

16   A silence had fallen. I was one of those born into that silence. The bison had perished; the Sioux no longer rode. Only the yellow dust of the cyclonic twisters still marched across the landscape. I knew the taste of that dust in my youth. I knew it in the days of the dust bowl. No matter how far I travel it will be a fading memory upon my tongue in the hour of my death. It is the taste of one dust only, the dust of a receding ice age.

17   So much for my mother, the mad Shepards, and the land, but this is not all, certainly not. Some say a child's basic character is formed by the time he is five. I can believe it, I who begged for peace at four and was never blessed for long by its presence.

18   The late W. H. Auden once said to me over a lonely little dinner in New York before he left America, "What public event do you re-

member first from childhood?" I suppose the massive old lion was in his way encouraging a shy man to speak. Being of the same age we concentrated heavily upon the subject.

19 "I think for me, the Titanic disaster," he ventured thoughtfully.

20 "Of course," I said. "That would be 1912. She was a British ship and you British have always been a sea people."

21 "And you?" he questioned, holding me with his seamed features that always gave him the aspect of a seer.

22 I dropped my gaze. Was it 1914? Was it Pancho Villa's raid into New Mexico in 1916? All westerners remembered that. We wandered momentarily among dead men and long-vanished events. Auden waited patiently.

23 "Well," I ventured, for it was a long-held personal secret, "It was an escape, just an escape from prison."

24 "Your own?" Auden asked with a trace of humor.

25 "No," I began, "it was the same year as the Titanic sinking. He blew the gates with nitroglycerin. I was five years old, like you." Then I paused, considering the time. "You are right," I admitted hesitantly. "I was already old enough to know one should flee from the universe but I did not know where to run." I identified with the man as I always had across the years. "We never made it," I added glumly, and shrugged. "You see, there was a warden, a prison, and a blizzard. Also there was an armed posse and a death." I could feel the same snow driving beside the window in New York. "We never made it," I repeated unconsciously.

26 Auden sighed and looked curiously at me. I knew he was examining the pronoun. "There are other things that constitute a child," I added hastily. "Sandpiles, for example. There was a lot of building being done then on our street. I used to spend hours turning over the gravel. Why, I wouldn't know. Finally I had a box of pretty stones and some fossils. I prospected for hours alone. It was like today in book stores, old book stores," I protested defensively.

27 Auden nodded in sympathy.

28 "I still can't tell what started it," I went on. "I was groping, I think, childishly into time, into the universe. It was to be my profession but I never understood in the least, not till much later. No other child on the block wasted his time like that. I have never understood my precise motivation, never. For actually I was retarded in the reading

of clock time. Was it because, in the things found in the sand, I was already lost and wandering instinctively—amidst the debris of vanished eras?"

29   "Ah," Auden said kindly, "who knows these things?"

30   "Then there was the period of the gold crosses," I added. "Later, in another house, I had found a little bottle of liquid gilt my mother used on picture frames. I made some crosses, carefully whittled out of wood, and gilded them till they were gold. Then I placed them over an occasional dead bird I buried. Or, if I read of a tragic, heroic death like those of the war aces, I would put the clipping—I could read by then—into a little box and bury it with a gold cross to mark the spot. One day a mower in the empty lot beyond our backyard found the little cemetery and carried away all of my carefully carved crosses. I cried but I never told anyone. How could I? I had sought in my own small way to preserve the memory of what always in the end perishes: life and great deeds. I wonder what the man with the scythe did with my crosses. I wonder if they still exist."

31   "Yes, it was a child's effort against time," commented Auden. "And perhaps the archaeologist is just that child grown up."

32   It was time for Auden to go. We stood and exchanged polite amenities while he breathed in that heavy, sad way he had. "Write me at Oxford," he had said at the door. But then there was Austria and soon he was gone. Besides one does not annoy the great. Their burdens are too heavy. They listen kindly with their eyes far away.

33   After that dinner I was glumly despondent for days. Finally a rage possessed me, started unwittingly by that gentle, gifted man who was to die happily after a recitation of his magnificent verse. For nights I lay sleepless in a New York hotel room and all my memories in one gigantic catharsis were bad, spewed out of hell's mouth, invoked by that one dinner, that one question, *what do you remember first?* My God, they were all firsts. My brain was so scarred it was a miracle it had survived in any fashion.

34   For example, I remembered for the first time a ruined farmhouse that I had stumbled upon in my solitary ramblings after school. The road was one I had never taken before. Rain was falling. Leaves lay thick on the abandoned road. Hesitantly I approached and stood in the doorway. Plaster had collapsed from the ceiling; wind mourned through the empty windows. I crunched tentatively over shattered glass upon the floor. Papers lay scattered about in wild disorder. Some looked like

school examination papers. I picked one up in curiosity, but this, my own mature judgment tells me, no one will believe. The name Eiseley was scrawled across the cover. I was too shocked even to read the paper. No such family had ever been mentioned by my parents. We had come from elsewhere. But here, in poverty like our own, at the edge of town, had subsisted in this ruined house a boy with my own name. Gingerly I picked up another paper. There was the scrawled name again, not too unlike my own rough signature. The date was what might have been expected in that tottering clapboard house. It read from the last decade of the century before. They were gone, whoever they were, and another Eiseley was tiptoing through the ruined house.

35   All that remained in a room that might in those days have been called the parlor were two dice lying forlornly amidst the plaster, forgotten at the owners' last exit. I picked up the pretty cubes uncertainly in the growing sunset through the window, and on impulse cast them. I did not know how adults played, I merely cast and cast again, making up my own game as I played. Sometimes I thought I won and murmured to myself as children will. Sometimes I thought I lost, but I liked the clicking sound before I rolled the dice. For what stakes did I play, with my childish mind gravely considering? I think I was too naive for such wishes as money and fortune. I played, and here memory almost fails me. I think I played against the universe as the universe was represented by the wind, stirring papers on the plaster-strewn floor. I played against time, remembering my stolen crosses, I played for adventure and escape. Then, clutching the dice, but not the paper with my name, I fled frantically down the leaf-sodden unused road, never to return. One of the dice survives still in my desk drawer. The time is sixty years away.

36   I have said that, though almost ostracized, we loved each other fiercely there in the silent midcountry because there was nothing else to love, but was it true? Was the hour of departure nearing? My mother lavished affection upon me in her tigerish silent way, giving me cakes when I should have had bread, attempting protection when I was already learning without brothers the grimness and realities of the street.

37   There had been the time I had just encountered the neighborhood bully. His father's shoulder had been long distorted and rheumatic from the carrying of ice, and the elder son had just encountered the law and gone to prison. My antagonist had inherited his brother's status in the black Irish gang that I had heretofore succeeded in avoiding by journeying homeward from school through alleys and occasional thickets

best known to me. But now brother replaced brother. We confronted each other on someone's lawn.

38 "Get down on your knees," he said contemptuously, knowing very well what was coming. He had left me no way out. At that moment I hit him most inexpertly in the face, whereupon he began very scientifically, as things go in childish circles, to cut me to ribbons. My nose went first.

39 But then came the rage, the utter fury, summoned up from a thousand home repressions, adrenalin pumped into me from my Viking grandfather, the throwback from the long ships, the berserk men who cared nothing for living when the mood came on them and they stormed the English towns. It comes to me now that the Irishman must have seen it in my eyes. By nature I was a quiet reclusive boy, but then I went utterly mad.

40 The smashed nose meant nothing, the scientific lefts and rights slicing up my features meant nothing. I went through them with body punches and my eyes. When I halted we were clear across the street and the boy was gone, running for home. Typically I, too, turned homeward but not for succor. All I wanted was access to the outside watertap to wash off the blood cascading down my face. This I proceeded to do with the stoical indifference of one who expected no help.

41 As I went about finishing my task, my mother, peering through the curtains, saw my face and promptly had hysterics. I turned away then. I always turned away. In the end, not too far distant, there would be an unbridgeable silence between us. Slowly I was leaving the world she knew and desperation marked her face.

42 I was old enough that I obeyed my father's injunction, reluctantly given out of his own pain. "Your mother is not responsible, son. Do not cross her. Do you understand?" He held me with his eyes, a man I loved, who could have taken the poor man's divorce, desertion, at any moment. The easy way out. He stayed for me. That was the simple reason. He stayed when his own closest relatives urged him to depart.

43 I cast down my eyes. "Yes, father," I promised, but I could not say for always. I think he knew it, but work and growing age were crushing him. We looked at each other in a blind despair.

44 I was like a rag doll upon whose frame skins were tightening in a distorted crippling sequence; the toddler begging for peace between his parents at midnight; the lad suppressing fury till he shook with it; the solitary with his books; the projected fugitive running desperately

through the snows of 1912; the dice player in the ruined house of his own name. Who was he, really? The man, so the psychologists would say, who had to be shaped or found in five years' time. I was inarticulate but somewhere, far forward, I would meet the running man; the peace I begged for between my parents would, too often, leave me sleepless. There was another thing I could not name to Auden. The fact that I remember it at all reveals the beginning of adulthood and a sense of sin beyond my years.

45   To grow is a gain, an enlargement of life; is not this what they tell us? Yet it is also a departure. There is something lost that will not return. We moved one fall to Aurora, Nebraska, a sleepy country town near the Platte. A few boys gathered to watch the van unload. "Want to play?" ventured one. "Sure," I said. I followed them off over a rise to a creek bed. "We're making a cave in the bank," they explained. It was a great raw gaping hole obviously worked on by more than one generation of troglodytes. They giggled. "But first you've got to swear awful words. We'll all swear."

46   I was a silent boy, who went by reading. My father did not use these words. I was, in retrospect, a very funny little boy. I was so alone I did not know how to swear, but clamoring they taught me. I wanted to belong, to enter the troglodytes' existence. I shouted and mouthed the uncouth, unfamiliar words with the rest.

47   Mother was restless in the new environment, though again my father had wisely chosen a house at the edge of town. The population was primarily Scandinavian. She exercised arbitrary judgment. She drove good-natured, friendly boys away if they seemed big, and on the other hand encouraged slighter youngsters whom I had every reason to despise.

48   Finally, because it was farmland over which children roamed at will, mother's ability to keep track of my wide-ranging absences faltered. On one memorable occasion her driving, possessive restlessness passed out of bounds. She pursued us to a nearby pasture and in the rasping voice of deafness ordered me home.

49   My comrades of the fields stood watching. I was ten years old by then. I sensed my status in this gang was at stake. I refused to come. I had refused a parental order that was arbitrary and uncalled for and, in addition, I was humiliated. My mother was behaving in the manner of a witch. She could not hear, she was violently gesticulating without dignity, and her dress was somehow appropriate to the occasion.

50   Slowly I turned and looked at my companions. Their faces could not be read. They simply waited, doubtless waited for me to break the apron strings that rested lightly and tolerably upon themselves. And so in the end I broke my father's injunction; I ran, and with me ran my childish companions, over fences, tumbling down haystacks, chuckling, with the witch, her hair flying, her clothing disarrayed, stumbling after. Escape, escape, the first stirrings of the running man. Miles of escape.

51   Of course she gave up. Of course she never caught us. Walking home alone in the twilight I was bitterly ashamed. Ashamed for the violation of my promise to my father. Ashamed at what I had done to my savage and stone-deaf mother who could not grasp the fact that I had to make my way in a world unknown to her. Ashamed for the story that would penetrate the neighborhood. Ashamed for my own weakness. Ashamed, ashamed.

52   I do not remember a single teacher from that school, a single thing I learned there. Men were then drilling in a lot close to our house. I watched them every day. Finally they marched off. It was 1917. I was ten years old. I wanted to go. Either that or back to sleeping the troglodyte existence we had created in the cave bank. But never home, not ever. Even today, as though in a far-off crystal, I can see my running, gesticulating mother and her distorted features cursing us. And they laughed, you see, my companions. Perhaps I, in anxiety to belong, did also. That is what I could not tell Auden. Only an unutterable savagery, my savagery at myself, scrawls it once and once only on this page.

QUESTIONS

Ideas

1. Eiseley's images seem especially vivid in this remembrance. What one comes immediately to your mind? Eiseley uses narrative, anecdotes, and significant moments from his experiences, but what do these pictures convey to you? Who is this essay about? Is it about Eiseley as a child or as an adult? Or is it about his mother?

2. What is Eiseley's purpose in writing this essay? Does he hope to do something for himself? Is he trying to learn something, discover something? Consider especially paragraphs 5 and 6.

3. Does Eiseley himself realize that he is not "sticking to the topic" as the essay opens, that he seems to be wandering? But does he? Read the first and the last four paragraphs again. Do you see connections to the rest of the piece?

4. What is all this business about being an "American man"? Is Eiseley trying to connect his life to yours in some way? Do you accept the notion that one life can represent the experiences of all Americans?

5. Eiseley denies that he is "harsh, embittered" about his relationship with his mother. What do you think? In this sense, what do you make of the last paragraph? How about the first sentence of paragraph 2?

6. What exactly do you think Eiseley means by "It was for nothing"?

7. What do you make of Eiseley's comment on the writing of autobiography: "To tell the story of a life one is bound to linger about gravestones where memory blurs and doors can be pushed ajar, but never opened"? What does Eiseley seem to be implying in this paragraph about the difference between writing about one's life and living it? Look especially at the last sentence.

8. Based on paragraphs 11 and 12, what do you make of Eiseley's wagon dream?

9. Before Eiseley begins his anecdote about Auden (paragraph 18) he writes a short "introductory" paragraph about inner peace. Why does he do this, and what expectations does this raise about the subsequent narrative?

10. In the tale Eiseley tells Auden, what do you think he means by "I was already old enough to know one should flee from the universe but I did not know where to run"?

11. Why did a rage possess Eiseley after his dinner with Auden? In his attempts to remember, Eiseley narrates a series of anecdotes: about his finding dice in a ruined farmhouse, his encounter with the neighborhood bully, and, finally, his running from his "violently gesticulating" mother. What is the point of these stories? Do they make concrete and specific a generalization? Look especially at the concluding paragraph to his bully story ("As I went about . . .") and the elaborate build-up to the running-away scene (the four paragraphs preceding "Finally, because it was farm land . . . "). Do you see common threads among these tales? Are they in sequence, leading somewhere?

12. Why could he not tell Auden this last episode, yet could "scrawl it once and once only on this page"?

13. What is meant by "The Running Man"? Try to suggest several different possibilities.

Organization

14. Eiseley begins and ends this essay with thoughts of his mother. Where does the introduction end? The conclusion begin?
15. List in order all the incidents in this piece. What holds them all together?

Sentences

16. Eiseley has a reputation for lyrical, evocative prose. Cite some examples. What makes them poetic?
17. Read the last three paragraphs out loud. What do you notice about Eiseley's style? How does he use repetition? Modifiers? Sentence fragments? Parallelism? Sentence length?

Words

18. Make a list of all the words Eiseley uses to describe himself. What impression do they add up to? Do the same for words describing his mother.

Suggestion for Writing

From vividly drawn episodes in his life, Eiseley tries to assemble recurring patterns to define himself, to create an image of who he is. Try to remember two or three incidents from your childhood. Just free-write for fifteen minutes on each one, until some narrative line begins to emerge.

Read over your writing, looking for possible consistent themes, key terms, gestures, beginnings, and endings. That is, can you, like Eiseley, see in that distant self beginnings of your adult self; can you see hopes, fears, likes, curiosities, needs, predictable reactions, in these brief jottings of yours? Be aware that defining yourself in a narrative is often as much a process of interpretation as of discovery.

Now try to arrange your writing in a simple pattern. Begin with a generalization, a broad theme (see Eiseley's paragraph "To grow is a gain . . .") and then get more specific about yourself. Then support that assertion with one or two brief anecdotes. Conclude with a present view of that incident (see especially Eiseley's penultimate paragraph, "Of course she gave up . . .").

TWELVE

Norman Mailer
(1923–   )

As a writer and a public personality, Norman Mailer wants to affect the consciousness of his time; he wants to alter history. Since these are hardly modest goals, Mailer is often thought of as an outrageous character: egocentric, posturing, quixotic. He probably is. But he is also a generous, inspired scholar and a gifted writer of a remarkably rich and varied body of nonfiction. He is many people, sometimes in the same book. He simply refuses to conform to traditional notions of what is normal. He resists harmony and balance. And he abhors consistency, which he suspects is another name for inertia.

Mailer's writing and life-style are restless, robust, and intellectually awesome. He is challenging. He does not talk or write simply. He wants you to think—he demands that you do. If you want to keep up with his fertile and energetic mind, you must concentrate. His thought is often filled with idiosyncratic digression, foolish posturing, and brilliant flashes of insight. His prose is a record of an intricate and complex mind at work. He has written books about the first journey to the moon, boxing, women's liberation, the anti-war movement, film stars, other writers, and politics. And, of course, he has also written novels—among them, *The Naked and the Dead, An American Dream, The Deer Park,* and *Why Are We in Vietnam?*—plays, movies, and short stories. He has punched strangers and friends in bars and at society parties; he stabbed one of his four wives with a penknife; he has been abrasive and obscene to talk-show hosts; he boxed with José Torres on television; he ran for mayor of New York City; he has been arrested, praised, condemned, and honored.

Because Mailer is dedicated to avoiding the easy answer and typical response, his writing is often unpredictable. For Mailer, composing is a quest for truth, not merely a record of it. Because he knows he is searching, his writing does appear to wander at times. Some critics, in fact, are upset by his taste for long sentences and "associative rambling." But Mailer has made a conscious artistic choice to do just that. He wants to let his writing be exploratory, to look this way and that for possible answers. He doesn't want to give the impression that truth can be just simply stated and defended. So his style and content mirror truth's complexity.

In *The Armies of the Night*, for example, he jumps from one thought to the next, in a dizzying array of allusions to history, politics, sex, drugs, and technology. He uses this stylistic technique to suggest his own uncertainty about what is going on. He is trying to explore the confusion of the march on the Pentagon from as many angles as he can. So the "tributary contributions to the main direction" that perplex the critics are really attempts to be accurate and honest. Style becomes a way to understand.

Closely related to style are Mailer's innovative ideas on persona. He is often a character in his own books. In *Of a Fire on the Moon*, he calls himself Aquarius and writes about his observation of the moon shot in the third person. In *The Armies of the Night*, he is "Mailer" or the "novelist" or sometimes just "he." In an extreme form of New Journalism, Mailer actually participates in the event he has come to write about. His presence at the Pentagon is, in fact, a good deal of the story. Still, Norman Mailer the writer is not identical with this participant. In an attempt to go beyond the conventional "objective" accounts of this massive protest, Mailer the writer describes Mailer the participant's perceptions of what is going on; hence, the reader gets a double vision, from both the inside and the outside. For Mailer, the multiplex nature of such an enormous event demands an innovative perspective.

In "A Confrontation by the River," the reader is invited to join "Mailer" as he runs past MPs to be arrested. But later on, in "Why Are We in Vietnam?" (also from *The*

Armies of the Night), the writer changes this almost adolescent persona into a voice that seems quite reasonable, balanced, and credible. Mailer has many personalities, and he is not afraid to switch, midstream if need be. And he is even willing to disappear altogether. In the opening pages of *The Fight* ("Carnal Indifference"), he is obviously watching Ali at his training camp, but he refrains from participating. He reports. He adapts his style to the occasion, using energetic, snappy sentences laced with fight jargon and expertise.

Norman Mailer graduated from Boys High in Brooklyn, New York, and entered Harvard in 1939, where he majored in aeronautical engineering. In his freshman year he discovered the modern American novel. This discovery so reshaped his mind and heart that he decided then to become a major American writer. After graduation he fought in World War II, mostly in the Philippines. *The Naked and the Dead*, a spectacularly successful novel of this war, was published in 1947. Later he helped to found *The Village Voice*, an avant-garde newspaper on the arts and politics.

During the 1950s he lived in Greenwich Village. For Mailer this was a time of turbulent experimentation in his personal life. His repuation as a reckless drinker and ruffian became widely known. He seemed to be obsessed with overturning the foundations of traditional American values. But this rebellion against convention did not improve his declining reputation as a novelist. When *The Deer Park* (1955), an ironic and complex novel about a Hollywood resort, received mixed reviews, Mailer became frustrated with his fictional failures and wrote *Advertisements for Myself*, a collection of nonfiction exploring his own character.

Although racy and sensational copy still followed him, Mailer's critical reputation as a journalist began to increase. In fact, his aggressive public performances seem to have helped him clarify and understand his complex personality. *The Presidential Papers* (1963) and *Cannibals and Christians* (1966) established Mailer as one of America's leading social and political critics. His more recent nonfiction, *The Prisoner of Sex* (1971), *Marilyn* (1973), *Genius and Lust* (1976), and *The Faith of Graffiti* (1974), have solidified his stature as a writer of prodigious range and talent. His imagination, intelligence, and "extraordinary powers of expressiveness" have widened the artistic and intellectual possibilities of nonfiction. Through his innovative use of style and persona to reinforce meaning, he has demonstrated that skilled writers create their own rules, by working against the obvious and the trite.

Carnal Indifference

---

1   There is always a shock in seeing him again. Not *live* as in television but standing before you, looking his best. Then the World's Greatest Athlete is in danger of being our most beautiful man, and the vocabulary of Camp is doomed to appear. Women draw an *audible* breath. Men look *down*. They are reminded again of their lack of worth. If Ali never opened his mouth to quiver the jellies of public opinion, he would still inspire love and hate. For he is the Prince of Heaven—so says the silence around his body when he is luminous.

2   When he is depressed, however, his pale skin turns the color of coffee with milky water, no cream. There is the sickly green of a depressed morning in the muddy washes of the flesh. He looks not quite well. That may be a fair description of how he appeared at his training camp in Deer Lake, Pennsylvania, on a September afternoon seven weeks before his fight in Kinshasa with George Foreman.

3   His sparring was spiritless. Worse. He kept getting hit with stupid punches, shots he would normally avoid, and that was not like Ali! There was an art to watching him train and you acquired it over the years. Other champions picked sparring partners who could imitate the style of their next opponent and, when they could afford it, added a fighter who was congenial: someone they could hit at will, someone fun to box. Ali did this also, but reversed the order. For the second fight with Sonny Liston, his favorite had been Jimmy Ellis, an intricate artist who had nothing in common with Sonny. As boxers, Ellis and Liston had such different moves one could not pass a bowl of soup to

the other without spilling it. Of course, Ali had other sparring partners for that fight. Shotgun Sheldon comes to mind. Ali would lie on the ropes while Sheldon hit him a hundred punches to the belly—that was Ali conditioning stomach and ribs to take Liston's pounding. In that direction lay his duty, but his pleasure was by way of sparring with Ellis as if Ali had no need to study Sonny's style when he could elaborate the wit and dazzle of his own.

4   Fighters generally use a training period to build confidence in their reflexes, even as an average skier, after a week of work on his parallel, can begin to think he will yet look like an expert. In later years, however, Ali would concentrate less on building his own speed and more on how to take punches. Now, part of his art was to reduce the force of each blow he received to the head and then fraction it further. Every fighter does that, indeed a young boxer will not last long if his neck fails to swivel at the instant he is hit, but it was as if Ali were teaching his nervous system to transmit shock faster than other men could.

5   Maybe all illness results from a failure of communication between mind and body. It is certainly true of such quick disease as a knockout. The mind can no longer send a word to the limbs. The extreme of this theory, laid down by Cus D'Amato when managing Floyd Patterson and José Torres, is that a pugilist with an authentic desire to win cannot be knocked out if he sees the punch coming, for then he suffers no dramatic lack of communication. The blow may hurt but cannot wipe him out. In contrast, a five-punch combination in which every shot lands is certain to stampede any opponent into unconsciousness. No matter how light the blows, a jackpot has been struck. The sudden overloading of the victim's message center is bound to produce that inrush of confusion known as coma.

6   Now it was as if Ali carried the idea to some advanced place where he could assimilate punches faster than other fighters, could literally transmit the shock through more parts of his body, or direct it to the best path, as if ideally he were working toward the ability to receive that five-punch combination (or six or seven!) yet be so ready to ship the impact out to each arm, each organ and each leg, that the punishment might be digested, and the mind remain clear. It was a study to watch Ali take punches. He would lie on the ropes and paw at his sparring partner like a mother cat goading her kitten to belt away. Then

Ali would flip up his glove and let the other's punch bounce from that glove off his head, repeating the move from other angles, as if the second half of the art of getting hit was to learn the trajectories with which punches glanced off your gloves and still hit you; Ali was always studying how to deaden such shots or punish the glove that threw the punch, forever elaborating his inner comprehension of how to trap, damp, modify, mock, curve, cock, warp, distort, deflect, tip, and turn the bombs that came toward him, and do this with a minimum of movement, back against the ropes, languid hands up. He invariably trained by a scenario that cast him as a fighter in deep fatigue, too tired to raise his arms in the twelfth round of a fifteen-round fight. Such training may have saved him from being knocked out by Frazier in their first fight, such training had been explored by him in every fight since. His corner would scream "Stop playing!," the judges would score against him for lying on the ropes, the fight writers would report that he did not look like the old Ali and all the while he was refining methods.

7   This afternoon, however, in Deer Lake it looked as if he were learning very little. He was getting hit by stupid punches and they seemed to take him by surprise. He was not languid but sluggish. He looked bored. He showed, as he worked, all the sullen ardor of a husband obliging himself to make love to his wife in the thick of carnal indifference.

QUESTIONS

Ideas

1. How did you respond to the first paragraph? Do "men look down," literally? What do you think Mailer means by calling Ali "the Prince of Heaven"?

2. This little snapshot of Ali is punctuated by ideas from boxing theory. What are some of the skills Mailer most admires in Ali? What principles is Ali violating as Mailer watches?

3. Mailer clearly sees Ali as more than a mere fighter. Why do you think this is? Is it something in Ali or a need in Mailer for a hero larger than life? Is the concluding analogy meant to be amusing? Shocking? Thought-provoking?

Organization

4. Which paragraphs are about what is actually taking place in Deer Lake and which are not?
5. What is the topic sentence (implied or direct) in the penultimate paragraph? Do all the sentences here relate directly to this general idea? Is there a beginning, middle, and end to this paragraph? What term does Mailer use in the first sentence that he returns to in the last?

Sentences

6. Why does Mailer decide to begin the last four sentences with "He"? Is this effective?
7. Why does Mailer write, "He looks not quite well"? Does this sound natural?

Words

8. What is the function of "however" in the second and last paragraphs?
9. What purpose does "Now" serve in the penultimate paragraph?
10. What does "luminous" mean? Is there any boxing jargon or argot here? What function do these terms serve?

Suggestions for Writing

A. Rewrite the sentence in the penultimate paragraph that begins, "Then Ali would flip . . ." Try for four or five varied sentences.
B. Can you remember meeting an impressive person? Write a short piece describing the person and your response to the meeting.
C. Write an editorial supporting or opposing boxing.

The Siege of Chicago

1   **M**eanwhile, a mass meeting was taking place about the bandshell in Grant Park, perhaps a quarter of a mile east of Michigan Avenue and the Conrad Hilton The meeting was under the auspices

of the Mobilization, and a crowd of ten or fifteen thousand appeared.
The Mayor had granted a permit to assemble, but had refused to allow
a march. Since the Mobilization had announced that it would attempt,
no matter how, the march to the Amphitheatre that was the first purpose
of their visit to Chicago, the police were out in force to surround the
meeting.

2   An episode occurred during the speeches. Three demonstrators
climbed a flag pole to cut down the American flag and put up a rebel
flag. A squad of police charged to beat them up, but got into trouble
themselves, for when they threw tear gas, the demonstrators lobbed the
canisters back, and the police, choking on their own gas, had to fight
their way clear through a barrage of rocks. Then came a much larger
force of police charging the area, overturning benches, busting up
members of the audience, then heading for Rennie Davis at the bull-
horn. He was one of the coordinators of the Mobilization, his face was
known, he had been fingered and fingered again by plainclothesmen.
Now urging the crowd to sit down and be calm, he was attacked from
behind by the police, his head laid open in a three-inch cut, and he
was unconscious for a period. Furious at the attack, Tom Hayden, who
had been in disguise these last two days to avoid any more arrests for
himself, spoke to the crowd, said he was leaving to perform certain
special tasks, and suggested that others break up into small groups and
go out into the streets of the Loop "to do what they have to do." A few
left with him; the majority remained. While it was a People's Army
and therefore utterly unorganized by uniform or unity, it had a variety
of special troops and regular troops; everything from a few qualified
Kamikaze who were ready to charge police lines in a Japanese snake
dance and dare on the consequence, some vicious beatings, to various
kinds of small saboteurs, rock-throwers, gauntlet-runners—some of the
speediest of the kids were adept at taunting cops while keeping barely
out of range of their clubs—not altogether alien to running the bulls
at Pamplona. Many of those who remained, however, were still nom-
inally pacifists, protesters, Gandhians—they believed in non-violence,
in the mystical interposition of their body to the attack, as if the violence
of the enemy might be drained by the spiritual act of passive resistance
over the years, over the thousands, tens of thousands, hundreds of
thousands of beatings over the years. So Allen Ginsberg was speaking
now to them.

3   The police looking through the plexiglass face shields they had flipped down from their helmets were then obliged to watch the poet with his bald head, soft eyes magnified by horn-rimmed eyeglasses, and massive dark beard, utter his words in a croaking speech. He had been gassed Monday night and Tuesday night, and had gone to the beach at dawn to read Hindu Tantras to some of the Yippies, the combination of the chants and the gassings had all but burned out his voice, his beautiful speaking voice, one of the most powerful and hypnotic instruments of the Western world was down to the scrapings of the throat now, raw as flesh after a curettage.

4   "The best strategy for you," said Ginsberg, "in cases of hysteria, overexcitement or fear, is still to chant 'OM' together. It helps to quell flutterings of butterflies in the belly. Join me now as I try to lead you."

5   The crowd chanted with Ginsberg. They were of a generation which would try every idea, every drug, every action—it was even possible a few of them had made out with freaky kicks on tear gas these last few days—so they would chant OM. There were Hindu fanatics in the crowd, children who loved India and scorned everything in the West; there were cynics who thought the best thing to be said for a country which allowed its excess population to die by the millions in famine-ridden fields was that it would not be ready soon to try to dominate the rest of the world. There were also militants who were ready to march. And the police there to prevent them, busy now in communication with other detachments of police, by way of radios whose aerials were attached to their helmets, thereby giving them the look of giant insects.

6   A confused hour began. Lincoln Park was irregular in shape with curving foot walks; but Grant Park was indeed not so much a park as a set of belts of greenery cut into files by major parallel avenues between Michigan Avenue and Lake Michigan half a mile away. Since there were also cross streets cutting the belts of green perpendicularly, a variety of bridges and pedestrian overpasses gave egress to the city. The park was in this sense an alternation of lawn with superhighways. So the police were able to pen the crowd. But not completely. There were too many bridges, too many choices, in effect, for the police to anticipate. To this confusion was added the fact that every confrontation of demonstrators with police, now buttressed by the National Guard, attracted hundreds of newsmen, and hence began a set of attempted negotiations

between spokesmen for the demonstrators and troops the demonstrators finally tried to force a bridge and get back to the city. Repelled by tear gas, they went to other bridges, still other bridges, finally found a bridge lightly guarded, broke through a passage and were loose in the city at six-thirty in the evening. They milled about in the Loop for a few minutes, only to encounter the mules and three wagons of the Poor People's Campaign. City officials, afraid of provoking the Negroes on the South Side, had given a permit to the Reverend Abernathy, and he was going to march the mules and wagons down Michigan Avenue and over to the convention. An impromptu march of the demonstrators formed behind the wagons immediately on encountering them and ranks of marchers, sixty, eighty, a hundred in line across the width of Michigan Avenue began to move forward in the gray early twilight of 7 P.M.; Michigan Avenue was now suddenly jammed with people in the march, perhaps so many as four or five thousand people, including onlookers on the sidewalk who jumped in. The streets of the Loop were also reeking with tear gas—the wind had blown some of the gas west over Michigan Avenue from the drops on the bridges, some gas still was penetrated into the clothing of the marchers. In broken ranks, half a march, half a happy mob, eyes red from gas, faces excited by the tension of the afternoon, and the excitement of the escape from Grant Park, now pushing down Michigan Avenue toward the Hilton Hotel with dreams of a march on to the Amphitheatre four miles beyond, and in the full pleasure of being led by the wagons of the Poor People's March, the demonstrators shouted to everyone on the sidewalk, "Join us, join us, join us," and the sidewalk kept disgorging more people ready to march.

7   But at Balbo Avenue, just before Michigan Avenue reached the Hilton, the marchers were halted by the police. It was a long halt. Perhaps thirty minutes. Time for people who had been walking on the sidewalk to join the march, proceed for a few steps, halt with the others, wait, get bored, and leave. It was time for someone in command of the hundreds of police in the neighborhood to communicate with his head-quarters, explain the problem, time for the dilemma to be relayed, alternatives examined, and orders conceivably sent back to attack and disperse the crowd. If so, a trap was first set. The mules were allowed to cross Balbo Avenue, then were separated by a line of police from the marchers, who now, several thousand compressed in this one place, filled the intersection of Michigan Avenue and Balbo. There, dammed

by police on three sides, and cut off from the wagons of the Poor People's March, there, right beneath the windows of the Hilton which looked down on Grant Park and Michigan Avenue, the stationary march was abruptly attacked. The police attacked with tear gas, with Mace, and with clubs, they attacked like a chain saw cutting into wood, the teeth of the saw the edge of their clubs, they attacked like a scythe through grass, lines of twenty and thirty policemen striking out in an arc, their clubs beating, demonstrators fleeing. Seen from overhead, from the nineteenth floor, it was like a wind blowing dust, or the edge of waves riding foam on the shore.

8   The police cut through the crowd one way, then cut through them another. They chased people into the park, ran them down, beat them up; they cut through the intersection at Michigan and Balbo like a razor cutting a channel through a head of hair, and then drove columns of new police into the channel who in turn pushed out, clubs flailing, on each side, to cut new channels, and new ones again. As demonstrators ran, they reformed in new groups only to be chased by the police again. The action went on for ten minutes, fifteen minutes, with the absolute ferocity of a tropical storm, and watching it from a window on the nineteenth floor, there was something of the detachment of studying a storm at evening through a glass, the light was a lovely gray-blue, the police had uniforms of sky-blue, even the ferocity had an abstract elemental play of forces of nature at battle with other forces, as if sheets of tropical rain were driving across the street in patterns, in curving patterns which curved upon each other again. Police cars rolled up, prisoners were beaten, shoved into wagons, driven away. The rain of police, maddened by the uncoiling of their own storm, pushed against their own barricades of tourists pressed on the street against the Hilton Hotel, then pressed them so hard—but here is a quotation from J. Anthony Lukas in *The New York Times*:

> Even elderly bystanders were caught in the police onslaught. At one point, the police turned on several dozen persons standing quietly behind police barriers in front of the Conrad Hilton Hotel watching the demonstrators across the street.
>
> For no reason that could be immediately determined, the blue-helmeted policemen charged the barriers, crushing the spectators against the windows of the Haymarket Inn, a restaurant in the hotel. Finally the window gave way, sending screaming middle-aged women and children backward through the broken shards of glass.

The police then ran into the restaurant and beat some of the victims who had fallen through the windows and arrested them.

9   Now another quote from Steve Lerner in *The Village Voice*:

When the charge came, there was a stampede toward the sidelines. People piled into each other, humped over each other's bodies like coupling dogs. To fall down in the crush was just as terrifying as facing the police. Suddenly I realized my feet weren't touching the ground as the crowd pushed up onto the sidewalk. I was grabbing at the army jacket of the boy in front of me; the girl behind me had a stranglehold on my neck and was screaming incoherently in my ear.

10   Now, a longer quotation from Jack Newfield in *The Village Voice*. (The accounts in *The Voice* of September 5 were superior to any others encountered that week.)

At the southwest entrance to the Hilton, a skinny, long-haired kid of about seventeen skidded down on the sidewalk, and four overweight cops leaped on him, chopping strokes on his head. His hair flew from the force of the blows. A dozen small rivulets of blood began to cascade down the kid's temple and onto the sidewalk. He was not crying or screaming, but crawling in a stupor toward the gutter. When he saw a photographer take a picture, he made a V sign with his fingers.

A doctor in a white uniform and Red Cross arm band began to run toward the kid, but two other cops caught him from behind and knocked him down. One of them jammed his knee into the doctor's throat and began clubbing his rib cage. The doctor squirmed away, but the cops followed him, swinging hard, sometimes missing.

A few feet away a phalanx of police charged into a group of women, reporters, and young McCarthy activists standing idly against the window of the Hilton Hotel's Haymarket Inn. The terrified people began to go down under the unexpected police charge when the plate glass window shattered, and the people tumbled backward through the glass. The police then climbed through the broken window and began to beat people, some of whom had been drinking quietly in the hotel bar.

At the side entrance of the Hilton Hotel four cops were chasing one frightened kid of about seventeen. Suddenly, Fred Dutton, a former aide to Robert Kennedy, moved out from under the marquee and interposed his body between the kid and the police.

"He's my guest in this hotel," Dutton told the cops.

The police started to club the kid.

Dutton screamed for the first cop's name and badge number. The cop grabbed Dutton and began to arrest him, until a Washington *Post* reporter identified Dutton as a former RFK aide.

Demonstrators, reporters, McCarthy workers, doctors, all began to stagger into the Hilton lobby, blood streaming from face and head wounds. The lobby smelled from tear gas, and stink bombs dropped by the Yippies. A few people began to direct the wounded to a makeshift hospital on the fifteenth floor, the McCarthy staff headquarters.

Fred Dutton was screaming at the police, and at the journalists to report all the "sadism and brutality." Richard Goodwin, the ashen nub of a cigar sticking out of his fatigued face, mumbled, "This is just the beginning. There'll be four years of this."

The defiant kids began a slow, orderly retreat back up Michigan Avenue. They did not run. They did not panic. They did not fight back. As they fell back they helped pick up fallen comrades who were beaten or gassed. Suddenly, a plainclothesman dressed as a soldier moved out of the shadows and knocked one kid down with an overhand punch. The kid squatted on the pavement of Michigan Avenue, trying to cover his face, while the Chicago plainclothesman punched him with savage accuracy. Thud, thud, thud. Blotches of blood spread over the kid's face. Two photographers moved in. Several police formed a closed circle around the beating to prevent pictures. One of the policemen then squirted Chemical Mace at the photographers, who dispersed. The plainclothesman melted into the line of police.

11   Let us escape to the street. The reporter, watching in safety from the nineteenth floor, could understand now how Mussolini's son-in-law had once been able to find the bombs he dropped from his airplane beautiful as they burst, yes, children, and youths, and middle-aged men and women were being pounded and clubbed and gassed and beaten, hunted and driven, sent scattering in all directions by teams of policemen who had exploded out of their restraints like the bursting of a boil, and nonetheless he felt a sense of calm and beauty, void even of the desire to be down there, as if in years to come there would be beatings enough, some chosen, some from nowhere, but it was as if the war had finally begun, and this was therefore a great and solemn moment, as if indeed even the gods of history had come together from each side to choose the very front of the Hilton Hotel before the television cameras of the world and the eyes of the campaign workers and the delegates' wives, yes, there before the eyes of half the principals at the convention was this drama played, as if the military spine of a great liberal party

had finally separated itself from the skin, as if, no metaphor large enough to suffice, the Democratic Party had here broken in two before the eyes of a nation like Melville's whale charging right out of the sea.

12   A great stillness rose up from the street through all the small noise of clubbing and cries, small sirens, sigh of loaded arrest vans as off they pulled, shouts of police as they wheeled in larger circles, the intersection clearing further, then further, a stillness rose through the steel and stone of the hotel, congregating in the shocked centers of every room where delegates and wives and Press and campaign workers innocent until now of the intimate working of social force, looked down now into the murderous paradigm of Vietnam there beneath them at this huge intersection of this great city. Look—a boy was running through the park, and a cop was chasing. There he caught him on the back of the neck with his club! There! The cop is returning to his own! And the boy stumbling to his feet is helped off the ground by a girl who has come running up.

13   Yes, it could only have happened in a meeting of the Gods, that history for once should take place not on some back street, or some inaccessible grand room, not in some laboratory indistinguishable from others, or in the sly undiscoverable hypocrisies of a committee of experts, but rather on the center of the stage, as if each side had said, "Here we will have our battle. Here we will win."

14   The demonstrators were afterward delighted to have been manhandled before the public eye, delighted to have pushed and prodded, antagonized and provoked the cops over these days with rocks and bottles and cries of "Pig" to the point where police had charged in a blind rage and made a stage at the one place in the city (besides the Amphitheatre) where audience, actors, and cameras could all convene, yes, the rebels thought they had had a great victory, and perhaps they did; but the reporter wondered, even as he saw it, if the police in that half hour of waiting had not had time to receive instructions from the power of the city, perhaps the power of the land, and the power had decided, "No, do not let them march another ten blocks and there disperse them on some quiet street, no, let it happen before all the land, let everybody see that their dissent will soon be equal to their own blood; let them realize that the power is implacable, and will beat and crush and imprison and yet kill before it will ever relinquish the power. So let them see before their own eyes what it will cost to continue to mock us, defy us, and resist. There are more millions behind us than behind them,

more millions who wish to weed out, poison, gas, and obliterate every flower whose power they do not comprehend than heroes for their side who will view our brute determination and still be ready to resist. There are more cowards alive than the brave. Otherwise we would not be where we are," said the Prince of Greed.

15   Who knew. One could thank the city of Chicago where drama was still a property of the open stage. It was quiet now, there was nothing to stare down on but the mules, and the police guarding them. The mules had not moved through the entire fray. Isolated from the battle, they had stood there in harness waiting to be told to go on. Only once in a while did they turn their heads. Their role as actors in the Poor People's March was to wait and to serve. Finally they moved on. The night had come. It was dark. The intersection was now empty. Shoes, ladies' handbags, and pieces of clothing lay on the street outside the hotel.

QUESTIONS

Ideas

1. What is Mailer's purpose in this piece? To report? To entertain? To persuade?

2. Do you think the persona Mailer has adopted here is effective? Is he stating the facts or interpreting them? Is there a difference?

3. Examine the descriptions of the police and of the demonstrators in paragraphs 2, 3, and 5. How does Mailer reveal his attitude toward each?

4. In his descriptions of the demonstrators, Mailer is careful to show their heterogeneity, their differences from one another. Why? Does he do the same thing in the descriptions of the police?

5. Since there is no explicit conclusion, Mailer invites the reader to decide who won and who lost. In the next-to-last paragraph, who do you think is right?

Organization

6. How is the essay organized? Divide it into sections and give each section a title. Explain the purpose of each section and explain how the parts are related.

7. Why does Mailer include news accounts of the incident and print them intact within his own account? How do the accounts compare with one another and with Mailer's own version? Do you think these reports are a representative cross section of the reporting that went on? How could you verify this?

8. Where is Mailer as he reports on the scene? Where is his vantage point, and how does this affect his perspective on the scene he witnesses?

Sentences

9. Throughout the essay, Mailer employs short sentences. Explain how the short sentences at the beginning of the following paragraphs work: 2, 5, 6, 9, 11, 15. What is the effect of the series of short sentences at the end of the essay?

10. The final sentence of paragraph 6 is a long periodic sentence in which a series of modifiers precedes the main clause. State the main clause and give your reaction to the way the sentence is constructed. What is the effect of accumulating many details and of putting them at the beginning?

11. A loose sentence, on the other hand, begins with the main clause and then adds modifiers. Look, for example, at the second sentence in paragraph 8. Find other examples of loose and periodic sentences. Why does Mailer choose each?

12. The next-to-last sentence of paragraph 7 runs together a number of actions and details. Would these have been better separated into discrete, simple sentences? Explain.

13. Paragraph 11 consists of two sentences, one very short and one very long. Examine the long sentence and explain how Mailer keeps it going, how he extends it, adds on to it, without losing control of either his idea or his language, without losing us along the way, as he attempts to understand his feelings about what he has seen, as he tries to explain its meaning to us and to himself.

14. Explain how the series of short sentences in the final paragraph affects the tone of the entire paragraph.

Words

15. In paragraph 2 Mailer describes the protesters as a People's Army. He also compares some of them to Kamikaze pilots and to the people who run the bulls at Pamplona. How do these comparisons help characterize the demonstrators? What do they reveal of Mailer's attitude toward the protesters? Look also at paragraph 5.

16. At the end of paragraph 7 Mailer describes the police attack on the crowd. What do the comparisons in this account have in common, and what is their cumulative effect?
17. The description of the attack is continued in paragraph 8, with more comparisons. How do these relate to, extend, and develop those used in the previous paragraph?
18. Examine the verbs in the last two sentences of paragraph 7 and throughout paragraph 8. Which are repeated? Why? To what effect?
19. What are the tone and effect of the speech Mailer imagines given by the "Prince of Greed"? (paragraph 14).
20. In the final three paragraphs Mailer introduces and sustains the imagery of drama and theater. What point does he make by means of this extended comparison?

Suggestions for Writing

A. Write sentences imitating Mailer's use of the dash and double dash in paragraph 2; the front-loaded sentence from paragraph 6; the run-together sentence of paragraph 7; the long sentence of paragraph 11.
B. Write an imitation of paragraph 15 using all short sentences.
C. Write a paragraph imitating Mailer's technique of using one short and one long sentence (as in paragraph 11).
D. Write an essay analyzing Mailer's use of metaphor in this essay. Explain how he uses metaphor, where and why he uses it, and what he achieves through its repeated use.
E. Write an essay challenging Mailer's description of the scene. You might consider writing a letter to Mailer asking him why he wrote the piece and what he hoped to accomplish with it. You might explain why you like or dislike the piece, what you think about the political viewpoint expressed in it, perhaps even including some of your own ideas about politics, protest, and police.

Into Orbit

1   Just as the Greeks could be confident they had discovered the secret of beauty because the aesthetic of their sculptors permitted no blemish to the skin, because their sculptors said in fact that the

surface of marble was equal to the surface of skin, so classical physics remained simple because it did not try to deal with anything less than ideal form. Later, Western aesthetics was sufficiently ambitious to wish to discover the laws of beauty in skins with blemish and bodies with twisted limbs (and indeed would never quite succeed), just indeed as engineering could never prove simple and comprehensible to amateurs. At its best engineering was a judicious mixture of physics and a man's life-experience with machines: one insignificant dial on one bank of instruments was often the product of the acquired wisdom of a good engineer who had put in years of work reducing the deviations of an imperfect instrument of measure.

2   Any attempt to explain the mechanics of the flight of Apollo II in engineering terms is then near to impossible for one would be obliged to rewrite a set of extracts from technical manuals, and each manual would finally prove nothing but an extract from other more detailed manuals, which in turn would be summaries of the verbally trans-mittable and therefore less instinctive experience of veteran engineers. Yet, the pure physics of the flight was still simple, so simple and pleased with itself as a Greek statue.

3   The rocket rose because the forces which were pushing it up were larger than the forces which held it down. The thrust of its motors was greater than the heft of its bulk. So it rose upward, even as we can jump in the air for a moment because for just a moment the push in our legs up against our body is greater than our weight. Speak of potency!—the force of our legs immediately ceases; almost immediately we descend. While the rocket had no legs to propel it upward, it had rather a burning gas expelled from its rear, and this force did not cease. So the rocket continued to rise. In the beginning it did not rise very quickly. Seven million seven hundred thousand pounds pushed upward against six million five hundred thousand pounds of weight which pressed down-ward. The difference was therefore to be calculated at one million two hundred thousand. That was the same as saying that if the rocket had been mounted on wheels in order to travel down a level road (and so did not have to be lifted), one million two hundred thousand pounds would be pushing the same six million five hundred thousand pounds of rocket. It can be remarked in anticipation that as this force continued to push, the rocket would begin to go faster. Its velocity would increase at an even rate if the push remained the same and the weight remained

the same. If at the end of a second, its measured speed was about what it should be—five feet a second—it would reach fifty feet a second after ten seconds, and one hundred feet a second after twenty. The reason was not complex. The push did not diminish. Therefore the rocket would go five feet faster every second than the second just before. After two seconds it would be going at ten feet a second because five feet a second would have been added in that second interval of measure to the first five feet a second. After three seconds, fifteen feet a second would be its speed. The velocity would increase five feet a second, every second, so long as the push remained steady on that rocket rolling on wheels down that level road. At the end of seventeen and a half minutes the rocket we have used for an imaginary model would be moving at an imaginary speed of a mile every second.

4   Yet that hypothetical rocket is still traveling at a much slower rate than Apollo-Saturn. When Apollo-Saturn went into orbit one hundred miles up and fifteen hundred miles out, not twelve minutes were gone, yet it was traveling at five miles a second or eighteen thousand miles an hour.

5   The explanation is agreeable to a liberal mentality, for it suggests that expenditure is power. The greatest weight in the rocket is fuel, and the fuel is being consumed. The rocket loses weight at a rate as immense as thirty-five hundred gallons of fuel each second. Somewhere about thirty-five thousand pounds of weight vanish in the same interval, which comes out by calculation as close to two million pounds a minute. At the end of a minute, seven million seven hundred thousand pounds are pushing not six and a half million pounds but four and a half million. Thus, the ship is accelerating more rapidly each instant. Its speed of increase now would be not five feet a second but more than twenty. Since the engines, however, also increase their effectiveness as the rocket takes on high altitude and the near-vacuum of the thinning atmosphere offers less resistance to the fires of the exhaust, so at the end of two minutes and fifteen seconds of flight the thrust has actually reached over nine million pounds and is then pushing only a little more than two and a half million pounds. Now the rocket is being propelled by a force almost four times as great as itself: so its acceleration would be not five feet a second as at lift-off nor twenty feet a second at the end of a minute, but more like ninety feet a second.

6   Apollo-Saturn however does not travel that fast for long. It takes

two minutes and fifteen seconds to reach such acceleration, and then the center motor is shut down. The thrust reduces to seven million two hundred thousand pounds from the four continuing engines. Twenty-five seconds later the outboard motors are cut off. A few more seconds, and the first stage is released. The rocket begins to travel on the motors of the second stage, and these next five engines are not nearly so powerful. Never again will Apollo-Saturn pick up speed so quickly.

7   It hardly matters. The more modest acceleration of the second stage is added onto the high velocities already attained by the first stage. Apollo-Saturn will increase its speed to four and a half miles a second, and will be altogether out of sight when the second stage is discarded after nine minutes and twelve seconds of flight. Stripped of its first stage and its second stage, powered now by but a single motor which develops hardly one part in forty of the force the first engines developed to get off the ground, the ship now weighs only four hundred thousand pounds, or a sixteenth of its original weight. Drastically reduced, it is still in need of a little more speed, and the third stage will give it that, the third stage will take it up to something near five miles a second, or eighteen thousand miles an hour. To reach the moon it will yet have to go faster, it will have to reach twenty-five thousand miles an hour to escape the force of the earth's gravity. But that is a subsequent step. Now the ship is wheeling through the near-heavens. A little bit more than one hundred miles overhead, it proceeds to circumnavigate the earth every hour and twenty-eight minutes. Its weight, fuel of the third stage partially consumed, is now down to three hundred thousand pounds and it is in that magical condition of defiance to gravity which is known as orbit.

QUESTIONS

Ideas

1. What is the point of Mailer's opening comparison? Why doesn't Mailer explain Apollo's trip in engineering terms? What terms does he use?
2. What does Mailer mean by "pleased with itself as a Greek statue"?
3. Describe in your own words the process Apollo uses to get into orbit.

Organization

4. Describe the function of paragraphs 1 and 2. How about paragraph 4?
5. The bulk of the orbital process is described in paragraphs 5 and 7. How does Mailer organize these two chunks of discourse?
6. Which paragraphs have first sentences that refer to ideas in the preceding paragraph? Why does he do this?

Sentences

7. Try to write the first sentence three or four different ways.
8. If you were Mailer's editor, what might you suggest as a revision of the last sentence?

Words

9. Rewrite the first sentence of paragraph 5 using a primer vocabulary.
10. From the context, what does Mailer mean by "aesthetic"?

Suggestion for Writing

Using Mailer's discursive style as a model, describe a complicated process you know well, for example, driving a truck, developing film, playing a guitar, surfing, or skiing. Try to begin with an analogy.

Why Are We in Vietnam?

He knew the arguments for the war, and against the war—finally they bored him. The arguments in support of the war were founded on basic assumptions which had not been examined and were endlessly repeated—the arguments to withdraw never pursued the consequences.

He thought we were in the war as the culmination to a long sequence of events which had begun in some unrecorded fashion toward the end of World War II. A consensus of the most powerful middle-aged and elderly Wasps in America—statesmen, corporation executives, generals, admirals, newspaper editors, and legislators—had pledged an intellectual troth: they had sworn with a faith worthy of medieval knights that Communism was the deadly foe of Christian culture. If it were not resisted in the postwar world, Christianity itself would perish. So had begun a Cold War with intervals of overt war, mixed with periods of modest collaboration. As Communist China grew in strength, and her antagonisms with the Soviet Union quickened their pace, the old troth of the Wasp knights had grown sophisticated and abstract. It was now a part of the technology of foreign affairs, a thesis to be called upon when needed. The latest focus of this thesis was of course to be found in Vietnam. The arguments presented by the parties of war suggested that if Vietnam fell to the Communists, soon then would Southeast Asia, Indonesia, the Philippines, Australia, Japan, and India fall also to the Chinese Communists. Since these Chinese Communists were in the act of developing a nuclear striking force, America would face eventually a united Asia (and Africa?) ready to engage America (and Russia?) in a suicidal atomic war which might level the earth, a condition to the advantage of the Chinese Communists, since their low level of subsistence would make it easier for them to recover from the near to unendurable privations of the postatomic world.

Like most simple political theses, this fear of a total nuclear war was not uttered aloud by American statesmen, for the intimations of such a thesis are invariably more powerful than the thesis itself. It was sufficient that a paralysis of thought occurred in the average American at the covert question: should we therefore bomb the nuclear installations of the Chinese now? Obviously, public discussion preferred to move over to the intricate complexities of Vietnam. Of course, that was an ugly unattractive sometimes disgraceful war, murmured the superior apologists for the Hawks, perhaps the unhappiest war America had ever fought, but it was one of the most necessary, for (1) it demonstrated to China that she could not advance her guerrilla activities into Asia without paying a severe price; (2) it rallied the small Asian powers to confidence in America; (3) it underlined the depth of our promise to defend small nations; (4) it was an inexpensive means of containing a great power, far more inexpensive than fighting the power itself; and (5) it was probably superior to starting a nuclear war on China.

In answer, the debaters best armed for the Doves would reply that it was certainly an ugly disgraceful unattractive war but not necessary to our defense. If South Vietnam fell to the Vietcong, Communism would be then not 12,000 miles from our shores, but 11,000 miles. Moreover, we had not necessarily succeeded in demonstrating to China that guerrilla wars exacted too severe a price from the Communists. On the contrary, a few more guerrilla wars could certainly bankrupt America, since we now had 500,000 troops in South Vietnam to the 50,000 of the North Vietnamese, and our costs for this one small war had mounted to a figure between $25,000,000,000 and $30,000,000,000 a year, not so small an amount if one is reminded that the Second World War cost a total of $300,000,000,000 over four years, or less than three times as much on an average year as Vietnam! (Of course, there has been inflation since, but still! What incredible expense for so small a war—what scandals of procurement yet to be uncovered. How many more such inexpensive wars could the economy take?)

The Doves picked at the seed of each argument. Yes, they said, by fulfilling our commitments to South Vietnam, we have certainly inspired confidence in the other small Asian powers. But who has this confidence? Why the most reactionary profiteers of the small Asian nations now have the confidence; so the small Asian nations are polarized, for the best of their patriots, foreseeing a future plunder of Asia by Asian Capitalists under America's protection, are forced over to the Communists.

Yes, the Doves would answer, it is better to have a war in Vietnam than to bomb China, but then the war in Vietnam may serve as the only possible pretext to attack China. Besides the question of Chinese aggression has been begged. China is not, by its record, an aggressive nation, but a timid one, and suffers from internal contradictions which will leave her incapable for years of even conceiving of a major war.

This was not the least of the arguments of the Doves: they could go on to point out that North Vietnam had been occupied for centuries by China, and therefore was as hostile to China as Ireland was to England—our intervention had succeeded therefore in bringing North Vietnam and China closer together. This must eventually weaken the resistance of other small Asian powers to China.

Besides, said the Doves, part of the real damage of Vietnam takes place in America where civil rights have deteriorated into city riots, and

an extraordinary number of the best and most talented students in
America are exploring the frontiers of nihilism and drugs.

The Doves seemed to have arguments more powerful than the
Hawks. So the majority of people in America, while formidably patriotic
were also undecided and tended to shift in their opinion like the weather.
Yet the Hawks seemed never too concerned. They held every power
securely but one, a dependable consensus of public opinion. Still this
weakness left them unperturbed—their most powerful argument remained inviolate. There, the Doves never approached. The most powerful argument remained: what if we leave Vietnam, and all Asia eventually goes Communist? all of Southeast Asia, Indonesia, the
Philippines, Australia, Japan, and India?

Well, one could laugh at the thought of Australia going Communist. The Hawks were nothing if not humorless. If Communist
China had not been able to build a navy to cross the Straits of Formosa
and capture Taiwan, one did not see them invading Australia in the
next century. No, any decent Asian Communist would probably shud-
der at the thought of engaging the Anzacs, descendants of the men who
fought at Gallipoli. Yes, the Hawks were humorless, and Lyndon Johnson was shameless. He even invoked the defense of Australia.

But could the Dove give bona fides that our withdrawal from
Vietnam would produce no wave of Communism through Asia? Well,
the Dove was resourceful in answers, and gave many. The Dove talked
of the specific character of each nation, and the liberal alternatives of
supporting the most advanced liberal elements in these nations, the
Dove returned again and again to the profound weaknesses of China,
the extraordinary timidity of Chinese foreign policy since the Korean
war, spoke of the possibility of enclaves, and the resources of adroit,
well-managed economic war in Asia.

Yet the Doves, finally, had no answer to the Hawks. For the
Doves were divided. Some of them, a firm minority, secretly desired
Asia to go Communist, their sympathies were indeed with Asian peas-
ants, not American corporations, they wanted what was good for the
peasant, and in private they believed Communism was probably better
suited than Capitalism to introduce the technological society to the
peasant. But they did not consider it expedient to grant this point, so
they talked around it. The others, the majority of the Doves, simply

refused to face the possibility. They were liberals. To explore the dimensions of the question, might have exploded the foundation of their liberalism, for they would have had to admit they were willing to advocate policies which could conceivably end in major advances of Asian Communism, and this admission might oblige them to move over to the Hawks.

Mailer was bored with such arguments. The Hawks were smug and self-righteous, the Doves were evasive of the real question.

Mailer was a Left Conservative. So he had his own point of view. To himself he would suggest that he tried to think in the style of Marx in order to attain certain values suggested by Edmund Burke. Since he was a conservative, he would begin at the root. He did not see all wars as bad. He could conceive of wars which might be noble. But the war in Vietnam was bad for America because it was a bad war, as all wars are bad if they consist of rich boys fighting poor boys when the rich boys have an advantage in the weapons. He recollected a statistic: it was droll if it was not obscene. Next to every pound of supplies the North Vietnamese brought into South Vietnam for their soldiers, the Americans brought in one thousand pounds. Yes, he would begin at the root. All wars were bad which undertook daily operations which burned and bombed large numbers of women and children; all wars were bad which relocated populations (for the root of a rich peasant lore was then destroyed) all wars were bad which had no line of battle or discernible climax (an advanced notion which supposes that wars may be in part good because they are sometimes the only way to define critical conditions rather than blur them) certainly all wars were bad which took some of the bravest young men of a nation and sent them into combat with outrageous superiority and outrageous arguments: such conditions of combat had to excite a secret passion for hunting other humans. Certainly any war was a bad war which required an inability to reason as the price of retaining one's patriotism; finally any war which offered no prospect of improving itself as a war—so complex and compromised were its roots—was a bad war. A good war, like anything else which is good, offers the possibility that further effort will produce a determinable effect upon chaos, evil, or waste. By every conservative measure (reserving to Conservatism, the right to approve of wars) the war in Vietnam was an extraordinarily bad war.

Since he was also a *Left* Conservative, he believed that radical measures were sometimes necessary to save the root. The root in this case was the welfare of the nation, not the welfare of the war. So he had an answer to the Hawks. It was: pull out of Vietnam completely. Leave Asia to the Asians. What then would happen?

He did not know. Asia might go to the Communists, or it might not. He was certain no one alive knew the answer to so huge a question as that. It was only in the twentieth century, in the upper chambers of technology land (both Capitalist *and* Communist) that men began to believe there must be concrete answers to every large question. No! So far as he had an opinion (before the vastness of this question) his opinion existed on the same order of magnitude of undiscovered ignorance as the opinion of any Far Eastern expert. While he thought it was probable most of Asia would turn to Communism in the decade after any American withdrawal from that continent, he did not know that it really mattered. In those extraordinary World War II years when the Wasp admirals, generals, statesmen, legislators, editors and corporation presidents had whispered to each other that the next war was going to be Christianity versus Communism, the one striking omission in their Herculean crusade was the injunction to read Marx. They had studied his ideas, of course; in single-spaced extracts on a typewritten page! but because they had not read his words, but merely mouthed the extracts, they had not had the experience of encountering a mind which taught one to reason, even to reason away from his own mind; so the old Wasps and the young Wasps in the power elite could not comprehend that Communists who read their Marx might come to reason away from the particular monoliths of Marxism which had struck the first spark of their faith. It seemed never to occur to the most powerful Wasps that one could count quite neatly on good Communists and bad Communists just as one would naturally expect good Christians and bad. In fact, just as Christianity seemed to create the most unexpected saints, artists, geniuses, and great warriors out of its profound contradictions, so Communism seemed to create great heretics and innovators and converts (Sartre and Picasso for two) out of the irreducible majesty of Marx's mind (perhaps the greatest single tool for cerebration Western man had ever produced). Or at least—and here was the kernel of Mailer's sleeping thesis—Communism would continue to produce heretics and great innovators just so long as it expanded. Whenever it ceased to expand, it would become monolithic again, mediocre, and malign. An ogre.

An explanation? A submersion of Asia in Communism was going to explode a shock into Marxism which might take a half century to digest. Between Poland and India, Prague and Bangkok, was a diversity of primitive lore which would jam every fine gear of the Marxist. There were no quick meals in Asia. Only indigestion. The real difficulty might be then to decide who would do more harm to Asia, Capitalism or Communism. In either case, the conquest would be technological, and so primitive Asian societies would be uprooted. Probably, the uprooting would be savage, the psychic carnage unspeakable. He did not like to contemplate the compensating damage to America if it chose to dominate a dozen Asian nations with its technologies and its armies while having to face their guerrilla wars.

No, Asia was best left to the Asians. If the Communists absorbed those countries, and succeeded in building splendid nations who made the transition to technological culture without undue agony, one would be forced to applaud; it seemed evident on the face of the evidence in Vietnam, that America could not bring technology land to Asia without bankrupting itself in operations ill-conceived, poorly comprehended, and executed in waste. But the greater likelihood was that if the Communists prevailed in Asia they would suffer in much the same fashion. Divisions, schisms, and sects would appear. An endless number of collisions between primitive custom and Marxist dogma, a thousand daily pullulations of intrigue, a heritage of cruelty, atrocity, and betrayal would fall upon the Communists. It was not difficult to envision a time when one Communist nation in Asia might look for American aid against another Communist nation. Certainly Russia and China would be engaged in a cold war with each other for decades. Therefore, to leave Asia would be precisely to gain the balance of power. The answer then was to get out, to get out any way one could. Get out. There was nothing to fear—perhaps there never had been. For the more Communism expanded, the more monumental would become its problems, the more flaccid its preoccupations with world conquest. In the expansion of Communism, was its own containment. The only force which could ever defeat Communism, was Communism itself.

QUESTIONS

Ideas

1. Although Mailer is again writing about himself in the third person ("he"), his stance seems more serious than usual, more objective. Do you think he is objective, or is he only giving the appearance of giving both sides a fair chance?

2. In the second paragraph Mailer gives an explanation of the Vietnam war. Does it make sense to you? Does he offer any evidence for the intellectual pledge? Does he have to?

3. Does Mailer allow the Hawks' solid arguments for their side? Do the Doves' answers to the five defenses for the war seem fair? Does he seem to favor one side?

4. How does he deal with the "arguments to withdraw"?

5. From the evidence given, what do you think Mailer's definition of a "Left Conservative" is?

6. Does Mailer think all communists are bad?

7. What are some of the elements of a bad war? Do you agree with him that there could be a good war?

8. What does Mailer think will happen if Asia goes communist? Do you agree with this speculative idea?

9. What is his final position in the last paragraph? Does it take into consideration the arguments of the Doves and the Hawks?

Organization

10. Mailer uses comparison and contrast here as a way to persuade. He is trying to convince you to change your mind. To do this he adopts a certain persona. Do you think he chose an appropriate one? What if he had used his persona from "A Confrontation by the River"?

11. What is the sequence of Mailer's argument? Notice that he says in the first paragraph that he is bored by the arguments of the Hawks and the Doves. Does he support that statement? Where is this feeling repeated?

12. Does Mailer use the metaphor of the medieval knights developed in the second paragraph in other places in the essay? What is the purpose of this technique?

13. Writers sometimes use a short transitional paragraph to build a bridge between one section of a long essay and another. Find an example of this device here.

14. Some writers think it is wise to hold your best argument for last. Does Mailer? What would have been another possible organization strategy for this piece?

Sentences

15. Compare Mailer's sentences in "A Confrontation by the River" with those in "Why Are We in Vietnam?" Consider sentence forms, length, and tone.

16. What do you think are Mailer's most effective sentences here, i.e., which ones did you respond to most favorably? Was it the conversational ones— "No, Asia was best left to the Asians"—or the clear, assertive ones—"The only force which could ever defeat Communism, was Communism itself"? Or did you prefer the ones with imagery and literary diction—"A consensus of the most powerful . . ."?

Words

17. What does "truth" mean? Why did Mailer choose this word instead of "pledge"?

18. In the third paragraph from the end, Mailer writes, ". . . it would become monolithic again, mediocre, and malign. An ogre." What do these words mean? Did he choose them for meaning, for sound? Why "ogre" and not "monster" or "beast"?

Suggestions for Writing

A. Write a persuasive essay about a controversial subject in which you carefully analyze the position of both sides before developing your own argument. Be sure to state the opposing points of view as objectively as you can before you explain their flaws. Try to imitate the "searching-for-the-truth" persona Mailer adopts.

B. Write a paragraph in which you adopt a biased, extremist position about a controversial issue. Cast the opposing side's argument in the worst possible light. All right is on your side. Now do the same thing taking the completely opposite side.

A Confrontation by the River

It was not much of a situation to study. The MPs stood in two widely spaced ranks. The first rank was ten yards behind the rope, and each MP in that row was close to twenty feet from the next man. The second rank, similarly spaced, was ten yards behind the first rank and perhaps thirty yards behind them a cluster appeared, every fifty yards or so, of two or three U. S. Marshals in white helmets and dark blue suits. They were out there waiting. Two moods confronted one another, two separate senses of a private silence.

It was not unlike being a boy about to jump from one garage roof to an adjoining garage roof. The one thing not to do was wait. Mailer looked at Macdonald and Lowell. "Let's go," he said. Not looking again at them, not pausing to gather or dissipate resolve, he made a point of stepping neatly and decisively over the low rope. Then he headed across the grass to the nearest MP he saw.

It was as if the air had changed, or light had altered; he felt immediately much more alive—yes, bathed in air—and yet disembodied from himself, as if indeed he were watching himself in a film where this action was taking place. He could feel the eyes of the people behind the rope watching him, could feel the intensity of their existence as spectators. And as he walked forward, he and the MP looked at one another with the naked stricken lucidity which comes when absolute strangers are for the moment absolutely locked together.

The MP lifted his club to his chest as if to bar all passage. To Mailer's great surprise—he had secretly expected the enemy to be calm and strong, why should they not? they had every power, all the guns— to his great surprise, the MP was trembling. He was a young Negro, part white, who looked to have come from some small town where perhaps there were not many other Negroes; he had at any rate no Harlem smoke, no devil swish, no black, no black power for him, just a simple boy in an Army suit with a look of horror in his eye, "Why, why did it have to happen to me?" was the message of the petrified marbles in his face.

"Go back," he said hoarsely to Mailer.

"If you don't arrest me, I'm going to the Pentagon."

"No. Go back."

The thought of a return—"since they won't arrest me, what can I do?"—over these same ten yards was not at all suitable.

As the MP spoke, the raised club quivered. He did not know if it quivered from the desire of the MP to strike him, or secret military wonder was he now possessed of a moral force which implanted terror in the arms of young soldiers? Some unfamiliar current, now gyroscopic, now a sluggish whirlpool, was evolving from that quiver of the club, and the MP seemed to turn slowly away from his position confronting the rope and the novelist turned with him, each still facing the other until the axis of their shoulders was now perpendicular to the rope, and still they kept turning in this psychic field, not touching, the club quivering, and then Mailer was behind the MP, he was free of him, and he wheeled around and kept going in a half run to the next line of MPs and then on the push of a sudden instinct, sprinted suddenly around the nearest MP in the second line, much as if he were a back cutting around the nearest man in the secondary to break free—that was actually his precise thought—and had a passing perception of how simple it was to get past these MPs. They looked petrified. Stricken faces as he went by. They did not know what to do. It was his dark pinstripe suit, his vest, the maroon and blue regimental tie, the part in his hair, the barrel chest, the early paunch—he must have looked like a banker himself, a banker gone ape! And then he saw the Pentagon to his right across the field, not a hundred yards away, and a little to his left, the marshals, and he ran on a jog toward them, and came up, and they glared at him and shouted, "Go back."

He had a quick impression of hard-faced men with gray eyes burning some transparent fuel for flame, and said, "I won't go back. If you don't arrest me, I'm going on to the Pentagon," and knew he meant it, some absolute certainty had come to him, and then two of them leaped on him at once in the cold clammy murderous fury of all cops at the existential moment of making their bust—all cops who secretly expect to be struck at that instant for their sins—and a surprising force came to his voice, and he roared, to his own distant pleasure in new achievement and new authority—"Take your hands off me, can't you see? I'm not resisting arrest," and one then let go of him, and the other stopped trying to pry his arm into a lock, and contented himself with a hard hand under his armpit, and they set off walking across the field at a rapid intent quick rate, walking parallel to the wall of the Pentagon, fully visible on his right at last, and he was arrested, he had succeeded in that, and without a club on his head, the mountain air in his lungs as thin and fierce as smoke, yes, the livid air of tension on this livid side promised a few events of more interest than the routine wait to be free, yes he was more than a visitor, he was in the land of the enemy now, he would get to see their face.

QUESTIONS

Ideas

1. Do you think Mailer has, as he speculates, "gone ape"? Are you surprised that a famous writer would act in such a way?
2. When Mailer finally decides to go, what new feelings does he experience? Does this seem like a normal reaction?
3. Why do you think the MPs allow him to get as far as he does? What do you think of Mailer's characterization of the "murderous fury of all cops"?
4. Based on the last sentence, what do you think Mailer's motives are?
5. Do you think that this passage is more like fiction than history? Why? Is Mailer the writer trying to create a sense of objectivity by writing about himself in the third person as Mailer the participant?

Organization

6. Although this essay is essentially a narrative, it also has description, dialogue, speculation, and analysis. Does the narrative conform to the traditional structure of beginning, middle, and end?
7. In what ways does Mailer create unity in this piece? Are phrases, words, or ideas repeated in various places? Look, for example, at the first two words of the first three paragraphs.

Sentences

8. Most readers assume that Mailer writes mostly complex sentences with lots of subordinate clauses. Is this true? Look carefully at the sentence structure of the first paragraph.
9. What is Mailer's point in making the last sentence so long, so involved?

Words

10. What does Mailer mean by "no Harlem smoke, no devil swish"?
11. What does "existential moment" mean? What do "gyroscopic" and "sluggish whirlpool" mean?

Suggestions for Writing

A. Rewrite the last sentence in two different ways. Try first to use a series of short sentences, then your own preference.
B. Rewrite the sentence that begins, "Some unfamiliar current, now gyroscopic . . .".
C. Write a narrative paragraph about an event you recently participated in using Mailer's technique of writing in the third person. Now rewrite the paragraph using "I." Is there a difference? Do you simply change the pronoun reference or do other elements also have to change? Under what circumstances would each technique be more effective?

THIRTEEN

James Baldwin
(1924–   )

James Baldwin was born in Harlem, the son of fundamentalist religious parents. Baldwin followed his father's vocation and became, at fourteen, a preacher. At seventeen he abandoned the ministry and devoted himself to the craft of writing. He had been writing all along, from early childhood, but this writing had been discouraged by his family in favor of the religion that overshadowed it.

Baldwin received institutional support in the form of fellowships to help sustain him while he wrote and published his first two novels: *Go Tell It on the Mountain* (1953) and *Giovanni's Room* (1956), both of which were written abroad. Sandwiched between these works was a collection of essays, *Notes of a Native Son* (1955), which many readers consider his finest work. More fiction and essays followed: *Nobody Knows My Name* (essays, 1961), *Another Country* (a novel, 1962), *The Fire Next Time* (a polemical essay, 1963), *Going to Meet the Man* (stories, 1965)—and more.

In his early essays, for which he has received considerable praise, Baldwin struggled to define himself—as an American, as a writer, and as a black. (And for Baldwin the three are inextricably intertwined.) In coming to terms with what was, for him, the most difficult thing in his life—the fact that he was born a Negro, "and was forced, therefore, to effect some kind of truce with this reality"—Baldwin revealed himself to be a passionate and eloquent writer. His most frequent subject has been the relations between the races, about which he notes sardonically, "the color of my skin makes me, automatically, an expert."

Baldwin has written of pain, of rage and bitterness,

of persecution and paranoia, of identity and responsibility, of the relations between fathers and sons, and of the search for equanimity, understanding, and love. Regardless of title, occasion, and place of composition, his essays revolve around these subjects and often stress the importance of accepting and understanding one another, whatever our differences of race, sex, culture, religion, or intellectual disposition.

In "Autobiographical Notes" Baldwin explores the meaning and purpose of his vocation, which he describes simply as to be "a good writer," to get his work done. But the essay explores something more: the fact of Baldwin's blackness and its effect on both his life and his writing. Another essay that explores Baldwin's identity as a writer and as a black is "The Discovery of What It Means to Be an American," an essay whose title reveals a third dimension of Baldwin's identity—his American-ness. This last element of his identity Baldwin examines with thoroughness and acuity by developing a set of contrasts between the social and cultural contexts available to a writer in Europe and in America.

"Fifth Avenue Uptown: A Letter from Harlem" and "Notes of a Native Son" are devoted more specifically and more fully to the problem of race relations in America. In "Fifth Avenue" Baldwin works largely by description and comparison, providing commentary after he takes us on a "tour" of Harlem. His purpose is to help us understand the despair and hopelessness of the black ghetto. In "Notes of a Native Son" Baldwin is more strictly autobiographical than in any of his other essays. This piece combines a reminiscence of his father with an account of the day of his father's funeral. And it includes as well a narrative of an unpleasant incident that brought home to Baldwin a painful social fact concerning his race and an important and even more painful personal revelation of his feelings toward white people. As one of Baldwin's most impressive attempts to explore problematic social issues through personal experience, "Notes of a Native Son" fulfills what Baldwin sees as one of the most important obligations of the writer: "to examine attitudes, to go beneath the surface, to tap the source."

In the prefatory essay to the collection *Notes of a*

Native Son, Baldwin stressed the absolute priority of his personal experience for his writing. He put it this way: "One writes out of one thing only—one's own experience. . . . Everything depends on how relentlessly one forces from this experience the last drop, sweet or bitter, it can possibly give." That Baldwin's experience was bitter helped his writing as much as it may have hindered it. For he himself noted that "any writer . . . finds that the things which hurt him and the things which helped him cannot be divorced from each other." Baldwin's anguished experience thus was essential for his acute understanding of the hatred and bitterness in his own heart and of the bitter hatred at the heart of the racial antagonisms existing between many Americans.

Although Baldwin may have resigned from his religious ministry at seventeen, his writing, nonetheless, is strongly influenced by the style of pulpit oratory. It possesses the same strong emotional cast, a similar quality of exhortation, and a common vision of apocalypse. In its rhythm, in its imagery, and in its ethical imperatives, Baldwin's style reveals the influence of both the King James Bible and the storefront church—the two influences he specifically mentions as formative.

Preacher, polemicist, social critic, autobiographer, essayist—Baldwin brings together repeatedly, in deeply affecting ways, public issues and private agonies with relentless candor and inexorable logic. On the success of his best essays rest his fame and fate as a writer, on what he himself claims ·· the only real concern of the artist: "to recreate out of the disorder of life that order which is art."

Autobiographical Notes

---

1   **I** was born in Harlem thirty-one years ago. I began plotting novels at about the time I learned to read. The story of my childhood is the usual bleak fantasy. and we can dismiss it with the restrained

observation that I certainly would not consider living it again. In those days my mother was given to the exasperating and mysterious habit of having babies. As they were born, I took them over with one hand and held a book with the other. The children probably suffered, though they have since been kind enough to deny it, and in this way I read *Uncle Tom's Cabin* and *A Tale of Two Cities* over and over and over again; in this way, in fact, I read just about everything I could get my hands on—except the Bible, probably because it was the only book I was encouraged to read. I must also confess that I wrote—a great deal—and my first professional triumph, in any case, the first effort of mine to be seen in print, occurred at the age of twelve or thereabouts, when a short story I had written about the Spanish revolution won some sort of prize in an extremely short-lived church newspaper. I remember the story was censored by the lady editor, though I don't remember why, and I was outraged.

2   Also wrote plays, and songs, for one of which I received a letter of congratulations from Mayor La Guardia, and poetry, about which the less said, the better. My mother was delighted by all these goings-on, but my father wasn't; he wanted me to be a preacher. When I was fourteen I became a preacher, and when I was seventeen I stopped. Very shortly thereafter I left home. For God knows how long I struggled with the world of commerce and industry—I guess they would say they struggled with *me*—and when I was about twenty-one I had enough done of a novel to get a Saxton Fellowship. When I was twenty-two the fellowship was over, the novel turned out to be unsalable, and I started waiting on tables in a Village restaurant and writing book reviews—mostly, as it turned out, about the Negro problem, concerning which the color of my skin made me automatically an expert. Did another book, in company with photographer Theodore Pelatowski, about the store-front churches in Harlem. This book met exactly the same fate as my first—fellowship, but no sale. (It was a Rosenwald Fellowship.) By the time I was twenty-four I had decided to stop reviewing books about the Negro problem—which, by this time, was only slightly less horrible in print than it was in life—and I packed my bags and went to France, where I finished, God knows how, *Go Tell It on the Mountain.*

3   Any writer, I suppose, feels that the world into which he was born is nothing less than a conspiracy against the cultivation of his talent—which attitude certainly has a great deal to support it. On the other

hand, it is only because the world looks on his talent with such a frightening indifference that the artist is compelled to make his talent important. So that any writer, looking back over even so short a span of time as I am here forced to assess, finds that the things which hurt him and the things which helped him cannot be divorced from each other; he could be helped in a certain way only because he was hurt in a certain way; and his help is simply to be enabled to move from one conundrum to the next—one is tempted to say that he moves from one disaster to the next. When one begins looking for influences one finds them by the score. I haven't thought much about my own, not enough anyway; I hazard that the King James Bible, the rhetoric of the storefront church, something ironic and violent and perpetually understated in Negro speech—and something of Dickens' love for bravura—have something to do with me today; but I wouldn't stake my life on it. Likewise, innumerable people have helped me in many ways; but finally, I suppose, the most difficult (and most rewarding) thing in my life has been the fact that I was born a Negro and was forced, therefore, to effect some kind of truce with this reality. (Truce, by the way, is the best one can hope for.)

4   One of the difficulties about being a Negro writer (and this is not special pleading, since I don't mean to suggest that he has it worse than anybody else) is that the Negro problem is written about so widely. The bookshelves groan under the weight of information, and everyone therefore considers himself informed. And this information, furthermore, operates usually (generally, popularly) to reinforce traditional attitudes. Of traditional attitudes there are only two—For or Against—and I, personally, find it difficult to say which attitude has caused me the most pain. I am speaking as a writer; from a social point of view I am perfectly aware that the change from ill-will to good-will, however motivated, however imperfect, however expressed, is better than no change at all.

5   But it is part of the business of the writer—as I see it—to examine attitudes, to go beneath the surface, to tap the source. From this point of view the Negro problem is nearly inaccessible. It is not only written about so widely; it is written about so badly. It is quite possible to say that the price a Negro pays for becoming articulate is to find himself, at length, with nothing to be articulate about. ("You taught me language," says Caliban to Prospero, "and my profit on't is I know how to curse.") Consider: the tremendous social activity that this problem generates imposes on whites and Negroes alike the necessity of looking

forward, of working to bring about a better day. This is fine, it keeps the waters troubled; it is all, indeed, that has made possible the Negro's progress. Nevertheless, social affairs are not generally speaking the writer's prime concern, whether they ought to be or not; it is absolutely necessary that he establish between himself and these affairs a distance which will allow, at least, for clarity, so that before he can look forward in any meaningful sense, he must first be allowed to take a long look back. In the context of the Negro problem neither whites nor blacks, for excellent reasons of their own, have the faintest desire to look back; but I think that the past is all that makes the present coherent, and further, that the past will remain horrible for exactly as long as we refuse to assess it honestly.

6   I know, in any case, that the most crucial time in my own development came when I was forced to recognize that I was a kind of bastard of the West; when I followed the line of my past I did not find myself in Europe but in Africa. And this meant that in some subtle way, in a really profound way, I brought to Shakespeare, Bach, Rembrandt, to the stones of Paris, to the cathedral at Chartres, and to the Empire State Building, a special attitude. These were not really my creations, they did not contain my history; I might search in them in vain forever for any reflection of myself. I was an interloper; this was not my heritage. At the same time I had no other heritage which I could possibly hope to use—I had certainly been unfitted for the jungle or the tribe. I would have to appropriate these white centuries, I would have to make them mine—I would have to accept my special attitude, my special place in this scheme—otherwise I would have no place in any scheme. What was the most difficult was the fact that I was forced to admit something I had always hidden from myself, which the American Negro has had to hide from himself as the price of his public progress; that I hated and feared white people. This did not mean that I loved black people; on the contrary, I despised them, possibly because they failed to produce Rembrandt. In effect, I hated and feared the world. And this meant, not only that I thus gave the world an altogether murderous power over me, but also that in such a self-destroying limbo I could never hope to write.

7   One writes out of one thing only—one's own experience. Everything depends on how relentlessly one forces from this experience the last drop, sweet or bitter, it can possibly give. This is the only real concern of the artist, to recreate out of the disorder of life that order

which is art. The difficulty then, for me, of being a Negro writer was the fact that I was, in effect, prohibited from examining my own experience too closely by the tremendous demands and the very real dangers of my social situation.

8   I don't think the dilemma outlined above is uncommon. I do think, since writers work in the disastrously explicit medium of language, that it goes a little way towards explaining why, out of the enormous resources of Negro speech and life, and despite the example of Negro music, prose written by Negroes has been generally speaking so pallid and so harsh. I have not written about being a Negro at such length because I expect that to be my only subject, but only because it was the gate I had to unlock before I could hope to write about anything else. I don't think that the Negro problem in America can be even discussed coherently without bearing in mind its context; its context being the history, traditions, customs, the moral assumptions and preoccupations of the country; in short, the general social fabric. Appearances to the contrary, no one in America escapes its effects and everyone in America bears some responsibility for it. I believe this the more firmly because it is the overwhelming tendency to speak of this problem as though it were a thing apart. But in the work of Faulkner, in the general attitude and certain specific passages in Robert Penn Warren, and, most significantly, in the advent of Ralph Ellison, one sees the beginnings—at least—of a more genuinely penetrating search. Mr. Ellison, by the way, is the first Negro novelist I have ever read to utilize in language, and brilliantly, some of the ambiguity and irony of Negro life.

9   About my interests: I don't know if I have any, unless the morbid desire to own a sixteen-millimeter camera and make experimental movies can be so classified. Otherwise, I love to eat and drink—it's my melancholy conviction that I've scarcely ever had enough to eat (this is because it's *impossible* to eat enough if you're worried about the next meal)—and I love to argue with people who do not disagree with me too profoundly, and I love to laugh. I do *not* like bohemia, or bohemians, I do not like people whose principal aim is pleasure, and I do not like people who are *earnest* about anything. I don't like people who like me because I'm a Negro; neither do I like people who find in the same accident grounds for contempt. I love America more than any other country in the world, and, exactly for this reason, I insist on the right to criticize her perpetually. I think all theories are suspect, that the finest principles may have to be modified, or may even be pulverized

by the demands of life, and that one must find, therefore, one's own moral center and move through the world hoping that this center will guide one aright. I consider that I have many responsibilities, but none greater than this: to last, as Hemingway says, and get my work done. 10   I want to be an honest man and a good writer.

QUESTIONS

1. Baldwin, like many writers, says he read voraciously as a child. And he says also that he wrote a lot as well. Do you think there is any connection between these two facts? What is the relationship between reading and writing?

2. Does Baldwin seem honest in this brief overview of his life as a writer? Does he seem boastful? Modest? Paranoid? Cite specific sentences where you sense strongly his tone.

3. In paragraph 3 Baldwin discusses the effect of circumstance on a writer's talent. How, specifically, does he apply that point to his own situation? What is the single most important fact of his life—the fact that conditions, influences, and affects all others?

4. How do you explain this remark of Baldwin's: "I suppose the most difficult (and most rewarding) thing in my life has been the fact that I was born a Negro and was forced, therefore, to come to some kind of truce with reality. (Truce, by the way, is the best one can hope for.)" How does this statement tie in with his earlier statement that a writer "finds that the things which hurt him and the things which helped him cannot be divorced from each other"?

5. In paragraph 4 Baldwin makes a distinction between how the changes in the civil status of blacks affect him as a man and how they affect him as a writer. Why is or isn't this a valid and useful distinction?

6. What does Baldwin see as the business of the writer? Should a writer be more concerned with art and craft or with ideas and values, perhaps even with social change? Does Baldwin seem to stress one or the other? (See paragraphs 5 and 7.)

7. Baldwin states that "the past is all that makes the present coherent." From what you have learned about Baldwin in reading this essay, and perhaps others, how has this been true for him? Is it true for you? How?

8. Baldwin makes two complex and important points in paragraph 6. One concerns his attitude toward the cultural monuments of Western civilization. What is this point? Can it be extended to others besides blacks?

9. The second important point of paragraph 6 comes at the end, where Baldwin says he hated both white and black people. Why is this an important aspect of his experience?

10. In paragraph 8 Baldwin remarks: "I have not written about being a Negro at such length because I expect that to be my only subject, but only because it was the gate I had to unlock before I could write about anything else." Explain.

11. The last long paragraph of the essay (paragraph 9) contains a miscellany of things Baldwin does and does not like. Which do you think is the most important? Is there any relationship between this point and the final sentence of the essay: "I want to be an honest man and a good writer"?

12. Reread the first sentence of each paragraph. What do these opening sentences reveal about the organization of "Autobiographical Notes"?

Suggestions for Writing

A. Write your own "Autobiographical Notes," perhaps focusing on one central fact of your life such as your race, religion, ethnic background, special talents, place of birth. You could, if you wish, structure your essay as Baldwin structures his: facts in the opening and closing paragraphs, longer speculations and explanations in the middle.

B. Write an essay discussing, exploring, examining one of the ideas raised in Baldwin's essay—perhaps hatred, the white world, or blackness.

C. Compare the views on writing expressed by Didion in her essay "Why I Write" with those expressed here by Baldwin.

The Discovery of What It Means to Be an American

1   "It is a complex fate to be an American," Henry James observed, and the principal discovery an American writer makes in Europe is just how complex this fate is. America's history, her aspirations, her peculiar triumphs, her even more peculiar defeats, and her position in the world—yesterday and today—are all so profoundly and

stubbornly unique that the very word "America" remains a new almost completely undefined and extremely controversial proper noun. No one in the world seems to know exactly what it describes not even we motley millions who call ourselves Americans.

2   I left America because I doubted my ability to survive the fury of the color problem here. (Sometimes I still do.) I wanted to prevent myself from becoming *merely* a Negro; or, even, merely a Negro writer. I wanted to find out in what way the *specialness* of my experience could be made to connect me with other people instead of dividing me from them. (I was as isolated from Negroes as I was from whites, which is what happens when a Negro begins, at bottom, to believe what white people say about him.)

3   In my necessity to find the terms on which my experience could be related to that of others, Negroes and whites, writers and non-writers, I proved, to my astonishment, to be as American as any Texas G.I. And I found my experience was shared by every American writer I knew in Paris. Like me, they had been divorced from their origins, and it turned out to make very little difference that the origins of white Americans were European and mine were African—they were no more at home in Europe than I was.

4   The fact that I was the son of a slave and they were the sons of free men meant less, by the time we confronted each other on European soil, than the fact that we were both searching for our separate identities. When we had found these, we seemed to be saying, why, then, we would no longer need to cling to the shame and bitterness which had divided us so long.

5   It became terribly clear in Europe, as it never had been here, that we knew more about each other than any European ever could. And it also became clear that, no matter where our fathers had been born, or what they had endured, the fact of Europe had formed us both was part of our identity and part of our inheritance.

6   I had been in Paris a couple of years before any of this became clear to me. When it did, I, like many a writer before me upon the discovery that his props have all been knocked out from under him, suffered a species of breakdown and was carried off to the mountains of Switzerland. There, in that absolutely alabaster landscape, armed with two Bessie Smith records and a typewriter, I began to try to re-

create the life that I had first known as a child and from which I had spent so many years in flight.

7   It was Bessie Smith, through her tone and her cadence, who helped me to dig back to the way I myself must have spoken when I was a pickaninny, and to remember the things I had heard and seen and felt. I had buried them very deep. I had never listened to Bessie Smith in America (in the same way that, for years, I would not touch watermelon), but in Europe she helped to reconcile me to being a "nigger."

8   I do not think that I could have made this reconciliation here. Once I was able to accept my role—as distinguished, I must say, from my "place"—in the extraordinary drama which is America, I was released from the illusion that I hated America.

9   The story of what can happen to an American Negro writer in Europe simply illustrates, in some relief, what can happen to any American writer there. It is not meant, of course, to imply that it happens to them all, for Europe can be very crippling, too; and, anyway, a writer, when he has made his first breakthrough, has simply won a crucial skirmish in a dangerous, unending and unpredictable battle. Still, the breakthrough is important, and the point is that an American writer, in order to achieve it, very often has to leave this country.

10   The American writer, in Europe, is released, first of all, from the necessity of apologizing for himself. It is not until he *is* released from the habit of flexing his muscles and proving that he is just a "regular guy" that he realizes how crippling this habit has been. It is not necessary for him, there, to pretend to be something he is not, for the artist does not encounter in Europe the same suspicion he encounters here. Whatever the Europeans may actually think of artists, they have killed enough of them off by now to know that they are as real—and as persistent—as rain, snow, taxes or businessmen.

11   Of course, the reason for Europe's comparative clarity concerning the different functions of men in society is that European society has always been divided into classes in a way that American society never has been. A European writer considers himself to be part of an old and honorable tradition—of intellectual activity, of letters—and his choice of a vocation does not cause him any uneasy wonder as to whether or

not it will cost him all his friends. But this tradition does not exist in America.

12   On the contrary, we have a very deep-seated distrust of real intellectual effort (probably because we suspect that it will destroy, as I hope it does, that myth of America to which we cling so desperately). An American writer fights his way to one of the lowest rungs on the American social ladder by means of pure bull-headedness and an indescribable series of odd jobs. He probably *has* been a "regular fellow" for much of his adult life, and it is not easy for him to step out of that lukewarm bath.

13   We must, however, consider a rather serious paradox: though American society is more mobile than Europe's, it is easier to cut across social and occupational lines there than it is here. This has something to do, I think, with the problem of status in American life. Where everyone has status, it is also perfectly possible, after all, that no one has. It seems inevitable, in any case, that a man may become uneasy as to just what his status is.

14   But Europeans have lived with the idea of status for a long time. A man can be as proud of being a good waiter as of being a good actor, and, in neither case, feel threatened. And this means that the actor and the waiter can have a freer and more genuinely friendly relationship in Europe than they are likely to have here. The waiter does not feel, with obscure resentment, that the actor has "made it," and the actor is not tormented by the fear that he may find himself, tomorrow, once again a waiter.

15   This lack of what may roughly be called social paranoia causes the American writer in Europe to feel—almost certainly for the first time in his life—that he can reach out to everyone, that he is accessible to everyone and open to everything. This is an extraordinary feeling. He feels, so to speak, his own weight, his own value.

16   It is as though he suddenly came out of a dark tunnel and found himself beneath the open sky. And, in fact, in Paris, I began to see the sky for what seemed to be the first time. It was borne in on me—and it did not make me feel melancholy—that this sky had been there before I was born and would be there when I was dead. And it was up to me, therefore, to make of my brief opportunity the most that could be made.

17   I was born in New York, but have lived only in pockets of it. In Paris, I lived in all parts of the city—on the Right Bank and the Left,

among the bourgeoisie and among *les misérables,* and knew all kinds of people, from pimps and prostitutes in Pigalle to Egyptian bankers in Neuilly. This may sound extremely unprincipled or even obscurely immoral: I found it healthy. I love to talk to people, all kinds of people, and almost everyone, as I hope we still know, loves a man who loves to listen.

18   This perceptual dealing with people very different from myself caused a shattering in me of preconceptions I scarcely knew I held. The writer is meeting in Europe people who are not American, whose sense of reality is entirely different from his own. They may love or hate or admire or fear or envy this country—they see it, in any case, from another point of view, and this forces the writer to reconsider many things he had always taken for granted. This reassessment, which can be very painful, is also very valuable.

19   This freedom, like all freedom, has its dangers and its responsibilities. One day it begins to be borne in on the writer, and with great force, that he is living in Europe as an American. If he were living there as a European, he would be living on a different and far less attractive continent.

20   This crucial day may be the day on which an Algerian taxi-driver tells him how it feels to be an Algerian in Paris. It may be the day on which he passes a café terrace and catches a glimpse of the tense, intelligent and troubled face of Albert Camus. Or it may be the day on which someone asks him to explain Little Rock and he begins to feel that it would be simpler—and, corny as the words may sound, more honorable—to *go* to Little Rock than sit in Europe, on an American passport, trying to explain it.

21   This is a personal day, a terrible day, the day to which his entire sojourn has been tending. It is the day he realizes that there are no untroubled countries in this fearfully troubled world; that if he has been preparing himself for anything in Europe, he has been preparing himself—for America. In short, the freedom that the American writer finds in Europe brings him, full circle, back to himself, with the responsibility for his development where it always was: in his own hands.

22   Even the most incorrigible maverick has to be born somewhere. He may leave the group that produced him—he may be forced to—but nothing will efface his origins, the marks of which he carries with

everywhere. I think it is important to know this and even find it a matter for rejoicing, as the strongest people do, regardless of their station On this acceptance, literally, the life of a writer depends.

23 The charge has often been made against American writers that they do not describe society, and have no interest in it. They only describe individuals in opposition to it, or isolated from it. Of course, what the American writer is describing is his own situation. But what is *Anna Karenina* describing if not the tragic fate of the isolated individual, at odds with her time and place?

24 The real difference is that Tolstoy was describing an old and dense society in which everything seemed—to the people in it, though not to Tolstoy—to be fixed forever. And the book is a masterpiece because Tolstoy was able to fathom, and make us see, the hidden laws which really governed this society and made Anna's doom inevitable.

25 American writers do not have a fixed society to describe. The only society they know is one in which nothing is fixed and in which the individual must fight for his identity. This is a rich confusion, indeed, and it creates for the American writer unprecedented opportunities.

26 That the tensions of American life, as well as the possibilities, are tremendous is certainly not even a question. But these are dealt with in contemporary literature mainly compulsively; that is, the book is more likely to be a symptom of our tension than an examination of it. The time has come, God knows, for us to examine ourselves, but we can only do this if we are willing to free ourselves of the myth of America and try to find out what is really happening here.

27 Every society is really governed by hidden laws, by unspoken but profound assumptions on the part of the people, and ours is no exception. It is up to the American writer to find out what these laws and assumptions are. In a society much given to smashing taboos without thereby managing to be liberated from them, it will be no easy matter.

28 It is no wonder, in the meantime, that the American writer keeps running off to Europe. He needs sustenance for his journey and the best models he can find. Europe has what we do not have yet, a sense of the mysterious and inexorable limits of life, a sense, in a word, of tragedy. And we have what they sorely need: a new sense of life's possibilities.

29 In this endeavor to wed the vision of the Old World with that of the New, it is the writer, not the statesman, who is our strongest arm.

Though we do not wholly believe it yet, the interior life is a real life, and the intangible dreams of people have a tangible effect on the world.

QUESTIONS

Ideas

1. Why is to be an American a "complex fate"? Why, particularly, was it a complex fate for Baldwin?
2. What does Baldwin suggest about origins—about what and where a person is born and how he is raised? Why does he mention Bessie Smith?
3. Throughout the second and third parts of this essay, Baldwin contrasts Europe with America. What differences does he emphasize? And what are the reasons for and the focus of his contrasts?
4. How can living in another country help a writer—or any artist? (See especially paragraph 18.)

Organization

5. Why is the essay divided into three sections? What are the focus and emphasis of each?
6. How does Baldwin achieve coherence and continuity in this essay? Look closely at the first sentence of each paragraph of section two, for example. What words and phrases link the thought of each opening sentence to the idea of the paragraph before it? Look also at paragraph 20. Notice how Baldwin begins each sentence in that paragraph:

   This crucial day may be the day on which . . .
   It may be the day on which . . .
   Or it may be the day on which . . .

   And then paragraph 21:

   This is a personal day, a terrible day, the day to which . . .
   It is the day . . .

   Are these repetitions necessary? Helpful? Monotonous? Explain.

Sentences

7. Read paragraphs 11–15, noting particularly the length of Baldwin's sentences. In that five-paragraph stretch, do you find any consistency in the kind of sentence Baldwin uses or in how he begins and ends his paragraphs?

8. Baldwin uses balance and parallelism of syntax throughout the essay. Here are two brief examples:

This reassessment, which can be very painful,
is also   very valuable.

This freedom, like all freedom, has its dangers
                                    and its responsibilities.

In both of these simple sentences Baldwin interrupts the direct flow of syntax with interpolated phrases or clauses. These interruptions change the rhythm of the sentences, making them more emphatic. Analyze the repetitions, balances, and interruptions of the following two sequential sentences from paragraph 5:

It became terribly clear in Europe,
    as it never had been here,
        that we knew more about each other than any
        European ever could.

And it also became   clear   that,
        no matter where our fathers had been born,
    or   what   they   had endured,
            the fact of Europe had formed us both,
                                was part of our identity
                    and   part of our inheritance.

9. Baldwin varies the rhythm of his sentences and achieves emphasis and expansiveness by careful use of punctuation. Consider, for example, the commas in paragraphs 16–19. Read the sentences aloud, noting the pauses and the pacing. Try reading the same paragraphs as if the commas had been omitted.

10. Baldwin interrupts his sentences with the dash as well as with the comma. Consider the dashes in the following paragraphs: 1, 8, 10, 11, 15, 16, and 17. What kind of information is interpolated between the dashes? Can we remove the words between dashes, thus eliminating the internal punctuation of those sentences? In reading the sentences aloud, what tone of voice would you use and why?

11. In paragraphs 2 and 7, Baldwin could have used dashes or commas instead of parentheses. Try reading the sentences aloud, testing in turn parentheses, dashes, commas. What differences do you hear?

Words

12. Many words in the essay convey the meaning of division or separation.

Reread paragraphs 2–12, marking off these words as well as those suggesting an opposite idea, that of unity or reconciliation.

13. In paragraph 9, Baldwin uses a central metaphor—that for the writer life is a battle. What specific words and phrases carry the comparison between life and war? What is the point of the paragraph overall, and how do the comparisons help to convey it?

14. How would you describe Baldwin's language in this essay? Is it formal, informal, serious, casual, heavy, or light? How, for example, would you classify the language of the following phrases: "the mysterious and inexorable limits of life" (28), "incorrigible maverick" (22), "obscure resentment" (14)? Is the essay written primarily in this style of language? In another?

15. Why does Baldwin use quotation marks around the following words: "nigger" (7), "place" (8), "regular guy" (10), "made it" (14)?

Suggestions for Writing

A. Write an essay explaining what it means to be an American, especially what it means to be a particular kind of American, such as a Jewish or Chinese American or an American traveling abroad. Try to focus on your identity as this particular kind of American—or upon the reactions of other people to you as a particular kind of American. Has it been a complex fate for you to be an American? Explain.

B. Write an essay in which you identify and define yourself as belonging to a particular social group or as being one of a particular type of people. You might explain what it means, for example, for you to be a musician, an athlete, a feminist, a science fiction fan, or a moviegoer.

C. In the last section of "The Discovery of What It Means to Be an American," and especially in paragraphs 22–27, Baldwin comments on the American writer and his relation to American society. Apply any one of Baldwin's remarks on this subject to a writer whose work you know (perhaps Baldwin) and develop an essay either confirming or refuting Baldwin's assertion. You might take, for example, one of the following comments:

> The charge has often been made against American writers that they do not describe society, and have no interest in it. They only describe individuals in opposition to it, or isolated from it. (23)

> American writers do not have a fixed society to describe. The only society they know is one in which nothing is fixed and in which the individual must fight for his identity. (25)

> [The tensions of American life] are dealt with in contemporary literature mainly compulsively; that is, the book is more likely to be a symptom of our tension than an examination of it. (26)

Fifth Avenue, Uptown:
A Letter from Harlem

1   There is a housing project standing now where the house in which we grew up once stood, and one of those stunted city trees is snarling where our doorway used to be. This is on the rehabilitated side of the avenue. The other side of the avenue—for progress takes time— has not been rehabilitated yet and it looks exactly as it looked in the days when we sat with our noses pressed against the windowpane, longing to be allowed to go "across the street." The grocery store which gave us credit is still there, and there can be no doubt that it is still giving credit. The people in the project certainly need it—far more, indeed, than they ever needed the project. The last time I passed by, the Jewish proprietor was still standing among his shelves, looking sadder and heavier but scarcely any older. Farther down the block stands the shoe-repair store in which our shoes were repaired until reparation became impossible and in which, then, we bought all our "new" ones. The Negro proprietor is still in the window, head down, working at the leather.

2   These two, I imagine, could tell a long tale if they would (perhaps they would be glad to if they could), having watched so many, for so long, struggling in the fishhooks, the barbed wire, of this avenue.

3   The avenue is elsewhere the renowned and elegant Fifth. The area I am describing, which, in today's gang parlance, would be called "the turf," is bounded by Lenox Avenue on the west, the Harlem River on the east, 135th Street on the north, and 130th Street on the south. We never lived beyond these boundaries; this is where we grew up. Walking along 145th Street—for example—familiar as it is, and similar, does not have the same impact because I do not know any of the people on the block. But when I turn east on 131st Street and Lenox Avenue, there is first a soda-pop joint, then a shoeshine "parlor," then a grocery store, then a dry cleaners', then the houses. All along the street there are people who watched me grow up, people who grew up with me, people I watched grow up along with my brothers and sisters; and, sometimes in my arms, sometimes underfoot, sometimes at my shoul-

der—or on it—their children, a riot, a forest of children, who include my nieces and nephews.

4   When we reach the end of this long block, we find ourselves on wide, filthy, hostile Fifth Avenue, facing that project which hangs over the avenue like a monument to the folly, and the cowardice, of good intentions. All along the block, for anyone who knows it, are immense human gaps, like craters. These gaps are not created merely by those who have moved away, inevitably into some other ghetto; or by those who have risen, almost always into a greater capacity for self-loathing and self-delusion; or yet by those who, by whatever means—War II, the Korean war, a policeman's gun or billy, a gang war, a brawl, madness, an overdose of heroin, or, simply, unnatural exhaustion—are dead. I am talking about those who are left, and I am talking principally about the young. What are they doing? Well, some, a minority, are fanatical churchgoers, members of the more extreme of the Holy Roller sects. Many, many more are "moslems," by affiliation or sympathy, that is to say that they are united by nothing more—and nothing less— than a hatred of the white world and all its works. They are present, for example, at every Buy Black street-corner meeting—meetings in which the speaker urges his hearers to cease trading with white men and establish a separate economy. Neither the speaker nor his hearers can possibly do this, of course, since Negroes do not own General Motors or RCA or the A & P, nor, indeed, do they own more than a wholly insufficient fraction of anything else in Harlem (those who *do* own anything are more interested in their profits than in their fellows). But these meetings nevertheless keep alive in the participators a certain pride of bitterness without which, however futile this bitterness may be, they could scarcely remain alive at all. Many have given up. They stay home and watch the TV screen, living on the earnings of their parents, cousins, brothers, or uncles, and only leave the house to go to the movies or to the nearest bar. "How're you making it?" one may ask, running into them along the block, or in the bar. "Oh, I'm TV-ing it"; with the saddest, sweetest, most shamefaced of smiles, and from a great distance. This distance one is compelled to respect; anyone who has traveled so far will not easily be dragged again into the world. There are further retreats, of course, than the TV screen or the bar. There are those who are simply sitting on their stoops, "stoned," animated for a moment only, and hideously, by the approach of someone who may

lend them the money for a "fix." Or by the approach of someone from whom they can purchase it, one of the shrewd ones, on the way to prison or just coming out.

5   And the others, who have avoided all of these deaths, get up in the morning and go downtown to meet "the man." They work in the white man's world all day and come home in the evening to this fetid block. They struggle to instill in their children some private sense of honor or dignity which will help the child to survive. This means, of course, that they must struggle, stolidly, incessantly, to keep this sense alive in themselves, in spite of the insults, the indifference, and the cruelty they are certain to encounter in their working day. They patiently browbeat the landlord into fixing the heat, the plaster, the plumbing; this demands prodigious patience; nor is patience usually enough. In trying to make their hovels habitable, they are perpetually throwing good money after bad. Such frustration, so long endured, is driving many strong, admirable men and women whose only crime is color to the very gates of paranoia.

6   One remembers them from another time—playing handball in the playground, going to church, wondering if they were going to be promoted at school. One remembers them going off to war—gladly, to escape this block. One remembers their return. Perhaps one remembers their wedding day. And one sees where the girl is now—vainly looking for salvation from some other embittered, trussed, and struggling boy— and sees the all-but-abandoned children in the streets.

7   Now I am perfectly aware that there are other slums in which white men are fighting for their lives, and mainly losing. I know that blood is also flowing through those streets and that the human damage there is incalculable. People are continually pointing out to me the wretchedness of white people in order to console me for the wretchedness of blacks. But an itemized account of the American failure does not console me and it should not console anyone else. That hundreds of thousands of white people are living, in effect, no better than the "niggers" is not a fact to be regarded with complacency. The social and moral bankruptcy suggested by this fact is of the bitterest, most terrifying kind.

8   The people, however, who believe that this democratic anguish has some consoling value are always pointing out that So-and-So, white, and So-and-So, black, rose from the slums into the big time. The existence—the public existence—of, say, Frank Sinatra and Sammy

Davis, Jr. proves to them that America is still the land of opportunity and that inequalities vanish before the determined will. It proves nothing of the sort. The determined will is rare—at the moment, in this country, it is unspeakably rare—and the inequalities suffered by the many are in no way justified by the rise of a few. A few have always risen—in every country, every era, and in the teeth of regimes which can by no stretch of the imagination be thought of as free. Not all of these people, it is worth remembering, left the world better than they found it. The determined will is rare, but it is not invariably benevolent. Furthermore, the American equation of success with the big times reveals an awful disrespect for human life and human achievement. This equation has placed our cities among the most dangerous in the world and has placed our youth among the most empty and most bewildered. The situation of our youth is not mysterious. Children have never been very good at listening to their elders, but they have never failed to imitate them. They must, they have no other models. That is exactly what our children are doing. They are imitating our immorality, our disrespect for the pain of others.

9   All other slum dwellers, when the bank account permits it, can move out of the slum and vanish altogether from the eye of persecution. No Negro in this country has ever made that much money and it will be a long time before any Negro does. The Negroes in Harlem, who have no money, spend what they have on such gimcracks as they are sold. These include "wider" TV screens, more "faithful" hi-fi sets, more "powerful" cars, all of which, of course, are obsolete long before they are paid for. Anyone who has ever struggled with poverty knows how extremely expensive it is to be poor; and if one is a member of a captive population, economically speaking, one's feet have simply been placed on the treadmill forever. One is victimized, economically, in a thousand ways—rent, for example, or car insurance. Go shopping one day in Harlem—for anything—and compare Harlem prices and quality with those downtown.

10   The people who have managed to get off this block have only got as far as a more respectable ghetto. This respectable ghetto does not even have the advantages of the disreputable one—friends, neighbors, a familiar church, and friendly tradesmen; and it is not, moreover, in the nature of any ghetto to remain respectable long. Every Sunday, people who have left the block take the lonely ride back, dragging their increasingly discontented children with them. They spend the day talk-

ing, not always with words, about the trouble they've seen and the trouble—one must watch their eyes as they watch their children—they are only too likely to see. For children do not like ghettos. It takes them nearly no time to discover exactly why they are there.

11 The projects in Harlem are hated. They are hated almost as much as policemen, and this is saying a great deal. And they are hated for the same reason: both reveal, unbearably, the real attitude of the white world, no matter how many liberal speeches are made, no matter how many lofty editorials are written, no matter how many civil-rights commissions are set up.

12 The projects are hideous, of course, there being a law, apparently respected throughout the world, that popular housing shall be as cheerless as a prison. They are lumped all over Harlem, colorless, bleak, high, and revolting. The wide windows look out on Harlem's invincible and indescribable squalor: the Park Avenue railroad tracks, around which, about forty years ago, the present dark community began; the unrehabilitated houses, bowed down, it would seem, under the great weight of frustration and bitterness they contain; the dark, the ominous schoolhouses from which the child may emerge maimed, blinded, hooked, or enraged for life; and the churches, churches, block upon block of churches, niched in the walls like cannon in the walls of a fortress. Even if the administration of the projects were not so insanely humiliating (for example: one must report raises in salary to the management, which will then eat up the profit by raising one's rent; the management has the right to know who is staying in your apartment; the management can ask you to leave, at their discretion), the projects would still be hated because they are an insult to the meanest intelligence.

13 Harlem got its first private project, Riverton*—which is now, naturally, a slum—about twelve years ago because at that time Negroes

---

*The inhabitants of Riverton were much embittered by this description; they have, apparently, forgotten how their project came into being; and have repeatedly informed me that I cannot possibly be referring to Riverton, but to another housing project which is directly across the street. It is quite clear, I think, that I have no interest in accusing any individuals or families of the depredations herein described: but neither can I deny the evidence of my own eyes. Nor do I blame anyone in Harlem for making the best of a dreadful bargain. But anyone who lives in Harlem and imagines that he has *not* struck this bargain, or that what he takes to be his status (in whose eyes?) protects him against the common pain, demoralization, and danger, is simply self deluded.

were not allowed to live in Stuyvesant Town. Harlem watched Riverton go up, therefore, in the most violent bitterness of spirit, and hated it long before the builders arrived. They began hating it at about the time people began moving out of their condemned houses to make room for this additional proof of how thoroughly the white world despised them. And they had scarcely moved in, naturally, before they began smashing windows, defacing walls, urinating in the elevators, and fornicating in the playgrounds. Liberals, both white and black, were appalled at the spectacle. I was appalled by the liberal innocence—or cynicism, which comes out in practice as much the same thing. Other people were delighted to be able to point to proof positive that nothing could be done to better the lot of the colored people. They were, and are, right in one respect: that nothing can be done as long as they are treated like colored people. The people in Harlem know they are living there because white people do not think they are good enough to live anywhere else. No amount of "improvement" can sweeten this fact. Whatever money is now being earmarked to improve this, or any other ghetto, might as well be burnt. A ghetto can be improved in one way only: out of existence.

14   Similarly, the only way to police a ghetto is to be oppressive. None of the Police Commissioner's men, even with the best will in the world, have any way of understanding the lives led by the people they swagger about in twos and threes controlling. Their very presence is an insult, and it would be, even if they spent their entire day feeding gumdrops to children. They represent the force of the white world, and that world's real intentions are, simply, for that world's criminal profit and ease, to keep the black man corraled up here, in his place. The badge, the gun in the holster, and the swinging club make vivid what will happen should his rebellion become overt. Rare, indeed, is the Harlem citizen, from the most circumspect church member to the most shiftless adolescent, who does not have a long tale to tell of police incompetence, injustice, or brutality. I myself have witnessed and endured it more than once. The businessmen and racketeers also have a story. And so do the prostitutes. (And this is not, perhaps, the place to discuss Harlem's very complex attitude toward black policemen, nor the reasons, according to Harlem, that they are nearly all downtown.)

15   It is hard, on the other hand, to blame the policeman, blank, good-natured, thoughtless, and insuperably innocent, for being such a perfect representative of the people he serves. He, too, believes in good

intentions and is astounded and offended when they are not taken for the deed. He has never, himself, done anything for which to be hated—which of us has?—and yet he is facing, daily and nightly, people who would gladly see him dead, and he knows it. There is no way for him not to know it: there are few things under heaven more unnerving than the silent, accumulating contempt and hatred of a people. He moves through Harlem, therefore, like an occupying soldier in a bitterly hostile country; which is precisely what, and where, he is, and is the reason he walks in twos and threes. And he is not the only one who knows why he is always in company: the people who are watching him know why, too. Any street meeting, sacred or secular, which he and his colleagues uneasily cover has as its explicit or implicit burden the cruelty and injustice of the white domination. And these days, of course, in terms increasingly vivid and jubilant, it speaks of the end of that domination. The white policeman standing on a Harlem street corner finds himself at the very center of the revolution now occurring in the world. He is not prepared for it—naturally, nobody is—and, what is possibly much more to the point, he is exposed, as few white people are, to the anguish of the black people around him. Even if he is gifted with the merest mustard grain of imagination, something must seep in. He cannot avoid observing that some of the children, in spite of their color, remind him of children he has known and loved, perhaps even of his own children. He knows that he certainly does not want *his* children living this way. He can retreat from his uneasiness in only one direction: into a callousness which very shortly becomes second nature. He becomes more callous, the population becomes more hostile, the situation grows more tense, and the police force is increased. One day, to everyone's astonishment, someone drops a match in the powder keg and everything blows up. Before the dust has settled or the blood congealed, editorials, speeches, and civil-rights commissions are loud in the land, demanding to know what happened. What happened is that Negroes want to be treated like men.

16   *Negroes want to be treated like men:* a perfectly straightforward statement, containing only seven words. People who have mastered Kant, Hegel, Shakespeare, Marx, Freud, and the Bible find this statement utterly impenetrable. The idea seems to threaten profound, barely conscious assumptions. A kind of panic paralyzes their features, as though they found themselves trapped on the edge of a steep place. I

once tried to describe to a very well-known American intellectual the conditions among Negroes in the South. My recital disturbed him and made him indignant; and he asked me in perfect innocence, "Why don't all the Negroes in the South move North?" I tried to explain what *has* happened, unfailingly, whenever a significant body of Negroes move North. They do not escape Jim Crow: they merely encounter another, not-less-deadly variety. They do not move to Chicago, they move to the South Side; they do not move to New York, they move to Harlem. The pressure within the ghetto causes the ghetto walls to expand, and this expansion is always violent. White people hold the line as long as they can, and in as many ways as they can, from verbal intimidation to physical violence. But inevitably the border which has divided the ghetto from the rest of the world falls into the hands of the ghetto. The white people fall back bitterly before the black horde; the landlords make a tidy profit by raising the rent, chopping up the rooms, and all but dispensing with the upkeep; and what has once been a neighborhood turns into a "turf." This is precisely what happened when the Puerto Ricans arrived in their thousands—and the bitterness thus caused is, as I write, being fought out all up and down those streets.

17   Northerners indulge in an extremely dangerous luxury. They seem to feel that because they fought on the right side during the Civil War, and won, they have earned the right merely to deplore what is going on in the South, without taking any responsibility for it; and that they can ignore what is happening in Northern cities because what is happening in Little Rock or Birmingham is worse. Well, in the first place, it is not possible for anyone who has not endured both to know which is "worse." I know Negroes who prefer the South and white Southerners, because "At least there, you haven't got to play any guessing games!" The guessing games referred to have driven more than one Negro into the narcotics ward, the madhouse, or the river. I know another Negro, a man very dear to me, who says, with conviction and with truth, "The spirit of the South is the spirit of America." He was born in the North and did his military training in the South. He did not, as far as I can gather, find the South "worse"; he found it, if anything, all too familiar. In the second place, though, even if Birmingham *is* worse, no doubt Johannesburg, South Africa, beats it by several miles, and Buchenwald was one of the worst things that ever happened in the entire history of the world. The world has never lacked for horrifying examples; but I

do not believe that these examples are meant to be used as justification for our own crimes. This perpetual justification empties the heart of all human feeling. The emptier our hearts become, the greater will be our crimes. Thirdly, the South is not merely an embarrassingly backward region, but a part of this country, and what happens there concerns every one of us.

18   As far as the color problem is concerned, there is but one great difference between the Southern white and the Northerner: the Southerner remembers, historically and in his own psyche, a kind of Eden in which he loved black people and they loved him. Historically, the flaming sword laid across this Eden is the Civil War. Personally, it is the Southerner's sexual coming of age, when, without any warning, unbreakable taboos are set up between himself and his past. Everything, thereafter, is permitted him except the love he remembers and has never ceased to need. The resulting, indescribable torment affects every Southern mind and is the basis of the Southern hysteria.

19   None of this is true for the Northerner. Negroes represent nothing to him personally, except, perhaps, the dangers of carnality. He never sees Negroes. Southerners see them all the time. Northerners never think about them whereas Southerners are never really thinking of anything else. Negroes are, therefore, ignored in the North and are under surveillance in the South, and suffer hideously in both places. Neither the Southerner nor the Northerner is able to look on the Negro simply as a man. It seems to be indispensable to the national self-esteem that the Negro be considered either as a kind of ward (in which case we are told how many Negroes, comparatively, bought Cadillacs last year and how few, comparatively, were lynched), or as a victim (in which case we are promised that he will never vote in our assemblies or go to school with our kids). They are two sides of the same coin and the South will not change—*cannot* change—until the North changes. The country will not change until it re-examines itself and discovers what it really means by freedom. In the meantime, generations keep being born, bitterness is increased by incompetence, pride, and folly, and the world shrinks around us.

20   It is a terrible, an inexorable, law that one cannot deny the humanity of another without diminishing one's own: in the face of one's victim, one sees oneself. Walk through the streets of Harlem and see what we, this nation have become.

QUESTIONS

Ideas

1. What is implied by the title of the essay? Consider individually three elements of the title: Fifth Avenue, Harlem, Letter.
2. What is Baldwin's purpose in writing this essay, this letter from Harlem? Who is his implied audience? What is his major point?
3. In paragraph 4 Baldwin suggests that the projects are "a monument to the folly, and the cowardice, of good intentions." What does he mean? And whose "folly," "cowardice," and "good intentions" is he referring to?
4. In describing Harlem, or at least in describing the section he knows well, Baldwin contrasts what he remembers from his childhood with what he sees later as an adult. What does he remember, what does he see, and what is the significance of the difference?
5. Twice in "Fifth Avenue" Baldwin considers counterarguments, alternate explanations for why slums exist (paragraphs 8 and 13). What are Baldwin's views about this problem, and what are the counterviews? Which do you find more persuasive and why?
6. Children are mentioned five times in the essay—in paragraphs 3, 5, 6, 10, and 15. What common thread ties together the references to children? What point does Baldwin make when he mentions them?
7. What does Baldwin say about the relationship between the police and the people of Harlem? Reread paragraph 15, then outline the pattern of cause and effect that Baldwin provides as an explanation for why riots occur.
8. Why does Baldwin discuss the South? Why does he bring South Africa and Buchenwald into the argument? What justification for crime does he offer? Is it persuasive? Is it valid? Why or why not?
9. The final paragraph of the essay makes one of Baldwin's most important points: that in diminishing other people we diminish ourselves. Explain how this is or is not true.

Organization

10. One way of looking at the structure of "Fifth Avenue" is to see it as composed of two major parts: paragraphs 1–10 and paragraphs 11–20 Provide a title for each part and explain how the two parts are related
11 Another way of looking at the organization of the essay is to see it as oscillating between description and argumentation How are the descriptive sections related to the polemical sections?

12. Baldwin structures part of the essay as a walk through Harlem. Where does the tour begin and end? How does Baldwin lead into and slide out of this section?

Sentences

3. Paragraph 2 is only a single sentence. Why? Would this sentence be better attached to paragraph 1 or 3? Explain.

14. The last sentence of paragraph 5 packs in many details. Why does Baldwin cram them into one sentence? Would these details be more effectively presented in a series of short sentences? How are the length, shape, and style of the sentence as Baldwin wrote it related to the point he makes in it?

15. The end of paragraph 15 and the beginning of paragraph 16 contain the same sentence—or part of the same sentence. What does Baldwin gain by repeating it this way?

16. Read the final sentences of the following paragraphs: 7–13, 15, 19–20. What do you notice about how Baldwin concludes his paragraphs?

Words

17. What is the tone of the opening paragraphs? Consider especially the word "rehabilitated" (paragraphs 2 and 3) and the clause "for progress takes time" (paragraph 1).

18. Paragraphs 4–6 contain highly charged, emotional language. Which words carry especially strong connotations? Of these, which have positive and which negative connotations? What point does Baldwin make with this strongly connotative language?

19. Throughout the essay Baldwin places many words in quotation marks. Explain the tone of each word, especially the following: "the turf" (3), "moslems" (4), "the man" (5), "powerful" (9), and "improvement" (13). Explain also the tone and point of the sentences quoted in paragraphs 4, 16, and 17.

Suggestions for Writing

A. Write a polemical essay about a social problem, using a place as the central focus. Try to mix description of the location of the problem with an analysis of how it got that way. Decide whether you want primarily to persuade readers to do something about the problem or whether you want simply to enable them to better understand it. Decide on the relative proportions of description, explanation, and analysis—but only after you write a couple of rough drafts.

B. Argue with or support Baldwin. Choose one of the following statements from "Fifth Avenue" and write an essay confirming or refuting Baldwin's idea.

Negroes want to be treated like men. (15, 16)

It is a terrible, an inexorable, law that one cannot deny the humanity of another without diminishing one's own: in the face of one's victim, one sees oneself. (20)

Children have never been very good at listening to their elders, but they have never failed to imitate them. (8)

Notes of a Native Son

I

1   On the 29th of July, in 1943, my father died. On the same day, a few hours later, his last child was born. Over a month before this, while all our energies were concentrated in waiting for these events, there had been, in Detroit, one of the bloodiest race riots of the century. A few hours after my father's funeral, while he lay in state in the undertaker's chapel, a race riot broke out in Harlem. On the morning of the 3rd of August, we drove my father to the graveyard through a wilderness of smashed plate glass.

2   The day of my father's funeral had also been my nineteenth birthday. As we drove him to the graveyard, the spoils of injustice, anarchy, discontent, and hatred were all around us. It seemed to me that God himself had devised, to mark my father's end, the most sustained and brutally dissonant of codas. And it seemed to me, too, that the violence which rose all about us as my father left the world had been devised as a corrective for the pride of his eldest son. I had declined to believe in that apocalypse which had been central to my father's vision; very well, life seemed to be saying, here is something that will

certainly pass for an apocalypse until the real thing comes along. I had inclined to be contemptuous of my father for the conditions of his life, for the conditions of our lives. When his life had ended I began to wonder about that life and also, in a new way, to be apprehensive about my own.

3   I had not known my father very well. We had got on badly, partly because we shared, in our different fashions, the vice of stubborn pride. When he was dead I realized that I had hardly ever spoken to him. When he had been dead a long time I began to wish I had. It seems to be typical of life in America, where opportunities, real and fancied, are thicker than anywhere else on the globe, that the second generation has no time to talk to the first. No one, including my father, seems to have known exactly how old he was, but his mother had been born during slavery. He was of the first generation of free men. He, along with thousands of other Negroes, came North after 1919 and I was part of that generation which had never seen the landscape of what Negroes sometimes call the Old Country.

4   He had been born in New Orleans and had been a quite young man there during the time that Louis Armstrong, a boy, was running errands for the dives and honky-tonks of what was always presented to me as one of the most wicked of cities—to this day, whenever I think of New Orleans, I also helplessly think of Sodom and Gomorrah. My father never mentioned Louis Armstrong, except to forbid us to play his records; but there was a picture of him on our wall for a long time. One of my father's strong-willed female relatives had placed it there and forbade my father to take it down. He never did, but he eventually maneuvered her out of the house and when, some years later, she was in trouble and near death, he refused to do anything to help her.

5   He was, I think, very handsome. I gather this from photographs and from my own memories of him, dressed in his Sunday best and on his way to preach a sermon somewhere, when I was little. Handsome, proud, and ingrown, "like a toe-nail," somebody said. But he looked to me, as I grew older, like pictures I had seen of African tribal chieftains: he really should have been naked, with war-paint on and barbaric mementos, standing among spears. He could be chilling in the pulpit and indescribably cruel in his personal life and he was certainly the most bitter man I have ever met; yet it must be said that there was something else in him, buried in him, which lent him his tremendous power and, even, a rather crushing charm. It had something to do with

his blackness, I think—he was very black—with his blackness and his beauty, and with the fact that he knew that he was black but did not know that he was beautiful. He claimed to be proud of his blackness but it had also been the cause of much humiliation and it had fixed bleak boundaries to his life. He was not a young man when we were growing up and he had already suffered many kinds of ruin; in his outrageously demanding and protective way he loved his children, who were black like him and menaced, like him; and all these things some-times showed in his face when he tried, never to my knowledge with any success, to establish contact with any of us. When he took one of his children on his knee to play, the child always became fretful and began to cry; when he tried to help one of us with our homework the absolutely unabating tension which emanated from him caused our minds and our tongues to become paralyzed, so that he, scarcely know-ing why, flew into a rage and the child, not knowing why, was punished. If it ever entered his head to bring a surprise home for his children, it was, almost unfailingly, the wrong surprise and even the big water-melons he often brought home on his back in the summertime led to the most appalling scenes. I do not remember, in all those years, that one of his children was ever glad to see him come home. From what I was able to gather of his early life, it seemed that this inability to establish contact with other people had always marked him and had been one of the things which had driven him out of New Orleans. There was something in him, therefore, groping and tentative, which was never expressed and which was buried with him. One saw it most clearly when he was facing new people and hoping to impress them. But he never did, not for long. We went from church to smaller and more improbable church, he found himself in less and less demand as a minister, and by the time he died none of his friends had come to see him for a long time. He had lived and died in an intolerable bitterness of spirit and it frightened me, as we drove him to the graveyard through those unquiet, ruined streets, to see how powerful and over-flowing this bitterness could be and to realize that this bitterness now was mine.

6   When he died I had been away from home for a little over a year. In that year I had had time to become aware of the meaning of all my father's bitter warnings, had discovered the secret of his proudly pursed lips and rigid carriage: I had discovered the weight of white people in the world. I saw that this had been for my ancestors and now would

be for me an awful thing to live with and that the bitterness which had
helped to kill my father could also kill me.

7   He had been ill a long time—in the mind, as we now realized,
reliving instances of his fantastic intransigence in the new light of his
affliction and endeavoring to feel a sorrow for him which never, quite,
came true. We had not known that he was being eaten up by paranoia,
and the discovery that his cruelty, to our bodies and our minds, had
been one of the symptoms of his illness was not, then, enough to enable
us to forgive him. The younger children felt, quite simply, relief that
he would not be coming home anymore. My mother's observation that
it was he, after all, who had kept them alive all these years meant
nothing because the problems of keeping children alive are not real for
children. The older children felt, with my father gone, that they could
invite their friends to the house without fear that their friends would
be insulted or, as had sometimes happened with me, being told that
their friends were in league with the devil and intended to rob our
family of everything we owned. (I didn't fail to wonder, and it made
me hate him, what on earth we owned that anybody else would want.)

8   His illness was beyond all hope of healing before anyone realized
that he was ill. He had always been so strange and had lived, like a
prophet, in such unimaginably close communion with the Lord that
his long silences which were punctuated by moans and hallelujahs and
snatches of old songs while he sat at the living-room window never
seemed odd to us. It was not until he refused to eat because, he said,
his family was trying to poison him that my mother was forced to accept
as a fact what had, until then, been only an unwilling suspicion. When
he was committed, it was discovered that he had tuberculosis and, as
it turned out, the disease of his mind allowed the disease of his body
to destroy him. For the doctors could not force him to eat, either, and,
though he was fed intravenously, it was clear from the beginning that
there was no hope for him.

9   In my mind's eye I could see him, sitting at the window, locked
up in his terrors; hating and fearing every living soul including his
children who had betrayed him, too, by reaching towards the world
which had despised him. There were nine of us. I began to wonder
what it could have felt like for such a man to have had nine children
whom he could barely feed. He used to make little jokes about our
poverty, which never, of course, seemed very funny to us; they could
not have seemed very funny to him, either, or else our all too feeble

response to them would never have caused such rages. He spent great energy and achieved, to our chagrin, no small amount of success in keeping us away from the people who surrounded us, people who had all-night rent parties to which we listened when we should have been sleeping, people who cursed and drank and flashed razor blades on Lenox Avenue. He could not understand why, if they had so much energy to spare, they could not use it to make their lives better. He treated almost everybody on our block with a most uncharitable asperity and neither they, nor, of course, their children were slow to reciprocate.

10   The only white people who came to our house were welfare workers and bill collectors. It was almost always my mother who dealt with them, for my father's temper, which was at the mercy of his pride, was never to be trusted. It was clear that he felt their very presence in his home to be a violation: this was conveyed by his carriage, almost ludicrously stiff, and by his voice, harsh and vindictively polite. When I was around nine or ten I wrote a play which was directed by a young, white schoolteacher, a woman, who then took an interest in me, and gave me books to read and, in order to corroborate my theatrical bent, decided to take me to see what she somewhat tactlessly referred to as "real" plays. Theatergoing was forbidden in our house, but, with the really cruel intuitiveness of a child, I suspected that the color of this woman's skin would carry the day for me. When, at school, she suggested taking me to the theater, I did not, as I might have done if she had been a Negro, find a way of discouraging her, but agreed that she should pick me up at my house one evening. I then, very cleverly, left all the rest to my mother, who suggested to my father, as I knew she would, that it would not be very nice to let such a kind woman make the trip for nothing. Also, since it was a schoolteacher, I imagine that my mother countered the idea of sin with the idea of "education," which word, even with my father, carried a kind of bitter weight.

11   Before the teacher came my father took me aside to ask *why* she was coming, what *interest* she could possibly have in our house, in a boy like me. I said I didn't know but I, too, suggested that it had something to do with education. And I understood that my father was waiting for me to say something—I didn't quite know what; perhaps that I wanted his protection against this teacher and her "education." I said none of these things and the teacher came and we went out. It was clear, during the brief interview in our living room, that my father was agreeing very much against his will and that he would have refused

permission if he had dared. The fact that he did not dare caused me to despise him: I had no way of knowing that he was facing in that living room a wholly unprecedented and frightening situation.

12   Later, when my father had been laid off from his job, this woman became very important to us. She was really a very sweet and generous woman and went to a great deal of trouble to be of help to us, particularly during one awful winter. My mother called her by the highest name she knew. she said she was a "christian ' My father could scarcely disagree but during the four or five years of our relatively close association he never trusted her and was always trying to surprise in her open, Midwestern face the genuine, cunningly hidden, and hideous motivation. In later years, particularly when it began to be clear that this "education" of mine was going to lead me to perdition, he became more explicit and warned me that my white friends in high school were not really my friends and that I would see, when I was older, how white people would do anything to keep a Negro down. Some of them could be nice, he admitted, but none of them were to be trusted and most of them were not even nice. The best thing was to have as little to do with them as possible. I did not feel this way and I was certain, in my innocence, that I never would.

13   But the year which preceded my father's death had made a great change in my life. I had been living in New Jersey, working in defense plants, working and living among southerners, white and black. I knew about the south, of course, and about how southerners treated Negroes and how they expected them to behave, but it had never entered my mind that anyone would look at me and expect *me* to behave that way. I learned in New Jersey that to be a Negro meant, precisely, that one was never looked at but was simply at the mercy of the reflexes the color of one's skin caused in other people. I acted in New Jersey as I had always acted, that is as though I thought a great deal of myself— I had to *act* that way—with results that were, simply, unbelievable. I had scarcely arrived before I had earned the enmity, which was extraordinarily ingenious, of all my superiors and nearly all my co-workers. In the beginning, to make matters worse, I simply did not know what was happening. I did not know what I had done, and I shortly began to wonder what *anyone* could possibly do, to bring about such unanimous, active, and unbearably vocal hostility. I knew about jim-crow but I had never experienced it. I went to the same self-service restaurant three times and stood with all the Princeton boys before the counter,

waiting for a hamburger and coffee; it was always an extraordinarily long time before anything was set before me; but it was not until the fourth visit that I learned that, in fact, nothing had ever been set before me: I had simply picked something up. Negroes were not served there, I was told, and they had been waiting for me to realize that I was always the only Negro present. Once I was told this, I determined to go there all the time. But now they were ready for me and, though some dreadful scenes were subsequently enacted in that restaurant, I never ate there again.

14   It was the same story all over New Jersey, in bars, bowling alleys, diners, places to live. I was always being forced to leave, silently, or with mutual imprecations. I very shortly became notorious and children giggled behind me when I passed and their elders whispered or shouted—they really believed that I was mad. And it did begin to work on my mind, of course; I began to be afraid to go anywhere and to compensate for this I went places to which I really should not have gone and where, God knows, I had no desire to be. My reputation in town naturally enhanced my reputation at work and my working day became one long series of acrobatics designed to keep me out of trouble. I cannot say that these acrobatics succeeded. It began to seem that the machinery of the organization I worked for was turning over, day and night, with but one aim: to eject me. I was fired once, and contrived, with the aid of a friend from New York, to get back on the payroll; was fired again, and bounced back again. It took a while to fire me for the third time, but the third time took. There were no loopholes anywhere. There was not even any way of getting back inside the gates.

15   That year in New Jersey lives in my mind as though it were the year during which, having an unsuspected predilection for it, I first contracted some dread, chronic disease, the unfailing symptom of which is a kind of blind fever, a pounding in the skull and fire in the bowels. Once this disease is contracted, one can never be really carefree again, for the fever, without an instant's warning, can recur at any moment. It can wreck more important things than race relations. There is not a Negro alive who does not have this rage in his blood—one has the choice, merely, of living with it consciously or surrendering to it. As for me, this fever has recurred in me, and does, and will until the day I die.

16   My last night in New Jersey, a white friend from New York took me to the nearest big town, Trenton, to go to the movies and have a

few drinks. As it turned out, he also saved me from, at the very least, a violent whipping. Almost every detail of that night stands out very clearly in my memory. I even remember the name of the movie we saw because its title impressed me as being so patly ironical. It was a movie about the German occupation of France, starring Maureen O'Hara and Charles Laughton and called *This Land Is Mine.* I remember the name of the diner we walked into when the movie ended: it was the "American Diner." When we walked in the counterman asked what we wanted and I remember answering with the casual sharpness which had become my habit: "We want a hamburger and a cup of coffee, what do you think we want?" I do not know why, after a year of such rebuffs, I so completely failed to anticipate his answer, which was, of course, "We don't serve Negroes here." This reply failed to discompose me, at least for the moment. I made some sardonic comment about the name of the diner and we walked out into the streets.

17   This was the time of what was called the "brown-out," when the lights in all American cities were very dim. When we re-entered the streets something happened to me which had the force of an optical illusion, or a nightmare. The streets were very crowded and I was facing north. People were moving in every direction but it seemed to me, in that instant, that all of the people I could see, and many more than that, were moving toward me, against me, and that everyone was white. I remember how their faces gleamed. And I felt, like a physical sensation, a *click* at the nape of my neck as though some interior string connecting my head to my body had been cut. I began to walk. I heard my friend call after me, but I ignored him. Heaven only knows what was going on in his mind, but he had the good sense not to touch me— I don't know what would have happened if he had—and to keep me in sight. I don't know what was going on in my mind, either; I certainly had no conscious plan. I wanted to do something to crush these white faces, which were crushing me. I walked for perhaps a block or two until I came to an enormous, glittering, and fashionable restaurant in which I knew not even the intercession of the Virgin would cause me to be served. I pushed through the doors and took the first vacant seat I saw, at a table for two, and waited.

18   I do not know how long I waited and I rather wonder, until today, what I could possibly have looked like. Whatever I looked like, I frightened the waitress who shortly appeared, and the moment she appeared

all of my fury flowed towards her. I hated her for her white face, and for her great, astounded, frightened eyes. I felt that if she found a black man so frightening I would make her fright worth-while.

19   She did not ask me what I wanted, but repeated, as though she had learned it somewhere, "We don't serve Negroes here." She did not say it with the blunt, derisive hostility to which I had grown so accustomed, but, rather, with a note of apology in her voice, and fear. This made me colder and more murderous than ever. I felt I had to do something with my hands. I wanted her to come close enough for me to get her neck between my hands.

20   So I pretended not to have understood her, hoping to draw her closer. And she did step a very short step closer, with her pencil poised incongruously over her pad, and repeated the formula: ". . . don't serve Negroes here."

21   Somehow, with the repetition of that phrase, which was already ringing in my head like a thousand bells of a nightmare, I realized that she would never come any closer and that I would have to strike from a distance. There was nothing on the table but an ordinary water-mug half full of water, and I picked this up and hurled it with all my strength at her. She ducked and it missed her and shattered against the mirror behind the bar. And, with that sound, my frozen blood abruptly thawed, I returned from wherever I had been, I *saw*, for the first time, the restaurant, the people with their mouths open, already, as it seemed to me, rising as one man, and I realized what I had done, and where I was, and I was frightened. I rose and began running for the door. A round, potbellied man grabbed me by the nape of the neck just as I reached the doors and began to beat me about the face. I kicked him and got loose and ran into the streets. My friend whispered, "*Run!*" and I ran.

22   My friend stayed outside the restaurant long enough to misdirect my pursuers and the police, who arrived, he told me, at once. I do not know what I said to him when he came to my room that night. I could not have said much. I felt, in the oddest, most awful way, that I had somehow betrayed him. I lived it over and over and over again, the way one relives an automobile accident after it has happened and one finds oneself alone and safe. I could not get over two facts, both equally difficult for the imagination to grasp, and one was that I could have been murdered. But the other was that I had been ready to commit

murder. I saw nothing very clearly but I did see this: that my life, my *real* life, was in danger, and not from anything other people might do but from the hatred I carried in my own heart.

II

23   I had returned home around the second week in June—in great haste because it seemed that my father's death and my mother's confinement were both but a matter of hours. In the case of my mother, it soon became clear that she had simply made a miscalculation. This had always been her tendency and I don't believe that a single one of us arrived in the world, or has since arrived anywhere else, on time. But none of us dawdled so intolerably about the business of being born as did my baby sister. We sometimes amused ourselves, during those endless, stifling weeks, by picturing the baby sitting within in the safe, warm dark, bitterly regretting the necessity of becoming a part of our chaos and stubbornly putting it off as long as possible. I understood her perfectly and congratulated her on showing such good sense so soon. Death, however, sat as purposefully at my father's bedside as life stirred within my mother's womb and it was harder to understand why he so lingered in that long shadow. It seemed that he had bent, and for a long time, too, all of his energies towards dying. Now death was ready for him but my father held back.

24   All of Harlem, indeed, seemed to be infected by waiting. I had never before known it to be so violently still. Racial tensions throughout this country were exacerbated during the early years of the war, partly because the labor market brought together hundreds of thousands of ill-prepared people and partly because Negro soldiers, regardless of where they were born, received their military training in the south. What happened in defense plants and army camps had repercussions, naturally, in every Negro ghetto. The situation in Harlem had grown bad enough for clergymen, policemen, educators, politicians, and social workers to assert in one breath that there was no "crime wave" and to offer, in the very next breath, suggestions as to how to combat it. These suggestions always seemed to involve playgrounds, despite the fact that racial skirmishes were occurring in the playgrounds, too. Playground or not, crime wave or not, the Harlem police force had been augmented in March, and the unrest grew—perhaps, in fact, partly as a result of

the ghetto's instinctive hatred of policemen. Perhaps the most revealing news item, out of the steady parade of reports of muggings, stabbings, shootings, assaults, gang wars, and accusations of police brutality is the item concerning six Negro girls who set upon a white girl in the subway because, as they all too accurately put it, she was stepping on their toes. Indeed she was, all over the nation

25   I had never before been so aware of policemen, on foot, on horseback, on corners, everywhere, always two by two. Nor had I ever been so aware of small knots of people. They were on stoops and on corners and in doorways, and what was striking about them, I think, was that they did not seem to be talking. Never, when I passed these groups, did the usual sound of a curse or a laugh ring out and neither did there seem to be any hum of gossip. There was certainly, on the other hand, occurring between them communication extraordinarily intense. Another thing that was striking was the unexpected diversity of the people who made up these groups. Usually, for example, one would see a group of sharpies standing on the street corner, jiving the passing chicks; or a group of older men, usually, for some reason, ir the vicinity of a barber shop, discussing baseball scores, or the numbers or making rather chilling observations about women they had known Women, in a general way, tended to be seen less often together—unless they were church women, or very young girls, or prostitutes met togethei for an unprofessional instant. But that summer I saw the strangest combinations: large, respectable, churchly matrons standing on the stoops or the corners with their hair tied up, together with a girl in sleazy satin whose face bore the marks of gin and the razor, or heavy-set, abrupt, no-nonsense older men, in company with the most disreputable and fanatical "race" men, or these same "race" men with the sharpies, or these sharpies with the churchly women. Seventh Day Adventists and Methodists and Spiritualists seemed to be hobnobbing with Holyrollers and they were all, alike, entangled with the most flagrant disbelievers; something heavy in their stance seemed to indicate that they had all, incredibly, seen a common vision, and on each face there seemed to be the same strange, bitter shadow.

26   The churchly women and the matter-of-fact, no-nonsense men had children in the Army. The sleazy girls they talked to had lovers there, the sharpies and the "race" men had friends and brothers there. It would have demanded an unquestioning patriotism, happily as uncommon in this country as it is undesirable, for these people not to

have been disturbed by the bitter letters they received, by the newspaper stories they read, not to have been enraged by the posters, then to be found all over New York, which described the Japanese as "yellow-bellied Japs." It was only the "race" men, to be sure, who spoke ceaselessly of being revenged—how this vengeance was to be exacted was not clear—for the indignities and dangers suffered by Negro boys in uniform; but everybody felt a directionless, hopeless bitterness, as well as that panic which can scarcely be suppressed when one knows that a human being one loves is beyond one's reach, and in danger. This helplessness and this gnawing uneasiness does something, at length, to even the toughest mind. Perhaps the best way to sum all this up is to say that the people I knew felt, mainly, a peculiar kind of relief when they knew that their boys were being shipped out of the south, to do battle overseas. It was, perhaps, like feeling that the most dangerous part of a dangerous journey had been passed and that now, even if death should come, it would come with honor and without the complicity of their countrymen. Such a death would be, in short, a fact with which one could hope to live.

27　　It was on the 28th of July, which I believe was a Wednesday, that I visited my father for the first time during his illness and for the last time in his life. The moment I saw him I knew why I had put off this visit so long. I had told my mother that I did not want to see him because I hated him. But this was not true. It was only that I *had* hated him and I wanted to hold on to this hatred. I did not want to look on him as a ruin: it was not a ruin I had hated. I imagine that one of the reasons people cling to their hates so stubbornly is because they sense, once hate is gone, that they will be forced to deal with pain.

28　　We traveled out to him, his older sister and myself, to what seemed to be the very end of a very Long Island. It was hot and dusty and we wrangled, my aunt and I, all the way out, over the fact that I had recently begun to smoke and, as she said, to give myself airs. But I knew that she wrangled with me because she could not bear to face the fact of her brother's dying. Neither could I endure the reality of her despair, her unstated bafflement as to what had happened to her brother's life, and her own. So we wrangled and I smoked and from time to time she fell into a heavy reverie. Covertly, I watched her face, which was the face of an old woman; it had fallen in, the eyes were sunken and lightless; soon she would be dying, too.

29　　In my childhood—it had not been so long ago—I had thought her beautiful. She had been quick-witted and quick-moving and very generous with all the children and each of her visits had been an event. At one time one of my brothers and myself had thought of running away to live with her. Now she could no longer produce out of her handbag some unexpected and yet familiar delight. She made me feel pity and revulsion and fear. It was awful to realize that she no longer caused me to feel affection. The closer we came to the hospital the more querulous she became and at the same time, naturally, grew more dependent on me. Between pity and guilt and fear I began to feel that there was another me trapped in my skull like a jack-in-the-box who might escape my control at any moment and fill the air with screaming.

30   She began to cry the moment we entered the room and she saw him lying there, all shriveled and still, like a little black monkey. The great, gleaming apparatus which fed him and would have compelled him to be still even if he had been able to move brought to mind, not beneficence, but torture; the tubes entering his arm made me think of pictures I had seen when a child, of Gulliver, tied down by the pygmies on that island. My aunt wept and wept, there was a whistling sound in my father's throat; nothing was said; he could not speak. I wanted to take his hand, to say something. But I do not know what I could have said, even if he could have heard me. He was not really in that room with us, he had at last really embarked on his journey; and though my aunt told me that he said he was going to meet Jesus, I did not hear anything except that whistling in his throat. The doctor came back and we left, into that unbearable train again, and home. In the morning came the telegram saying that he was dead. Then the house was suddenly full of relatives, friends, hysteria, and confusion and I quickly left my mother and the children to the care of those impressive women, who, in Negro communities at least, automatically appear at times of bereavement armed with lotions, proverbs, and patience, and an ability to cook. I went downtown. By the time I returned, later the same day, my mother had been carried to the hospital and the baby had been born.

III

31   For my father's funeral I had nothing black to wear and this posed a nagging problem all day long. It was one of those problems,

simple, or impossible of solution, to which the mind insanely clings in order to avoid the mind's real trouble. I spent most of that day at the downtown apartment of a girl I knew, celebrating my birthday with whiskey and wondering what to wear that night. When planning a birthday celebration one naturally does not expect that it will be up against competition from a funeral and this girl had anticipated taking me out that night, for a big dinner and a night club afterwards. Sometime during the course of that long day we decided that we would go out anyway, when my father's funeral service was over. I imagine *I* decided it, since, as the funeral hour approached, it became clearer and clearer to me that I would not know what to do with myself when it was over. The girl, stifling her very lively concern as to the possible effects of the whiskey on one of my father's chief mourners, concentrated on being conciliatory and practically helpful. She found a black shirt for me somewhere and ironed it and, dressed in the darkest pants and jacket I owned, and slightly drunk, I made my way to my father's funeral.

32   The chapel was full, but not packed, and very quiet. There were, mainly, my father's relatives, and his children, and here and there I saw faces I had not seen since childhood, the faces of my father's one-time friends. They were very dark and solemn now, seeming somehow to suggest that they had known all along that something like this would happen. Chief among the mourners was my aunt, who had quarreled with my father all his life; by which I do not mean to suggest that her mourning was insincere or that she had not loved him. I suppose that she was one of the few people in the world who had, and their incessant quarreling proved precisely the strength of the tie that bound them. The only other person in the world, as far as I knew, whose relationship to my father rivaled my aunt's in depth was my mother, who was not there.

33   It seemed to me, of course, that it was a very long funeral. But it was, if anything, a rather shorter funeral than most, nor, since there were no overwhelming, uncontrollable expressions of grief, could it be called—if I dare to use the word—successful. The minister who preached my father's funeral sermon was one of the few my father had still been seeing as he neared his end. He presented to us in his sermon a man whom none of us had ever seen—a man thoughtful, patient, and forbearing, a Christian inspiration to all who knew him, and a model for

his children. And no doubt the children, in their disturbed and guilty
state, were almost ready to believe this; he had been remote enough to
be anything and, anyway, the shock of the incontrovertible, that it was
really our father lying up there in that casket, prepared the mind for
anything. His sister moaned and this grief-stricken moaning was taken
as corroboration. The other faces held a dark, non-committal thought-
fulness. This was not the man they had known, but they had scarcely
expected to be confronted with *him*; this was, in a sense deeper than
questions of fact, the man they had not known, and the man they had
not known may have been the real one. The real man, whoever he
had been, had suffered and now he was dead: this was all that was sure
and all that mattered now. Every man in the chapel hoped that when
his hour came he, too, would be eulogized, which is to say forgiven,
and that all of his lapses, greeds, errors, and strayings from the truth
would be invested with coherence and looked upon with charity. This
was perhaps the last thing human beings could give each other and it
was what they demanded, after all, of the Lord. Only the Lord saw the
midnight tears, only He was present when one of His children, moaning
and wringing hands, paced up and down the room. When one slapped
one's child in anger the recoil in the heart reverberated through heaven
and became part of the pain of the universe. And when the children
were hungry and sullen and distrustful and one watched them, daily,
growing wilder, and further away, and running headlong into danger,
it was the Lord who knew what the charged heart endured as the strap
was laid to the backside; the Lord alone who knew what one *would*
have said if one had had, like the Lord, the gift of the living word. It
was the Lord who knew of the impossibility every parent in that room
faced: how to prepare the child for the day when the child would be
despised and how to *create* in the child—by what means?—a stronger
antidote to this poison than one had found for oneself. The avenues,
side streets, bars, billiard halls, hospitals, police stations, and even the
playgrounds of Harlem—not to mention the houses of correction, the
jails, and the morgue—testified to the potency of the poison while
remaining silent as to the efficacy of whatever antidote, irresistibly
raising the question of whether or not such an antidote existed; raising,
which was worse, the question of whether or not an antidote was desirable; perhaps poison should be fought with poison. With these several
schisms in the mind and with more terrors in the heart than could be

named, it was better not to judge the man who had gone down under an impossible burden. It was better to remember: *Thou knowest this man's fall; but thou knowest not his wrassling.*

34   While the preacher talked and I watched the children—years of changing their diapers, scrubbing them, slapping them, taking them to school, and scolding them had had the perhaps inevitable result of making me love them, though I am not sure I knew this then—my mind was busily breaking out with a rash of disconnected impressions. Snatches of popular songs, indecent jokes, bits of books I had read, movie sequences, faces, voices, political issues—I thought I was going mad; all these impressions suspended, as it were, in the solution of the faint nausea produced in me by the heat and liquor. For a moment I had the impression that my alcoholic breath, inefficiently disguised with chewing gum, filled the entire chapel. Then someone began singing one of my father's favorite songs and, abruptly, I was with him, sitting on his knee, in the hot, enormous, crowded church which was the first church we attended. It was the Abyssinia Baptist Church on 138th Street. We had not gone there long. With this image, a host of others came. I had forgotten, in the rage of my growing up, how proud my father had been of me when I was little. Apparently, I had had a voice and my father had liked to show me off before the members of the church. I had forgotten what he had looked like when he was pleased but now I remembered that he had always been grinning with pleasure when my solos ended. I even remembered certain expressions on his face when he teased my mother—had he loved her? I would never know. And when had it all begun to change? For now it seemed that he had not always been cruel. I remembered being taken for a haircut and scraping my knee on the footrest of the barber's chair and I remembered my father's face as he soothed my crying and applied the stinging iodine. Then I remembered our fights, fights which had been of the worst possible kind because my technique had been silence.

35   I remembered the one time in all our life together when we had really spoken to each other.

36   It was on a Sunday and it must have been shortly before I left home. We were walking, just the two of us, in our usual silence, to or from church. I was in high school and had been doing a lot of writing and I was, at about this time, the editor of the high school magazine. But I had also been a Young Minister and had been preaching from

the pulpit. Lately, I had been taking fewer engagements and preached as rarely as possible. It was said in the church, quite truthfully, that I was "cooling off."

37   My father asked me abruptly, "You'd rather write than preach, wouldn't you?"

38   I was astonished at his question—because it was a real question. I answered, "Yes."

39   That was all we said. It was awful to remember that that was all we had *ever* said.

40   The casket now was opened and the mourners were being led up the aisle to look for the last time on the deceased. The assumption was that the family was too overcome with grief to be allowed to make this journey alone and I watched while my aunt was led to the casket and, muffled in black, and shaking, led back to her seat. I disapproved of forcing the children to look on their dead father, considering that the shock of his death, or, more truthfully, the shock of death as a reality, was already a little more than a child could bear, but my judgment in this matter had been overruled and there they were, bewildered and frightened and very small, being led, one by one, to the casket. But there is also something very gallant about children at such moments. It has something to do with their silence and gravity and with the fact that one cannot help them. Their legs, somehow, seem *exposed*, so that it is at once incredible and terribly clear that their legs are all they have to hold them up.

41   I had not wanted to go to the casket myself and I certainly had not wished to be led there, but there was no way of avoiding either of these forms. One of the deacons led me up and I looked on my father's face. I cannot say that it looked like him at all. His blackness had been equivocated by powder and there was no suggestion in that casket of what his power had or could have been. He was simply an old man dead, and it was hard to believe that he had ever given anyone either joy or pain. Yet, his life filled that room. Further up the avenue his wife was holding his newborn child. Life and death so close together, and love and hatred, and right and wrong, said something to me which I did not want to hear concerning man, concerning the life of man.

42   After the funeral, while I was downtown desperately celebrating my birthday, a Negro soldier, in the lobby of the Hotel Braddock, got into a fight with a white policeman over a Negro girl. Negro girls, white

policemen, in or out of uniform, and Negro males—in or out of uniform—were part of the furniture of the lobby of the Hotel Braddock and this was certainly not the first time such an incident had occurred. It was destined, however, to receive an unprecedented publicity, for the fight between the policeman and the soldier ended with the shooting of the soldier. Rumor, flowing immediately to the streets outside, stated that the soldier had been shot in the back, an instantaneous and revealing invention, and that the soldier had died protecting a Negro woman. The facts were somewhat different—for example, the soldier had not been shot in the back, and was not dead, and the girl seems to have been as dubious a symbol of womanhood as her white counterpart in Georgia usually is, but no one was interested in the facts. They preferred the invention because this invention expressed and corroborated their hates and fears so perfectly. It is just as well to remember that people are always doing this. Perhaps many of those legends, including Christianity, to which the world clings began their conquest of the world with just some such concerted surrender to distortion. The effect, in Harlem, of this particular legend was like the effect of a lit match in a tin of gasoline. The mob gathered before the doors of the Hotel Braddock simply began to swell and to spread in every direction, and Harlem exploded.

43   The mob did not cross the ghetto lines. It would have been easy, for example, to have gone over Morningside Park on the west side or to have crossed the Grand Central railroad tracks at 125th Street on the east side, to wreak havoc in white neighborhoods. The mob seems to have been mainly interested in something more potent and real than the white face, that is, in white power, and the principal damage done during the riot of the summer of 1943 was to white business establishments in Harlem. It might have been a far bloodier story, of course, if, at the hour the riot began, these establishments had still been open. From the Hotel Braddock the mob fanned out, east and west along 125th Street, and for the entire length of Lenox, Seventh, and Eighth avenues. Along each of these avenues, and along each major side street—116th, 125th, 135th, and so on—bars, stores, pawnshops, restaurants, even little luncheonettes had been smashed open and entered and looted—looted, it might be added, with more haste than efficiency. The shelves really looked as though a bomb had struck them. Cans of beans and soup and dog food, along with toilet paper, corn flakes,

sardines and milk tumbled every which way, and abandoned cash reg-
isters and cases of beer leaned crazily out of the splintered windows and
were strewn along the avenues. Sheets, blankets, and clothing of every
description formed a kind of path, as though people had dropped them
while running. I truly had not realized that Harlem *had* so many stores
until I saw them all smashed open; the first time the word *wealth* ever
entered my mind in relation to Harlem was when I saw it scattered in
the streets. But one's first, incongruous impression of plenty was countered immediately by an impression of waste. None of this was doing
anybody any good. It would have been better to have left the plate glass
as it had been and the goods lying in the stores.

44   It would have been better, but it would also have been intolerable,
for Harlem had needed something to smash. To smash something is
the ghetto's chronic need. Most of the time it is the members of the
ghetto who smash each other, and themselves. But as long as the ghetto
walls are standing there will always come a moment when these outlets
do not work. That summer, for example, it was not enough to get into
a fight on Lenox Avenue, or curse out one's cronies in the barber shops.
If ever, indeed, the violence which fills Harlem's churches, pool halls,
and bars erupts outward in a more direct fashion, Harlem and its citizens
are likely to vanish in an apocalyptic flood. That this is not likely to
happen is due to a great many reasons, most hidden and powerful
among them the Negro's real relation to the white American. This
relation prohibits, simply, anything as uncomplicated and satisfactory
as pure hatred. In order really to hate white people, one has to blot so
much out of the mind—and the heart—that this hatred itself becomes
an exhausting and self-destructive pose. But this does not mean, on the
other hand, that love comes easily: the white world is too powerful, too
complacent, too ready with gratuitous humiliation, and, above all, too
ignorant and too innocent for that. One is absolutely forced to make
perpetual qualifications and one's own reactions are always canceling
each other out. It is this, really, which has driven so many people mad,
both white and black. One is always in the position of having to decide
between amputation and gangrene. Amputation is swift but time may
prove that the amputation was not necessary—or one may delay the
amputation too long. Gangrene is slow, but it is impossible to be sure
that one is reading one's symptoms right. The idea of going through
life as a cripple is more than one can bear, and equally unbearable is

the risk of swelling up slowly, in agony, with poison. And the trouble, finally, is that the risks are real even if the choices do not exist.

45   "But as for me and my house," my father had said, "we will serve the Lord." I wondered, as we drove him to his resting place, what this line had meant for him. I had heard him preach it many times. I had preached it once myself, proudly giving it an interpretation different from my father's. Now the whole thing came back to me, as though my father and I were on our way to Sunday school and I were memorizing the golden text: *And if it seem evil unto you to serve the Lord, choose you this day whom you will serve; whether the gods which your fathers served that were on the other side of the flood, or the gods of the Amorites, in whose land ye dwell: but as for me and my house, we will serve the Lord.* I suspected in these familiar lines a meaning which had never been there for me before. All of my father's texts and songs, which I had decided were meaningless, were arranged before me at his death like empty bottles, waiting to hold the meaning which life would give them for me. This was his legacy: nothing is ever escaped. That bleakly memorable morning I hated the unbelievable streets and the Negroes and whites who had, equally, made them that way. But I knew that it was folly, as my father would have said, this bitterness was folly. It was necessary to hold on to the things that mattered. The dead man mattered, the new life mattered; blackness and whiteness did not matter; to believe that they did was to acquiesce in one's own destruction. Hatred, which could destroy so much, never failed to destroy the man who hated and this was an immutable law.

46   It began to seem that one would have to hold in the mind forever two ideas which seemed to be in opposition. The first idea was acceptance, the acceptance, totally without rancor, of life as it is, and men as they are: in the light of this idea, it goes without saying that injustice is a commonplace. But this did not mean that one could be complacent, for the second idea was of equal power: that one must never, in one's own life, accept these injustices as commonplace but must fight them with all one's strength. This fight begins, however, in the heart and it now had been laid to my charge to keep my own heart free of hatred and despair. This intimation made my heart heavy and, now that my father was irrecoverable, I wished that he had been beside me so that I could have searched his face for the answers which only the future would give me now.

QUESTIONS

Ideas

1. In section I Baldwin describes his father and characterizes him. Where does this begin and end? What does Baldwin say about his father? What observations about his father does Baldwin make in section III, and how do they echo his observations and descriptions of section I?

2. In the descriptions of his father, Baldwin also reveals things about himself, particularly, of course, about his relationship with his father. What kind of relationship was it? What is Baldwin's final assessment of his father— of his life and character?

3. We might say that Baldwin uses description and narration throughout the essay in the service of argumentation. What point does Baldwin make in narrating the restaurant incident? What point is made by the description of Harlem as he rides through in a car on the day of his father's funeral?

4. In the second paragraph of section II, Baldwin moves out in thought. Up to that point—in section I and in the first paragraph of section II—he has been describing his family. What new considerations are introduced, and how are they related to the facts and actions presented in section I?

5. Trace the sequence of ideas—and the pattern of cause and effect—through paragraphs 24, 25, and 26. What is Baldwin's point here?

6. What ironies of circumstance does Baldwin indicate in the first paragraph of section III? What other ironies do you detect in the essay?

7. What is the point of mentioning who attended the funeral? What does Baldwin mean when he suggests that his aunt was one of the few people in the world who had loved his father, and yet "their incessant quarreling proved precisely the strength of their tie"?

8. In paragraph 45 Baldwin brings together the personal and the social, the private and public, his father and Harlem. What conclusions does he draw about his relationship to his father and about the hatred and rage and bitterness that sparked the riots? Explain the final sentence of the paragraph: "Hatred, which could destroy so much, never failed to destroy the man who hated and this was an immutable law."

9. "Notes of a Native Son" ends with a pair of contradictory impulses, with two irreconcilable ideas. What are they, and how does Baldwin both emphasize them and tie them in with what has gone before?

Organization

10. The essay is divided into three major sections. Provide a title for each, explain the main point of each, and comment on the relationship among the three sections.

11. Take any one of the three sections and examine its structure. Explain how it begins, where it goes, and how it ends. Explain how each of its parts fits into the whole section and into the entire essay.

12. As you reread the first paragraph of section II, think back or look back to the opening of section I. What connections do you notice? Why does Baldwin begin section II this way? How does this opening tie in to the essay as a whole?

13. The third paragraph of section III (33) splits in half. In the first part Baldwin mentions that his father was eulogized, that the preacher's description of the man he and his brothers and sisters had known was strikingly different from the reality. Yet Baldwin finds comfort and meaning in this discrepancy. Why? In the second part of this paragraph Baldwin himself eulogizes his father—but not only his father. He presents an imaginative and sympathetic account of how his father and other men under similar pressures of prejudice, fear, insecurity, and bitterness must have felt and why they must be forgiven this bitter hatred. Find the place where Baldwin shifts from one concern to the other. How, specifically, does he accomplish the shift?

14. How does Baldwin manage the shift from the preacher's sermon to happier memories of his childhood? (Consider paragraph 34.) Paragraphs 35–39 form a unit. What is the point of this highly condensed segment, and why is it so brief?

Sentences

15. Baldwin ends many of his paragraphs with emphatic, vivid sentences. Read through the final sentences of all the paragraphs in section I in sequence. What do you notice?

16. What balances and parallels does Baldwin include in his opening sentences? How do the rhythm and the word order of the third and fourth sentences continue the rhythm and structure established in the first and second sentences? What is the effect of this structural and rhythmic patterning? "or convenience, here are the first four sentences of the essay:

> On the 29th of July, in 1943, my father died. On the same day, a few hours later, his last child was born. Over a month before this, while all our energies were concentrated in waiting for these events, there had

been, in Detroit, one of the bloodiest race riots of the century. A few hours after my father's funeral, while he lay in state in the undertaker's chapel, a race riot broke out in Harlem. On the morning of the 3rd of August, we drove my father to the graveyard through a wilderness of smashed plate glass.

17. In paragraph 2 of section I Baldwin again uses parallel sentences. Look especially at sentences 3 and 4 and at sentences 5 through 7. Read the sentences aloud, noting pacing and pauses.

18. Reread one of Baldwin's paragraphs, mentally deleting all material between commas. What happens to the sound and the weight of the sentences?

19. Here is one of Baldwin's paragraphs without punctuation. Punctuate it, then compare your version with those of other students and with Baldwin's punctuation. What differences in tone, rhythm, and emphasis do you notice?

> My friend stayed outside the restaurant long enough to misdirect my pursuers and the police who arrived he told me at once I do not know what I said to him when he came to my room that night I could not have said much I felt in the oddest most awful way that I had somehow betrayed him I lived it over and over and over again the way one relives an automobile accident after it has happened and one finds oneself alone and safe I could not get over two facts both equally difficult for the imagination to grasp and one was that I could have been murdered but the other was that I had been ready to commit murder I saw nothing very clearly but I did see this that my life my real life was in danger and not from anything other people might do but from the hatred I carried in my own heart.

20. In the third paragraph from the end of the essay, Baldwin uses two unusual sentence patterns: a sentence beginning with an infinitive; another sentence beginning with a nominalization:

> *infinitive:* To smash something is the ghetto's chronic need.
> *nominalization:* That this is not likely to happen is due to a great many reasons, most hidden and powerful among them the Negro's real relation to the white American.

In this paragraph also, Baldwin mixes and varies his sentences in length, form, and opening phrasing. Examine the paragraph from these standpoints.

21. The final paragraph of the essay achieves coherence, continuity, and emphasis, mainly by careful repetition of words and phrases. Circle or underline the words and phrases that establish this coherence and continuity.

Words

22. There are two vocabularies in "Notes of a Native Son": simple, common words; more formal and unusual longer words, usually of Latin derivation. Read paragraphs 2 and 3, marking off words of each type. Then find a passage of five or six sentences where Baldwin blends the two kinds of diction. What is the effect of the mixture?

23. In the narrative portions of the essay, especially in paragraphs 17, 21, and 22, Baldwin employs comparisons. What is the point of each?

24. Explain how Baldwin uses imagery—especially comparisons—to make his point in paragraphs 28, 29, 30, and 45.

25. Read the following passage, noting especially its sound effects of assonance, consonance, rhyme, and alliteration:

> He could be chilling in the pulpit and indescribably cruel in his personal life and he was certainly the most bitter man I have ever met; yet it must be said that there was something else in him, buried in him, which lent him .s tremendous power and, even, a rather crushing charm. It had something to do with his blackness, I think—he was very black—with his blackness and beauty, and with the fact that he knew that he was black but did not know that he was beautiful. He claimed to be proud of his blackness but it had also been the cause of much humiliation and it had fixed bleak boundaries to his life.

26. In paragraph 43 Baldwin describes the effects of the looting. What comparisons does he use and how effective are they? In the next paragraph (44) he uses the language of disease to express the consequences for blacks of race relations in the United States. What psychological difference is Baldwin suggesting by means of describing the physical differences between gangrene and amputation?

Suggestions for Writing

A. Baldwin ends section I with a narrative account of an episode at a New Jersey restaurant. He begins this account with an idea and he ends it with one. Write an essay in which you describe something that happened to you, something that made you aware of yourself, or something that made you aware of a social, political, religious, or racial situation. Begin and end your account, as Baldwin does, with an idea.

B. Write your own "Notes of a Native Sor or Daughter." Try to come to terms with your ethnic or racial heritage and with your place in relation to the society of which you are a part.

C. Describe one of your parents or relatives, examining your relationship with that person. Or compare your parents or two of your other relatives.

D. Reread the last paragraph of section I and of section III. Discuss the ideas in an essay.

E. Write imitations of the sentences discussed in questions 15–21.

F. Discuss the following poem by Stephen Crane in relation to what Baldwin says about himself in the final paragraph of section I.

A MAN FEARED

A man feared that he might find an assassin;
Another that he might find a victim.
One was more wise than the other.

About the Editors

John Clifford is presently an assistant professor at the University of North Carolina at Wilmington. He has taught literature and writing at Queens College, CUNY, and the University of Pennsylvania. During the academic year 1980–1981 he was an NEH Fellow-in-Residence in Literature and Literacy at the University of Southern California. He also attended the NDEA Seminar in Composition and Linguistics at Drake University in 1968 when he was chairman of a high school English department in Brooklyn, N.Y. Dr. Clifford's publications include the instructor's manual for *The Random House Guide to Writing* and numerous articles on composition and literature for such journals as *Research in the Teaching of English, English Journal,* and *College Composition and Communication.* He was a consultant for Daiker, Kerek, and Morenberg's *A Writer's Options* (Harper & Row) and also for the *Random House Handbook* and the *Random House Reader.* He has a doctorate from New York University

Robert DiYanni, assistant professor of English at Pace University, teaches courses in British and American literature and in composition. He has also taught at Queens College and at Long Island University He received his B.A. from Rutgers and his Ph.D. from the City University of New York.

Among his scholarly interests are seventeenth-century British literature, nineteenth-century American literature, and rhetoric and composition. He has published articles in all three fields, and he is currently working on three projects: a rhetoric-reader, *Connections,* to be published by Boynton/Cook; an anthology of essays about music, *Writing About Music;* and a collection of new essays, co-edited with Edmund Miller, on the works of George Herbert.